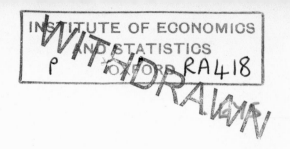

THE CAUSES AND EFFECTS OF SMOKING

'The question seems to be a serious one; when is serious investigation going to begin?' *Sir Ronald Fisher, F.R.S.*

H. J. EYSENCK Ph.D., D.Sc.

Institute of Psychiatry, University of London

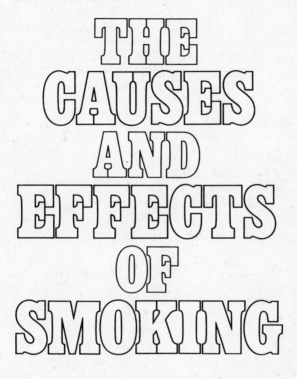

THE CAUSES AND EFFECTS OF SMOKING

with contributions by Dr L. J. EAVES, University of Oxford

MAURICE TEMPLE SMITH

First published in Great Britain in 1980 by
Maurice Temple Smith Ltd
37 Great Russell Street, London WC1

© 1980 H. J. Eysenck, L. J. Eaves, J. Kasriel

ISBN   0 85117 186 9

Printed in Great Britain by

Billing and Sons,
London, Guildford,
Worcester and Oxford

Typeset in India by
Tata Press Ltd
Bombay 400 025

Contents

Introduction

In the 1950s, studies of the relation between smoking and lung cancer among British doctors suggested a statistical link, and American studies soon confirmed the British findings. Since then, many other diseases have been linked with smoking, also largely using epidemiological and statistical evidence. We are now assured by the British Minister of Health that 50,000 lives a year could be saved in Great Britain by smokers ceasing to smoke, and along similar lines his American counterpart asserts that 320,000 lives could thus be saved in his country. Several reports from the Royal College of Physicians, and from the Surgeon General's Office, have given substance to these hypotheses, and it is nowadays taken for granted that lung cancer, coronary heart disease, and many other lethal and terrible illnesses are the direct consequence of smoking cigarettes.

From the beginning, however, competent statisticians have voiced grave doubts about the validity of the arguments used, the evidence adduced, and the statistical methods employed. As Sir Ronald Fisher pointed out: 'There is nothing to stop those who greatly desire it from believing that lung cancer is caused by smoking cigarettes. They should also believe that inhaling cigarette smoke is a protector. [The original study by R. Doll and A. Bradford Hill showed a negative correlation between inhaling and lung cancer.] To believe either is, however, to run the risk of failing to recognize, and therefore failing to prevent, other and more genuine causes.' Many other statisticians have since followed Fisher in criticizing the large number of studies which succeeded the pioneering work of Doll and Hill. Thus Professor Theodor D. Sterling (1973), in a report which formed part of the

Washington University Project on the review of crucial data bearing on the smoking and health issue, devoted eighty pages to an impartial and critical review of the evidence available by 1971, and found it still unconvincing and full of ambiguities. As he said: 'It would be very desirable if the antecedent for lung cancer turned out to be, or only depended on such a simple event as smoking. The readiness with which the existing evidence has been accepted as demonstrating causality for cigarette smoking perhaps is the best measure of the desire to keep our world simple and orderly. But cancer is a complex disease. . . .There is real danger that, having cast cigarettes as the prime villain, scientific interest and effort will turn to needs that appear more pressing.'

The contradictory nature of much of the evidence, already highlighted by Fisher's mention of the curious inhalation effects, was further emphasized by Professor Leo Katz (1969), in a hearing before a Committee of the US House of Representatives. He said: 'It has been suggested, not entirely facetiously, that since light smokers . . . showed, generally, lower morbidity and lower disability than non-smokers, it is advisable for all non-smokers immediately to commence smoking at the moderate rate of one half pack per day or less. Further, according to this theory, since former smokers are, almost uniformly across conditions, worse off in respect to both morbidity and disability than present smokers, it is equally advisable that present smokers should not under any circumstances consider quitting' (p. 861). (Whitby (1979), an eminent physician and surgeon, has seriously suggested that 'smoking is good for you'!)

In a more serious vein, Professor Katz continued: 'Overall, our information regarding the observed association between smoking and disease is remarkably little different than that when the Surgeon General's Committee report appeared in 1964. Instead of devoting its considerable resources to answering the basic questions raised by that report and trying to unravel the biomechanisms of the disease, the PHS has been engaged in a public relations campaign to "meet smoking's grave challenge" and in putting forth conjectures about the biomechanisms as though these were made gospel by the act of inclusion in printed documents' (p. 806). (Similar problems have arisen in relation to the role of cholesterol in coronary heart disease —McMichael (1979).)

Many similar doubts, reservations and criticisms will be found on later pages; the major problem with the existing evidence is simply that it concerns correlation, not causation; because A and B are correlated we cannot conclude that A has caused B. Such a conclusion must be based on a type of investigation altogether different in nature, and much more complicated and difficult to instigate. If we could assign 50,000 people at birth to a smoking group, on a random basis, and another 50,000 to a non-smoking group; if we could then follow them through to death and calculate accurately differences in longevity and in causes of death, then we would have available the sort of material on which a causal conclusion might be based. In the absence of this sort of material we have to consider alternative possibilities to the causal one for the observed correlations between smoking and disease. Among these alternative possibilities Fisher originally suggested the genetic one — perhaps people who are genetically predisposed to smoke are also predisposed to fall prey to certain types of disease? Another possibility, originally suggested by R. Pearl, and not incompatible with Fisher's suggestion, is that people are differentiated by their life style, or their 'rate of living'; thus we may deal with a complex intertwining of many different and correlated behaviours of which smoking is only one. The cause of observed differences in mortality may thus be any one or more of these intertwined behaviours, and it would be unscientific to single out one of these (e.g. smoking) as *the* cause of death. Smoking has been found to be correlated with drinking, with womanizing, with changing jobs, and with many other behaviours; it is also correlated with antisocial behaviour and criminality. Thus style of life may be a more important variable than smoking by itself.

In this book I have tried to take a new look at the evidence concerning both the establishment theory, and also Fisher's genetic theory, in the light of the evidence now available. In doing this, I have gone a long way beyond simply looking at disease as an effect of smoking; I have looked at many other, more positive effects of smoking as well, particularly in so far as these are related to motivation. The desire to smoke is so universal, and the difficulties of giving it up so immense, that clearly there must be some consequences of smoking which are regarded as supremely positive by the people concerned. Smokers have been threatened with the death penalty, or have had their ears cut off for smoking; nevertheless they persisted. Smokers are threatened with death by lung cancer and coronary heart disease by the establishment; nevertheless the great majority persist in smoking *even when they believe in the reality of the threat!* Hence we must look seriously at the evidence concerning the positive effects of smoking—what do people get out of it, and what makes them continue to smoke? The results of such studies may also give us some information on possible genetic bases for the continuance of the smoking habit, and on the personality correlates we may expect to find.

A survey of the evidence concerning the personality correlates of smoking thus constitutes another important part of this survey. If there is any truth in the genetic hypothesis, then smokers and non-smokers should be differentiated in terms of their general behaviour patterns and personality traits; even their physiques would be expected to be different. The data support such a view, and they tie up very neatly with the causal factors implicated in the continuance of the smoking habit. We are thus beginning to get a more thorough grasp on the physiology and psychology of the smoking habit, and we are beginning to see a pattern emerging which may in due course explain more clearly precisely what the causes and the effects of smoking really are. Without such knowledge of the complex interactions involved we are unlikely to come to any wise decisions in this difficult field.

The genetic hypothesis demands not only that smokers and non-smokers should differ in physique and personality; it also demands that genetic factors should be responsible for these differences. Here too there is much evidence to support such a view. Further than that, of course, the theory demands that there should be genetic factors involved in lung cancer, coronary heart disease, and the other diseases linked with smoking, and that this predisposition to disease itself should be correlated with personality. The evidence on this point is less reliable, and certainly there is much less of it; unfortunately few investigators have been willing to give time and energy to a search which for many of them seemed doomed to failure. The existing evidence does not support such pessimism. There seems to be little doubt about the existence of some genetic predisposition to lung cancer and coronary heart disease, and equally about the existence of some quite strong relations between susceptibility to the diseases in question, and personality, even though it is much too early to be dogmatic about the precise nature of these relations. Further research on this point is urgently required.

Finally, the genetic hypothesis demands that smoking itself, and in particular the continuance of the smoking habit, should be determined in part at least by genetic factors. Here, while there is much evidence in the literature, it consists mainly of simple comparisons of the concordance rates of identical and fraternal twins; this is not a very illuminating type of analysis, although it does seem to establish the importance of the genetic contribution. Jointly with a professional geneticist, Dr Lindon Eaves of Oxford University, I carried out a number of studies of twins, adopted children, and familial relationships in order to try and extract more detailed knowledge on this point than is possible by the use of traditional methods; in the course of this work, reported here in Chapters 3, 4 and 5, we had to solve a number of interesting statistical problems, but we believe that the outcome justifies the long time it took us to complete this section of the book. Inevitably the treatment is somewhat technical, but the non-statistical reader, by judicious skipping, should be able to get the main drift of the argument, and the implications of the major conclusions, provided he is willing to take our statistics for granted.

There are three appendices, reporting some additional investigations which are of relevance to the main topic of this book. Thus with the help of the Gallup Poll organization I looked at the effects of giving up smoking (successfully or unsuccessfully!), and the differences in personality, socio-economic status and other characteristics of smokers and non-smokers, successful and unsuccessful givers-up. It was found, as had been suspected, that those who give up successfully are constitutionally more like non-smokers, while those who fail to give up smoking are constitutionally more like smokers. This is an important finding; it shows that studies comparing the health of smokers and former smokers are not dealing with comparable groups, so that their conclusions are vitiated to an unknown degree by dissimilarity of the groups with respect to constitutional factors. Friedman et al. (1979) have found similar differences, antedating the time of giving up or not giving up smoking, with respect to mental and physical healh records; thus genetic factors not only cause us to smoke, but also cause us to give up smoking!

A final word may be said concerning my own interest in this field. It may seem odd that an experimental psychologist, specializing in personality research, should enter what may at first sight seem to be a medical field. There is a natural explanation. Having tried to clarify the nature of the major dimensions of personality (Eysenck, 1967), I went on to consider the social relevance and importance of these personality differences. In doing so I looked at such behaviour patterns as neurosis (Eysenck & Rachman, 1964; Eysenck, 1977b), anti-social behaviour and criminality (Eysenck, 1977a), sex (Eysenck,

1976a) social and political behaviour (Eysenck, 1954), the relation
between personality and ideology (Eysenck & Wilson, 1978), education (Eysenck, 1978), drug taking and influence (Eysenck, 1963a;
1972), and many others. Inevitably, smoking and drinking emerged
as suitable topics of investigation — particularly as my theory
enabled me to make predictions regarding both the causes and the
effects of drug taking in this particular context. It was as a consequence of this rather specialized interest that I was brought up
against the problems outlined in the first few paragraphs of this Introduction, and recognized, as had Fisher so much earlier, that while
the problems of lung cancer and coronary heart disease are ultimately medical, the epidemiological aspects of these problems are
statistical, and closely related to constitutional differences in personality, of just the sort I was studying.

In thus constructing a model of smoking behaviour (Eysenck,
1973), I was hoping to make a contribution, not only to psychology,
but also to the much wider field of disease prevention. In collaboration
with the late Dr D. M. Kissen I extended my work on personality to
a consideration of the relation between personality and disease, in
particular lung cancer; the details of our findings will be discussed in
the body of the book. Unlikely as it might have seemed at first sight,
we found quite a close relationship. Unfortunately, relatively
little follow-up work has been done to exploit these original observations; possibly the untimely death of Dr Kissen delayed recognition of his important contribution. I still believe that such exploitation
of the implications of our joint work could be of great importance; if
highly emotional people are seemingly protected from lung cancer,
an investigation of the causes (biochemical, physiological, neuro-
logical) of this protection might give us an important lead to the
prevention of lung cancer, or its treatment.

I would not like to leave the reader with the impression that the
model of smoking behaviour, personality and disease that is beginning to emerge is more clearly defined, or more advanced, than it
is. Some of its outlines are beginning to emerge pretty clearly; others
are little more than rough lines on paper suggesting the path future
research might take. There is a desperate shortage of workers taking
an interest in these heterodox lines of research; practically all the
official money is devoted to often meaningless replications of faulty
researches leading nowhere — and recognized as leading nowhere. This
is one of the consequences, already foreseen by Fisher, of the accept-

ance of the belief, unjustified by the existing evidence though of course possibly correct, that 'smoking causes cancer' (and coronary heart disease, and all sorts of other diseases). While simple-minded theories of this sort are given official recognition, leading to political propaganda and wide dispersion by the media, it is inevitable that the climate is inimical to the development of theories, and the undertaking of research projects, concerned with an alternative, though possibly complementary view of the observed relationships. It is hoped (though not expected with any degree of confidence!) that the appearance of this book, marshalling as it does much of the evidence for such an alternative view, and many of the criticisms of the orthodox view, may hasten the day when full recognition is given to the existence of both of these alternative theories, and when research is organized in such a way as to make possible a more just and equitable decision as to their mutual merits.

Readers may wonder how it is possible that one side of a scientific dispute can be so vociferous, while the other side remains almost completely suppressed. This is by no means rare in the history of science; we need only think of Newton's corpuscular theory of light which was later challenged by men like Thomas Young. Young was a successful physician; he did not dare publish his theories and experimental results, advocating a wave theory of light, for fear of putting off his patients by having the temerity to contradict Newton! Similarly, Harvey suffered considerably for daring to put forward his unorthodox theory of the circulation of the blood; he too was a physician, and lost the confidence of many of his patients. Scientists, like ordinary mortals, are subject to the 'law of certainty' proclaimed by Thoulless in 1935. The law states: 'When, in a group of persons, there are influences acting both in the direction of acceptance and of rejection of a belief, the result is not to make the majority adopt a lower degree of conviction, but to make some hold the belief with a high degree of conviction, while others reject it also with a high degree of conviction.' I have adduced much evidence for the truth of this law (Eysenck, 1954), and history does not suggest that it is confined in its application to non-scientists! Hence the somewhat rhetorical and often hostile diatribes found in the smoking field between believers and non-believers. Such an attitude is not conducive to that impartial, unbiased approach to truth that is the ideal of all scientists, and I may perhaps express the hope that calmer counsels will prevail, and that we may all go forward together in the search for a solution to a complex, difficult and altogether puzzling problem, a problem moreover which has grave social consequences.

Different parts of the research have been supported, in whole or in part, by many different organizations; acknowledgement will be found in the original journal articles in question. The special study of the genetics of smoking behaviour here published for the first time was supported in part by a grant from the Council for Tobacco Research USA Inc., to whom I wish to express my gratitude. Needless to say, the conclusions derived from the work in this book are my own, and do not commit the Council in any way. During the analysis of the data, Dr L. Eaves was supported by a grant from the Medical Research Council to the University of Birmingham. I also wish to acknowledge the help and sage advice received from Professor P. Burch, from Professor J. Jinks, and from Mr E. Jacobs; faults that remain are entirely my own. We thank Mrs P. Parsons and Mrs S. Chumbley, and Mrs M. Johnson and Miss S. Pipe for patiently typing Parts 1 and 2 of the manuscript, respectively.

PART ONE

Smoking, Health and Personality

H. J. Eysenck

CHAPTER 1

Smoking and Health: Does Smoking Cause Disease?

The epidemiological argument

In this chapter we shall consider the evidence relating to the now very popular hypothesis that smoking causes lung cancer, heart disease, and many other types of illness. This hypothesis, and the surveys and analyses on which it is based, has found many critics, and an alternative hypothesis has been put forward by Fisher (1958a, 1959), Berkson (1960), Brownley (1965), Eysenck (1965) and Burch (1976). On this hypothesis, smoking is not the cause of lung cancer, but rather both the development of lung cancer and the maintenance of the smoking habit are produced by genetic or constitutional factors which are responsible for the observed correlation. The two theories are of course not mutually exclusive, and both may contain some truth. We shall consider in this chapter the environmental ('smoking causes cancer') theory, and will then go on in the next chapter to discuss research related to a more specific genetic theory than that originated by Fisher.

There has been a tremendous literature on the topic in question, including three reports from the Royal College of Physicians of London (1962, 1971, 1977), and four major reports by the American Surgeon General (1964, 1971, 1972, and 1973). There has also been a report by the World Health Organization (1960), as well as several other reports from the same Organization somewhat less relevant. In addition to these official reports, we have had many books and even more articles, setting forth various views either supportive or critical of the theory that smoking causes cancer and other diseases, particularly coronary heart disease. There would be little point in reviewing all the literature again here, particularly as the problem is not central to our research interest, although we believe that our research does throw a certain amount of light on the debate.

Essentially the argument of those who support the hypothesis that smoking causes disease is based on a statistical finding, namely that *smokers of a given age and sex die more frequently of a given disease than do non-smokers.* This difference can be expressed as a 'mortality ratio' (age-standardized mortality rate, or SMR), indicating the proportion of smokers to non-smokers who are certified as having died of a particular disease. Table 1 gives an indication of the kind of data used for this purpose (Eysenck, 1965). The heading 'observed' refers to actual deaths in the population under study; 'expected' refers to deaths among non-smokers. Column D gives the absolute difference between the first two columns, thus 4,746 more persons died of coronary artery disease in the USA than would have been expected to do so if they had none of them smoked. The column headed 'mortality ratio' gives the ratio Observed/Expected; in the case of lung cancer this is 10.8, indicating that almost eleven times as many people died of this disease than would have been expected to do so if none had smoked. It will be seen that there are a large number of different diseases with mortality ratios above 1, indicating the possibility that smoking may have increased the chances of a given individual of succumbing to these diseases.

It is not always realized that ratios may be below 1 as well as above, apparently indicating a beneficent effect of smoking. Thus Kahn (1966) found a mortality ratio of 0.90 for cancer of the rectum. Hammond (1966) found mortality ratios of 0.78 and 0.66 respectively for colorectal cancer in women who smoked or smoked heavily; for males the mortality ratios were just over 1. Choi, Schuman & Gullen (1970) found a negative correlation of primary central nervous system neoplasms with cigarette smoking; they found a similar negative association between such neoplasms and alcohol consumption. (As we shall see later, alcohol consumption and cigarette smoking are definitely correlated in the general population.)

Another disease in which negative correlations have been found

TABLE 1

Mortality ratios, and expected and observed deaths for a number of diseases which have been linked with smoking

	Expected	Observed	D	Mortality ratio
Cancer of the lung	170	1,833	1,657	10.8
Bronchitis and emphysema	90	546	456	6.1
Cancer of the larynx	14	75	61	5.4
Cancer of oral cavity	37	152	115	4.1
Cancer of oesophagus	34	113	79	3.4
Stomach and duodenal ulcers	105	294	189	2.8
Other circulatory diseases	254	649	395	2.6
Cirrhosis of liver	169	379	210	2.2
Cancer of bladder	112	216	104	1.9
Coronary artery disease	6,431	11,177	4,746	1.7
Other heart diseases	526	868	342	1.7
Hypertensive heart disease	409	631	222	1.5
General arteriosclerosis	211	310	99	1.5
Cancer of kidney	79	120	41	1.5
All other cancer	1,061	1,524	463	1.4
Cancer of stomach	285	413	128	1.4
Influenza, pneumonia	303	415	112	1.4
All other causes	1,509	1,946	437	1.3
Cerebral vascular lesions	1,462	1,844	382	1.3
Cancer of prostate	253	318	65	1.3
Accidents, suicides, violence	1,063	1,310	247	1.2
Nephritis	156	173	17	1.1
Rheumatic heart disease	291	309	18	1.1
Cancer of rectum	208	213	5	1.0

consistently is Parkinson's disease. Kahn (1966) reported a mortality ratio of 0.26; Hammond (1966) one of 0.81 for an older group; Nefzger et al. (1968) found that among 138 patients with Parkinson's disease, only 70 per cent had ever smoked compared with 84 per cent of 166 controls. The differences in smoking habits were established prior to the onsets of the disease, and hence the negative correlation was not brought about by the disease itself. Kessler (1972) found similar results, as did Westlund (1970) in Norway. The figures for Parkinson's disease are particularly striking, but other diseases, such as trigeminal neuralgia (Rothman & Monson, 1973) and diabetes (Hirayama, 1972), can also be mentioned here. If we can interpret positive mortality ratios as indicative of nefarious effects of smoking, can we interpret ratios below unity as indicative of beneficial effects of smoking? The answer is probably no. If smoking had a prophylactic effect, we would expect a secular decrease in morbidity and mortality as a consequence of the secular increase in smoking; this has not been found with respect to Parkinson's disease (Westlund, 1970). Perhaps we are equally wrong in interpreting the positive correlation indicated by elevated mortality ratios in a causal manner.

It is a well-known error in statistics to interpret correlations in terms of causation. The fact that A is correlated with B may mean that A causes B, that B causes A, that both to some degree cause each other, that C causes A and B, that C causes A while D causes B, and that C and D are correlated because both are caused by E, or any other of a large number of possible contingencies. Consider Figure 1. This shows, on the ordinate, meat consumption in 23 countries in terms of grammes per person per day, while the abscissa shows the annual incidence of cancer of the large intestine among women in these countries, in terms of incidence per 100,000 population. The data are adjusted to eliminate differences in age distribution in the population. An obvious explanation of the quite close relationships between the two variables might be that high meat consumption produces cancer of the intestine. A more likely explanation perhaps would be that cancer of the large intestine is due to a low consumption of cereals; there is a high correlation between high meat consumption and low cereal consumption. Thus possibly the causal chain might start with poverty causing people to eat little meat, and a lot of cereals; cereal consumption protects against cancer of the large intestine. Thus the observed correlation between meat consumption and cancer is not indicative of any direct causal influence of the one on the other, but both are produced by a fairly complex chain of events. We do not know of course what the precise answer may be to the problem of cancer of the large intestine and its relationship to meat consumption, cereal consumption, etc.; we are merely pointing out that the existence of a quite close correlation (much closer than that found for different countries between smoking and lung cancer) does not tell us anything about the causal features involved.

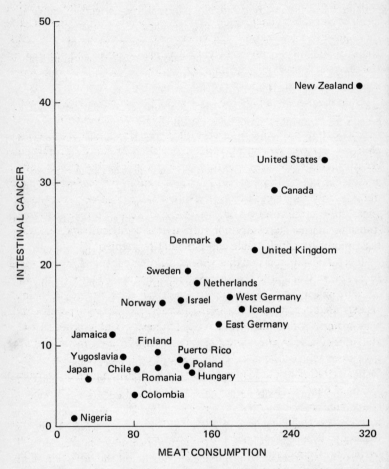

Figure 1 Meat consumption (grammes per person per day), plotted against incidence per 100,000 population of cancer of the large intestine.

To take another example, a study of statistics will show that users of tranquillizer pills are far more prone to acute nervous tension than non-users. Does this prove that tranquillizers cause nervousness? Does the correlation between taking insulin and diabetes show that insulin causes diabetes? These are extreme examples to demonstrate the absurdity of taking correlation to be a safe guide to causation. On a more serious note, Wakefield et al. (1973) showed that occupation of the husband was strongly correlated with mortality from cancer of the cervix in women. It would indeed be interesting to know the causal relations involved, if any.

Even if we were to take the correlation between smoking and lung cancer seriously as proof of causal connections, we would still have to conclude that smoking was neither a necessary nor a sufficient cause. Roughly speaking (figures differ considerably from country to country), only one heavy smoker in ten dies of lung cancer; thus smoking is not a sufficient cause. One person in ten of those who die of lung cancer is a non-smoker; thus smoking is not a necessary cause. Clearly the establishment of firm causal links when the presumed 'cause' is neither necessary nor sufficient is a difficult and awkward task, requiring considerable experimental refinement.

It is not always realized that what should be a medical problem has in fact been turned into a statistical one, and that the statistics put forward by physicians and others concerned with the writing of official reports are not always of the highest order. It is an indisputable fact that professional statisticians have been openly contemptuous of the statistics offered by those who support the official doctrine that smoking causes cancer (Berkson, 1958, 1960; Berkson & Elveback, 1960; Fisher, 1958a; Katz, 1969; Sterling, 1973; Mainland & Herrera, 1956). Thus Sterling (1973) says that 'the deceptive simplicity of the original problems may be one of the major sources of unsatisfactory answers that have been offered. There are . . . a number of confounding variables that need and indeed should be adequately controlled but, for the most part, were ignored . . . . Most statisticians may well be aware of the prevalence of statistical malpractices in public health matters, but at the same time, most of them avoid involvement in controversies over which they have little control'. Berkson (1962) is even more scathing when he says that 'in view of the brain washing that the general public and even the scientific world has been subjected to, at the hands of self-constituted arbiters of complex scientific questions who have already decided that we know the answer, . . . an open-minded investigative programme is unlikely. It is an old and, to a professional statistician, a sad and humiliating story. Non-statisticians have noted that "statistics is used as an inebriated gentleman uses the lamppost, not for the light it casts on the subject, but for the support it gives his position".'

Eysenck (1965) has enumerated some of the many errors in the design of epidemiological studies (Reid, 1975), in their statistical treatment, and in their evaluation which have been noted by statisticians; in this book we do not wish to go over this field again (Burch, 1979). It may, however, be useful to quote a summary by Berkson (1958) of these criticisms which unfortunately still apply. This is what he says:

> In the first place, virtually all the evidence is obtained from statistical studies. . .we are not dealing with the results of laboratory experiments, or even with placebo-controlled clinical trials. Nor is the conclusion based on a synthesis, by a 'chain of reasoning', of relevant scientific knowledge from many different sources. Such statistical evidence, for a question like the identification of a cause of a disease, at best, can be only presumptive. But even as statistical investigations, I do not find the published studies so sound or convincing as they apparently have been widely assumed to be. In the studies that have been called 'retrospective', as well as those called 'prospective', I find questionable and even paradoxic elements.

Berkson goes on to discuss such a paradoxic element in two prominent prospective studies.

> These studies were projected as a check on the theory that smoking causes cancer of the lung, a theory derived from previous observations pointing to that specific conclusion. What the prospective studies actually revealed was an association of smoking, not specifically with lung cancer, but with a wide variety of diseases, including diseases that never have been conceived to have the same aetiology as cancer. It is not logical to take such a set of results as confirming the theory that tobacco smoke contains carcinogenic substances which, by contact with the pulmonary tissues, initiate cancerous changes at the site of contact. Nor is it wise to look aside from positive findings that do not neatly fit the simple theory that initiated the investigation. . . The results suggest that in data which have been obtained as these data have been collected there are factors

which produce a statistical association between smoking and the death rate from disease generally.

Berkson suggests three explanations for the association. The first is that 'the observed associations are spurious, that is they have no biological significance but are the result of interplay of various subtle and complicated "biases"'. The second possibility suggested is that the observed associations have a constitutional basis. 'Persons who are non-smokers, or relatively light smokers, are the kind of people who are biologically self-protective, and biologically this is correlated with robustness in meeting normal stress from disease generally.' The third possibility suggested is that smoking increases the 'rate of living' (Pearl, 1928); smokers at a given age are, biologically, at an age older than their chronological age. 'As a result, smokers (in particular, heavy smokers), are subject to the death rates of non-smokers or relatively light smokers who are chronologically older. Diseases like cancer and heart disease, the death rates for which have a pronounced gradient with age, will be considerably more prominent in heavy smokers than in non-smokers or relatively light smokers of the same age.' Since these words were written, there appears to have been little improvement in the statistical sophistication of the studies that have been carried out, nor has there been an improvement in the methodology of data collection. As Sterling (1973) says, 'ordinarily, results from a study such as Doll's in which over 30 per cent of the queried population did not participate will be considered, if at all, with greatest suspicion, especially if, as is freely admitted, the responders were quite different from the reference population'. One feels like echoing Sir Ronald Fisher's (1959) remarks in relation to this controversy: 'The question seems to be a serious one; when is serious investigation going to begin?'

The concentration on statistical proof of correlation has led to a relative neglect of the medical study of causal factors. Possible mechanisms by which associations between cigarette smoking and the occurrence of disease might arise were given in an introductory statement to the Surgeon General's 1971 report. Five possibilities are listed. (a) Cigarette smoking produces specific, progressive, irreversible damage. (b) Cigarette smoking initiates a disease process, at first corrected by continual repair and recovery, until at some critical point the process is no longer reversible. (c) Cigarette smoking promotes or contributes to the development of a disease process by reducing the ability of the organism to recover. (d) Cigarette smoking produces a set of temporary conditions that increase the probability of a critical catastrophic event, which also becomes more likely if the temporary conditions are produced by other means than smoking. (e) Cigarette smoking may be artificially related to excess disability or death because it is associated with another damaging condition or exposure that is more common among smokers than among non-smokers and the latter condition itself is responsible for the disease. Elevated mortality ratios for suicide are a good example of condition (e), where clearly any direct influence of smoking on suicide can be eliminated. However, the recognition that such possibilities exist must be borne in mind in evaluating the high mortality ratios for lung cancer, coronary heart disease, and other disorders.

The correlational argument on which the environmental hypothesis is based posits two major sources of correlations. Within a given population, we would expect smoking to be correlated with liability to death from lung cancer, a correlation usually expressed in terms of the age-corrected mortality ratios already discussed. Between countries, we would expect national death rates from lung cancer in one country to correlate with the effective tobacco consumption in that country, or perhaps even more closely with the cigarette consumption of people in that country. We would hardly expect a perfect correlation because of differences in the type of tobacco smoked, the use among smokers of filters, the accuracy of diagnostic techniques used in that country, manner of smoking (e.g. length of stub left when extinguishing cigarette), etc. Figure 2, taken from Burch (1976) shows for 21 countries the death rates from lung cancer in males, in relation to national consumption of manufactured cigarette tobacco; the figures on which the table is based were given by Beese (1968). The consumption of cigarettes was calculated for the year 1950; the death rates for 1960-61. If it is assumed that there is a thirty-year delay between smoking and death from cancer, then the ten-year period intervening here is too short; however, the relative standing in the smoking league of these countries has not changed very much over time, and this factor can hardly be responsible for the obvious failure of a close relationship to emerge. The relationship is certainly very much weaker than that between incidence of cancer of the large intestine and meat consumption illustrated in Figure 1. Even if the correlation were more pronounced than it is, it would obviously be hazardous to make any deductions from it; as the figures stand they can hardly support the environmental hypothesis.

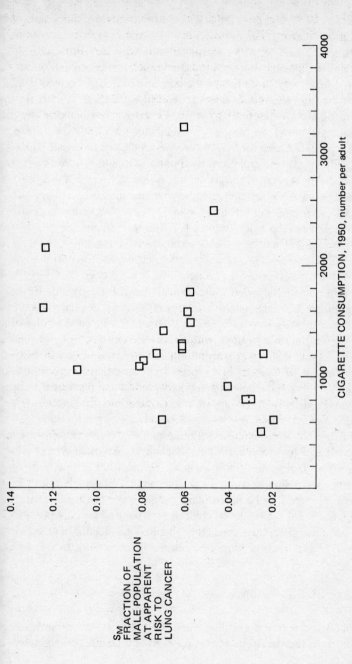

Figure 2   Death rates from lung cancer in males for 21 different populations, in relation to national consumption of manufactured cigarette tobacco. (From Burch, 1976)

Stocks (1970) has reported statistical tests for the significance of correlations between the mean annual consumption of cigarettes in 20 countries, and the mean age-adjusted death rate from cancer in various sites. For cancer of the lung and bronchus, the association was just significantly positive for males, but failed to reach conventional significance for females. Stocks carried out a total of 26 statistical tests, using a total of 15 sites; 15 of these statistical tests gave negative associations, 4 of them statistically significant, while the remaining 11 gave positive associations, only one of which was minimally significant. The negative correlations with national cigarette consumption were found for cancers of the buccal cavity and pharynx in males only; stomach in males and females; rectum in males and females; liver and bile passages in males only; larynx in males only; bladder in males and females; prostate, ovaries, uterus (in the appropriate sex only, of course!); and leukaemia in males and females.

As Burch comments, 'The meanings to be attached to correlations and *P* values in this context are somewhat obscure, but I find it difficult to believe that the negative associations, even the highly significant ones, signify a prophylactic action of cigarette smoking . . . perhaps the chief merit of such studies is to demonstrate the utter absurdity of relying upon mortality ratios, and/or correlations between national death rates and cigarette consumption, as evidence for causal relations. If *recorded* national death rates from specific cancers depend primarily on the frequency of genetically predisposed persons and the accuracy of diagnosis, the apparent contradictions disappear.' It is certainly notable that these negative correlations over nations bear out the negative correlations within nations, at least in certain cases. In other cases (cancers of the buccal cavity, pharynx and larynx in men), where high mortality ratios have been found, the patterns of correlations are simply contradictory, although, as we shall see, in these cases there may be no secular change in the disease pattern to parallel the secular changes in cigarette smoking. The only possible conclusion for these disorders is that there is no evidence of cigarette smoking as the main or even contributory cause of death.

An alternative hypothesis

In order to understand the literature critical of the environmental hypothesis, it may be useful at this point to outline quite briefly what has emerged as the major genetic theory in the field of lung cancer. This theory has led to certain types of analysis which are very relevant to the proper understanding of the argument. The theory is due to Professor P. R. J. Burch (1976), who argues that all well-defined natural diseases with a reproducible age pattern result from some specific breakdown in the central nervous system that, in health, regulates growth and controls the size of tissues. Such diseases are called 'auto-aggressive' because one part of the body attacks another part, the target tissue. Specific auto-aggressive diseases are confined to persons possessing a specific genetic predisposition for that disease, and the age of onset is largely determined by the prior occurrence of somatic gene mutations. These mutations cause changes in messages from particular genes and stem cells of the central growth-control system.

Burch's main suggestion is that a stem cell with the full complement of specifically mutant genes divides to propagate a 'forbidden clone' of descendant cells. More than one such forbidden clone may be needed for the onset of certain diseases. Peripheral cells of the forbidden clone, or humoral products secreted by these clones, attack complementary target cells at one or more anatomic locations to produce the symptoms and signs of disease. Essential for the investigation of such diseases is the study of their sex- and age-dependence. Burch plotted age-specific death rates for a given calendar year, or a few (consecutive) years, and found results such as those shown in Figures 3 and 4. Figure 3 shows data from cancer registries for sex-specific and age-specific onset rates in England and Wales, 1962. These rates for older men climb to a peak more steeply than for women, and then fall sharply from about seventy years of age onwards. (Age-specific death rates exhibit a similar behaviour because on the average the interval between onset and death from lung cancer is short.) Figure 4 shows similar age-specific death rates for men in Finland 1960-61, the European country with the (then) second highest rates, and for men in Portugal, the European country with the (then) lowest recorded rates. These curves are quite typical of many others analysed and reproduced by Burch in his book.

Mathematical analysis of the curves enables Burch to calculate n, the number of forbidden clones, and r, the number of somatic mutations required to initiate each forbidden clone. The numbers are given in the figure. Burch also gives a formula describing these curves containing in addition two major variables. One is S, which represents the proportion of the population at risk with respect to diagnosis of the on-

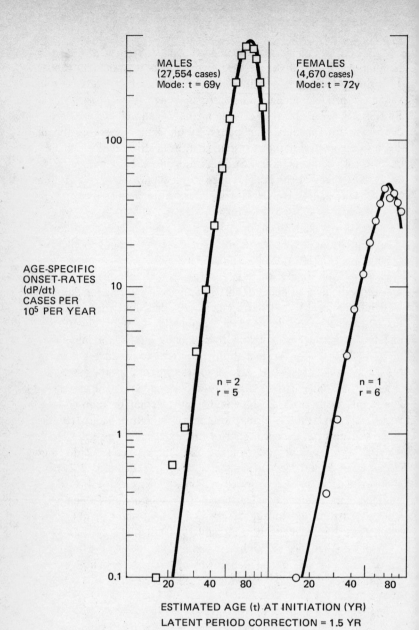

Figure 3 Sex-specific and age-specific onset rates of lung cancer at initiation, plotted on log scales, for males and females. Data refer to full regions of England and Wales, 1962. (From Burch, 1976)

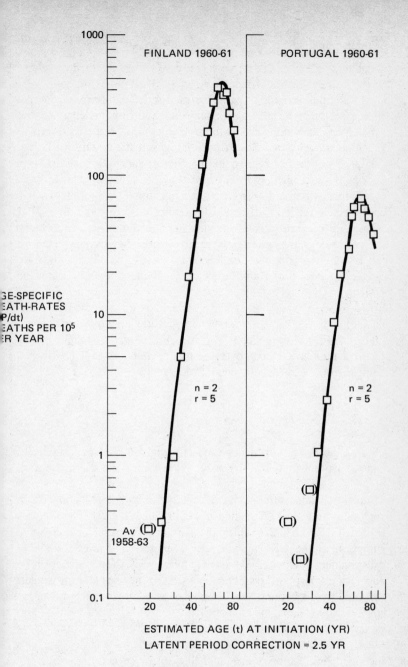

Figure 4   Age specific death rates (male) versus estimated age at initiation. Data on the left are for Finland, 1960-61, and on the right for Portugal, 1960-61. (From Burch, 1976)

set of lung cancer, and the other is k, which is a kinetic constant related to the average rate at which each forbidden clone is initiated.

Burch finds that the age pattern in men is always different from that in women, which he interprets as showing that the genetic factors that predispose men to lung cancer differ in at least one respect from those that predispose women. So do the initiating somatic mutations. Values for S, the proportion of the population that appears to be 'at risk' to lung cancer, is much greater for women than for men; furthermore the values for S differ widely from country to country. Values of k (which are inversely related to the modal age of onset) are generally similar from country to country and have remained almost constant during the first half of the century, although latterly they have appeared to fall. Burch claims that these findings conflict with the idea that cigarette smoke acts as an initiator of lung cancer, which would raise the value of k.

The particular method of analysis of cancer data adopted by Burch enables us to test the environmental hypothesis in a number of ways. One of the most interesting is by comparing the rates, and changes in rates, of men and women over the past seventy years or so. Such a comparison is given in the next section.

Sex distribution of lung cancer

Of the many deductions which can be drawn from the 'smoking causes cancer' hypothesis, one of the strongest relates to the sex distribution of the disease. Women in England began to smoke cigarettes only some thirty years after men had begun to do so; the comparison springs to the eye when the figures are graphed (Fig. 5). The figure is taken from Burch (1976) and shows, in the lower panel, cigarette consumption in the UK by five-yearly averages. If cigarette smoking causes cancer, then we would confidently expect S, the proportion of the population at risk with respect to diagnosis of the onset of lung cancer, to follow a similar course. As the upper panel shows, this is by no means so; the rise in S_F begins at about the same time as that for S_M, and proceeds *pari passu,* although always at a lower level. As Burch points out, in England and Wales the apparent proportion of males (S_M) has increased by a factor of around 120 during this century, while the apparent increase in S_F is a factor of about 25. In another graph, Burch analyses the data from the previous figure to show the fine structure of

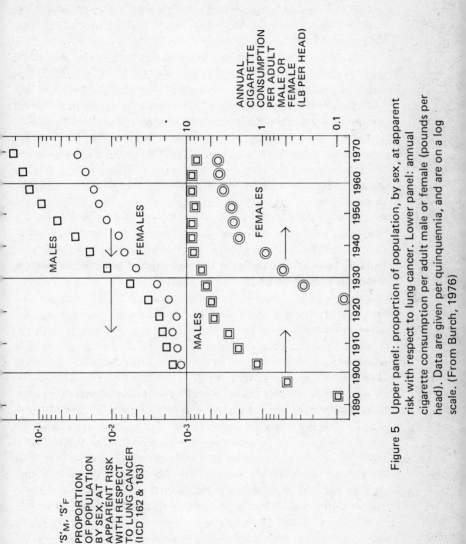

Figure 5   Upper panel: proportion of population, by sex, at apparent risk with respect to lung cancer. Lower panel: annual cigarette consumption per adult male or female (pounds per head). Data are given per quinquennia, and are on a log scale. (From Burch, 1976)

secular change in S_M and S_F. The ordinate of Figure 6 shows the increments in S_M and S_F from one five-year period to the next. With one exception, these increments are larger for men than for women, but largely or wholly synchronous, and unrelated to the secular increases in cigarette consumption.

The same point, in a slightly different way, is made by Rosenblatt (1974). As he points out, 'the pattern of sex distribution of lung cancer, with predominance of males, has not changed since the 19th century, when cigarette consumption was relatively insignificant. Several authorities in the 1890s reported that lung cancer was predominantly a male disease with sex ratios ranging from 3:1 to 13:1. The ratio did not change in the early decades of the 20th century when cigarette smoking was still not very popular. Ratios between 4:1 and 6:1 were reported by Dr. W. Berlinger between 1925 and 1933. Professor Richard Passey in his study of the teaching hospitals in Great Britain found between 1894 and 1918, 579 cases of lung cancer in males and 182 cases in females.' What we find, therefore, is a completely different picture for cigarette smoking, but a closely similar picture of cancer liability between the sexes. The increase in smoking of the men, as compared with the women, from 1890 to 1920 is not mirrored by any corresponding increase in their proportion of lung cancer cases, and the rapid increase in smoking of the women, as compared with the men, from 1920 to 1940, is not mirrored by any corresponding increase in their proportion of lung cancer cases. These facts are truly astounding if smoking really plays any part in the causation of cancer, and urgently require explanation.

If smoking causes cancer, then it should have produced a superabundance of cancers in the men who took up smoking from 1890 to 1920, as compared to the women who did not take up smoking, and similarly the large number of women who took up smoking from 1920 to 1940 should have produced a superabundance of cancers, compared to the men who hardly increased their smoking of cigarettes during this period. It is often assumed that there is a thirty-year delay period before the effects of smoking are shown up in actual lung cancer, but this delay period fails to show up in the respective changes in incidence of cancer of men and women; increases and decreases for the two sexes clearly occur *pari passu,* and are completely in step. These two facts, based as they are on very complete statistics embracing very large numbers of cases, are quite incompatible with the 'smoking causes cancer' hypothesis. Can they be explained in terms of a genetic

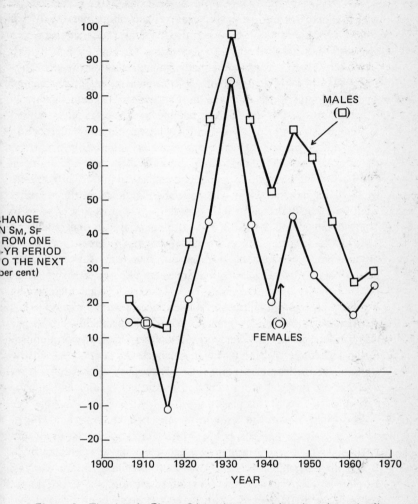

Figure 6 The data in Figure 3 have been reanalysed to show the fine structure of secular change in S_M and S_F. The ordinate gives the increments in S_M and S_F from one five-year period to the next. Increments are larger for men than women, but are always in step. (From Burch, 1976)

hypothesis?

Such an hypothesis requires two assumptions. In the first place, we need to explain the increase in lung cancer cases altogether during this period; we shall discuss this point presently, and argue that changes in diagnostic accuracy are largely responsible for this change, which would affect men and women equally, thus preserving the sex ratios observed prior to the increase in lung cancer diagnoses. In the second place, we would have to argue that men and women have unequal genetic predispositions to develop cancer, and to take up cigarette smoking. Such assumptions are difficult to prove, but they do serve to suggest novel experiments which might throw light on these matters. As we shall show in the next chapter, personality traits which differentiate between men and women have also been found to differentiate smokers and non-smokers, and both these traits, and the smoking habit, are largely determined by genetic factors; this would seem to argue in favour of the genetic hypothesis. Comparative studies of male and female lung cancer patients in terms of personality, and of physical and constitutional factors differentiating the sexes (e.g. pelvic shape—Eysenck, 1976a), would seem likely to shed some light on this theory. The prediction would be that when matched on a variety of relevant variables, male cancer patients should differ from male non-patients as female cancer patients should from female non-patients, i.e. by having more masculine personality and constitutional characteristics, e.g. having a shorter distance between the ischial tuberosities. This point will not be pursued here as future chapters are devoted to a discussion of the personality and genetic evidence relevant to this proposal.

Sex differences in the sense that men started to smoke cigarettes approximately thirty years before women did can also be used very effectively to rule out a number of other types of cancer, for which the standardized mortality rates are high, and for whom therefore smoking has been suspected as a causal agent. Thus, for instance, we are able to compare the secular trends in the two sexes for cancer of the pancreas. When these are plotted they can be seen to run almost parallel from 1905 onwards, and there is no suggestion of an initial rise in death rate among men preceding a rise among women. Yet mortality ratios (e.g. Hirayama, 1967, 1972) of large populations in Japan showed results of about 2 for both men and women!

When we look at cancers of the stomach, bladder, buccal sites and pharynx, plotted against calendar year, it can be seen that none of the secular trends bear the expected relation to those observed in cigarette consumption. Cancer of the pharynx, which has a mortality ratio of 9.0, shows a slight increase in both sexes from 1911-20 to 1931-40, followed by a slight decrease over the next decade; this continues for males but is reversed for females over the final period. Despite the large mortality ratio, therefore, factors other than smoking must obviously be responsible for the secular trends observed.

Buccal cancer, which has the moderately large mortality ratio of 3.8, actually shows a decrease in death rate. As far as stomach and bladder cancers are concerned, the secular trends in the standardized mortality rates for the two sexes diverge at the end of the period in question when they might be expected to converge, due to the greater similarity and smoking habits of the two sexes. Here too, therefore, there is no suggestion in the figures that smoking has any causal connection with these types of cancer (Burch, 1976).

Figures on cancer of the oesophagus, larynx, and kidney similarly fail to bear out secular trend theories, either predicting a general rise for both men and women, or predicting a differential rise for the two sexes as a function of the thirty-year interval in the inception of smoking. Data instead show a very flat pattern, with little increase or decrease over time, and with the two sexes showing parallel fluctuations. Cancer of the larynx is particularly interesting as it has a mortality ratio of 9.5, rather similar to that for the pharynx; yet the very slight upward trend for the two sexes is strikingly parallel, with no thirty-year delay period in evidence (Stell, 1972). Burch (1976) has summarized the data as follows:

> When both sexes are at risk, the secular trends of SMRs for men roughly parallel those for women. No sign of the expected thirty-year lag of increase in women can be discerned in any of the data. If we wish to retain the causal hypothesis we have to invoke a different set of *ad hoc* arguments to explain the trends for each site. Factors that were responsible for the changes in SMR at a given site with time had, in the main, a rather similar and *simultaneous* impact on the two sexes. Generally, the timing of the impact of these factors differed from site to site. Clearly, no corroboration of the causal interpretation of mortality ratios can be expected from this study of secular trends.

As Burch also comments, it is curious that so little attention should have been directed at these paradoxes. They would seem to rule out almost completely any explanation of these many types of cancer in terms of cigarette smoking, in spite of the middling to high or very high age-standardized mortality rates shown by the various disorders.

An added complication in all this work is the differentiation made by Leiv Kreyberg (see Eysenck, 1965) of two main distinct histological types of lung cancer. Primary epithelial lung tumours of one type, which he calls Group 1 lung tumours, are made up of epidermoid carcinomas, and small cell anaplastic carcinomas; Group 2 lung tumours are made up of adenocarcinomas and bronchial or alveolar cell types. Kreyberg related the average amount smoked by his cancer patients to the estimated risk of contracting the disease of the sufferers from Group 1 lung cancer and those of Group 2 lung cancer; the results showed no relationship whatsoever between smoking and Group 2 lung cancer, but a very marked straight-line relationship between smoking and Group 1 lung cancer. Thus lung cancer clearly is not just one undifferentiated entity; we are dealing with presumably at least two and possibly more quite different types of disease, and each of these different types has different relationships with smoking. The widespread acceptance of Kreyberg's hypothesis has led to certain complications which are exemplified in the work of Belcher (1971, 1975) and Kennedy (1973). It has been shown that the proportion of patients with adenocarcinoma in the surgical series had not altered with the passage of time; during a period of fifteen years when the incidence of bronchial carcinoma in Britain had risen dramatically, the proportion of patients with adenocarcinoma had not changed. As Belcher points out, 'if the epidemic was due to smoking and adenocarcinoma was not, this proportion should have fallen, and it had not'.

Again, the incidence of adenocarcinoma in both men and women in the Far East is very much higher than that in Western countries, being about 40 per cent as against 20 per cent in Europe and North America. But, there also, there has been a rise in the incidence of bronchial carcinoma of almost epidemic proportions during the last two decades, it having gone up almost three times in ten years in Japan and Taiwan. As Belcher argues, 'If this rise is to be attributed to cigarette consumption, which in Japan at least has been as high as that in many European countries for years, and adenocarcinoma is not due to smoking, the proportion of tumours of this type should have fallen to an even greater extent than that which might have been expected in Europe. It has not done so. The figure still stands at 40 per cent in both men and women. Either the epidemic is due to smoking and so is adenocarcinoma, or neither is.'

Kennedy has suggested that the relationship of adenocarcinoma to smoking may be different in the two sexes. He also makes the point that the influence of smoking on adenocarcinoma is different in English patients from that of their North American counterparts. While adenocarcinoma in women in America is unrelated to smoking habits, Kennedy found no evidence for Kreyberg's hypothesis in the proportions of the cell types in female smokers and non-smokers in UK.

To all this confusion should be added certain racial differences. As Belcher (1971) has shown, the sex ratio of the incidence of bronchial carcinoma varies widely in different parts of the world, ranging from 13.5 : 1 in Holland to 1 : 1 in Nigeria. Furthermore, the incidence, the proportion of cell types and the site of the growth in European peoples are different from those among non-European peoples. In fact, he suggests that on the basis of lung cancer sex ratios, the world can be divided into two groups: Europeans and people elsewhere in the world of predominantly European origin, and non-Europeans. He also showed that there was no relationship between the sex ratio and the total tobacco consumption in different countries, and from the finding that the differences in sex ratio tended to follow the pattern of that of the ethnic group and peoples living in the same country, he deduced that there is a genetic factor in the aetiology of bronchial carcinoma. This point will be taken up again in the next chapter.

Diagnosis and secular changes in lung cancer

One of the major objections to the genetic theory of lung cancer, whether in the form given it by Burch or by other authors, is undoubtedly the very rapid rise in the diagnosis of lung cancer during the past seventy years (see Figure 5). It is quite implausible to argue that there have been genetic changes of such a size and nature as to cause such a manifold increase in the diagnosis of lung cancer, and consequently, it is argued, environmental changes (air pollution, cigarette smoking, etc.) must be considered responsible. An alternative suggestion is that the increase in deaths diagnosed as lung cancer has been due to improvements in diagnostic techniques, and is therefore more apparent than real. This is the argument put forward by Burch (1976), and we will here briefly consider it. As a beginning, consider a paper by Sehrt (1904), in which are described 178 cases of lung cancer discovered at necropsy at the beginning of this century; only 6 of these had been recognized during life! If we take this ratio of 172 failures to diagnose lung cancer, as compared with 6 successful diagnoses of lung cancer, in 1904, and argue that with our modern techniques all or most of the 178 cases of lung cancer would have been so diagnosed, then it seems quite reasonable to assume that much if not all of the apparent increase in deaths from lung cancer may have been due to improvements in diagnostic techniques.

Burch is not the only expert to doubt whether there has been an actual increase in deaths from lung cancer. Rigdon & Kirchoff (1953) concluded that claims of genuine increase in the frequency of lung cancer were 'open to question'. Willis (1967), after an extensive review of the literature, concluded: 'it is not possible either to affirm or to deny that there has been a real increase'. Similarly, Feinstein (1968) concluded his historical discussion by stating that diagnostic changes have played the most important role in the increase in death rate from lung cancer.

If the reliability of the diagnosis given on death certificates at the turn of the century or earlier is very low, it must also be doubted whether the reliability of more recent diagnoses so recorded is very high. Several authors have indicated that there are frequent disagreements between clinicians and pathologists over the diagnosis of lung cancer. Heasman & Kipworth (1966) reported on post-mortem examinations and compared results with diagnoses made by clinicians. In the sample analysed, clinicians diagnosed 338 cases of primary cancer of the lung; 417 were diagnosed so at necropsy, but only 227 of these agreed with the clinicians' assessment. If we can assume that the pathologists' diagnosis was correct, then 33 per cent of the clinicians' diagnoses were false positive, while 46 per cent of lung cancer cases were myths! These authors also concluded that a large part of the increase in recorded mortality from cancer of the lung resulted from advances in diagnoses, and that even in 1959 there was 'still considerable room for further improvement'.

Bauer & Robbins (1972) reported a similar study from the Boston City Hospital, USA. Necropsies disclosed 446 cases of cancer of the lung, with an overall clinical diagnostic error of 49.1 per cent! 22 per cent of cases were overlooked by the clinical diagnosticians.

What causes false-positive diagnoses? Rosenblatt (1969) has suggested that in the post-1930 period, false-positive clinical diagnoses of lung cancer have often been reported due to metastases in the lung from primary loci at many different sites. He too believed that the very great increase in recorded lung cancer deaths over the past thirty years was not due to an extrinsic carcinogen, but resulted from the use of new diagnostic techniques (radiology, bronchoscopy, sputum examination, and surgery). He further suggests that the great interest in lung cancer stimulated by the suggestion that it might be due to smoking, has produced the tendency to over-diagnose this particular disorder, and Smithers (1953) discovered that even specialists in thoracic diseases were guilty of a large proportion of false positive diagnoses from 1944 to 1950.

Rosenblatt et al. (1971a, b) supported this argument by showing that at the Doctors Hospital, New York, clinical diagnosis of lung cancer was over twice as frequent as diagnosis following necropsy! As Burch points out, 'carcinoma of the lung was the only neoplasm to be greatly over-diagnosed clinically and in which no unsuspected cases were found at necropsy'. Primary lung cancer had been simulated by pulmonary metastases from carcinomas of the pancreas, kidney, stomach, breast and thyroid, and by malignant melanoma. Burch adds the comment: 'It is of great interest that the 5.5 per cent of lung cancers found in this recent New York necropsy series of malignancies is *lower* than the proportions found among several necropsy series from Austria, Germany and the U.S. published at the end of the 19th and the beginning of the 20th century. In five such series in which necropsy findings were the main basis of diagnosis, lung cancer diagnosis ranged from 8.3 to 11.5 per cent of all cancers.'

The problem of metastases to lung being erroneously diagnosed as lung cancer is emphasized by a study reported by Burch (1974); he found that a total of 747 primary lung cancers was recorded in a large-scale post-mortem study of the anatomical distribution of metastases in Swedish cancer cases, but some 2,079 metastases to the lung from primary sites outside the lung!

Burch gives many further instances, and it is difficult not to agree with him when he concludes: 'There can be no doubt, therefore, that diagnostic artefacts have contributed massively to the secular increases in recorded death rates from lung cancer . . . the beginning of the century was characterised by severe under-diagnosis, especially above the age of 40 years. However, in 1959, Heasman & Kipworth's (1966) study showed that although false-negative diagnoses were still common (46%), false-positive diagnoses were already making appreciable contributions (33%).' Burch ends the discussion by saying: 'We have now reached the following position: (a) a positive association between a habit such as smoking and a disease such as a specific cancer, is an unreliable indicator of a causal connection—to *assume* that a positive association implies causal connection is, of course, methodological outrage; and (b) the bulk of the enormous secular increase in death rates from lung cancer recorded during the century was a consequence of diagnostic error and cannot be attributed to tobacco.' These conclusions of course do not prove that smoking has not caused lung cancer in certain cases; the data merely throw severe doubt on the argument put forward by the environmentalist school.

It must not be assumed that autopsies will necessarily result in completely reliable results. Non-medical readers can have no idea of the unreliability of medical diagnoses, even when based on autopsies; to imagine that such diagnoses can be relied upon to give a reasonable picture of the actual condition of the patient is overtly optimistic. In a recent editorial (1971) in the *Annals of Thoracic Surgery* it was pointed out that 'the most experienced pathologists often disagree on classification of these tumours, and differential criteria are poorly defined'. Large bodies of data are available to indicate that the reliability of medical diagnosis, using pathological material relevant to respiratory diseases, is well below what would be regarded as acceptable in psychological tests. Among the papers on which this generalization is based are the following: Feinstein et al., 1970; Kern et al., 1968; McCarthy & Widmer, 1974; Reid & Rose, 1964; Stebbings, 1971; Thurlbeck et al., 1968; Wilson & Burke, 1957; Yesner, 1973; Yesner et al., 1965, 1973. It is odd that this unreliability has not been pointed out either by the proponents of the orthodox view (e.g. the various reports of the Royal College of Physicians, or the Surgeon General), or by the critics; both sides have treated the results of autopsy reports as inherently valid and reliable. The fact that this clearly is not so must make one even more suspicious of statistical treatment of unreliable data.

Dose-response relations between cigarette smoking and lung cancer

In pharmacological research, dose-response relations are among the most important parameters to be investigated. If there is a direct relation between a given drug and a given type of response, then the more of the drug is administered, the greater should be the response. Non-linear relations do of course exist, and deserve special study; as we shall see, the effects of nicotine on a person may be of this type. However, when the response is disease or death, monotonic relations are far more frequent than curvilinear ones, and indeed curvilinear relations may not exist at all. Under these circumstances, it is important to investigate the dose-response relationships between smoking and lung cancer.

A seminal investigation of this problem has been reported by Passey (1962). Having referred to the hypothesis of cancer of the lung as the result of the carcinogens contained in tobacco smoke, Passey queries whether there is a necessary connection, and asks: 'May not lung cancer be the result of altered conditions arising out of disease or damage of the respiratory system in which carcinogens need have played no part? This damage may have been induced by (a) irritating properties of tobacco or other smoke, (b) chronic respiratory disease, or (c) other injuries.'

Passey goes on to state: 'Nowhere has it been claimed that the heavy smoker is stricken with cancer *earlier* than the light smoker. If lung cancer in smokers is the result of direct carcinogenic action, one would certainly expect this to happen; for experiment has shown beyond question that a potent carcinogen induces tumours early.' Passey next examines the smoking histories of 499 men with lung cancer, grouping the cases according to the number of cigarettes smoked. He gives a table which shows 'that the amount smoked makes no appreciable difference to the mean age at which the person first reported to the clinic. The light smoker is afflicted with lung cancer at the same age as a heavy smoker. This is a surprising observation. The mean age at which smoking was started was 17; the average amount smoked daily was 23 cigarettes; and the mean age at which the patient presented at the clinic was 57 years . . . the mean smoking period was some 40 years.' Nor was it true, as might be thought, that the youngest of these patients with lung cancer might have smoked particularly heavily, and that the eldest had survived because they were specially moderate smokers. 'The amount smoked daily by old and young is not dissimilar. Yet the oldest patient had smoked for some 50 years longer than the youngest — this represents well over a quarter of a million more cigarettes. These figures suggest that there is no relation between the amount smoked daily and the age of onset of lung cancer.'

Passey's figures show clearly that lung cancer developed at approximately the same age in those who began to smoke earliest (between the ages of 6 and 10) and in those who started to smoke much later. Those who started early smoked for some 51 years, whereas the late starters smoked for only 31 years or so; yet there was no great difference between the daily amounts which patients in each group said they smoked. Each member of the group which began early must have smoked over 150,000 cigarettes more than the late starters! 'These figures offer the clearest evidence that the age when lung cancer develops is determined by neither the amount smoked nor the age at which smoking began. If this is true, tobacco smoke did not act as a carcinogen. It is apparently not the number of cigarettes smoked but something related to the age of the individual which determines when he dies from lung cancer.' This is an important conclusion which would seem to be very difficult to reconcile with a causal hypothesis of the 'smoking causes cancer' type. Taken together with the other anomalies and contradictions discussed, it would seem to present a considerable obstacle to the easy adoption of the currently orthodox view of the environmentalists. It is interesting that Passey's findings have been replicated by Pike & Doll (1965), on their sample of British doctors; they conclude that 'neither the amount smoked nor the age of starting made any substantial difference to the "period" average age at onset of the disease', and that these conclusions were also valid for the 'life-span' average under the conditions in which lung cancer is produced in man.

The effects of inhalation

One of the most obvious deductions from the environmentalist hypothesis that smoking causes cancer is that the inhalation of tobacco smoke must put the smoker at a greater risk than smoking without inhaling. In the 1971 report of the Royal College of Physicians, those who must smoke are exhorted to inhale less, thus accepting the soundness of the argument. Certainly the idea that cigarette smoke causes lung cancer makes its strong intuitive appeal because we can readily envisage airborne carcinogens passing through the mouth, past the larynx and pharynx, down through the trachea to the bronchi, and lodging in the lungs. Unless we inhale, however, most of this passage is aborted, and whatever airborne carcinogens might be in the smoke do not reach the lungs. If, as Popper and other philosophers of science assert, falsification of hypotheses is a true mark of scientific endeavour, then this would seem an excellent hypothesis to test, as negative results would seriously disconcert the 'smoking causes cancer' hypothesis. Positive results would not be fatal to the constitutional theory, because it could be asserted that the constitutional factors leading people to smoke might be the same as those which lead some of them to inhale, but clearly this would be something of an *ad hoc* argument, difficult to substantiate.

The findings concerning inhaling are inconsistent, but for the most part contradict the environmentalist hypothesis. What Burch calls 'the only numerically adequate survey in this country of the effect of inhaling' was based on 399 inhalers and 249 non-inhalers (Fisher, 1959). It showed that, when figures were standardized for the number of cigarettes smoked per day, inhalers suffered, on the average, a 10 per cent *lower* incidence of lung cancer than non-inhalers. This difference was found to be statistically significant at the 1 per cent level, and Fisher commented: 'Even equality would be a fair knock-out for the theory that smoke in the lung causes cancer.' In another, much smaller study, Doll & Hill (1964) found results suggesting that inhalers who were heavy smokers had a lower incidence of lung cancer than corresponding non-inhalers.

In the United States, Lombard & Snegireff (1959) found that the incidence of lung cancer in non-inhaling slight smokers was only 55 per cent of that in inhaling slight smokers; the incidence in non-inhaling heavy smokers was 88 per cent of that of inhaling heavy smokers. As Burch (1976) points out, there are statistical infelicities in the treatment of the data (statistical significances of differences are not given; no details of the numbers involved are stated; findings for medium smokers are not given, etc.). Data do seem to support the Doll & Hill finding, however, that for heavy smokers inhaling is less injurious than for light smokers, and may have no effect at all.

A similar finding emerges from the study by Schwartz et al. (1961) carried out in France. Light and medium smokers who inhaled suffered a significantly higher risk of lung cancer, but for those smoking thirty or more cigarettes a day, the risk among inhalers was only 60 per cent of that in non-inhalers! The authors of this study also found that cigarette smokers who, in addition, smoked a pipe incurred only half the risk of lung cancer, a prophylactic effect of the additional pipe smoking which was even more marked among heavy cigarette smokers who inhaled. The authors concluded that the explanation of that paradoxical finding must be sought in the smoker himself.

The figures as quoted seem to be definitely inconsistent with a causal theory of smoking causing lung cancer, but Burch (1976) has pointed out that this is not strictly true. As he says:

> The recorded age-dependence of lung cancer favours no form of [smoking] causal hypothesis, but it is least inconsistent with the idea that smoking precipitates the growth of forbidden clones. Precipitating action is more likely to take place centrally (perhaps in the bone marrow) than peripherally in the lungs and bronchi. Hence, even when the incidence of lung cancer in inhalers of certain types of tobacco smoke is indeed lower than non-inhalers ... this does not disprove the causal hypothesis as such. ... We are forced to conclude that the evidence for the effect of inhaling cannot provide definitive tests of all causal hypotheses, although it might help to define some of those anatomical sites where cigarette smoke does *not* exert a direct carcinogenic action.

This is true, but if we restrict ourselves to the theories advanced by orthodox defenders of the causal hypothesis, then the results must be seen as a definitive disconfirmation; it is only within Burch's theory that this disconfirmation is less than complete.

One difficulty which arises with the stated figures about the effects of inhalation derives from the well-known fact that statements about smoking habits are not very accurate, even when questions relate to amount smoked, type of cigarette smoked, etc. (Todd, 1966). The report of the Royal College of Physicians (1977) acknowledges the inaccuracy, particularly relating to statements about inhalation. They admit that: 'In several studies it has been found that among heavier smokers inhalers have a slightly lower risk than men who say they do not inhale.' They go on to say: 'Part of the explanation of this anomaly is that nearly all heavy cigarette smokers inhale to some degree and their statements about whether or not they inhale are inaccurate. Furthermore, it is possible that deep inhalation may deposit smoke in parts of the lungs that are less susceptible to cancer.'

There is no doubt that statements about inhaling are inherently inaccurate; we have found in our own work that people differ in their understanding of what the term means, and may give quite divergent replies depending on these differences in understanding. However, despite the fact that for light smokers differences in incidence of lung cancers related to inhaling can be observed, while for heavy smokers this incidence is reversed, one is chary of accepting the notion that the understanding of what inhaling means is more adequate in light smokers than in heavy smokers. It is an interesting comment on the lack of psychological expertise on the part of the physicians who have directed the enquiries into this aspect of the problem that they have only realized the difficulties attending the understanding of terms like 'inhaling' when confronted with paradoxical findings. Psychologists would have begun by examining the understanding of often badly educated and dull respondents of the terms used in their questions, and would have changed these in such a way as to maximize agreement on facts between respondents. This task is an obvious necessity if we are ever to get proper factual knowledge in this field, but to date, in spite of a recognition of the problem, this has not been done. Psychological enquiries of this kind should never be carried out without the advice of a properly qualified psychologist, experienced in questionnaire construction and large-scale testing. As they stand, the data are certainly inconsistent with the causal hypothesis, although certain implausible *ad hoc* hypotheses have been advanced to explain them away. We must await better designed and better controlled experiments, using well-known psychological techniques of test construction, before we are likely to have an adequate understanding of these facts.

Burch (1976) goes on from here to argue that: 'In view of the lack of consistent evidence for the effects of inhalation of cigarette smoke, we can conclude that the actual route of entry of carcinogens has rather little relevance. Accordingly, we might expect to find a simple correlation between the incidence of lung cancer and the concentration of chemical carcinogens in tobacco smoke.' Having reviewed some of the evidence on the nature of the chemical carcinogens in tobacco smoke, he concluded that: 'We will anticipate a much higher incidence of lung cancer in "pure" cigar and pipe smokers than in smokers of equivalent masses of cigarette tobacco.' As he goes on to say, 'In most studies, the reverse relation is found; pipe and "classical" cigar smokers suffer lower rates of lung cancer than cigarette smokers . . . . In France, Schwartz et al. (1961) found that pure pipe smoking was far more common, and heavier, among controls than among lung cancer cases . . . . Again, the important factor would appear to be the person who smokes (and his constitution) rather than the pipe of tobacco he smokes, and how he smokes it.' This argument is true only if we can indeed assume that type of tobacco smoked is irrelevant to the incidence of cancer; is this correct? The evidence suggests that there may be important differences between flue-cured tobacco and naturally cured tobacco. We must next turn to a brief review of this evidence.

Differential effects of alkaline and acid tobaccos

There is a considerable body of evidence to indicate that different types of tobacco have very different effects on smokers, a point fully discussed by Eysenck (1965), who also points out the curious reluctance of many textbooks and government reports to discuss this matter. The late Dr Jan Beffinger, who was born in Poland and was intimately concerned with the introduction of new methods of fermentation of tobacco, very forcefully drew attention to certain facts which are potentially of considerable importance in this connection. He takes his cue from the following observation. As he says, 'It is a statistical fact that in some countries like the Soviet Union, Poland and the Union of South Africa there is no increase in the rate of lung cancer to the same extent as in the USA and the UK — although in those countries the consumption of cigarettes is increasing at the same rate as in the USA and the UK.' Similarly, regarding Russian investigations on tobacco smoking and lung cancer, it has been reported by Dr A. B. Savittski of the USSR Academy of Medical Sciences that studies in Russia indicated that there was no relationship between the smoking of cigarettes and lung cancers: 'Russians do not deny that they have cases of lung cancer, especially in industrial areas, but they clearly state that they are not facing the problem to such a catastrophic extent as the UK and the USA.' A possible answer to this question may also give us an answer to the problem raised by the lack of deleterious consequences of smoking cigars and pipes.

As is well known, the tobacco used in the manufacture of cigarettes is quite different in many ways from the tobacco used for smoking in pipes and cigars. One of the main chemical differences is in the content of plant sugars. This difference is largely due to different means of curing the tobacco. Cigar tobacco (air-cured) has a low sugar content of between 0.5 per cent and 2 per cent, and gives rise to an alkaline smoke, whereas most cigarettes contain a proportion of, and in some countries consist entirely of, flue-cured tobacco, the sugar content of which may be as high as 20—25 per cent. These high-sugar-content cigarettes give rise to an acid smoke. The possibility suggests itself that the apparent health dangers of smoking may be largely related to the method of curing, flue-cured tobacco being much more dangerous than air-cured tobacco, and that the risks to health are mediated by the high sugar content and the acid smoke of the flue-cured tobaccos largely used in the manufacture of cigarettes. Conversely, smokers of pipes and cigars may be protected by the low sugar content and the alkaline smoke of the air-cured tobaccos used.

Some important experiments bearing on this point were published by Passey et al. (1971). In these experiments, groups of young rats were exposed to the smoke of either cigar tobacco or cigarette tobacco, with control groups being exposed to no tobacco smoke at all. A pilot experiment indicated that the smoke of cigar tobacco is relatively harmless compared with that of cigarette tobacco. Only five animals in the cigarette group survived to the 70th day, whereas after much heavier and longer exposure to cigar smoke six animals in the cigar group were alive on the 251st day, presenting little or no cellular damage to their respiratory systems, with even the cilia in the trachea and bronchi remaining intact. Further experiments were undertaken, and 'the results were substantially the same as in the pilot experiment in that the animals exposed to the smoke of flue-cured tobacco consistently suffered much more than those exposed to the smoke of cigar and other air-cured tobaccos'. Post-mortem findings supported these conclusions, as did experiments by Lamb and Reid (1969), which effectively replicated the work of Passey and his colleagues.

Elson, Betts and Passey (1972) followed this finding with a detailed analysis of the pH of smoke of different tobaccos when smoked in a pipe or as a cigarette. They conclude that:

> The main differences in smoking characteristics between cigarettes and cigars and pipes would appear from our work to be: (1) the high sugar content of many—particularly the so-called 'mild'—cigarettes, which results in the production of the smoke of acid pH, becoming progressively *more acid* during the course of smoking; (2) the low sugar content of cigar tobacco, and of the air-dried tobacco used in cigarettes of certain countries, which

gives a smoke of less acid pH, becoming progressively more *alkaline* during the course of smoking; (3) the conditions of smoking in a pipe, whereby the smoke from all types of tobacco, with both high and low sugar content, is less acid than that of most cigarettes and becomes progressively *more alkaline* during the course of smoking.

Elson et al. go on to say:

> Since the satisfaction derived from smoking is mainly due to the pharmacological effects of nicotine (Ashton & Watson, 1970), the lower lung cancer incidence in cigar and pipe smokers may be related to the fact that nicotine is more readily absorbed in the form of the free base (at alkaline pH, up to pH 9) than in the form of a stable salt (at acid pH, from about pH 5-4). To obtain the same degree of 'nicotine satisfaction' as in smoking a pipe or cigar, the smoker of cigarettes giving an acid smoke would tend to encourage more prolonged and extensive contact with the mucus membranes of the mouth and bronchus, and *to take the smoke into his lungs,* which would thus suffer greater exposure to the 'carcinogenic' effects of the smoke than would be the case with pipe or cigar smokers.... The 'acid buffering capacity' of the smoke also increases progressively during the course of smoking, the increase being particularly great during the smoking from a 30mm to a 10mm butt length. The 'absorbability' of the nicotine thus becomes progressively less, and the tendency to inhale to keep up the 'nicotine satisfaction' will be greatest at the time when the tar content of the smoke is also at its highest.

Exactly the opposite is true of cigarettes made from air-cured (low sugar) tobacco and with cigars and pipes, where the smoke becomes progressively more alkaline and the 'alkaline buffering capacity' increases as smoking proceeds, reaching its highest values in smoking from a 30mm to a 10mm butt length. The 'absorbability' of the nicotine thus increases during the course of smoking so that any tendency to inhale would be least in the period when the tar is at its maximum. This theoretical course of smoke inhalation is of course related to disease only on the hypothesis that inhalation in actual fact increases risk; as we have seen, this is a very doubtful proposition. Nevertheless the 'buffering capacity' of the smoke may have other important consequences.

Results from rats of course do not necessarily transfer to humans, and it is essential to test the Beffinger hypothesis directly, by comparing death rates from cancer in different countries where different types of tobacco are smoked. A beginning has been made by Elson & Betts (1972). As they state their objective: 'We are investigating the relation between sugar content of the tobacco and pH of the smoke of a range of cigarettes drawn from different countries. One objective is to ascertain whether the differences in lung cancer death rates in different countries have any connection with the predominant type of cigarettes smoked in these countries.'

In this study, the authors examined more than 150 brands of cigarettes, covering a total sugar content ranging from 0.5 to 20.5 per cent, and a pH ranging from 4.3 to 8.4, when cigarettes were smoked to a 20mm butt length, and 4.0 to 8.7 when smoked to a 10mm butt length. As regards national differences, they emphasize the striking difference between Great Britain and France. In Great Britain, which has the highest lung cancer death rate in the world, most of the cigarettes smoked over the past fifty years have been composed entirely of flue-cured tobacco of high sugar content (average about 18 per cent). In France, a country of relatively low lung cancer death rates (about one third of that of England and Wales), the cigarettes most commonly smoked have been consistently those made of air-cured tobacco of low sugar content (average about 2 per cent). This is an important difference difficult to explain in terms other than the type of smoke produced by these different types of tobacco.

In two further important papers, Betts & Elson (1974) and Elson, Betts & Darcy (1973) have shown that an increase in the serum levels of the $\alpha 1$ — acute phase protein, indicative of local tissue damage, has been shown in rats exposed to cigarette smoke for periods of up to thirty days. These increases correlated well with the degree of damage to the respiratory system as evidenced by the pathological changes observed post-mortem in the lungs. The effect of smoking on the serum $\alpha 1$ — acute phase protein does not seem to bear any direct relation to the tar or nicotine content of the smoke, and it is suggested that it is the acid nature of the smoke of the high sugar content, flue-cured tobacco, which makes some contribution to the intensity of the $\alpha 1$ — protein response; Betts & Elson show quite clearly the differential effects on rats of flue-cured and air-cured tobacco currently smoked in England, France, Switzerland, Spain and the United States: increases in $\alpha 1$ — acute phase protein units for typical flue-cured English cigarettes range from 0.78 to 1.10, while those for air-cured cigarettes range from 0.05 to 0.54.

The $\alpha 1$ — acute phase globulin has not been determined in human serum, but as a possible human counterpart Elson et al. (1973) considered $\alpha 1$ — antitrypsin, serum levels of which are of significance in relation to conditions such as emphysema and chronic obstructive pulmonary disease. The levels of $\alpha 1$ — antitrypsin in the serum show an increase in response to inflammation, and the frequent findings of early emphysema in adults with inherited $\alpha 1$ — antitrypsin deficiency suggested a possible causal relationship; during inflammation their $\alpha 1$ — antitrypsin level was found to increase less than normally, suggesting an impaired protective mechanism.

Non-smokers were found to have a narrow range of antitrypsin levels, ranging symmetrically around the 100 per cent level. In cigarette smokers the levels showed a considerably wider divergence than those of non-smokers, and have a mean value of 117, which would appear to indicate a smoker's level of about 20 per cent higher than the non-smoker's normal level. This higher mean serum $\alpha 1$ — antitrypsin level in smokers could indicate a compensatory protective mechanism to inflammatory or other conditions in the lung induced by smoking; a high level in the smoker could be a warning of a high degree of inflammation or tissue damage. 'The finding of an antitrypsin level much below the "smoker mean" in a confirmed smoker could be an even more significant danger signal in that it could mean an impaired protection against the smoking hazard. Such a smoker could well be at a high lung cancer risk, and it appears possible that an investigation such as $\alpha 1$ — antitrypsin determination could constitute one approach in the direction of finding some answer to the much asked question "why do not all smokers get cancer?"'

It is interesting to note, in anticipation of the next chapter, that there is a definite genetic factor in the production of $\alpha 1$ — antitrypsin. As Prieto (1976) states, 'The synthesis of antitrypsin and its concentration in the serum are determined genetically.... The current theory about antitrypsin inheritance is known as autosomal co-dominance: a pair of genes is responsible for determining the type of antitrypsin which is synthesised (the phenotype); each member of the pair is capable of expressing itself, that is, of determining the production of antitrypsin of a given phenotype independently (to a certain extent at least) of the other. The serum concentration of antitrypsin is related to the phenotype.' The normal genes are known as Pi M (P stands for proteinase, i for inhibitor) and the normal phenotype as MM, a homozygous state where all antitrypsin is of the type M and has a normal concentration in serum. There are more than twenty mutant genes, distinguished by alphabetic superscripts such as Pi^F, Pi^S, and Pi^Z; these are related to the mobility of the corresponding antitrypsin during a special electrophoretic technique. Persons with very low antitryptic activity in their serum are a phenotype ZZ (two genes of PiZ). Such homozygous deficient patients have a very high probability of contracting emphysema; one study found twenty-three cases with emphysema out of thirty-three homozygous deficient patients (Mittman, 1972).

It seems clear that the hypothesis linking type of tobacco smoke with disease and danger to health finds considerable support in these figures, which also suggest important physiological correlates (e.g. $\alpha1$—antitrypsin) related both to disease, smoking, and type of tobacco smoked. Although these theories have been around for quite a long time now, no determined effort seems to have been made to investigate the crucial question of the direct relation between type of tobacco smoked and lung cancer. This could easily be done in a country like Germany, where in certain provinces (e.g. Hessen) both types of tobacco are used for the manufacture of cigarettes, and are freely available and widely used. While a comparison of the types of tobacco smoked by lung cancer patients, as compared with those smoked by controls, would not constitute a crucial experiment (crucial experiments hardly exist in science!), nevertheless such an experiment, if properly controlled for personality, socio-economic status, sex and other important variables, could be of the utmost value in shedding further light on this important question. The environmentalist hypothesis would be considerably strengthened if it could be shown that lung cancer was related much more closely to the smoking of flue-cured tobaccos than to the smoking of air-cured tobaccos; the failure to find such a difference would weaken the environmentalist and strengthen the genetic hypothesis.

We must also consider the important practical consequences which might follow from such an experiment, provided that differences in the predicted direction were to be found. The idle search for artificial materials to constitute 'safe' cigarettes has led to the waste of between £20 and £50 million in this country alone, only to result in cigarettes which smokers refused to use. If air-cured tobaccos could be shown to be relatively safe, as compared with flue-cured tobaccos, then clearly we would here have a ready-made 'safe' material for the making of cigarettes which would satisfy smokers in a realistic manner. It is astonishing that these possibilities have not led to a large number of investigations into this area.

The effects of giving up smoking

We have so far discussed two of the three major arguments favouring the contention that smoking causes lung cancer. The first argument was the high mortality ratio for smokers as opposed to non-smokers; the second was the correlation over countries between smoking and lung cancer. The third argument, featured in the second report of the Royal College of Physicians (1971), relates to changes in mortality for British doctors as compared with those for the general population. The report features a table containing secular comparisons for the death rates during 1953-57 and 1962-65 of two groups of men aged 35 to 64. One group was taken from a sample of British doctors studied by R. Doll and A. B. Hill; the other group was assembled from the Registrar General's data for England and Wales. According to the RCP report, the contrasted data constitute 'the strongest evidence there is of the value of giving up cigarettes'. The following detailed claims were made. (1) The death rate of British doctors declined more than that of the general population in the interval between the time periods 1953-57 and 1962-65. (2) In the category 'major diseases related to cigarette smoking', the death rates declined for the British doctors but increased in the general population. (3) In the category 'all unrelated causes' death rates declined equally in British doctors and in the general population.

The RCP also argued, from data published elsewhere in the report, that British doctors' cigarette smoking declined by about 50 per cent between 1951 and 1965, but 'there was little corresponding change in the smoking habits of the general population during the same period'. The argument put forward by the RCP report was essentially that as cigarette smoking declined more for British doctors than for the general population, so the death rate between the two time periods declined more for the doctors than for the general population. Furthermore, although the British doctors and the general population had similar changes in death rates for diseases 'unrelated' to cigarette smoking, the death rates for the 'major diseases related to cigarette smoking' declined for the doctors but not for the general population. The argument certainly seems a very strong one, but unfortunately, as Seltzer (1972b) has shown, it is not firmly based on evidence, and contains certain very dubious manipulations of the data. We will now turn to consideration of Seltzer's re-analysis of the data.

Seltzer's first argument relates to the data about cigarette smoking. He makes a thorough analysis of available data and concludes that 'these data do support the RCP contention that the proportion of cigarette smoking British doctors fell between 1951 and 1965, but they do not support the statement about "little corresponding change" in the general population. From 1956 to 1965 the non-smokers in the general population increased at a rate similar to that shown by British doctors. From 1961 to 1965 the percentage of cigarette smokers decreased at about the same rate in both the general population and the doctors'. Thus the major plank in the RCP argument falls to the ground; both doctors and general population show similar changes in smoking, both groups increasing at a similar rate as far as non-smokers are concerned.

Seltzer puts forward but does not stress an argument which to us seems a very strong one, namely that even if all the facts were as stated by the RCP, nevertheless no conclusions could be drawn from them because doctors are not a typical sample of the general population, differing from the rest of the population in education, socio-economic status, professional knowledge, and in many other ways. The RCP arguments would only be valid if the sub-group studied (i.e. British doctors) were representative of the total group (i.e. the general population). Lack of comparability makes it impossible to derive any sensible kind of argument from differences that might be found in the secular changes in disease rates obtained for these two groups. However, as Seltzer goes on to show, it is not necessary to rely on this methodological argument, strong as it may be, because of the many other errors contained in the RCP demonstration.

Seltzer goes on to point out that while the RCP report used the original figures produced by Doll and Hill in their work, they changed the classification of various diseases, re-classifying many of Doll and Hill's 'unrelated diseases' to the category of 'related diseases'; some examples are rheumatic fever, rheumatic pericarditis, endocarditis and myocarditis, diseases of the mytral, aortic and tricuspit valve, acute and subacute bacterial endocarditis, gangrene, varicose veins and haemorrhoids. Seltzer points out that 'no explanation is provided for these changes in the Doll/Hill classification, although the RCP report relied so heavily on other aspects of the Doll/Hill data'. This unexplained change in the 'rules of the game' (which actually did not alter conclusions very much) would certainly be a disturbing feature of the report were it not put in the shade by even more disturbing aspects.

Seltzer points out certain restrictions of the data used by the RCP report. Thus it is restricted to men in England and Wales, whereas the Doll/Hill sample was drawn from the UK (Scotland and Northern Ireland, as well as England and Wales). The contrasted populations are thus geographically different, and a more suitable comparison for the British doctors would be with all men in the United Kingdom, since the male death rate of the UK may differ from those of only England and Wales. The RCP report also contains an age restriction; data are restricted to men aged 35 to 64, although the data for all adult ages would ordinarily extend from ages 35 to 84. As Seltzer states, 'Since the RCP statements are not confined to conclusions about the health of cigarette smokers only at ages 35 to 64, the absence for all adult ages would be a significant limitation on the RCP conclusion.'

Another major restriction relates to the time periods sampled. The RCP compared death rates for the period 1953 to 1957 (period 1) and 1962 to 1965 (period 3), omitting 1958 to 1961 (period 2). When two separated periods in time are compared without regard to the intervening period, any conclusions about the trend are tenuous, because the intermediate data may alter any trend found between the two extremes of time. In line with these arguments, Seltzer concluded that 'Since the missing data might help clarify some of the issues, a reanalysis of the RCP contention seems desirable, with the data extended to include geographic, age and temporal information that had been omitted in the RCP report.'

We can here only note the main conclusions from Seltzer's reanalysis of the expanded data. He first looked at the claim that total death rates of doctors decline more than those of the general population. He found that the death rate for the British doctors increased by 4 per cent from period 1 to period 2, despite the concomitant decrease in cigarette smoking. Over the same interval the death rate for the general population declined by 1 per cent. From period 2 to period 3, British doctors' overall death rate declined more than that of the general population which showed essentially no change, despite the drop in cigarette smoking. The data do not agree with the RCP report's conclusion.

The next claim looked at by Seltzer is that the death rates for the category of 'all unrelated causes' declined equally in British doctors and in the general population. He points out, 'This claim is not supported by the data for age 35 to 84. Between periods 1 and 3, the reduction in death rates for "unrelated causes" in the general population (11%) is almost twice as great as a comparable decline in the British doctors (6%). Thus the general population showed a much greater decline than the British doctors in death from unrelated causes.'

The third major claim made by the RCP report was that the death rates of 'major diseases related to cigarette smoking' declined in the British doctors but increased in the general population. Looking at periods 1 and 3, the death rates for 'related' diseases increased in both populations, rising by 2 per cent in British doctors and by 4 per cent in all men in England and Wales. Thus we do not have a decrease, as claimed, but an increase in British doctors! Changes from period 1 to period 2 in fact show a larger increase in death from 'related' causes in British doctors (4 per cent) than in the general population (1 per cent). It is only for the interval between periods 2 and 3 that the RCP claim can receive some support; during this interval the death rates of doctors declined by 2 per cent, while those of the general population increased by 3 per cent. 'Thus, the apparent contradiction of the rising death rate during a fall in smoking occurred in British doctors for the first interval and in the general population for the second.'

Seltzer also found many inconsistencies in patterns of specific diseases. For instance, death rates from periods 1 to 3 in British doctors increased by 8 per cent for coronary heart disease, during a period of declining cigarette smoking! In the category of 'other cardiovascular diseases', there was no change in British doctors, but death rates for the same diseases declined by 21 per cent in all men in the general population of England and Wales. The death rates for 'all cardiovascular disease' increased by 4 per cent in British doctors, in contrast with essentially no change for all men in England and Wales. Lastly, Seltzer notes that 'A curious feature of Doll and Hill's (1964) report on British doctors is that the death rates of former cigarette smokers (less than five years after stopping smoking) fell more for "unrelated causes" than for "related causes". This inconsistency is also found in the RCP report, where for British doctors the death rates for "unrelated causes" fell by 17 per cent, compared to a 10 per cent for "major diseases related to cigarette smoking".' No one can read Seltzer's re-analysis and discussion without coming to the conclusion that if the RCP report is

indeed the strongest evidence there is of the value of giving up cigarettes, then it must remain very doubtful whether giving up smoking
will indeed have any effect at all on a person's health. The fact that any
effect on death rates is stronger for diseases unrelated to smoking than
for diseases related to smoking must make one equally dubious about
the relevance of these data to a discussion of the environmental
hypothesis.

It is interesting to note how the medical establishment, as represented by the editors of *The Lancet*, received Seltzer's thoughtful critique.
They looked at the figure relating to the RCP's incorrect claim that
doctors change their smoking habits to a greater extent than other
men of similar age, and concluded that 'it is difficult to justify the
College's claim save on the basis of common experience and the knowledge that the overall consumption of tobacco in the country as a whole
has changed very little'. Having thus agreed that the major prop of the
RCP's argument has been knocked away, they conclude that 'Seltzer
may have succeeded in confusing the issue, but he has not thrown
doubt on the conclusion that the changes in mortality among British
doctors provide strong evidence that stopping smoking increases the
expectation of life'. Their main reason for making this statement
appears to be a large body of evidence from a number of prospective
studies, showing that the difference between the age-standardized death
rates of ex-smokers and non-smokers decreases steadily with the passage
of time after smoking has stopped, and disappears almost entirely after
it has been stopped for more than ten years. The editors of *The Lancet*
realize some of the difficulties involved in drawing conclusions from
such data, but curiously enough they do not seem to realize the most
important limitation on data of this kind, a limitation that also applies
to the comparison of British doctors who have given up smoking and
the general population. The point is that on the constitutional hypothesis people who give up smoking are constitutionally different from
those who continue, and thus have a lower constitutional predisposition to lung cancer (or whatever other disease is in question). Evidence
is at present being collected on this point, and it appears to show conclusively that smokers who give up smoking are more similar to non-
smokers than to smokers who continue smoking in their past medical
and psychological history (Friedman et al., *in press*). The failure of the
editors of *The Lancet* to realize the importance of this variable makes
even more strange their conclusion that 'Seltzer may have succeeded
in confusing the issue'; it would be more accurate to say that he has

pointed out very serious errors in the RCP report which would have led the unwary reader to quite erroneous conclusions. We must conclude that the contentions of the RCP report are not supported by the available data, and that the third argument supporting the environmental hypothesis is as lacking in strength as are the other two.

Coronary heart disease and smoking

After this fairly lengthy discussion of the alleged effect of smoking on lung and other types of cancer, we must turn at least briefly to a consideration of the effects of smoking on coronary heart disease (CHD). This is important because, although the mortality ratio for heart disease is much lower than that for lung cancer, nevertheless the numbers involved are much larger. Coronary heart disease is now the leading cause of death in many countries, and in Britain, for instance, the number of deaths attributed to it has been rising steadily over the past forty years. In the study of British doctors it was found that lung cancer was responsible for 19 per cent of the excess mortality in smokers; by contrast, all cardiovascular diseases account for 52 per cent of the excess, 31 per cent arising from CHD. All authorities agree that a strong *statistical* association between smoking and heart disease exists; the crucial question is whether or not there is a *causal* relation. The 1964 Surgeon General's report concluded that 'it is not clear that the association has causal significance'. The 1977 report of the Royal College of Physicians, here as always more ready to jump to possibly unjustified conclusions, decided that 'the association between smoking and heart disease is largely one of cause and effect'. Is this true?

It is widely recognized that certain factors other than smoking predispose to the condition, or are associated with an increased incidence of CHD. Among those recognized by the Surgeon General's report are age, sex, morphological constitution, heredity, occupations involving responsibility and stress, low levels of physical activity, diets high in saturated fats, high blood pressure, high serum cholesterol levels, and excessive obesity. It was also recognized that if it could be shown that cigarette smokers and non-smokers had significant constitutional differences apart from any differences that might be caused by smoking itself, then the possibility would exist that some predisposition of smokers to the disease might also be of constitutional origin and not caused by smoking.

Only one example of the complexities introduced by extraneous constitutional factors will be given. Seltzer et al. (1974) took three measures of pulmonary function, forced vital capacity, forced expiratory volume in one second, and peak expiratory flow, in a population of 65,086 white, black and oriental cigarette smokers and non-smokers, 20–79 years of age. The expected relationships with age and sex were noted for each of the racial groups. Whites showed markedly higher mean pulmonary function values than blacks and orientals when the same age, sex, and smoking categories were compared. Important racial distinctions between smokers and non-smokers were found with respect to the three measures of pulmonary function used. For the white group, larger mean pulmonary function values were found among non-smokers in comparison with cigarette smokers in virtually every age grouping and for both sexes. For blacks and orientals, however, no such differences between smokers and non-smokers were noted! The virtual absence of appreciable differences between smokers and non-smokers in pulmonary function values in blacks and orientals, in contrast to those of whites, could not be explained by the analysis of data related to amount of smoking, duration of smoking, and inhalation of cigarette smoke. Similarly no explanations were readily available for a lack of significant differences in mean pulmonary function values between smokers who inhale and those who do not. These data indicate clearly that generalizations which leave out constitutional, racial, and other important factors can have no meaning in this very complex field.

Additional evidence on this point comes from the very large-scale studies of Japanese men living in Japan, Hawaii and California (Kagan et al., 1975; Marmot et al., 1975; Nichaman et al., 1975; Rhoads et al., 1978; Stemmermann et al., 1976; Syme et al., 1975; Winkelstein et al., 1975; Worth et al., 1975). In these studies, it was shown that among men of Japanese ancestry, there is a gradient in CHD mortality increasing from Japan to Hawaii to California, although rates of smoking of these men are not substantially different. Findings in these papers are too detailed to discuss here, and such a discussion would be largely irrelevant anyway; what is demonstrated is the complex intermingling of racial and environmental influences on the causation of coronary heart disease. This result should be compared with the similar results of Belcher (1971) on social differences in lung cancer already mentioned.

Much work has been published since the publication of the Surgeon General's report, and this contains results which are conflicting, contradictory, and often hostile to a causal interpretation. All the data support the existence of a *statistical* relationship, of approximately the same size as that noted by the Surgeon General (SMR = 1.7). Angina pectoris has given rise to very contradictory results; thus in one large-scale study it was found that those who smoked twenty or more cigarettes per day had a lower morbidity ratio than non-cigarette smokers, giving rise to the conclusion that 'the risk of angina pectoris as the sole or initial manifestation of CHD appears to be unrelated to the tobacco habit'. Other studies give similar results (Seltzer, 1968); Cederlöf et al. (1965), in a study of morbidity among monozygotic twins from Sweden, found a similar frequency of angina pectoris among smokers and non-smokers, a finding also exonerating smoking as the causal factor in this disease. As Seltzer (1968) points out, 'Uncomplicated angina pectoris comprises about 20 per cent of all manifestations of CHD in men; elimination of such cases would mean elimination of a significant segment of CHD cases from consideration of being related to the tobacco habit.'

The evidence regarding the use of tobacco in other forms than cigarettes, i.e. cigar smoking, pipe smoking, etc., has indicated that there is no statistical relationship between CHD and these forms of smoking; indeed in the case of the Doll & Hill study of British doctors, 'Pipe or cigar smokers gave a lower death rate than the group of non-smokers. In the Dorn study of US veterans, the mortality ratios of persons who smoked cigars or a pipe were virtually the same as those of non-smokers. The Hammond study of American men showed that the pipe smokers on the whole had lower CHD death rates than non-smokers, while the cigar smokers tended to have slightly higher rates than the non-smokers.' When we add that the Doll & Hill study of British doctors showed no significant differences among cigarette smokers between the CHD death rates of inhalers and non-inhalers, then it will be realized that the results present a considerable anomaly, as nicotine in the tobacco smoke is regarded by many as the agent responsible for the effects on coronary heart disease. (Carbon monoxide is now often suggested as the most likely agent to be responsible, but the evidence here rests largely on Astrup's studies on rabbits, which the author himself was unable to replicate.) As Seltzer points out, 'For now, we can only conclude that this discrepancy between the mortality rate of cigarette smokers vs. those of cigar or pipe smokers is difficult to reconcile with the concept that tobacco smoking is causally related to excess death due to CHD.'

Another interesting anomaly is the effect of age. Seltzer (1975) has computed age-standardized CHD rates and mortality ratios from data available in four major prospective cohort investigations of smoking and health, and found that the data examined gave consistent results. 'For elderly men, there were no appreciable excess risks of CHD mortality or morbidity among cigarette smokers compared to ex-cigarette smokers and non-cigarette smokers. For elderly women, the CHD rates seemed lower in continuing cigarette smokers than in ex-cigarette smokers. . .among elderly people, the risk of CHD is essentially the same with persistence of cigarette smoking as with its cessation.' Thus even the statistical association breaks down over the age of sixty-four or thereabouts.

Dose-response relations provide another difficulty. Seltzer (1968) has reviewed a number of studies and concludes: 'Significantly, the majority of the new studies show inversions or inconsistencies in the gradient of mortality or morbidity with average number of cigarettes smoked daily. While it is true that in virtually all these instances, those who smoke the most cigarettes give consistently higher CHD and myocardiac infarction rates than those who smoke the least, the consistency of the gradient is broken down as between the groups which smoke the least and the intermediate groups, with the intermediate rates the same or lower than the rates of the groups which smoke the least. . . . The new data, with its many inconsistencies and inversions in the "rising gradient", indicate that this whole subject is not as clear-cut as it appeared at first blush.' Parenthetically, it is to be noted that almost identical inversions in body-build measurements according to the amount of cigarettes smoked have been described by Seltzer in a study of morphological constitution and smoking habits of Harvard College graduates (1963). These inversions have been found in countries where there exists a statistical relationship; it must be added, however, that in a multinational study, Keys (1962) found no association at all between cigarette smoking and CHD in Finland, The Netherlands, Yugoslavia, Italy, Greece, and Japan! Thus even a statistical relationship, however inconsistent, is confined to some countries and is not found in others.

Also relevant to the dose-response relationship is the fact that as in the case of lung cancer, there appears to be an absence of association between duration of heavy cigarette smoking and risk of myocardial infarction. Seltzer (1968) summarizes three studies, and concludes that 'it is notable that while duration of cigarette smoking is considered an important factor in connection with lung cancer mortality, the new evidence in the 1964 reports points to an exoneration of this important element with respect to CHD. The evidence would appear to be consistent with the conclusion of the authors of the combined Albany and Framingham study that it is not any cumulative effect of inhaling cigarette smoke which precipitates myocardial infarction and death from CHD.' This conclusion has led to a suggestion by the authors of the Framingham heart study that coronary heart disease is only *acutely* connected with cigarette smoking, and not *chronically,* acting by the 'triggering of a lethal arrhythmia or thrombosis in subjects predisposed by an already compromised coronary circulation'. If this were indeed true, then the effects of smoking would be limited solely to those persons with 'already compromised circulation'. Such a conclusion would seem to suggest that cigarette smoking is without deleterious effect on those with a normal, healthy coronary apparatus!

As in the case of lung cancer, so also in relation to CHD, inhalation gives contradictory and puzzling data. In the Doll & Hill study of British doctors, for instance, the authors stated that 'only small and statistically insignificant differences were observed in coronary disease without hypertension (3% excess in inhalers) . . .' Death rate for non-inhalers (5.09) was substantially higher than that for non-smokers (3.29). Hammond's (1966) prospective study, on the other hand, showed a tendency for CHD death rate to increase with degree of inhalation. Remembering the difficulty of establishing what constitutes 'inhaling', it is clear that much further work would need to be done to make it clear what the relationships really are.

Even more puzzling are data for ex-smokers. The Surgeon General's Report (1964) pointed out that 'men who stopped smoking have a lower death rate from coronary disease than those who continue'. Seltzer (1968) has reviewed a large body of literature which has appeared since then and documents the point that ex-smokers are at times intermediate between smokers and non-smokers with respect to CHD mortality, but may also appear significantly safer than non-smokers! The many pitfalls in this type of investigation are pointed out by him, and it is clear that much more decisive experiments and investigations are required before it can be said with any confidence that giving up smoking produces any differences in mortality rates as far as CHD is concerned.

Parallel with these statistical investigations of epidemiology are other investigations of a more medical kind, looking at the pathological, clinical and experimental evidence. This evidence has also been reviewed by Seltzer (1970). He concludes that 'the chronic effect of cigarette smoking is not clear and is inconsistent with other information. As far as acute effects are concerned, a series of physiological mechanisms have been advanced whereby cigarette smoking could trigger myocardial oxygen deficits of a critical degree in the presence of impaired coronary circulation due to CHD. This hypothesis has not been reasonably substantiated. Some of the evidence is provocative, but in many instances the hypothesised mechanisms are inadequately documented or not documented at all.' He goes on to say that the statistical association between cigarette smoking and CHD still remains to be explained, and states that 'an explanation may lie in a constitutional and genetic predisposition both to cigarette smoking and CHD. A genetic factor in the aetiology of CHD is well accepted, and there is a growing body of evidence that smokers are different from non-smokers in a large variety of biological ways and behaviour patterns, including "style of life". If smokers show a greater tendency towards heart disease than non-smokers because they are different kinds of people than non-smokers — more vulnerable constitutional types — this could explain the comparatively low degree of association (mortality ratio of 1.7) of excess heart disease among cigarette smokers.'

Conclusions

This is the end of our review of some of the anomalies, contradictions, and generally unsatisfactory features which attend the literature on the effects of smoking on health. It would be possible to extend this review almost indefinitely, and mention many more errors of methodology, of argument, and of conclusion than those with which we have dealt so far. One would have thought, in view of these many defects, that the conclusions drawn by responsible bodies, like the Surgeon General's Committee or the Royal College of Physicians, would be suitably low-key and cautious. What is so impressive, unfortunately, is that only very scant attention is paid to anomalies and criticisms, or to alternative hypotheses. Rather, very strong conclusions are based on weak and contradictory data. Quite generally, evidence apparently indicting cigarette smoking is mentioned prominently, while evidence indicative of lack of causal connection is either not mentioned, or dismissed without discussion or explanation (Katz, 1969).

Consider as one example the fact that in quite a number of countries no connection was found between CHD and smoking. This is all the comment made in the third report of the Royal College of Physicians: 'One report showed little or no connection between CHD and smoking in several countries where there was generally a low incidence of CHD, perhaps because of such favourable factors as low levels of blood cholesterol or high levels of physical activity. Similarly the smoking effect seems to be slight among those British civil servants with low levels of other risk factors.' The fact that there are many countries in which there is no statistical connection even between CHD and smoking, or that there are large groups in Britain where there is no such statistical connection, would seem to provide considerable difficulties for an acceptance of the causal connection between smoking and CHD. Yet the authors conclude without hesitation that 'if it were possible to abolish all the excess risk of heart disease in smokers, it has been estimated that there would be between 9,000 and 10,000 fewer deaths each year from CHD in men and women of working age in the United Kingdom'.

This conclusion, of course, is not a conclusion from the evidence at all; it is a hopeful statement which pertains more to the realm of propaganda than scientific evidence. It may be possible that the failure of a statistical association to emerge in certain countries may be due to 'such favourable factors as low levels of blood cholesterol or high levels of physical activity', but this is a purely *ad hoc* hypothesis, and there is no evidence for it. The majority of people in the countries concerned certainly do not show a higher level of physical activity than do people in Great Britain, France or elsewhere, and it is doubtful whether low levels of blood cholesterol are characteristic of all or even most of them.

Is it possible to arrive at any kind of general conclusions? We think that it is imperative to get away from the simple assertion that 'smoking causes disease', and treat different diseases under separate headings. Looking at those diseases which have shown a substantially elevated mortality rate when comparing smokers and non-smokers, we can first of all rule out suicides and certain types of accidents as being caused directly by cigarette smoking. What seems to be happening in these cases is that certain personality traits (e.g. extraversion) are responsible for both the smoking and the accidents, while others (e.g. neuroticism) may be responsible for both the smoking and the suicide. Whether this is or is not the true explanation does not matter for the moment; clearly direct action of smoking is ruled out.

As the second group we must consider various cancers (of the prostate, the pancreas, the stomach, the bladder, the pharynx and larynx, the oesophagus, the kidney, and buccal cancer) in which either there is disproportion between the secular changes in the disease and the secular increases in cigarette smoking, or there is a similar secular change for both sexes in spite of the fact that secular changes in smoking habits were significantly different between the two sexes, with the males starting the increase in cigarette smoking thirty years before the women. It would be difficult to make a case for a causal theory for these various disorders.

The third disorder to consider would be coronary heart disease, and as we have seen in the last few pages there are so many anomalies in the evidence, and so many weaknesses in the empirical studies cited, that no firm conclusion is possible. We can certainly rule out any causal effect in people over sixty-five, and we can equally rule out effects on angina pectoris; whether there is any causal effect on younger people at all remains questionable, although the possibility does exist that acute but not chronic effects may have to be recognized. This is a far cry from the exaggerated conclusion of the report of the Royal College of Physicians.

Last we come to lung cancer which may be regarded as a group by itself. Here too the evidence is contradictory and inconclusive, as we have pointed out; it is still possible for some authorities to argue as if the causal role of smoking had been definitively proved, while others (e.g. Burch, Berkson and Fisher) consider the evidence totally inadequate, and favour alternative theories. We would agree that the evidence is inconclusive, although we rate somewhat higher than some of the critics the positive evaluation of a causal influence of smoking on lung cancer. We also believe, however, that alternative theories are likely to play a vital part in a proper explanation of the phenomena, and will turn to a consideration of the genetic hypothesis in the next chapter. These various hypotheses, of course, are not incompatible, and some form of interaction between genetic and environmental factors may be the most promising type of theory to look for in the future (Cederlöf et al., 1977). It seems highly unlikely that the methods of investigation adopted hitherto (i.e. large-scale epidemiological studies) will give us results of any great scientific value. Instead what is needed are clearly defined and properly controlled experimental studies of specific hypotheses, such as those predicting different outcomes for the smoking of different types of tobacco. Equally important would be twin studies and half-sib studies which enable us to keep the genetic factor constant while varying the smoking factor. Much money and research time have been wasted on investigations which predictably gave doubtful, inconclusive and largely meaningless results. It is unfortunate that these investigations are still frequently cited as evidence of a causal relation when all they demonstrate is the possibility of a statistical relationship. The position here taken has been well defined by Hardy (1968) when he writes:

> I am not implying that research has exonerated the cigarette from suspicion as a possible health hazard. I neither take that position nor know of any responsible person who does. I do say, however, that the case against cigarettes has not been scientifically proved. The remaining 'gigantic areas for exploration' and 'puzzling anomalies' acknowledged even by the Surgeon General's Advisory Committee require much more objective research to either verify or refute the various hypotheses which have been proposed concerning the role of smoking in such diseases as lung cancer, heart disease, emphysema, and bronchitis.

This attitude contrasts startlingly with a statement made by the Chief of the Clearinghouse Community Program Development Section of the National Clearinghouse for Smoking and Health, who stated in 1966 that 'the goal is to find pertinent data that can be used for influencing smokers to stop smoking and non-smokers not to start'. The difference between scientific research and propaganda could hardly have been more felicitously put. It is unfortunate that many official publications in this field resemble the second more than the first.

CHAPTER 2

Smoking and Personality:
The Genetic Hypothesis

Introduction

We have already referred in passing to an alternative theory to the environmental one which alleges that 'smoking causes disease'. As we have seen, this is the constitutional theory first suggested by Fisher (1959), Berkson (1962), and others, and lately developed in great detail by Burch (1976). While suggestive, the writings of Fisher and Berkson are much too non-specific to be readily testable. The theory of Burch, on the other hand, is highly specific, but it relates only to the development of cancer, and is not concerned with many aspects of the problem that are to us of considerable interest. Burch is not concerned, for instance, with the important problem of constitutional and genetic predisposition to smoke, or the effect this might have on cancer proneness. While not denying the great importance of Burch's theory for the development of all auto-aggressive diseases, we have taken a rather different path in attempting to augment and make more precise the early suggestions of Fisher.

In doing so we shall attempt to look at the evidence concerning a number of questions all of which have to be answered in the affirmative if the constitutional theory is to be taken seriously. First of all it needs to be established that lung cancer and coronary heart disease (to name only the two most important disorders statistically linked with smoking) have a firm genetic basis. Next would come the equally important demonstration that smoking has a firm genetic basis; this point, however, constituting the central problem of our experimental studies, will be treated in detail in later chapters, and will therefore not be discussed here. The third question to be dealt with relates to the differences in physique, personality, and other aspects between smokers and non-smokers (and probably between both and previous smokers who have given up smoking); such differences must exist in demonstrable form if the constitutional hypothesis is to be considered seriously. This discussion will take up a good deal of our space in this chapter.

Next we will go on to consider the question of cancer and personality. If we are to find a causal chain from constitution to smoking and from constitution to cancer, then it would seem almost necessary that there should also be a demonstration of the relationship between cancer and personality, i.e. that certain types of persons develop cancer more readily. This is in part implied in a discovery of genetic factors for lung cancer and coronary heart disease, but there might be such a genetic determination without its manifesting itself also in a differential 'cancer personality'. This is certainly an important area which requires careful discussion.

We will end with a discussion of theories of smoking, i.e. the reasons why people smoke. Such a theory must also give an answer to the question why certain types of people smoke and others do not, i.e. it must give us at least a suggestive answer to the problem raised by the existence of individual differences in smokers and non-smokers. We believe that some evidence exists on all these points, although this evidence is by no means always conclusive, and although different investigators have not always come up with the same answers. We will attempt, nevertheless, to integrate as much of this information as possible into a general theory which can at least claim to be testable, and which may take its place beside the pure environmentalist theory which we have criticized in the first chapter. It must of course be remembered, as we have already pointed out, that the environmental and constitutional theories are not necessarily incompatible; they may rather turn out to be complementary. This indeed would appear to be the most likely outcome of the scientific study of the problem presented by the observed correlations between smoking and disease.

The inheritance of disease

We begin our discussion with a review of the evidence concerning the inheritance of lung cancer and coronary heart disease. 'In spite of the international concern with lung cancer the possible role of genetic factors has attracted little attention.' As Doll (1974) has remarked, 'few scientists have been sufficiently attracted by the hypothesis to mount the effort required to study large numbers of twins'. And the report of the Royal College of Physicians (1971) states that 'there is ... little evidence of any inherited tendency to lung cancer'. Burch (1976) comments: 'To be more precise, few studies have been made of the genetics of lung cancer. Indeed, only one large scale familial study has been carried out but, fortunately for the genetic hypothesis, it gave unambiguous results.'

The work referred to is that of Tokuhata (1964, 1973) and Tokuhata & Lilienfeld (1963a, b). These investigators studied first-degree relatives of 270 lung cancer probands and first-degree relatives of 270 controls, matched for race, sex, age and residence. Deaths from lung cancer among non-smoking first-degree relatives of probands were found to be 3.8 times greater than expected on the basis of those observed in non-smoking first-degree relatives of controls. The corresponding ratio among smokers was 2.3. Combining both sexes, as well as smokers and non-smokers, the probability that these differences between probands and controls could have arisen by chance was calculated at $p < 0.0006$. This seems incontrovertible evidence for the existence of a strong genetic predisposing factor in the development of lung cancer, a factor already suggested by the finding that smoking was neither a necessary nor a sufficient cause for lung cancer.

The same series of investigations resulted in a number of interesting findings which may be worthy of consideration. For all causes of death, there was a significantly higher rate in the relatives of probands than in the relatives of controls. For all cancers, the corresponding ratio was very much higher, with a level of significance at the $P = 0.00006$ level! It was found that 32 per cent of cancer diagnoses in the relatives of probands were of the respiratory system, in contrast to 20 per cent of the control relatives. Deaths from non-malignant diseases of the respiratory system were also more common in the relatives of probands than in the relatives of controls, by a factor of 1.66. The investigators were careful to check the possible influence of the home and the local environment, and compared death in spouses of probands with death of spouses of controls; no significant differences were found.

Of the 270 lung cancer cases, 250 were smokers; among the 270 controls only 160 were smokers. Thus we find here the usual statistical relationship between smoking and lung cancer. Among the relatives of probands, 41 per cent were smokers, as opposed to 37 per cent among relatives of controls; this is a highly significant statistical difference, and is consistent with evidence to be considered in the next chapter that points to genetic factors in smoking, although it might also reflect intrafamilial social pressures.

Burch (1976) presents an interesting argument by looking at the figures published by Tokuhata & Lilienfeld in a rather novel light. As he points out, 'The total number of deaths observed among case relatives was 796, as against 727.9 expected on the basis of mortality among control relatives. When we subtract the contribution to total deaths from all cancers and non-malignant respiratory diseases, we obtain for the remaining deaths, 463 observed among case relatives as against 523.1 expected. Remembering that these deaths include the large category of total cardiovascular disease, which is positively associated with smoking, it follows that many of the other causes of death must be appreciably negatively associated both with smoking and lung cancer.'

In a later study Tokuhata (1973) determined the frequency of cigarette smokers among the first-degree relatives of smoking and non-smoking probands and controls. In the proband group, when the lung cancer index subject was a smoker, 41.1 per cent of relatives smoked; when the index subject was a non-smoker, 40 per cent of relatives smoked. In the control group, 41.8 per cent of the relatives of smoking index subjects were smokers, in contrast to only 30.7 per cent of the relatives of non-smoking index subjects. These and other more complicated familial connections described in the original paper indicate that some non-smoking cancer cases nevertheless had a genetic predisposition to smoke, and/or that a marked positive association exists between the genotypes for lung cancer and cigarette smoking.

Burch concludes from these studies that '(a) smoking and lung cancer are positively associated; (b) certain genes predispose to lung cancer; (c) certain genes predispose to smoking; (d) the net positive familial association between lung cancer and all causes of death is genetically based; (e) the net positive familial association between lung cancer and all cancers has a genetic basis; (f) the net positive familial association between lung cancer and fatal, non-malignant respiratory diseases has a genetic basis; and (g) the net negative familial association between lung cancer and fatal diseases other than under (e) has a genetic basis. . . . Although these data support genetic hypotheses of positive and negative association between smoking and disease, they do not exclude additional causal factors.'

These findings are so clear-cut that it is most unfortunate that so few investigators have been drawn to this type of study, apparently preferring to replicate *ad nauseam* the useless and redundant correlational studies over large populations which originally suggested the hypothesis that smoking causes lung cancer. This would seem to be a waste of scientific energy, money and personnel, in that badly conceived investigations, however frequently repeated, cannot add to the power of proof of the original studies, unless the design is altered in such a way as to avoid the errors of the original studies. We agree with Burch that replication and extension of the Tokuhata studies is most urgently needed.

Of indirect relevance to the question of inheritance of lung cancer is the study by Harvald & Hauge (1973) in which they studied malignant growths in 1,038 pairs of twins. Concordance rates with regard to cancer of the same site were found in 14 out of 207 monozygotic twin pairs, and in 12 out of 397 dizygotic twin pairs. This difference is significant. These figures are for verified cancers; similar differences were obtained for cases where the cancer diagnosis was uncertain. For cancer rates of all sites there was no similar significant difference between monozygotic and dizygotic twins.

When we turn to coronary heart disease, the evidence suggests, as Rose (1977) points out, that 'the disease has a large genetic component, probably involving multiple genes'. De Faire (1974) has published some figures for the prevalence of ischaemic heart disease in survivors of 197 same-sex twin pairs. The prevalence of ischaemic heart disease in the survivors where the index case died of ischaemic heart disease was 94 per cent in monozygotic twins, but only 74 per cent in dizygotic twins. Where the index case died of other causes, the figures were 69 per cent and 62 per cent respectively, i.e. not different significantly from each other. These figures show a marked genetic determination of ischaemic heart disease.

Raised serum cholesterol levels have been implicated in ischaemic heart disease, and correlations in these levels have been found between sibs and child/parent pairs but not between mother/father pairs (Adlersberg et al., 1957). Studies comparing monozygotic with dizygotic twins have confirmed the presence of a genetic component controlling serum cholesterol levels. Pikkarainen et al. (1966) found a 56 per cent concordance rate in serum cholesterol levels between monozygotic twins and one of 37 per cent between dizygotic twins, indicating a fair degree of heritability. (Work on cholesterol should be viewed in the light of the new theories of high and low density lipoproteins as related to the effects of serum cholesterol.)

Another way of looking at the genetics of heart disease is by paying attention to population frequencies of histo-compatibility antigen, HLA-8 and haplotype 1-8 (Mathews, 1975). It has been suggested that HLA-8 is linked to genes which predispose to hypercholesterolaemia and ischaemic heart disease, and correlations over various populations come out at values of 0.64 and 0.84 respectively for HLA and haplotype 1-8.

In Liljefors' (1970) clinical twin study the hereditary aspects of coronary heart disease were carefully evaluated. When cumulative concordance rates, successively including different signs of coronary heart disease, were compared, it was found that the highest Mz/Dz ratio was 1.73. This ratio was reached when all signs of clinically overt coronary heart disease were included in the calculation. In a seven-year follow-up study by telephone (Liljefors, 1977) of the 37 pairs that had been discordant with respect to the presence of clinically overt coronary heart disease, it was found that nine monozygotic individuals and seven dizygotic individuals had developed symptoms of coronary heart disease during the intervening period, increasing concordance even further. It is difficult, in view of all these demonstrations, to doubt the hereditary nature of coronary heart disease.

This conclusion is strengthened by a consideration of the results of a large-scale study of the familial occurrence of hypertension and coronary artery disease (Thomas & Cohen, 1955). These authors studied the prevalence of hypertension and coronary artery disease among the parents, grandparents, aunts and uncles of 266 Johns Hopkins medical students. They found a strong degree of association between hypertension and coronary artery disease. A study of the incidence of coronary artery disease showed that it was nearly four times as prevalent among siblings of individuals with coronary artery disease as among siblings of persons without it. The incidence of the disease was also analysed by comparing its prevalence among the offspring of matings where both, one or neither of the parents were affected. 'In general, there was a distinct gradation among the offspring of these three types of matings, with the highest incidence among the offspring of two affected parents and the lowest among the offspring of two unaffected parents.' The actual percentages for these three types of matings are 13 per cent, 5 per cent and 3 per cent. The suggestion of a genetic link is inescapable, although no simple Mendelian formula, with either a dominant or a recessive single gene, fitted the data at all well.

Burch (1978b) has come to a similar conclusion along somewhat different lines of research. Burch carried out his analysis in terms of his theory of age-dependent auto-aggressive disease (although the conclusions are largely independent of that theory). The argument relates in the main to two parameters of the mathematical formulation of the theory: S, the fraction of the study population that is genetically predisposed to fatal CHD, and λ, the average latent period between the end of the intrinsic stochastic process of initiation and death from CHD. From published studies, Burch shows that the risk factors (cigarette smoking, high relative weight, hypercholesterolaemia) associate only with λ and not with S. High levels of these risk factors associate with low values of λ . Other risk factors, such as lack of exercise, hypertension and diabetes mellitus associate with both λ and S. 'The associations with S probably have a straightforward genetic interpretation: persons genetically predisposed to lack of exercise, hypertension and diabetes mellitus are more likely . . . to be genetically predisposed to CHD than persons in the general population.'

Burch goes on to raise the question of whether the negative associations between the level of a risk factor, and the average duration, λ , of the latent period, should be interpreted in 'causal' and/or genetic terms. 'Secular trends in sex-specific and age-specific death rates from CHD . . . give no indication of any appreciable shortening in λ . . . —in spite of increases in some major risk factors. The average latent period remains at about 10 years for men and 20 years for women throughout the period (from 1921 to 1973). A wide range of other pertinent epidemiological evidence is reviewed, all of which is consistent with the genetic interpretation and much of which is consistent with the 'causal' interpretation of the associations between the classical risk factors and λ .' Burch concludes that 'it is improbable that the classical risk factors make any appreciable causal contribution to the pathogenesis of CHD, but even if they do, the intrinsic biological process of initiation dominates the age dependence of CHD'. This strong conclusion seems well supported by the data cited, and the analysis performed.

The literature on the effects of genetic factors on disease is so vast that only a very small amount of the total work carried out in this field has been mentioned. The book *Cancer Genetics* by Lynch (1976) gives an excellent summary of relevant researches in the cancer field; its contents reinforce our main conclusion, that there can be no doubt regarding the importance of genetic factors in the causation of cancers, although of course cancers at different sites, and of different kinds, do not all behave in the same manner. As Anderson (1978) points out, 'the hereditary varieties of common cancers are characterized by a high degree of genetic heterogeneity. The specific types of hereditary cancers can be identified by focusing on the histological types and sites of involvement, not only of the primary neoplasms, but also associated neoplasms and associated conditions or stigmata, as well as by focusing on the age of the patient at the time of diagnosis, tumor localization and frequency, and the mode of inheritance' (p. 15). In general, 'it seems that for most tumors of man there exists a dominantly inherited form. In all instances the dominantly inherited form is characterised by . . . high risk for a specific kind of tumor; earlier age of occurrence of the tumor than is usual; and a multiplicity of primary tumors' (Knudson, 1978). (See also Jackson, 1978; Knudson et al., 1973; Knudson, 1977; Mulvihill, 1977; German, 1974.)

Personality and cancer

It seems likely that if there are strong genetic factors in the genesis of lung cancer, possibly all cancers, and of coronary heart disease, then patients suffering from these various disorders will be discriminable in terms of biochemical, physiological and personality characteristics. The hypothesis is a weak one because it does not predict specific characteristics of the disease-prone person, and consequently it cannot be disproved by failing to demonstrate the existence of specific relationships. Nevertheless, the approach is a promising and interesting one, and has given some positive results.

We shall begin with the demonstration of a negative relationship between lung cancer and neuroticism (Kissen & Eysenck, 1962). Neuroticism is one of the major personality traits widely recognized by psychologists; it is sometimes labelled 'anxiety' or 'emotionality', and may be symbolized by the letter N (Eysenck & Eysenck, 1969). There is a long history of theories linking emotion with cancer, going back to the Greek physician Galen (AD 131-201); more recent theories have been reviewed in a number of papers quoted by Kissen and Eysenck. The measuring instrument used in their research was a short form of the MPI, which measures neuroticism as well as extraversion, another widely recognized major dimension of personality. People scoring high on the neuroticism scale are tense, anxious, worried individuals with labile emotions generally; extraverted people tend to be sociable, impulsive, happy-go-lucky and histrionic. These two dimensions are quite uncorrelated.

The patients tested were 116 male lung cancer patients and 123 non-cancer controls, both groups being patients at surgical and medical chest units tested *before* diagnosis. Patients and controls were subdivided into age groups before a comparison of their scores was made. Patients were also subdivided into those with and without psychosomatic disorder. As regards extraversion, there were no differences between cancer and control patients without psychosomatic disorders, but, in comparing the groups with psychosomatic disorder, it was found that the cancer group was considerably more extraverted than the control group. This high extraversion score was found in all these age groups, but most strongly in the middle one (55 to 64 years). For the patients without psychosomatic disorders, a similar trend was found for the two younger age groups, but this violently reversed in the oldest of the three control groups; as this group was also the smallest, containing only ten cases, this may be a statistical freak, leaving open the possibility that in another sample a similar trend might be found to that in the other groups.

As regards neuroticism, the control group had much higher N scores than the cancer group, regardless of psychosomatic involvement. It was also found that the two psychosomatic groups (cancer and control) had somewhat higher neuroticism scores than did the non-psychosomatic groups. The results of the study therefore gave some support to the hypothesis that lung cancer patients differ from other patients with respect to personality, the major differences being with respect to lack of, or suppression of emotionality in cancer patients, and greater extraversion in cancer patients. These results, being statistically significant and obtained by means of objective tests, have been followed up by many investigators. The most directly relevant of these studies is a recently completed but not yet published investigation by Professor H. Berndt, undertaken at the Central Institute for Cancer Study of the Academy of Sciences of the DDR. Using Eysenck's EPI questionnaire, Berndt and his colleagues compared control groups of patients with patients who after completion of the questionnaire were found to suffer from breast cancer or bronchial carcinoma. The size of the female control group was 953; that of the breast cancer group was 231. The male control group numbered 195, and the male bronchial carcinoma group 123. The female bronchial carcinoma group was very small, numbering only 20, which makes it almost impossible for this group to give significant differences from the controls.

In all three groups the cancer patients had neuroticism scores *lower* than the controls, with the differences reaching a $P < .01$ level for the breast cancer group, and the male bronchial carcinoma group; for the female bronchial carcinoma group, because of the small number of patients, the result, although in the same direction, was not statistically significant. The mean differences on the N scale amounted to 1.0, 1.6, and 1.8 for the three comparisons. If it is permissible to use a one-tailed test for the female bronchial carcinoma group, i.e. if we agree to treat this study as a test of the hypothesis suggested by the Kissen and Eysenck study, then the difference observed there, which is actually the largest of the three, also reaches statistical significance. We may conclude that the Berndt investigation gives results essentially identical with those of the Kissen and Eysenck study.

Berndt and his colleagues did not find any significant differences for extraversion, but in this connection we should mention an even earlier study by Hagnell (1962), who reported on the results of an epidemiological survey of the 2,550 inhabitants of two adjacent rural parishes in the south of Sweden. This survey was started in 1947 and included an interview during which a personality assessment was made on each subject. Ten years later the procedure was repeated and the subsequent history of each subject examined. During this follow-up it was observed that a significantly high proportion of women who had developed cancer had been originally rated as extraverted. Actually, Hagnell used a rather different system of personality assessment to the one used by Kissen and Eysenck, but there is considerable evidence that the particular set of qualities which he found associated with cancer was in fact similar to or identical with what we have called extraversion. Hagnell's method of assessment was admittedly subjective, but as he did not start out with preconceived ideas it is unlikely that he would have been influenced in his assessment by hypothetical considerations. Hagnell was not concerned with lung cancer as such, but it is notable that he too found extraversion to be a crucial personality variable in relation to cancer.

The hypothesis that there might be a relationship between cancer and the personality traits of extraversion actually goes back quite a long time; in 1846, W. H. Walshe published a book entitled *Nature and Treatment of Cancer* in which he claimed there seemed to be general agreement that 'women of high colour and sanguinous temperament were more subject to mammary cancers than those of different constitutions'. As the description of the ancient 'temperament' of the sanguine personality is very similar to that of the (stable) extravert, we have here a startling anticipation of modern findings.

This finding was further strengthened by a study published by Coppen & Metcalfe (1963). They also used the MPI for their enquiry. Working in a general hospital, they used patients in two gynaecological and two surgical wards, and out-patients attending the surgical clinic. Questionnaires were first filled in by the patients, and at the end of the investigation the questionnaires were collected and scored and the diagnosis of each patient obtained. Forty-seven patients had a malignant tumour; 32 had cancer of the breast, 4 had cancer of the uterus and 11 had cancer in other parts of the body. Two control groups were used; one was a hospital control group made up of 129 patients with various gynaecological and surgical conditions. Care was taken that these should all fall into the same age group as the patients with cancer. The second control group of thirty-one subjects was obtained from a representative sample of the general population of the London area. This control group was somewhat younger than the hospital groups and therefore these subjects would be expected to have had higher extraversion scores than the cancer groups on account of their age alone. The mean extraversion scores of the hospital controls and the general population controls were very similar. The cancer group, however, had significantly higher extraversion scores than both control groups. The mean neuroticism scores did not differ significantly. The sub-groups of cancer patients had all very similar means.

Coppen & Metcalfe go on to discuss certain hormonal differences related to body build and personality. They conclude: 'Although the nature of this association is by no means clear one may perhaps speculate that certain constitutional factors predispose individuals to develop malignant tumours. Extraversion may be one manifestation of this constitutional difference which may also be related to physique and to hormonal activity.'

Kissen (1964a, b) took up the relationship between lung cancer and lack of neuroticism which appeared in the Kissen & Eysenck paper. In the 1964 paper he reports on the neuroticism scores on the MPI of lung cancer patients and other chest unit admissions. Again he found that the lung cancer patients had very significantly lower N scores than did the other patients. Kissen gives a rather interesting table in which he calculates lung cancer mortality rates per 100,000 men aged 25 and over by levels of neuroticism scores. He found that people with very low scores have a mortality rate of 296, those with intermediate scores have a mortality rate of 108, and those with very high scores have a mortality rate of only 56. He assumes, of course, that men aged 25 and over and suffering respectively from lung cancer and chest diseases can be taken as representing male lung cancer deaths and men generally in Scotland, an assumption which is almost certainly not an accurate representation of the facts, but which is perhaps not too far removed from the actual state of affairs to pass muster. One must also assume, of course, that samples of 100 each are large enough to make meaningful comparisons possible; clearly there is a wide margin here for considerable chance effects. Nevertheless, the figures are statistically significant and as they are quoted present quite amazingly great differences between people having high and low scores respectively on the neuroticism scale of the MPI. When it is realized that these are raw figures, i.e. uncorrected for attenuation due to lack of perfect reliability and validity of the scales, it will be realized that there is considerable support here for the assumption of a relationship between the development of lung cancer and constitutional personality factors. The figures also suggest the possibility of predicting who is likely to be 'at risk' as far as lung cancer is concerned. Very low scorers on N have about a six-fold possibility of developing lung cancer as compared with very high scorers.

Kissen in his paper failed to find any correlation between extraversion and lung cancer. Interestingly enough, he found significant differences between lung cancer inhalers and non-inhalers, the non-inhalers having a significantly lower N score than the inhalers. Thus inhaling, too, may be related to personality. Kissen concludes:

> The evidence given in this paper suggests that both cigarette smoking and a characteristic personality appear to be involved in the development of lung cancer. If one accepts the view that

lung cancer is of multiple aetiology and that among factors associated with its development are an exogenous one of exposure to cigarette smoke and an endogenous one of personality, it would appear that *the poorer the outlet for emotional discharge the less the exposure to cigarette smoke required to induce lung cancer.* Such an observation, based on the findings of this study, is consistent with some of the anomalous epidemiological findings regarding inhalation and may explain in part why some light smokers develop lung cancer while others who smoke more do not.

Kissen (1963a, b, 1964a, b) has published several more papers including one (Kissen, 1968) dealing with a general review of methodological problems. These papers report an extension of the work so far discussed, using different methods of personality assessment; the general findings tend to support the original relationship between lung cancer and low neuroticism/anxiety. Trends were also found for high extraversion in lung cancer patients, but the trend is rather weak.

Replication of studies by other workers is important, as authors testing their own hypotheses and replicating their own studies may be replicating errors as well. An interesting replication of the Kissen and Eysenck studies has been reported by Greer & Morris (1975), but using breast cancer cases instead of lung cancer cases. Thus their study widens the hypothesis linking lung cancer with low anxiety/neuroticism to include other cancers as well. A consecutive series of 160 women at hospital for breast tumour biopsy was studied by means of detailed structured interviews and standard tests, including the MPI. Interviews and testing were conducted on the day before operation without knowledge of the provisional diagnosis. Information obtained from patients was verified in almost all cases by separate interviews with husbands or close relatives. The published results are based on statistical comparisons between 69 patients found at operation to have breast cancer and a control group comprising the remaining 91 patients with benign breast disease.

The principal finding was the significant association between the diagnosis of breast cancer and the behaviour pattern, persisting throughout adult life, of abnormal release of emotions. 'This abnormality was, in most cases, extreme suppression of other feelings. Extreme expression of emotions, though much less common, also occurred in a higher proportion of cancer patients than controls.

Previous reports of correlations between breast cancer and extraversion, previous stress and depression were not confirmed.'

Another replication, this time concerned with lung cancer patients alone, was reported by Abse et al. (1974). They begin with a review of various psychoanalytic studies which have suggested certain personality characteristics in cancer patients, such as denial and repression, impaired self-awareness and introspective capacity, poor outlet for emotional discharge, little expression of aggression, self-sacrificing and self-blaming tendencies, rigid conventionality, predisposition for experienced hopelessness and despair, and other similar ones. In their own study, 59 male patients were interviewed, 31 of whom were later diagnosed as having lung cancer, and 28 as having other thoracic problems. An interview rating schedule was used, having relevance to the hypotheses in question. Age being considered an important variable, patients and controls were subdivided into old and young. Scores were derived from the interview procedure. A highly significant differentiation was obtained, particularly for the younger groups. Differentiation between lung cancer and control patients became *more* pronounced when comparisons were restricted to those patients who smoked more than one pack of cigarettes a day. The major differentiation showed that the (young) cancer patients showed a marked restriction in their interpersonal relationships, and reported less adequate or frequent sexual relationships. They appear to have more problems in the handling of dependency needs. All these differences are much less marked in the older patients who are relatively difficult to distinguish from their age-matched controls. On the whole, this study bears out the hypothesis of a relationship between lung cancer and low emotionality.

Indirect support for the hypothesis is given in a study by Ure (1969), who found a negative association between allergy and cancer. In a survey of 140 patients in the gynaecology ward of a large general hospital, the subjects were asked whether they suffered from any of the common hay-fever type allergies. An incidence of 20 per cent was established. Surgical and biopsy reports on this ward population established an incidence of malignant condition at the 28 per cent level. These two groups of comparable age turned out to be mutually exclusive. Reports of pregnancy nausea were also taken. Previous susceptibility to this varied from none to severe, and correlated positively with reports of common allergy-type reactions, and consequently inversely with liability to gynaecological cancers in later life. This study is relevant to our discussion because allergies and pregnancy nausea are to some extent indicative of high neuroticism, although the correlation is not particularly strong. In any event, the study does show that there are marked differences between cancer and non-cancer patients in areas not logically linked with cancer.

Also of relevance is a paper by Pettingale, Greer and Tee (1977) in which, as part of a multi-disciplinary study of 160 women admitted consecutively for breast tumour biopsy, they measured expression of anger and serum immunoglobulins before operation, i.e. when there was no knowledge of the provisional diagnosis, and three, twelve and twenty-four months after operation. Serum IgA levels were found to be significantly higher in patients who habitually suppressed anger than in those who were able to express anger ($p < 0.001$). This correlation was found before operation both in cancer patients and in those with benign breast disease. Over the subsequent two years, serum IgA levels remained consistently higher in all patients who suppressed anger, and the authors suggest how such an association might play a part in the pathogenesis of breast cancer. This is important in view of the possible use of the serum IgA level as a prognostic indicator, there being a significant positive correlation between serum IgA and advancing metastatic spread of breast cancer. Relationships have also been found between serum IgA level and breast cancer.

There are many other studies which, although they refer to personality-cancer relationships, are less directly relevant to our topic (e.g. Achterberg et al., 1976; Krasnoff, 1959). Others again refer to the relationship between personality and the progress of cancer in man, i.e. Burch's factor λ; among the more important are Achterberg et al. (1977), Evans et al. (1965), Kissen & Rowe (1969), and Stavraky (1968). All these studies strengthen the conclusion that there are important relations between personality on the one hand, and cancer and cancer outcome on the other. (Abse et al., 1974.)

Personality and coronary heart disease

Of particular interest in the study of personality as related to heart disease is the work of Caroline Thomas: her studies are connected with both cancer and heart diseases. Between 1946 and 1964, she collected data on 1,337 medical students at Johns Hopkins. Complete physical examinations, psychological profiles and family histories were recorded. These students were followed up through 1974; by that time, there had been 43 cases of cancer and 14 heart attacks. It was found that cancers tended to develop in people who were generally quiet, non-aggressive and emotionally contained; such persons scored low on tests of anxiety, anger and depression. The picture is very much like that found by Kissen and Eysenck. Coronary victims, on the other hand, scored high on depression, anxiety and nervous tension. They tended to suffer from insomnia, and were often tired in the morning. This still ongoing study (Thomas, 1976) provides excellent evidence of a prospective kind to link personality with disease, even though some of the tests used (like the Rorschach) have little validity or reliability; the information on which the above conclusions are based is fortunately derived from more secure foundations. (See also Thomas & Greenstreet, 1973, and Thomas & Duszynski, 1974.)

There is an interesting hypothesis regarding the relation between personality and coronary heart disease which has been developed by Thomas (1968). Referring to the literature on the relationship between personality and cigarette smoking, to be reviewed presently, she drew attention to the fact that 'outstanding characteristics differentiating cigarette smokers from non-smokers reside in the realm of personality', drawing particular attention to the role of anxiety. Thomas, Ross & Higginbottom (1962) also found that anxiety was the most important variable in a discriminatory analysis based on parental history of coronary heart disease. It was found that, on the average, the group with *fathers* affected by coronary heart disease reported a *higher* anxiety level than did the group with both parents unaffected, whereas the group whose *mothers* had coronary heart disease had lower anxiety scores than the group with two unaffected parents. Thus this and the preceding (Thomas, Ross & Higginbottom, 1962) study showed that the same psychological characteristic, anxiety, was an important single variable in distinguishing cigarette smokers from non-smokers and in distinguishing subjects with a positive parental history of coronary disease from subjects without such a history. Second, the subjects with a positive parental history of coronary disease fell on *opposite* sides of the negative parental coronary disease group in respect of their mean anxiety scores. Thomas cites other evidence for the relevance of anxiety under stress to coronary heart disease, such as the work of Dunbar (1943), Miles et al. (1954) and Ostfeld et al. (1964). Thomas finds indications in the studies that there may be *two* major coronary personality patterns which are diametrically opposed to each other. Bahnson & Wardwell (1962), for instance, discriminated between a mother-oriented group and a father-oriented group of patients, showing opposite personality characteristics. Ostfeld et al. (1964) found personality differences between patients with angina pectoris and those with myocardial infarctions, along similar lines. (See also Blumenthal et al., 1979, Dijl, 1979.)

Lastly, a series of well-known studies by Rosenman, Friedman and their colleagues used an interviewing technique and/or a questionnaire by which the specific behaviour patterns of the subject could be classified as type A or type B. They considered type A to be the coronary behaviour pattern; it is characterized by excessive drive, aggressiveness, ambition, competitiveness and a sense of time urgency. Type B, on the other hand, is described as a relative absence of these characteristics. There was a predominance of the type A behaviour among subjects who developed coronary disease, but as Thomas points out, 'It should be noted that a substantial number of type B men did develop coronary disease; again the evidence suggests that at least two precoronary personality types are involved.'

Many studies have since been carried out in relation to these two types, and their relation to coronary heart disease. The pattern of intense striving for achievement, competitiveness, easily-provoked impatience, time-urgency, abruptness of gesture and speech, hyper-alert posture, tense facial musculature, overcommitment to vocation or profession, and excessive drive and hostility has been shown to be definitely associated cross-sectionally with the presence of coronary heart disease, prospectively associated with the incidence of CHD, related to the recurrence of myocardial infarction in persons already having clinical CHD, and correlated with the severity of coronary atherosclerosis as determined angiographically. (Friedman, 1969; Jenkins, 1975, 1976; Jenkins, Rosenman & Friedman, 1967; Jenkins, Rosenman & Zyzanski, 1974; Rosenman, 1967; Rosenman, Friedman & Strauss, 1964; see also Floderns (1974), Siltanen et al. (1975), Greer (1979) and Rosenman & Chesrey (1980). But see Theorell et al. (1979). In the most recent study from this group, it was suggested that the different facets of the coronary-prone type

A behaviour pattern may be specifically associated with different clinical manifestations of coronary disease. It seems unfortunate that the two types, or rather the continuum involved, have not been studied very much in relation to more orthodox psychological personality variables; it would be interesting to see just where they fitted into some of the more widely recognized systems of personality description. (A good review of recent work is given by Glass, 1977.) Rake et al. (1978) failed to find evidence of genetic factors in an interview study, but their questionnaire work had an opposite result.

Thomas sums up her discussion by saying: 'Our own findings and those of others point to the existence of distinctive personality traits in cigarette smokers, on the one hand, and in precoronary individuals and coronary patients on the other. Inasmuch as a specific pattern of anxiety under stress was significantly related both to cigarette smoking and to parental coronary disease, anxiety appears to be one kind of denominator.' Thomas then refers to the involvement of genetic factors, and goes on to say that 'it seems likely that smoking habit patterns, too, are, to some extent, expressions of inborn differences'. This set of results, too, therefore supports the view that personality differences are related to CHD, and that genetic factors link these personality traits, and smoking, with disease.

Another line of research is reflected by the work of Bendien & Groen (1963). They examined the 'widespread impression that myocardial infarction occurs predominantly in individuals with a certain personality under frustration and certain interhuman conflict situations, to which they are more prone than others'. They decided to measure neuroticism and extraversion in twenty-five successive cases of myocardial infarction, comparing their scores with a control group of twenty-five patients carefully matched with the original probands. They found that 'there appeared to exist a definite difference in neuroticism score between infarct patients and control patients. . .the scores of the patients with myocardial infarction being lower than those of the other patients'. This difference, however, was not statistically significant. 'The extraversion scores showed the patients with myocardial infarction to be more extraverted than the control patients: this difference was statistically significant.'

What can we conclude from these and similar studies of the relationship between cancer and personality? At first sight the results seem to be reasonably consistent, and to bear out hypotheses previously voiced. We have mentioned the 1846 statement by Walshe who claimed that 'sanguinous temperament' was related to cancer; this would seem to fit in well with the results showing cancer patients to be more extraverted, and lower on N than controls. The 'sanguinous' temperament is indeed similar to that of the stable extravert (Eysenck, 1967), and so far, therefore, there seems to be a remarkable degree of concordance.

However, this concordance is more apparent than real. Galen is often quoted as stating that cancer was much more frequent in melancholic women; the melancholic temperament, however, is neurotic and introverted! Thus whatever the findings of modern researchers might be, it is always possible to discover some ancient scribe who said something apparently in line with the modern findings. This way lies self-deception.

Next we must note a number of criticisms of the research reported, such as those listed by Lebovits & Ostfeld (1971). They list the following ten criticisms. (1) Research in this area tends not to be based on theoretical treatments, and research is rarely based on conceptual hypotheses. (2) Large-scale systematic studies are few in number. (3) A large number of the studies are conceptually and methodologically weak, and lack conceptual sophistication. (4) The conclusions are drawn from inadequate and frequently invalid data. (5) Different concepts are referred to by identical terms, and common concepts used in several studies often are not identical or even comparable. (6) People are lumped together on the basis of superficially similar behaviour, i.e. smoking behaviour. For example, all cigarette smokers are treated as a homogeneous group. (7) A clear difference must be made between the factors that cause people to begin to smoke, and those that prompt them to continue, or to increase their consumption of tobacco. (8) There are few attempts to safeguard against deliberate or unconscious falsification of responses. (9) Poorly constructed and totally untested questionnaires are used. (10) Smoking habits are established through self-reports.

We have tried to concentrate on reports which are not subject to these criticisms, but inevitably the interpretation of the work reported must take into account the fact that while some studies deal with lung cancer, others deal with cancer of the breast, or all cancers; broad agreement on personality factors cannot disguise the diversity of diseases in question. Also, different criteria are often used in the personality field, and it cannot be assumed that inventory responses are equivalent to interview results. The results are clearly *suggestive* that extraversion and low neuroticism may be related to lung cancer, and possibly other cancers as well; it will require research carried out on a larger scale, and better controlled than heretofore, to put these suggestive findings on a secure basis.

Psychosis, cancer and metabolism

Much the same must be said of a series of studies carried out in an attempt to relate cancer to psychosis. Bahnson & Bahnson (1964a), as suggested in the title of their paper, consider 'Cancer is an alternative to psychosis', although elsewhere (Bahnson & Bahnson, 1964b) they also find some support for the theory that denial and repression of primitive impulses and of disturbing emotions is found most frequently in patients with malignant neoplasms. Rassidakis et al. (1971, 1972, 1973a, b, c, d) have shown that mentally ill populations, especially patients with schizophrenia, seem to be at relatively low risk for cancer. They found that the percentage of mental patients who died from cancer was considerably lower than that of the general population; 15 per cent of deaths were caused by malignant neoplasms in the general population compared with 4.9 per cent among the mentally ill. Other randomly selected causes of death (cardiovascular, diabetes) showed no appreciable differences. In England and Wales about 20 per cent of deaths are caused by neoplasms compared with 6.9 per cent of deaths in mentally ill populations; for Scotland the figures are 17 per cent and 5 per cent respectively. (The picture is confused by the fact that some authors (e.g. Bielianskas et al., 1979) find that cancer is significantly related to high scores on the depression scale of the MMPI. No differences between men dying of cancer and those who survived or who died from other causes were found on the other nine MMPI clinical scales. Why depression should differ in this way from neuroticism (with which it is usually highly correlated) and schizophrenia is not known.)

Schizophrenic patients seem to be more resistant to neoplasms than patients with other forms of mental illness. Of 2,145 State Hospital deaths over fifteen years, 16 were neoplastic and only 6 of these were amongst schizophrenics. The Kashenko Hospital in Moscow reports the incidence of death from malignant neoplasm in schizophrenics to be only 0.1 to 0.2 per cent from a yearly population of 2,500. Levi & Waxman (1975) cite other supportive evidence. They put forward the argument that the low incidence of cancer in schizophrenics may be related to a metabolic defect, related to a lack of labile methyl groups. They postulate that the schizophrenic patient is unable to utilize methionine as a methyl donor because of a deficiency of methionine adenosyltransferase. They argue that certain tumour tissues contain excessive methylated nucleic acids or differences in PNA and RNA methylation and methylating enzyme activities as compared to normal cells. Malignant cells require labile methyl groups derived electively from L-methionine. This suggests that tumour cells may be prevented from growing by restricting the supply of methionine. This hypothesis is developed in some detail by the authors, and it may account for the observed facts.

There does, however, seem to be no doubt that there is a (negative) relationship between cancer and schizophrenia, and probably psychosis as a whole. This again suggests that genetic factors play a part in determining who shall be at risk to cancer. This study leads us on to a consideration of various biochemical and other biological differences between cancer and non-cancer patients; this will be dealt with only very briefly because it goes rather beyond the major concerns of this book. Some of the work cited is relevant to the question of why cancer occurs in some people upon exposure to environmental or industrial carcinogens, and not in others.

In the late 1940s and the late 1950s, Drs J. A. and E. C. Miller initiated a series of experiments that demonstrated the presence of carcinogen-metabolizing enzymes in the endoplasmic reticulum of the liver cells. Studies by these authors indicated that many chemical carcinogens require metabolism to highly reactive intermediates that react with crucial cellular constituents to initiate the carcinogen event. The reactive intermediates may be detoxified by metabolism to non-carcinogenic substances or by interaction with non-critical cellular constituents.

Recent studies by Whitlocks, Cooper & Gelbrin (1972) and by Kellermann, Shaw and their associates (Busbee et al., 1972; Kellermann et al., 1973 a,b,c) discovered a way of assessing carcinogen metabolism in human tissues by measuring AHH activity in cultured human lymphocytes. The inductibility of AHH by a polycyclic hydrocarbon varied between 1.3 and 4.5 times the resting levels, and the population separated in the three groups consisting of low, medium and high inductibility. Kellermann et al. (1973) found that susceptibility to bronchogenic carcinoma is associated with the higher levels of inductible ayrl hydrocarbon hydroxylase activity, suggesting that the lungs of cigarette smokers in whom cancer develops may have higher levels of enzymes that metabolize BP and other polycyclic hydrocarbon carcinogens to reactive and toxic intermediates than the lungs of cigarette smokers in whom cancer does not develop. This work obviously contains a strong suggestion that susceptibility to lung cancer is genetically determined through differential inductibility of AHH activity. However, it should be noted that the work of Kellermann has been found difficult to replicate, and that there are many problems still unsolved in connection with it.

Another important line of study is that followed by Rao (1970, 1971, 1972). Rao's basic finding is that patients with lung cancer excrete less of the steroid hormone androsterone than the normal controls, and more of the group of steroids known as the 17-hydroxycorticosteroids. Rao in fact has shown that the ratio of 17-hydroxycorticosteroids to androsterone can be used as a diagnostic test for lung cancer. He also suggests that androsterone levels can be correlated with the length of survival of lung cancer patients. Whether or not they have undergone surgery, patients with low androsterone levels have a much worse prognosis than patients in the higher range. Rao concludes that the steroid might well be of therapeutic value to patients. This again is obviously an important line of research to follow up, demonstrating marked biochemical differences between lung cancer victims and non-victims.

Smoking and morphology

We turn next to the morphological-constitutional study of smokers and non-smokers. Here the major work is that of Seltzer (1963) who studied 922 members of the Harvard College class of 1946. The morphological material consists of a series of anthropometric measurements taken in the autumn of 1942 as part of the routine Harvard College medical examination by the author, a total of twelve measurements being obtained of various parts of the body, from which ten body ratios or indices were computed. Information with respect to the smoking habits of these Harvard men was obtained in the autumn of 1959 through the medium of a questionnaire sent to all members of the class for whom anthropometric measurements were available. At the time of their replies to the questionnaire, respondents were already thirteen years out of college and averaged thirty-five years of age. Thus body measurements were taken before smoking would have had any effect on constitution, making this in large part a prospective study.

Subjects were divided into non-smokers (234), pure cigarette smokers (445), pure pipe smokers (60) and pure cigar smokers (34), with mixed types disregarded. Details of all the measures, indices and significance ratios are given in the original paper, but as the author points out: 'The comparison between 234 non-smokers and 688 smokers leaves no doubt that the two groups are significantly differentiated in morphological dimensions and proportions. In every instance the smokers show larger mean dimensions than the non-smokers, and in all but one instance these differences are statistically significant. Some of the mean differences are quite substantial as, for example, in the case of body weight, in which smokers are on the average more than five pounds heavier than the non-smokers. Smokers are consistently greater than non-smokers in height and weight and in the dimensions of the head, face, shoulders, chest, hip, leg, and hand.'

The difference between non-smokers and smokers is not only a matter of size; significant differences are also evident in the case of a number of bodily proportions or indices. Smokers compared to non-smokers are narrower in shoulder breadth relative to chest circumference, greater in the width of the chest relative to the breadth of the shoulder, smaller in head circumference relative to chest circumference, greater in chest circumference relative to stature, and narrower in face breadth relative to chest breadth.

It appears also that significant morphological differences are to be found between non-smokers and the varieties of smoker types considered, i.e. the pure cigarette, pure pipe, pure cigar smokers. 'In every single measurement the exclusive smoker types have larger mean dimensions than those in the non-smoker category.' There appears to be a consistent rate of pattern of differentiation of the smoker types into a specific order of arrangement. 'The order of arrangement is as follows: non-smokers, pure cigarette, pure pipe, and pure cigar smokers. The pure cigarette smokers are the least differentiated in morphological features from the non-smokers, followed by the pure pipe smokers, while the pure cigar-smokers differ most in physical characteristics from the non-smoker group.' The *amount* of cigarette smoking, however, is not indexed by corresponding morphological differences; there is no gradient from little to much cigarette smoking as far as morphological constitution is concerned. Seltzer concludes:

It is clearly evident from the data presented in this paper that smokers as a group differ in their morphological characteristics as young adults from non-smokers. The differences between them are consistent, substantial, and pertain to both dimensions and proportions. It is also evident that the various smoking classes, non-smokers, cigarette smokers, pipe smokers, and cigar smokers, show manifold morphological differentiations. . . . The primary significance of our findings of body build differences among the various smoking classes lies in the constitutional and genetic implications. . . . The measures involved are on the whole clearly identifiable as having a strong genetic component. Such traits as stature, head circumference, biacromial diameter, and chest and hand dimensions are for the most part hereditary in nature. The intimate representation of skeletal dimensions by many of these traits lends added strength to their genetic determination, since skeletal dimensions have been shown to be only very slightly affected by environment during adolescence and maturity. Consequently, it is safe to conclude that the morphological differences ascertained are highly suggestive of genotypic deviations in the different smoking classes.

Seltzer has also documented anthropometric, somatotypical, occupational and educational differences between cigar smokers and pipe smokers, using a series of 1,698 white male veterans as his sample.

The results indicate that pure cigar smokers and pure pipe smokers are. . .quite different kinds of people. . . .The differential features between pure cigar smokers and pure pipe smokers reflect on the custom of combining them into and considering them as a single category. In studies which involve characterizing populations by smoking habits, such a combining practice can only serve to blur important associative differences, especially when considerations of body-build, education, and occupation are involved. In studies involving smoking and health, the practice of combining pure cigar smokers and pure pipe smokers into a single category will also have a blurring effect in those instances where the health or illness criteria are different for cigar and pipe smokers, as for example when considering morbidity or mortality, or both.

This is an important point to make in view of the fact that at least two population studies have shown manifold differences in mortality rates between pure cigar and pipe smokers; it is impossible to tell whether these observed differences are in any way related to the smoking habits of the participants, or to the associated typological characteristics.

More recent studies of constitutional differences have been summarized by Seltzer (1967) elsewhere; many of these suffer from the fact that the data accumulated may have been affected in turn by the smoking habits of the subjects investigated. This is not true of such studies as that of Thomas & Cohen (1960) on ability to taste phenylthiourea (Ptc), a trait which has been demonstrated to have a genetic basis; they found that heavy cigarette smokers showed a significantly higher proportion of tasters than did non-smokers. Seltzer also refers to an unpublished study of Harvard alumni in which it was found that future smokers, compared to future non-smokers, appeared to have smaller tidal air values, an increased frequency of sighs and swallows, greater respiratory rate, a somewhat higher recumbent pulse rate, more palpitations, more sinus arrhythmia, more constipation, more loss of appetite, and a greater frequency of urination. The future non-smokers, on the other hand, exhibited a consistent lack of physiological reaction to stress, suggesting that smokers are more prone to patterns of reducing anxiety which involve physiological change. This is in good agreement with the alleged tension-reducing properties of smoking.

Also of interest in connection with constitution are studies of ABO blood groups as related to smoking. Cohen & Thomas (1962) found a significant deficiency of group B individuals among heavy cigarette smokers and an excess of group B persons among non-smokers and occasional smokers. In a subsequent study of Welsh miners, Higgins et al. (1963) also found an excess of type B in non-smokers, but this did not reach the 5 per cent level of statistical significance. The authors commented: 'We must conclude, therefore, that while the present series provides no convincing evidence of an association between smoking and the ABO blood groups, it is not in serious conflict with Cohen and Thomas's data, and, combined with it, suggests that an association may exist.'

It is interesting in this connection to note that Angst & Maurer-Groeli (1974) have found significant relationships between blood groups and personality. They found that introversion is significantly more frequent among persons who have AB blood group, and that emotionality is significantly more frequent in persons having blood group B than in persons having blood group A. This would suggest that non-smokers as a group are more emotional than smokers, a finding which may tie up with the low N scores observed in lung cancer patients, who of course are frequently smokers. The whole field of genetic markers like blood groups deserves a much more detailed study than it has received so far.

Personality and smoking

The existence of constitutional differences between smokers and non-smokers suggests a relationship between personality and smoking. In looking at the evidence for such a relationship, we have paid particular attention to the three major dimensions of personality which emerge from a large number of empirical studies over the past fifty years (Royce, 1973). These three major type factors each represent the apex of a hierarchical system, produced by the intercorrelations between a number of different traits. Thus extraversion-introversion (E) is a concept based on the observed intercorrelations between traits such as sociability, impulsiveness, carefreeness, activity, etc. Neuroticism-stability (N) is based on the intercorrelations between such traits as worry, tenseness, anxiety, emotionality, etc. Psychoticism (P), the last of the three major dimensions, is based on the intercorrelations between such traits as emotional coldness, hostility, egocentricity, lack of superego control, etc. Details regarding the determination of these factors are given in Eysenck & Eysenck (1969; 1976).

There is good evidence for the genetic determination of these major personality variables (Eysenck, 1976c; Eaves & Eysenck, 1975, 1977). The behavioural manifestations of these personality traits would seem to be mediated through various anatomical and physiological features of the organism (Eysenck, 1967; Eysenck & Eysenck, 1976). Thus extraverts seem to be characterized by low resting levels of cortical arousal, whereas introverts have relatively high resting levels of cortical arousal; these levels are presumably mediated by the ascending reticular formation. Differences in emotionality, characteristic of N, are governed by the visceral brain or limbic system, coordinating the activity of the sympathetic and parasympathetic autonomic systems. As far as psychoticism is concerned, the evidence suggests some degree of hormonal control, related to sex hormones in particular; there is good evidence that males tend to have much higher P scores than females. There is a large body of experimental and physiological evidence relating to these hypotheses (Eysenck, 1976b; Eysenck & Eysenck, 1976), and for the purpose of this discussion we shall assume that these hypotheses are in the right direction.

We shall discuss presently the predictions as regards smoking which can be made on the basis of these general theories. Before doing so, however, it may be stated that in so far as evidence is available regarding specific traits, such as impulsiveness, which may contribute to one or more of these three major or super factors, such evidence will of course be mentioned in our discussion. Different investigators have approached the problem of personality-smoking correlations at different levels of the hierarchy, and while we consider the highest levels of these hierarchies to be the most important, nevertheless the lower levels will also be taken into account.

Smith (1967) has given an interesting discussion in which he relates the observed correlations between smoking and personality to the separation accuracy actually achieved. Figure 7 is taken from his paper. The figure shows that if the mean extraversion score of 100 smokers is 0.25 SD higher than that of 100 non-smokers, and if the extraversion scores are normally distributed and the two standard deviations are similar, assignment of group status (smokers vs. non-smokers) can be made with 55 per cent accuracy (i.e. 5 per cent above chance!) by simply designating as smokers the 100 subjects having extraversion scores above the combined mean of the two samples and designating as non-smokers those 100 who fall below the combined mean. When the means are separated by 0.50 SD, 1.00 SD, and 1.50 SD respectively, the accuracy of classification is 60 per cent, 69 per cent and 77 per cent, respectively. 'Examination of current literature concerning personality differences of smokers and non-smokers indicates that accuracy of classification typically ranges from 50 per cent (chance accuracy) to about 60 per cent (0.50 SD separation). Such accuracy offers only modest support for the hypothesis that smokers and non-smokers differ regarding certain constitutional variables.'

The point is an interesting one, but it underestimates the true differences between smokers and non-smokers. In the first place, such a statistical comparison leaves out the unreliability of the measuring instruments (personality, smoking history) which are being used. If we assume that the internal reliability of both the personality inventory used, and the smoking assessment made, is in the neighbourhood of 0.75, then by using more reliable tests we could increase the separa-

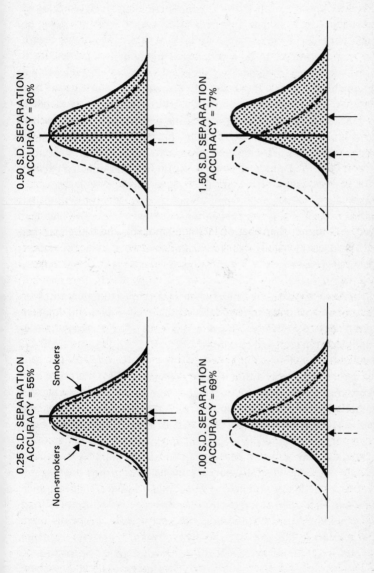

Figure 7 Separation accuracy achieved with different SD values, smokers vs. non-smokers. (From Smith, 1967)

tion between smokers and non-smokers very considerably. It can of course be objected that in actual fact these are the only measures that have been used, but this argument misses the point. If constitutional differences can be demonstrated significantly even with quite unreliable measures, then the true differences are likely to be considerably larger, and it is these true differences that we are fundamentally concerned with.

The second point to be made is that many of the investigations carried out were of the 'shot-gun' variety. In other words, what is done is to give either one or a number of personality inventories and trait measures, quite at random, and without any preconceived theory in mind. Many of these show no correlation with smoking at all, others show quite small correlations, and only a few show consistent and significant correlations. The negative outcome of some of these studies, however, does not prove that no constitutional differences exist; it simply demonstrates that instead of using the proper hypothetico-deductive approach, i.e. putting forward specific hypotheses and testing these, the investigators have chosen an approach which is not generally favoured by scientists in investigating complex problems of this kind. Positive and negative results cannot argue against any specific hypothesis because no specific hypotheses were put up in the first place.

The third argument is directed against the assumption, made in the discussion of Figure 7 given by Smith, that only one single trait is relevant. We shall see below that smokers tend to be extraverted, high on N, and also high on P; in other words they differ along all three dimensions of the three-dimensional personality model. Now it has often been shown that these three dimensions are essentially independent; it follows that we can add the 'separation accuracies' produced by each separately. Separations achieved by a single trait or factor may not be impressive, but when these can be added they may achieve a much more impressive degree of separation accuracy.

A fourth point will only be hinted at here but will be taken up again later on. Proper predictions of smoking behaviour are only possible in terms of a theory of smoking behaviour in general, i.e. a model which tells us something about the reasons why people smoke. Such a model will be presented presently, but for the moment let us merely consider that if different people smoke for different reasons, then these reasons should be related to personality in order to provide a meaningful prediction. To take a real differentiation, Frith (1971) has shown that men tend to smoke because they are bored, women because they are tense and nervous. If we correlated a measure of N with smoking in men, we would find no correlation; similarly, if we correlated E with smoking in women, we would find no correlation. It is the interaction between sex and personality which might be the crucial variable. Practically all the existing literature is concerned with overall correlations between smoking and some particular trait or factor of personality; few authors have paid even lip service to the complexities of the problem. If even these very superficial examinations find highly significant and replicable differentiation between smokers and non-smokers, it seems reasonable to expect that much bigger differentiations would be found if we took these complexities into account.

We may now turn to a consideration of the predictions which personality theory enables us to make of smoking behaviour. These predictions are phrased in a very general form, but they must of course be qualified by the properties of the smoking model to be introduced later. We will present the predictions in a rather abbreviated form as a more explicit statement has already been made elsewhere (Eysenck, 1973). We may begin with extraversion-introversion.

Extraverts are known to have low levels of cortical arousal, and there is good evidence to show that in general higher levels of arousal are preferred. This leads to a large number of predictions, such as that extraverts will tolerate boredom and sensory deprivation poorly, will like strong sensory stimuli, will habituate very quickly to repetitive stimulation, will change jobs, move house, and change sexual partners much more frequently than introverts, condition poorly to socializing stimuli, etc. (Eysenck, 1967, 1976a, b). These predictions have all been verified.

If extraverts seek for higher levels of cortical arousal, then it would seem that chemical agents such as nicotine, which has the effect of increasing cortical arousal (Weyer, 1967) would present them with a valuable means of achieving these higher levels of arousal. We would therefore predict that extraverts would smoke more than introverts, although, as we shall see presently, this prediction has to be qualified because of the nonlinear relation between amount of nicotine in the blood and cortical arousal.

Turning next to neuroticism, we must take seriously the view often voiced by smokers that smoking cigarettes makes them less tense, and reduces anxiety. If this is so, then we would predict that high N scorers would smoke more than low N scorers. We seem here to run into a theoretical problem, namely that extraverts smoke in order to increase their arousal while high N scorers smoke in order to decrease their arousal! As we shall see presently, this may be related to the dual function of nicotine, which acts to increase arousal when taken in small doses, but acts to decrease arousal when taken in larger doses.

Smoking is still regarded as a somewhat antisocial or asocial habit; it is more frequently indulged in by men (even nowadays), and criminals (who tend to be almost exclusively male) are known to smoke more than law-abiding citizens. Psychoticism is found more frequently in males, and it is related to antisocial behaviour, in children, adolescents and adults (Eysenck, 1977a). Furthermore, prisoners are known to have much higher P scores than non-prisoners. For all these reasons the prediction seems appropriate that high P scorers will smoke more than low P scorers. Again we shall have to qualify this prediction, and discuss it in more detail; at the moment we are merely concerned with indicating the direction which our prediction takes. We thus have a systematic view of smoking, predicting that it will be correlated with high scoring on P, E and N. The prediction relates specifically to cigarette smoking; it is difficult to make specific predictions for cigar and pipe smoking as these are much less frequent, are in part tied to social class, and use different types of tobacco, as already explained. We will discuss data on pipe and cigar smoking where they occur, but should note that our predictions are related most specifically to cigarette smoking.

Eysenck, Tarrant & Woolf (1960) and Eysenck (1963a) have carried out two studies specifically to test the hypotheses linking smoking with extraversion and neuroticism. Twenty-four groups of subjects were used, divided equally on the basis of age, class, and smoking habit. There were six different groups classified according to smoking habit: non-smokers, light smokers, medium smokers, heavy smokers, pipe smokers and ex-smokers. There were approximately 100 subjects in each of the twenty-four groups. Random samples of the population were obtained for each of these groups, about 7,000 contacts being made by interviewers in order to locate the requisite number of subjects. A very careful sampling design was used in order to make sure that the population did in fact amount to a proper representative sample of the British Isles.

The results of the study are shown in Figure 8. It will be seen that the amount of extraversion increases as we go from non-smokers to light, to medium and finally to heavy smokers, who are the most extraverted of all. Ex-smokers are situated between light and medium smokers so far as degree of extraversion is concerned; pipe smokers are the most introverted of all. The differences are fully significant statistically. In spite of the relatively large number of cases used there was no relationship between smoking and neuroticism, but it should be noted that the sample was restricted to males; as stated above, the relationship with neuroticism may be more apparent in females (e.g. Waters, 1971).

The second inquiry was carried out to make certain that the results obtained were not just statistical artefacts. Again twenty-four sub-groups were used, containing roughly 100 male subjects, all aged between 45 and 64 years. In this study, too, neuroticism and extraversion were measured, but in addition care was taken to include separate measures of impulsiveness and sociability. Figure 9 shows the results of this study. Again it will be seen that there is a regular progression in extraversion from non-smokers through light and medium to heavy smokers. Ex-smokers are between light and medium smokers, and pipe smokers are again the most introverted group. Again no relationship was found between smoking and neuroticism. The separate scoring of traits of sociability and impulsiveness did not add any information, as these traits are not related to smoking apart from the contribution they make to the measurement of extraversion.

Matarazzo & Saslow (1960) give a survey of a variety of findings in relation to cigarette smoking which support the view that extraversion is correlated with smoking. Consider the following findings. It has been shown that cigarette smokers also tend to partake more frequently of coffee and of alcoholic beverages; it has also been found that extraverts tend to drink more coffee and more liquor. Cigarette smokers are known to be more frequently involved in driving accidents; it has been found that extraverts tend to be more frequently involved in driving accidents than are introverts. It has been found that divorced people tend to smoke more whereas single people tend not to smoke; introverts tend to marry less, extraverts are more frequently involved in a change of marital partner. It has been found that people who change jobs frequently tend to smoke more; again extraverts are known to change jobs more frequently. Several studies

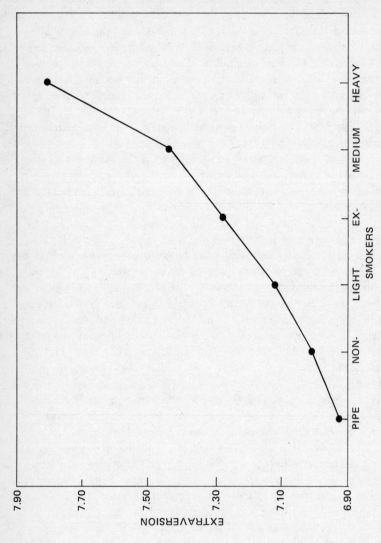

Figure 8 Relationship between extraversion and smoking habits. (After Eysenck, 1965)

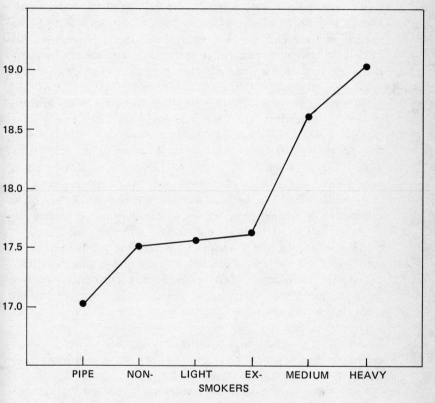

Figure 9   Replication of experimental results shown in Figure 8.

have tended to show that people who are relatively unsuccessful academically, both at school and university, tend to smoke more; it has also been found that introverts are more successful at school and at university. People who smoke a lot have been found to be 'chance oriented'; this agrees well with the finding that extraverts tend to be impulsive. Last, it has been found that on various personality questionnaires of gregariousness, social introversion, and the Pd scale of the MMPI, smokers go in the extraverted direction. All these findings come from American studies, and they all support the generalization that cigarette smoking is correlated with extraversion.

Many American studies have also been concerned with neuroticism or emotionality, and it must be said that here agreement is much less obvious. Most of the American studies have found a positive relationship between smoking and neuroticism. Admittedly many of these studies were carried out on relatively small groups, and in most cases the groups chosen were quite unrepresentative. Nevertheless, the amount of agreement reported must make one cautious of dismissing these results. The American report summarizes the findings in the following sentence: 'Despite the individual deficiencies of many of the studies, despite the great diversity in conceptualisation and research methods used and despite discrepancies in reported findings the presence of some comparability between them and the relative consistency of findings lends support to the existence of a relationship between the smoking habit and the personality configuration that is vaguely described as "neurotic".' The tortured structure and syntax of this sentence adequately indicate the difficulty which the authors had in coming to a conclusion on this point.

Since these early reports and studies were published, a number of further investigations have been carried out, some of which may be worthy of mention. One large-scale study is reported by Smith (1967) who used large samples of nursing students, female college freshmen, and two samples of male college freshmen, totalling almost 1,600 subjects in all. Personality questionnaires of various kinds and peer ratings of personality were used on different samples. It was found that among 512 nursing students, smokers scored significantly higher on extraversion than non-smokers; the two groups did not differ significantly on the neuroticism score. Use of the introversion scale permitted smokers and non-smokers to be classified quite accurately in 60 per cent of the cases. On the other inventories, relative to non-smokers, the smokers scored highly on the variable 'heterosexuality' and scored lower on the variables 'order' and 'deference'. 'Order, which reflects the degree of need for, or interest in, maintaining order and organisation in one's activities, gave the highest and most consistent separation between non-smokers and smokers of all the 15 traits (median accuracy of classification over 4 samples equals 59%).'

Peer ratings were organized by factor analysis into five clusters whose names will indicate the nature of the clusters. Relative to non-smokers, smokers are rated by their peers as being lower on 'agreeableness', i.e. they are less adaptable, tender, self-effacing, trusting and good-natured. They are also more prone to jealousy, assertive, attention-seeking and demanding. Attention-seeking, a very extraverted trait, gave the most definite discrimination between smokers and non-smokers.

On a factor of rated 'extraversion', smokers had higher scores than non-smokers, the best discrimination between the groups being achieved by a rating of 'retiring, shy', which applied most to non-smokers; the median accuracy for this rating was 63 per cent. On the next factor, 'strength of character', smokers scored lower than non-smokers. On the fourth factor, called 'emotionality', four out of five significant differences indicated a greater emotionality among smokers than non-smokers. The variable 'emotional' provided the best discrimination between the groups, with a median accuracy of 60 per cent, and it indicates that the smokers are more emotional than the non-smokers, a finding which would support the relationship with neuroticism. The last factor was called 'refinement, mannerliness'. The results show that students who smoke are rated as being significantly more crude and unmannerly than students who do not smoke. This variable discriminates between smokers and non-smokers with a median accuracy of 59 per cent. Results are also reported on discrimination between non-smokers and *heavy* smokers; here discrimination achieves a higher level (66 per cent for the two most discriminating variables). Finally, multiple discriminant analyses employing a composite score from each of five peer rating areas permitted discrimination between smokers and non-smokers with 68 per cent accuracy, and between non-smokers and heavy smokers with 76 per cent accuracy. The data on the whole are in good agreement with Eysenck's results, and demonstrate that personality is definitely related to smoking habits.

Several studies (e.g. Schubert, 1965; Brackenridge & Bloch, 1972; Rae, 1975) supported the contention that cigarette smokers are more extraverted than non-smokers, but there is no such consistency in the evidence for neuroticism. Brackenridge & Bloch (1972) found cigarette smokers higher on neuroticism than non-smokers, while Rae (1975) found no relationship, and Kanekar & Dolke (1970) found a negative one. Gupta, Sethi & Gupta (1976), working with male Indian students, found a positive relationship between the degree of smoking and the level of extraversion and neuroticism. 'Various sub-groups of smokers were found to have high neuroticism scores as compared to the non-smokers (0.001 level).' These data were derived from EPI questionnaires; 'observations of 16 PF were also substantially in support of these impressions . . . it may therefore be concluded that smokers have a higher level of neurotic tendency as well as extraversion'.

A study by Powell et al. (1979) is interesting as it deals with a sample of 808 middle-class children, in which more than half of the boys and girls had tried smoking cigarettes by the age of fifteen years. Table 2 shows the actual correlation between smoking and P, E and N for the various groups of boys and girls. It will be noted that the authors used the Junior EPQ (Eysenck & Eysenck, 1976) which also includes an L (lie or dissimulation) scale; under condi-

TABLE 2

Correlations of personality traits with smoking for boys and girls

		Boys			Girls
	11 yrs	13 yrs	15 yrs	13 yrs	15 yrs
P smoke	.281*	.345**	.193	.462**	.346**
E smoke	.020	.195	.093	.147*	.262*
N smoke	.228	.121	.289*	.357**	.236
L smoke	−.131	−.424**	−.121	−.428**	−.429**

*p<.05
**p<.01

(After Powell, 1978)

tions where dissimulation is not likely this scale measures personality traits of conformity and conservatism. It will be seen that all the correlations are in the expected direction, although of course there is quite a bit of variability in the size of the relationships. Canonical correlations for a combination of the four personality tests were carried out, resulting in coefficients averaging around 0.4. There seems to be little doubt that even in quite young children the same correlations between personality and smoking obtained as can be observed in older groups. It is interesting to note that Powell (1977) found that the pattern of personality relationships in children who smoked was identical to that of children who misbehaved and did not conform to a socialized pattern.

Jamison (1978) obtained similar results on another sample of children in the 4th and 5th grades. The main point of his study was the relationship between antisocial behaviour and personality, but the antisocial behaviour scale used also contained three questions relating to smoking (Item 4: Smoking during school hours; Item 35: Buying cigarettes to smoke yourself; Item 49: Smoking cigarettes). Table 3 shows the observed correlations between 'Yes' answers to these

TABLE 3

Correlations of personality traits with three smoking items for boys and girls

	Boys (N=781)			Girls (N=501)		
	I4	I35	I49	I4	I35	I49
P	.26	.28	.23	.42	.35	.34
E	.14	.14	.11	.23	.22	.34
N	.08	.10	.06	.09	.07	.08
L	− .22	− .28	− .29	− .22	− .21	− .24

(After Jamison, 1978)

three questions and the four personality scales of the Junior EPQ. Correlations with N are weaker, with E stronger, than in the Powell study; it is not obvious why there should be such differences. Correlations with P are strong in both studies. It is interesting that Jamison found almost identical correlations between personality and anti-social behaviour as between personality and smoking, suggesting that smoking in youngsters is in fact an antisocial activity.

This conclusion is supported by a study by Steward & Livson (1966) who tested the hypothesis that rebelliousness contributes to the aetiology of cigarette smoking. (See also Bartmann & Stäcker, 1974.) Using data from two longitudinal studies, the authors made comparisons between smokers and non-smokers (as determined at age thirty) in the pre-smoking years from kindergarten through high school on several measures of rebelliousness. In every comparison for both sexes the smokers showed greater rebelliousness; the difference was statistically significant in most instances. This difference persisted into adulthood; smokers of both sexes scored significantly lower on the socialization scale of the California Psychological Inventory. The evidence indicating rebelliousness was also found related to alcoholism and drug usage; it is interesting to note that smoking and drinking have always been found linked (e.g. Higgins et al., 1967), and that drug addicts too show the same pattern as Powell et al. found in smokers.

Along similar lines is a study by Jacobs & Spilken (1971) in which heavy smoking was hypothesized to be related to personality traits of defiance, impulsivity and danger-seeking, to manifest distress, and to a perception of having experienced minimal warmth, protection, and affection while growing up. Both self-rating scales and projective techniques were utilized to test the assumptions, and on all measures the heavy smokers scored significantly higher than the non-smokers. These results were interpreted as support for the view that although people smoke for a variety of reasons, the habituated or addicted smoker often engages in the practice as an extension of his personal style, and utilizes it to deal with characterologic as well as situational aspects of his life which may engender tension, irritation, or boredom.

Similar results have been reported from Schubert (1965), who found that in two groups studies, smokers scored significantly lower on the social introversion and lie scales of the MMPI and significantly higher on the hypomania scale. One group of smokers scored significantly higher on the psychopathic-deviate scale. An item analysis of the MMPI, and a cross-validation at another university, yielded fifty MMPI items which consistently differentiated smokers from non-smokers. Grouping these items by content revealed that smokers describe themselves (1) as being bored and seeking thrills, (2) as behaving in a socially unacceptable fashion (a trait which they also attribute to others), and (3) as having masculine traits. Smokers also scored significantly higher than non-smokers on an impulsivity scale. 'A trait of *arousal seeking* was suggested to account for these findings.'

Some further support for Eysenck's hypothesis regarding extraversion and arousal seeking comes from a study by Nilsson & Tibbling (1972), who studied the relationship between personality and consumption of tobacco, using the perceptual after-effect as a measure of personality. The study included the oculogyral illusion experiment and the serial colour word test. The results from both the instruments indicate that individuals 'hyposensitive' to after-effect experiences are heavier consumers of cigarettes than individuals 'who are sensitive or hypersensitive to such experiences'. Such sensitivity has been shown to be typical of introverted subjects (Eysenck, 1957).

Rather few studies have been conducted outside the Anglo-American circle, but those that have appeared have on the whole given similar results. Thus Gupta et al. (1976), working on an Indian sample, used the EPI and Cattell's 16 PF, and found significant differences between smokers and non-smokers, with the former more extraverted and more neurotic. In Germany, Arnold-Krüger (1973) and Lasogga (1978), the latter working with children, found evidence for the importance of N as a correlate of smoking, but Lasogga failed to obtain significant results for E. This is almost the only study to show such a failure; possibly an explanation may be found in the fact that the amount of pocket money the children obtained correlated quite highly with their expenditure on cigarettes! In Belgium, Rustin et al. (1978) found that cigarette smokers, as compared with non-smokers, were more frequently extravert and neurotic, and also less frequently of 'type A' personality; they also had a higher mean serum cholesterol level.

It is sometimes said that correlations between personality variables and smoking cannot establish a causal link; it may be that personality traits are influenced by smoking, rather than the other way around. This objection does not apply to a study by Cherry & Kiernan (1976; 1978), in which the short form of the Eysenck Maudsley Personality Inventory was administered at the age of sixteen, and information about smoking obtained at the age of twenty-five. There were 2,753 subjects included in this survey, and although the short form of the MPI is not as reliable as the longer form, the data are still of considerable importance. It was found that 'non-smokers are less extraverted and more stable than those who have ever been regular smokers (by the age of twenty-five years) and those who take up smoking early are more extraverted and more neurotic than those who start the habit after sixteen years'. Cherry & Kiernan fitted a logistic model to their data, and the resulting figures are shown in Table 4. (Only male subjects are used for this comparison. Figures for females are similar.) The progression of increasing smoking as we go from low to high extraversion, and from low to high neuroticism, is very clear. As the authors say, 'the analysis. . .is of interest in that it confirms the relationship between extraversion, neuroticism and smoking, and establishes that the position on the personality dimension pre-dated the smoking habit for those who took up smoking after sixteen years' (p. 14).

Before concluding this section we must return to the problem of emotionality, anxiety or neuroticism in relation to smoking. Nesbitt (1972) has put forward an interesting hypothesis, associated with his empirical finding of an association between chronic smoking and *low* emotionality. He found not only that smokers feel less emotional than non-smokers, but that they appear more emotional to others. After reviewing some studies such as that by Steward & Livson (1966) already mentioned, and one by Clausen (1968), who found that adolescent girls who were to become heavy

TABLE 4

Likelihood of men in sample taking up cigarette smoking by personality scores

	Neuroticism			
Extraversion	*Low*	*Medium*	*High*	*Number in sample*
Low	44%	55%	60%	382
Medium	48%	59%	64%	427
High	59%	69%	73%	489
Total number in sample	445	424	429	1298

(After Cherry & Kiernan, 1978)

smokers, reported themselves relatively *higher* on 'emotionality' and were also rated higher on 'expressiveness'. Nesbitt suggests the possibility that smokers are initially *more* emotional than non-smokers, taking up smoking perhaps because of its 'relaxing' effect. He goes on to say: 'It appears that smokers who have smoked the most feel the least emotional. One possible developmental sequence may be indicated in our finding that smokers tend to appear in general more insensitive to their internal physiological state. These results, while not by any means definitive, will still seem to argue plausibly for the conclusion that smokers' chronic emotional state is affected by their smoking habit.' This is an ingenious hypothesis which would seem to account for the curious contradictions that appear in the literature on the connection between smoking and emotionality; it deserves further study.

An alternative hypothesis is advanced by McArthur et al. (1958) and Emery et al. (1968) who find that both very anxious, agitated men, and emotionally constricted individuals tend to smoke; it is argued that both types are concerned with problems of affect control, that both show disturbances in this area, and that smoking is particularly appropriate in this context. Emery et al. succeeded in their investigation in replicating the relationship between extraversion and smoking; their data also suggest that neuroticism 'is measuring some personality factor which is central to the dynamics of smoking, particularly for women. It is closely related to those other scales measuring "emotionality" which are one of the determinants of "experience stress" central to smoking dynamics. . . . It is explicitly involved in situations where emotionality must clearly be controlled, that is, in situations necessitating concentration or requiring relief from boredom.'

Before presenting any conclusions, it may be worthwhile to draw attention to one further paper by Rae & McCall (1973) which is of particular interest as it relates extraversion to both smoking and lung cancer. The authors attempted to demonstrate that an association between cancer and personality holds internationally. National extraversion and anxiety levels in eight advanced countries, and statistics of the number of cigarettes smoked per adult per annum in these countries, have been provided by Lynn & Hayes, and mortality rates per 100,000 of the population due to lung cancer (males and females separately) and cancer of cervix (females) were also obtained for each of these countries.

Rank order correlations were then calculated between national personality levels and cancer mortality rates. There was a highly significant correlation between extraversion and male lung cancer (0.66) and between extraversion and female lung cancer (0.72). Corresponding correlations for cigarette consumption and lung cancer, for males and females combined, were quite insignificant (0.07). For cancer of the cervix, a correlation with extraversion was again significant (0.64), whereas for cigarette consumption it was insignificant (0.45).

Correlations between anxiety and lung cancer were negative in both sexes (−0.52 and −0.71). This is an interesting replication on an international scale of the findings of Kissen & Eysenck of a lower mean N score for lung cancer cases as compared with controls, mentioned on a previous page. This is an exceptionally interesting paper which deserves to be followed up on a much larger scale.

In summary of this large and varied literature, only very partially surveyed in the preceding few pages, it may perhaps be said that there is no doubt about the relationship between extraversion and smoking; in practically every study extraverts have been found to smoke cigarettes more than do introverts, and smoking has been related to a large number of behaviour patterns characteristic of extraverts. The high degree of introversion of pipe smokers would still remain to be explained, and it will be interesting to have some data on cigar smokers. It is interesting to note that the correlation between extraversion and smoking fits in well with the finding of Seltzer that smokers are larger in body-build; in terms of Sheldon's system, extraverts are either ectomorphic (sociable) or mesomorphic (impulsive), and consequently larger in body-build (Eysenck, 1970).

As far as psychoticism is concerned, the available data support the association with cigarette smoking, but there has not been sufficient replication (owing to the relative recency of the scales for the measurement of this variable) to be as certain of the association as we can be about that with extraversion. However, a number of the trait studies mentioned in the course of our discussion support this relationship, and it is unlikely not to be replicated in future research. There is an interesting study by Carney (1967) in which he found that smokers had more sex chromatine than did non-smokers. This is of interest in view of the relationship already mentioned between masculinity and high P, and may also be worthy of experimental follow-up.

Neuroticism, as we have seen, presents a rather more complicated pattern, in that some researchers have found positive associations with smoking, particularly in women, whereas others have not. We have noted possible hypotheses explaining this failure to replicate, but future work is urgently needed.

We have noted a negative correlation between conformity (as measured by the Lie scale), and smoking; this relationship comes out in many different studies, in various different guises, and may also be worthy of further study. Altogether the data leave no doubt that there are highly significant relationships between personality and smoking, most of them replicable, but some of them leading to rather anomalous and odd contradictions. Some of these at least may find explanation in terms of a proper model of the causes of smoking.

A model for smoking

We must next turn to the question of the general model of smoking, i.e. an overall theory of smoking behaviour. Why do people smoke? There have been many investigations to study the situations in which people smoke, hoping to deduce from this certain motivational laws governing smoking. One of the earliest and most influential psychosocial models proposed is that of Tomkins (1966, 1968). He sees smoking behaviour as motivated by affective states. Innate reinforcing properties combine with learning in such a way that smoking becomes capable of relieving any negative affective states, or evoking any positive affect. Tomkins posited smoker types corresponding to the affective significance of the smoking behaviour. Thus there are positive affect smokers, negative affect smokers and 'habitual' smokers for whom the affective involvement is minimal. He further described the 'addictive' smoker, characterized by learned dependence on smoking such that awareness of not smoking *per se* elicits negative affect and thus further smoking.

Ikard, Green & Horn (1969), in a factor analytic study using items reflecting these motives, lent support to Tomkins' theory; they added stimulation and sensory-motor manipulation motives to the model. Others (Mausner & Platt, 1971; McKennell, 1970; Russell, Peto & Patel, 1974) further stress the additional role played by social factors.

Best & Hakstian (1978) report a large-scale factor analysis, for men and women separately, of situations where people feel a desire to smoke; subjects were asked to indicate the amount of desire to smoke in those situations. They found several factors related to nervousness and the relief of tension; these may be related to the personality factor of neuroticism. The first of these factors they label 'nervous tension': people smoke when they feel nervous, when they are worried, when they feel tense, etc. The second factor was labelled 'frustration': you smoke when you feel annoyed, when you feel angry, when you feel frustrated. A third factor in this group was called 'relaxation': you smoke when you want to relax, when you feel tired, etc. The fourth factor, probably also connected with this group, was labelled 'discomfort': you smoke when you feel uncomfortable, when you feel embarrassed, when you want to cheer up, etc. Yet another factor in this group was called 'restlessness': you smoke when you feel restless, when you feel impatient, when you are overly excited, etc.

Another set of situations seems to be related to relief from low levels of arousal. This factor may have something to do with extra-version; extraverts, it will be remembered, tend to have low resting levels of cortical arousal. A major factor here was called 'inactive': you smoke when you feel bored. There were also several other factors which have nothing to do with either of these two types of reaction; one was the 'automatic' factor: you smoke when you simply become aware of the fact that you are not smoking, or you just realize you are lighting a cigarette even though you have just put one out. Another factor was the 'social' one: you smoke when you see others smoking, or when someone offers you a cigarette. Another factor which they call 'time structuring' seems to be rather similar: you smoke when you want to have time to think in a conversation, or when you want to fill a pause in a conversation. Yet another factor was labelled 'sensory stimulation': you smoke when you want something to do with your hands. These and one or two other factors are relatively minor, and just fill in the general picture, as does another odd factor called 'self-image': you smoke when you want to feel more attractive, or you smoke when you are in a situation in which you feel smoking is a part of your self-image.

It is possible to judge the urgency of the smoking motivation connected with each factor by looking at the mean rating; subjects were asked to give a rating from one to five depending on the urgency with which they wanted to smoke in a given situation. Nervous tension, frustration, restlessness and boredom rank highest in this league.

These results link up with a more basic and simplified model suggested by Eysenck (1973) and Frith (1971). A questionnaire was constructed listing 22 situations which might make it likely that a person would be tempted to light a cigarette; 12 of these were high-arousal and 10 were low-arousal situations. The questionnaire was constructed on the basis of Eysenck's theory that extraverts smoke in order to raise their unsatisfactorily low arousal level, while high N scorers smoke to lower their unsatisfactorily high arousal level. The actual list used is given in Table 5. A factor analysis of the intercorrelations gave the result shown in Figure 10.

In this figure, note the position of sex. Men clearly smoke more in *low*-arousal situations; this agreed well with the fact that males tend to be more *extraverted* than females. Women smoke more in high-arousal situations; this agrees well with the fact that they tend to be higher on N than males. Note also that the item 'cigarettes per day' is exactly intermediate between the two extremes of low-arousal and high-arousal situations; in other words, people who smoke a lot apparently tend to smoke in both types of situation. Similar results to those of Frith have been obtained by Elgerot (1977).

The distinction here drawn is similar in many ways to Tomkins' typology of smokers already referred to, particularly his two main types classified according to the distinction between positive-affect and negative-affect smoking. In the latter 'an individual smoked primarily to reduce his feelings of distress, or his fear, or his shame, or his disgust, or any combination of these. He is trying to sedate himself rather than to stimulate . . . himself' (p. 19).

In contrast, positive-affect smoking occurs in those individuals who characteristically smoke under pleasant circumstances which are relaxing — possibly so relaxing as to require some measure of arousal.

McKennell (1970) published data also supporting this type of analysis. Two major factors in his analysis were 'relaxation smoking' and 'nervous irritation smoking'; sex comparisons in his work gave results similar to Frith's. It is clear that for his adults, men exceed women for relaxation smoking, and women exceed men for nervous irritation smoking, when allowance is made for the fact that men are

Table 5

Situations in which people may smoke

Item number   *Situational statement*

1   You are having an important interview for a job.

2   You have to fill in a complicated tax form.

3   You have to look through several hundred coins to see if there are any rare and valuable ones.

4   You are having a quiet evening with friends.

5   You are witnessing a violent and horrifying film.

6   You have to drive at speed in heavy traffic.

7   You have to wait for your train home, which is very late.

8   You are having a restful evening alone reading a magazine.

9   You are sitting in a dentist's waiting room knowing that you are to have a particularly difficult filling.

10   You are trying to hold a conversation at a large and very noisy party.

11   You are very tired and need to keep awake.

12   You have to ask your boss for a raise at a time when he is known to be in a bad mood.

13   You are trying to account for the discrepancy between your spending for the month and your bank statement.

14   You are looking through a long list of names to see if you can find anyone you know.

15   You are chatting with friends during a tea-break.

16   You have just been informed of the death of a close friend.

17   You have to do some rapid mental arithmetic for an intelligence test.

18   You are travelling on a train for several hours.

19   You go for a solitary walk in quiet countryside.

20   You have just heard the announcement of a plane crash, and you think a friend may have been involved.

21   You are having an important telephone conversation in a very noisy office.

22   You have just had a very big meal.

(After Frith, 1971)

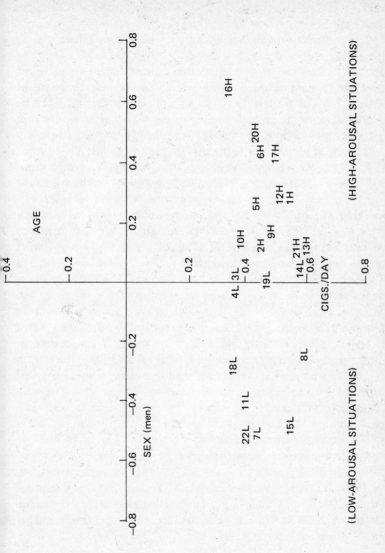

Figure 10 Factor analysis of Frith questionnaire (see Table 5). (After Frith, 1971)

heavier smokers than women. Other studies in support of the hypothesis are cited by Eysenck (1973).

Direct studies correlating 'reasons for smoking' and personality have only come to the fore recently. Bartol (1975), employing female smokers, found that extraverts indicated that they preferred to smoke in stressful situations whereas introverts preferred to smoke in non-stressful situations. Neurotics indicated a desire to smoke, greater than stables, in both situations, but with a greater difference in the stress situations. Barnes & Fishlinsky (1976) used a reducing — augmenting questionnaire (these concepts are related to E — Petrie, 1967), and found that extreme female augmenters tended to crave cigarettes more in low-arousal than in high-arousal situations. Knott (in press) used 100 male cigarette smokers who were divided into low-arousal and high-arousal groups according to their answers to a questionnaire. High arousal smokers were significantly more extraverted, more neurotic, and more reducing (on a reducing — augmenting questionnaire) than low-arousal smokers. The sedative smoking of neurotic subjects is in line with theory. The data on E and reducing — augmenting seem to go counter to hypothesis, but there are too many uncontrolled variables in verbal report situations to be confident on this point. The manner of smoking, the nicotine content of the cigarettes smoked, and many other variables can powerfully influence the situation. Furthermore, as Eysenck (1963b) has shown, for people who are high on neuroticism and extraversion, stimulant drugs have a calming effect and improve social behaviour. The issue is an important one, and deserves better-controlled studies. Such studies might also take into account the fact that Phelps & Gerdes (1978) have shown that the time of smoking, in relation to stress, is an important variable; they found that pre-stress smokers had significantly lower heart-rate increases during stress compared with other subjects, i.e. those who smoked during or after stress, and 'also reported significantly greater attributions for smoking as the cause of feeling states'. Extraverts and introverts may time their smoking differently in relation to stress.

Emphasis on two major factors in causing the maintenance of the smoking habit does not deny the fact that social factors, habit factors and other minor motivational causes may also play a part; we merely wish to suggest that there is strong evidence to show that nicotine plays an essential part in the maintenance of the smoking habit, and that the effects of the nicotine are most closely related to the two major factors emphasized in our theory. It seems likely that people who merely smoke for social reasons, or because the habit has developed but is no longer reinforced, would find it easier to give up smoking; it is those for whom the habit is reinforcing, because it changes the state of arousal in which they find themselves, who will find great difficulties in giving up the smoking habit. This does not mean that they are 'addicted' to smoking; it simply means that smoking produces positive or negative reinforcement for them which they find it difficult to forego.

One prediction which may be made from our theory is that under conditions of stress or overload, high neuroticism scoring subjects should benefit more from smoking than low neuroticism scoring subjects. Studies by Kucek (1975) and Warburton & Wesnes (1978) bear this out. In the former study, subjects were tested in an experiment under conditions of information overload (they were required to track a target and do mental arithmetic). Smoking had a beneficial effect on the performance of *neurotic* subjects allowed to smoke. In the Warburton & Wesnes study, an attentional vigilance task was used, and it was found that smoking helped high N scoring subjects, but not low N scoring subjects. The correlation between improvement and neuroticism was 0.68, which is astonishingly high, and indicates the importance of personality in evaluating the effects of smoking on performance.

The nicotine paradox

The hypothesis outlined above, and the model of smoking that it gives rise to, leads us straight to what Schachter (1973) has called 'Nesbitt's paradox'. As Schachter phrases it, 'the known physiological effects of smoking a cigarette are those that we consider as indicating states of activation or arousal. The psychological effects of smoking, at least as far as smokers describe them, are sedational.' This of course is not strictly accurate; many people smoke because they are bored and for them the activation or arousal factor is indeed an important one. We would word the paradox in a rather different manner, by saying that *some people smoke in order to achieve a reduction in activation or arousal, while others smoke in order to achieve an increment in activation or arousal.* In other words, the same activity is used by different people to produce quite contradictory results. How is that possible? Schachter suggests two possibilities, relying on some experiments by Nesbitt (1972). The first of his suggested explanations is based on the assumption that the intensity of an emotional state is a positively increasing function of deviation from the baseline level of autonomic activity. He goes on to argue that the cigarette that is actually smoked raises the ground level of sympathetic activity, and that the additional activation produced by external stimulation, and by worrying about external stimulation, is superimposed on this ground level. If we accept the 'law of initial values', it follows that the additional arousal induced by external stimulation and worrying about external stimulation will be least in those people who have achieved a high level of sympathetic activation by smoking, simply because this high level leaves little room for further increment in activation attributable to emotional experience.

An alternative hypothesis put forward by Schachter is essentially cognitive in nature, i.e. it is concerned with how the individual interprets and labels a set of internal physiological events that are set in motion by disturbing or frightening events. Such events are presumed to throw the autonomic nervous system into action, releasing epinephrine, sending up the heart rate and blood pressure, increasing blood sugar, etc. Now many of these physiological changes are precisely identical with the changes produced by smoking a cigarette. Schachter asks what happens, then, to the smoking smoker in a frightening situation? He feels the way he usually does when he is frightened, but he also feels the way he usually does when he is smoking a cigarette. Does he label his feelings as fright or as smoking a cigarette? 'I would suggest, of course, that to the extent that he attributes these physiological changes to smoking, he will not be frightened. And this, I propose, is the possible explanation for the strikingly calming effect that smoking a cigarette had on the chronic smokers in Nesbitt's experiments.'

Eysenck (1973) has suggested a third theory which has recently found some empirical support. He bases himself on two sets of findings. In the first place, it has been shown that the effects of nicotine are *biphasic,* there being a marked sequential effect, with the primary arousal phase being followed by a secondary depression phase. Thus Schaeppi (1967) concluded his survey by observing that 'EEG desynchronisation, retractions of the nictitating membrane, mydriasis and increase in blood pressure, which occur after the treatment of the cat's lower brain stem with nicotine, indicate an increase in the animal's level of vigilance. Conversely, the secondary phase, consisting of synchronisation, relaxation of the nictitating membrane, miosis and decrease in blood pressure indicate a low level of vigilance' (p. 47). Similarly Goldstein, Beck & Mundschenk (1967) comment that 'the electroencephalographic effects of nicotine start with an arousal reaction. By conventional methods of examination of cortical EEG and of behaviour, this arousal *per se* is not different, at least in animals, from the arousal elicited by a variety of other stimulant agents, such as amphetamine, caffeine, LSD, deanol, etc., or from that due to sensory stimulation alone. However, contrary to what is observed with a number of agents, the arousal in animals treated with very small doses of nicotine is of short duration and is followed by three distinct phases: the period of EEG alternation between sedation and excitation, the period of behavioural and EEG sedation and sleep, and, finally, a frequent occurrence of "paradoxical" or "activated" sleep' (p. 170). It thus seems that with identical doses of nicotine different effects may be obtained at different times after administration.

There is also evidence that while small doses have a positive effect on arousal, larger doses of nicotine may have a negative effect. Thus Armitage, Hall & Sellers (1969) found that doses of 2 mg/kg every thirty seconds for twenty minutes, given intravenously to cats, caused desynchronization of the electrocorticogram, indicating cortical activation, and an increase in the release of cortical acetylcholine. However, a larger dose given less frequently (4 mg/kg every minute for twenty minutes) caused sometimes an increase and sometimes a decrease in cortical activity, such changes being accompanied by an increase or a decrease in cortical acetylcholine output. Eysenck (1973), basing himself on these studies, suggested that the effects of nicotine depend primarily on the amount of nicotine in the blood stream. Small amounts of nicotine produce arousal, large amounts of nicotine produce reduction in arousal. This would resolve Nesbitt's paradox, and suggest a reason why some people smoke in order to increase arousal, while others smoke in order to decrease arousal. Recent evidence on humans by Ashton et al. (1976) is available which strongly supports this hypothesis; these authors injected nicotine into the blood stream of human volunteers and found the predicted curvilinear relationship, with small doses increasing arousal, and larger doses having an opposite effect. Provisionally, then, we may accept Eysenck's hypothesis, but without necessarily rejecting Schachter's two alternative theories; it is not impossible that all three may be correct and work together to produce the observed 'paradox'.

Quite recently, Roos (1977) has contributed a study which purports to examine Eysenck's theory. He grouped his 36 subjects into three groups of 12 each—non-smokers, light and medium-heavy smokers, respectively. EEG recordings were made while the subjects were presented with 14 stimuli while reclining on a bed with eyes closed. Stimuli included repeated sounds 'resembling machine-gun fire', and a door bell; also words differing in emotional loading, and cognitive tasks of different complexity. Lacey Autonomic Lability Scores were calculated, such that large decreases in the amount of alpha resulted in a large score. Auditory stimuli and the cognitive and task stimuli were grouped and analysed separately. It was found that the heavy smoking group was very heterogeneous, with the very heavy smokers giving quite different results from the medium smokers, and consequently this group was subdivided. When results were plotted, it was found that non-smokers and very heavy smokers had the lowest amount of alpha, i.e. might be considered the most aroused. These results are compatible with Eysenck's hypothesis that the mild and moderate smokers smoke to increase their arousal (lower their amount of alpha), while very heavy smokers smoke in order to lower their arousal (increase their amount of alpha). Roos seems to feel that his findings are contradictory to Eysenck's theory, but it is not apparent why he should think so.

In a second part of his study, Roos measured respiration rate, pulse volume, skin resistance and heart rate. Again using Autonomic Lability Scores, Roos found curvilinear relations between smoking and autonomic reactivity, very similar to those found for cortical arousal with the EEG. Heavy smokers showed trends opposite to those of medium smokers, and resembled rather non-smokers. The relationships obtained are nothing like as clear as in the case of the EEG. Roos explains this as follows: should the smoker smoke 'primarily for the effect the nicotine has on the CNS, it could be expected that the relationship between the activity of the CNS and smoking would be more perfect than that between the activity of the ANS and smoking'. This is a reasonable hypothesis.

The curvilinear regression of arousal on amount of nicotine may not be the only explanation of the paradox; another possibility is that arousal is a curvilinear function of arousal potential, using that term in the sense of Berlyne (1974). This arousal potential is made up of two major components, *internal* (e.g. extraversion—introversion differences) and *external* (outside stimulation, drugs, etc.). Eysenck & O'Connor (1979) have put forward the hypothesis that arousal would be higher in introverts than in extraverts (Eysenck, 1967), and that increasing the arousal potential by smoking would push the extraverts up to a higher level, but would push the introverts (hypothetically already at an optimal level of arousal) down beyond this point. Scores on the CNV (contingent negative variation)[1] measure of the EEG were used to indicate arousal level, and Figure 11 shows the predicted shifts with smoking. RS denotes real smoking of a cigarette, rate and duration of puffs being controlled and approximately equal for all subjects; SS denotes the control period of sham-smoking. The theory predicts an *increase* in CNV for *extraverts* after smoking, and a *decrease* for *introverts*. Using ISIs of 1 second and 4 seconds, this cross-over effect was found both for peak latencies and for peak amplitudes (Figures 12 and 13). It is thus apparent that in all experiments on the effects of smoking, personality differences must be controlled if replicable data are to be obtained (O'Connor, in press.)

The general picture may be rounded off with a description of a few recent researches which have been conducted with some such hypothesis as that outlined above in mind. The most important and relevant of these is the study by Ashton et al. (1976), which was carried out with the use of the contingent negative variation (CNV). Three series of experiments on the CNV were carried out. In the first of these 22 regular smokers were used, and the CNV was increased in size in 7, decreased in 11, and showed biphasic changes in 4. 'If it is assumed that an increase or decrease in CNV magnitude reflects stimulant or depressant actions on brain activity, it may be concluded that cigarette smoking can exert both effects on the CNV.' The authors also found that 'the dose of nicotine varies according to circumstances and is also related to the personality of the smoker. Thus, of 16 smokers, the 8 more extraverted subjects had a lower rate of nicotine intake which

[1]CNV is thought to reflect the degree of arousal, and possibly of attention, of the subject, and provides an objective measure with which to test the hypothesis that stimulant effects of nicotine on the brain might increase the magnitude of the CNV, whereas depressant effects might decrease it.

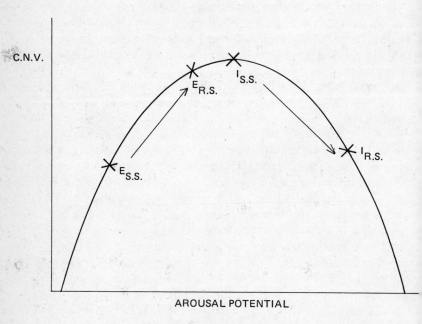

Figure 11 Relation of arousal, as measured by CNV, to arousal potential, for extraverts and introverts after real smoking (S.S.). (After Eysenck & O'Connor, 1979)

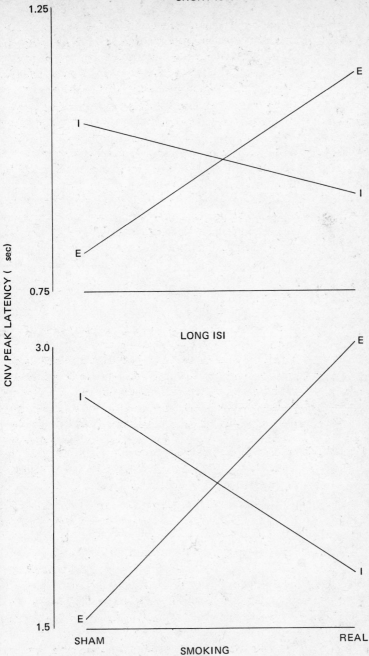

Figure 12 Change in peak latency of CNV for extraverts and introverts as a function of smoking, for short and long ISI. (After
Eysenck & O'Connor, 1979)

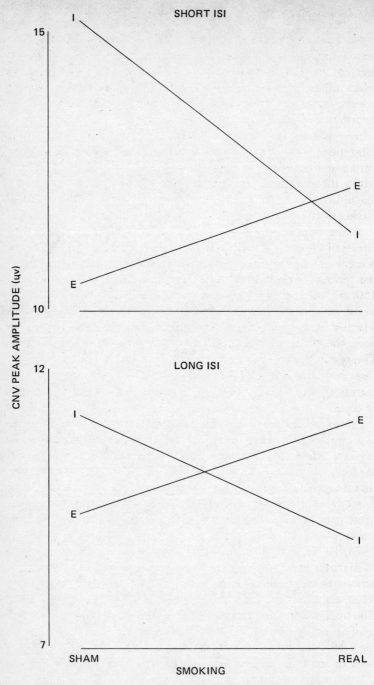

Figure 13 Change in peak amplitude of CNV for extraverts and introverts as a function of smoking, for short and long ISI.

produced the stimulant effect on the CNV whilst the 8 more intro-verted subjects had a higher rate of nicotine intake which de-pressed the CNV. It is concluded that smokers unconsciously select different doses of nicotine from a cigarette in order to achieve some optimum dose which meets their requirements, determined by circumstances and personality.'

In a second experiment Ashton et al. showed that the CNV is a valid measure of arousal by using known stimulant drugs (caffeine citrate and pemoline) which increase the magnitude of the CNV, whilst the depressant drugs nitrazepan and diazepan decrease the magnitude of the CNV. In the doses used, none of these drugs produced any subjective effects.

In the third experiment, the aim was to determine whether the effects of cigarette smoking could be accounted for by the nicotine content of the smoke. Intravenous nicotine was administered in the form of intermittent 'shots'. In some subjects five 'shots' of 150 mg of nicotine produced a stimulant effect in the CNV, whilst in others it had the opposite effect. In order to determine whether the response to nicotine depended on the subject or on the dose, the effects of a range of doses were studied in six subjects. The results showed that the dose-response curve is of an unusual form and that at first the magnitude of the CNV *increased* with increasing doses, but thereafter *decreased* with further increases of doses.

'From the results of all these experiments it was concluded that (1) cigarette smoking can produce either a stimulant or de-pressant effect on the human brain, (2) these effects of cigarette smoking are principally due to nicotine in the smoke and (3) nico-tine is capable of causing a biphasic response which is dose related. A study of the dose-response curve suggests that nicotine may exert part of its effects on the brain by the simultaneous stimu-lation of an excitatory and inhibitory system' (Ashton et al., 1974, 1975).

Myrsten et al. (1975) used a questionnaire concerning inter-actions between the need to smoke and the external situation to select eight 'low-arousal smokers' and eight 'high-arousal smokers'. The former were smokers who generally experienced their strongest need to smoke in low-arousal situations, characterized by mono-tony or boredom, whilst the latter experienced their strongest need to smoke in high-arousal situations, characterized by anxiety or excitement. Members of each group were examined under smoking and non-smoking conditions in a low-arousal situation, i.e. performing a vigilance-type sensory motor task, and in a high-arousal situation performing a complex sensory motor task. It was found that the two groups reacted differently to smoking in the two situations. In low-arousal smokers, performance and general well-being were favourably affected by smoking in the low-arousal situation only. Conversely, performance and well-being of the high-arousal smokers were enhanced by smoking in the high-arousal situation only. These results agree well with our hypothesis.

Knott (1976) and Knott & Venables (1977) reported recording EEG activity from non-smokers and smokers under smoking-deprived and non-deprived states, in sessions involving administration of tobacco and/or alcohol. Analysis of the tonic EEG data indicated deprived smokers to be characterized by a state of cortical hypoexcitation and for tobacco smoking, prior to and/or during alcohol ingestion, to counteract the alcohol-induced CNS depression which was observed in both deprived and non-smokers. Analysis of phasic EEG data indicated that tobacco smoking, in the non-deprived smokers, significantly enhanced the central nervous system's susceptibility to alcohol. Smoking generally increased dominant alpha frequency in deprived smokers to a level comparable to non-smokers and non-deprived smokers.

The authors conclude that 'the suggestion that individuals smoke to achieve. . .specific psychological states of increased vigilance and attention associated with high alpha frequency is persuasive in view of the following findings: (a) tobacco smoking improves efficiency and prevents deterioration of RT over time (Frankenhaeuser, Myrsten, Post & Johansson, 1971); (b) tobacco smoking prevents deterioration in signal detection tasks requiring sustained vigilance over time (Tarrière & Hartemann, 1964) and prevents normal accumulation of inhibition with tapping and pursuit rotor learning (Frith, 1967, 1968); (c) tobacco smoking improves visual discrimination (Warwick & Eysenck, 1963) and counteracts both the cortical depressant effects of alcohol on visual discrimination (Tong, Knott, McGraw & Leigh, 1974a, 1974b) and RT (Lyon, Tong, Leigh & Clare, 1975) and the distracting effects of noise on RT (Tong, Knott, McGraw & Leigh, 1974a, 1974b); and (d) tobacco smoke improves performance on learning and retention tasks (Carter, 1974; Anderson & Post, 1974; and Anderson, 1975)'. (See also works of Heimstra,

1973; Heimstra et al., 1967.)

Results of empirical studies have of course not always been favourable to the theory in question; there are also a few anomalies. Thus Kumar et al. (1977) carried out two experiments in which they examined the hypothesis that habitual smokers need nicotine, and that they regulate their intake of this drug. A laboratory test for smoking was devised which permitted the continuous monitoring of puffing as well as of selected physiological variables. The procedure was also designed to reduce the influence of smoking habits and rituals. In the first experiment, inhaled amounts of tobacco smoke reduced subsequent *ad libitum* smoking in a dose-related way. In the second experiment, comparable doses of nicotine were given intravenously to the same subjects, but they failed to affect ongoing smoking. However, both the inhaled and intravenous doses of the drug produced very similar physiological effects. These experiments do not, therefore, support the nicotine-dependence hypothesis. In view of the large number of experiments supporting the nicotine-dependence hypothesis, these results are unusual and would need to be replicated before being taken too seriously.

Glad & Adesso (1976) raised subjects' arousal level by anxiety manipulation, but failed to find an increase in smoking behaviour as compared to control groups. Thus their experiment was interpreted as a failure to demonstrate that anxiety reduction was an adequate explanation of cigarette smoking behaviour. Failure to control personality and other variables may account for this aberrant result. In spite of anomalies of this kind, the majority of studies strongly support the hypotheses outlined above.

It is important to look at the effects of nicotine, not in isolation, but in conjunction with the situation in which the nicotine is administered (i.e. where the situation is low-arousing, medium-arousing or high-arousing), and also in relation to the personality of the subject, i.e. whether he is extraverted (low resting arousal level), ambivert (medium resting arousal level), or introverted (high resting arousal level). The combination of these three factors (amount of nicotine taken in, arousal-producing situations, and low or high-arousal organism) determines the outcome of any experiment. In a similar manner the combination of organism and situation determines whether or not the given person will smoke, and also what kind of cigarette he will choose (high or low nicotine content), and how he will smoke this (i.e. a few well-spaced puffs or many puffs frequently taken).

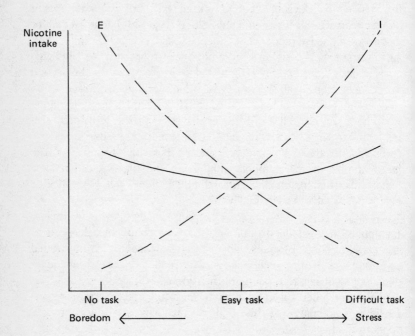

Figure 14 Predicted relation of nicotine intake under different task conditions, for extraverts and introverts.

Support for some such theory comes from the work of Ashton & Watson (1970), who used different filters to produce high nicotine and low nicotine cigarettes. They tested their subjects under three conditions: resting, easy simulated driving task, and stressful driving task. They found that

> during both of the driving tasks and during the resting period after the tasks the subjects smoking the low nicotine cigarette took more frequent puffs than those smoking the high nicotine cigarettes. . . . As would be expected from the increased puff frequency, the average time taken to finish a cigarette was less in the group smoking the low nicotine cigarettes. Records of respiration made during the smoking showed no differences in overall rate or in the depth of respiration at or after each puff between the two groups of smokers. Hence these results suggest that the subjects smoking the low nicotine cigarettes were attempting to compensate for the high filter retention of nicotine by a faster puffing rate. The puff volume appeared to be relatively constant though small differences may not have been detected.

It was also found that the resting puff rate was *significantly greater* during rest than during the easy task, and the nicotine obtained from the cigarettes per unit time was also significantly greater than during the task; this was true for both the 'high nicotine' and the 'low nicotine' group. 'This finding suggests the possibility that the subjects were striving for a higher nicotine dose during the resting period. There was also a tendency in both the high and low nicotine cigarette groups to take more puffs and obtain more nicotine during the level 2 (stressful) than during the level 1 (easy) task' (p. 680).

Figure 14 shows in diagrammatic form the outcome of the experiment. As predicted, the curve indicative of nicotine intake is bent, with least smoking occurring during the easy task, and most smoking during the no task period (boredom?) and the difficult task period (stress?). Also indicated are possible differential curves for extraverts and introverts, suggesting that personality differences may also play a part; unfortunately these were not included in the Ashton and Watson experiment. Their final conclusion is well in line with our theory; they conclude that 'these findings are thus consistent with the possibility that there exists an "optimum" nicotine dose for a given activity and that smokers unconsciously modify their smoking patterns in an attempt to obtain this dose' (p. 681). What our theory suggests in brief is that nicotine is a uniquely reinforcing agent, tending under all conditions (in suitable doses) to produce a shift in arousal directed towards the optimum degree. Possibly this is the reason why this habit is so difficult to give up, and so strongly reinforcing for so many people. Note the phrase 'in suitable doses', inserted in the sentence above, suggesting that the shift produced by nicotine in the arousal level could always be reinforcing. The smoker has 'fingertip control' over the actual uptake of nicotine; he can vary the inter-puff interval, the strength and length of puff, the total number of puffs taken; he can inhale or not as he pleases, and he can select cigarettes having a nicotine content most suitable for his habitual requirements. This then in brief is a kind of model of smoking behaviour which we feel accounts for many of the facts as we know them. The theory is presented in much greater detail by Eysenck (1973), but this would not be the place to pursue this point.

Smoking, health and personality

We have seen so far that there is a strong genetic component in the diseases which have been linked with smoking, and also that these genetic predispositions may be related to personality factors such as extraversion and neuroticism. Is it possible to make more specific this hypothesized relationship? There are several routes along which one might look for an answer. The first of these relates to specific personality factors related to the uptake of certain gases such as carbon dioxide (Clark & Cochrane, 1970; Saunders et al., 1972). In the Clark & Cochrane study, forty-four patients with chronic airways obstructions were tested by means of the Eysenck Personality Inventory. These authors took as their point of departure the known poor correlation obtained between the forced expired volume of air in one second (F.E.V.$_1$) and the CO_2 tension (PCO$_2$). Many patients have a PCO$_2$ much lower or higher than the mean value predicted by the regression equation linking the two variables, and Clark and Cochrane found that much of this variance was accounted for by the patients' extraversion score, those who are highly extravert being more likely to have a lower PVCO$_2$ at any F.E.V.$_1$ than patients more introverted. Neuroticism played no part in mediating any of the scatter.

Clark and Cochrane attempted an explanation of the finding by referring to the inverse relation between E score and the ability to be conditioned (Eysenck, 1967). 'From such a consideration it may be postulated that healthy individuals with a low E score are more readily conditioned and thus, in face of the stress of hindered breathing, are more likely to develop a tolerance to raised $PVCO_2$ caused by difficulty in CO_2 elimination. This tolerance is mediated by reduction in the excitability of respiratory motor neurones which is manifest by a fall in ventilatory response to CO_2.

Saunders et al. measured ventilatory response to carbon dioxide as an index of respiratory centre sensitivity in fifty normal subjects, also applying the Eysenck Personality Inventory. A significant correlation was found between extraversion score and ventilatory response to carbon dioxide in women ($P < 0.005$), but not in men. 'It is suggested that the degree of extraversion may play some part in determining the level of ventilation adopted, and hence of arterial carbon dioxide tension, if and when women develop lung disease such as asthma.'

Differences in the level of ventilation, such as appear in these studies, may be relevant to the development of cancer, in view of the fact that it is known that carbon monoxide interferes with the blood's capacity to carry oxygen and with the utilization of oxygen in the tissues. This has been suggested to be relevant to the production of cancer in the lung, and although of course there are differences between carbon monoxide and carbon dioxide, this seems an important line of research to develop, particularly in view of the current emphasis on possible relationships between carbon monoxide and cardiovascular disease.

Another line of research which is also suggested by the empirical findings is that relating low neuroticism with lung cancer. High and low N scorers are differentiated by the rapid and frequent development of strong emotional responses by the former, and it is well known that such strong emotional responses are mediated by physiological and humoral mechanisms which may protect the individual against the development of cancer. This is a second type of link between personality and cancer which, taken together with the links between personality and smoking, may mediate the relationships observed.

A third hypothesis, less direct but perhaps more immediately obvious than the other two, is the different 'life style' of different personality types. Extraverts not only smoke more than introverts, but also drink more alcohol, indulge in more sexual activities, are more active generally, move house and change jobs and marriage partners more frequently, and altogether seem to live at a faster rate than introverts. All these points have been documented in the references given in this chapter; they may link up with Pearl's (1928) theory of differential 'rates of living'. The existence of such different life styles, associated with personality factors, makes it impossible to concentrate attention on one of the many indices of such life styles (such as smoking), and use correlations found with that index to posit causal relationships. Cederlöf et al. (1975) have found that the age-adjusted risk for death from all causes was 1.4 for cigarette smokers who were not registered as alcoholics, and equally was 1.4 for registered alcoholics who never smoked. For alcoholics who smoked the risk was 1.9, indicating the difficulties one would have in sorting out the risk factors constituted by smoking and drinking if one did not have accurate information on both, as unfortunately is the case in most of the 'smoking causes disease' investigations.

Cederlöf et al. give another table in which they show that wealthy non-smokers have an age-adjusted risk of 1.0, whereas poor non-smokers have one of 1.6; wealthy smokers have a risk of 1.7, and poor smokers one of 2.7! Here is another variable which confounds any simple and straightforward correlation between smoking and disease.

The suggested equivalence of smoking and drinking comes out clearly in another table relating to suicide. Non-drinkers and non-smokers have a risk of 1.0; smokers who are non-drinkers have a risk of 1.8, whereas drinkers who are non-smokers also have a risk of 1.8! Clearly medical and behavioural risks should never be studied in relation to a single putative cause, such as smoking, when that cause is highly correlated with other putative causes, such as drinking, and the other components of 'rate of living'.

An added complication to all this is the fact that alcohol consumption and cigarette consumption show both synergistic and antagonistic interaction as far as behaviour is concerned. Interaction effects have also been found for caffeine consumption by Kozlowski (1976). She studied smokers who were light or heavy coffee drinkers, and who were provided with a cup of coffee and a pack of cigarettes each day for four days; the cigarettes were normal, but the coffee was doctored to contain different degrees of caffeine. None of the subjects noticed any difference between the various caffeine doses, but it was found that after a caffeine-free cup of coffee both cigarette and nicotine consumption were considerably higher. Heavy coffee drinkers were less influenced by the induced caffeine deficit and did not increase the nicotine intake as much. It is interesting to note that, of course, caffeine produces arousal effects similar to nicotine; the study also suggests the need to monitor coffee consumption in studies of smoking.

Certain clear-cut consequences follow from our discussion so far about the best method to be used for the epidemiological study of chronic diseases. The most important consequence that follows, as Cederlöf (1966) has so clearly indicated, is the use of the *twin method* to eliminate the many causes of error that we have discovered in this and the preceding chapter, errors which contaminate any possible relationships that are observed between environmental variables and disease when genetic variables are not controlled. Identical twins discordant for smoking are an ideal group for the study of the influence of smoking on health, and the methodology exists for making optimum use of such freaks of nature.

The report of an international symposium held in San Juan in 1969 (Report, Twin Registries in the Study of Chronic Disease, 1971) ends with a series of recommendations which are as apt today as they were when the symposium was held. The most important of these are:

(1) Twin studies should be expanded in a variety of populations and different geographical and ethnical settings. Special attention ought to be given to the inclusion of young age groups. New twin registries, suitable for epidemiological studies, should be established. (2) The cohorts representing the Swedish and the U.S. Twin Registry should be observed in longitudinal studies of both morbidity and mortality experience, with primary attention to certain cardiovascular and chronic pulmonary diseases. Other diseases which may be associated with smoking can be studied advantageously at the same time with little additional effort. (3) In order to interpret the role of smoking in disease, it will be essential to collect data on other living patterns and environmental factors, as well as personality types, behaviour and the more commonly recognised risk factors. In this fashion, associations and interactions between smoking and these factors can be assessed.

A series of reports of such studies has in fact been published by Cederlöf et al. (1965, 1967 a, b, 1969) and Lundman (1966); all this work has been reviewed and extended in a report of epidemio-

logical studies on the Swedish Twin Registries by Cederlöf, Friberg &
Lundman (1977). The outcome of these studies, too detailed to be
presented here, is briefly indicated in the following quotation:

> Even if quantitative assessments presently cannot be made of the
> relative roles of smoking, other risk factors and genetic disposi-
> tion, it seems that epidemiological investigations that have not
> controlled for factors referred to above may have overestimated
> the role of smoking as the causative factor in coronary heart
> disease and also, considering for example the distribution of sui-
> cides among smokers and non-smokers, that such studies have
> more than duly made smoking responsible as the causative factor
> for all excess deaths seen in smokers. On the other hand this should
> not be taken as evidence that smoking should be irrelevant as a
> precipitating factor for death in for example coronary heart
> disease. . . . The results from the twin study clearly demonstrate
> the importance of genetic, and several behavioural and psycho-
> social factors which have not been considered in conventional
> epidemiological studies. Such factors should as far as possible be
> included in future epidemiological research, not only in the
> context of smoking and health, but also in studies on other
> similar exposure factors that may be linked to risk factors of this
> type or to genetic predispositions. The twin approach certainly
> enhances the group comparability to a considerable extent not
> only with regard to genetic but also with respect to habitual and
> psycho-social factors that may be of aetiologic relevance.

The Swedish study also found that their

> results fit a model in which non-smokers and smokers are dif-
> ferent in regard to a life-style parameter of which smoking is but
> one index, others being alcohol drinking, drug abuse, psycho-
> social discord, etc. It may be assumed that this parameter ranges
> from a 'healthy' value at the one extreme to an 'unhealthy'
> value at the other extreme. The concordant non-smokers pro-
> bably have values close to the first mentioned extreme and
> concordant smokers close to the other, leaving the discordant
> smokers to occupy more 'undecided' values in the middle of
> the range. If this construct variable is associated with disease,
> which is highly probable, it is obvious that non-smokers in dis-
> cordant pairs should experience ill-health to a higher degree than

concordant non-smokers: whether the basic explanation is predominantly genetic or environmental may be open for speculation. However, from the analysis of the twin pairs, it does seem that monozygotes as a rule fit the model better than dizygotes as demonstrated by better control of most habitual and psychosocial traits, higher coincidence, and more pronounced lifestyle effects in the . . . analysis. These data point towards at least some influence of genetic factors.

The conclusions by Cederlöf and associates are conservative, but in broad outline they would probably command more agreement than the theories presented by Burch, which seem to rule out environmental effects on lung cancer and other cancers almost entirely. The Cederlöf group seems to occupy an intermediate position between the 100 per cent genetic determination advocated by Burch, and the almost complete disregard of genetic factors advocated by current orthodoxy, as represented by the Surgeon General in the United States, and the Royal College of Physicians in England. Our own position is probably most similar to that of Cederlöf and his colleagues, although they wrote their report before Burch's incisive critique of the orthodox position was published and consequently are perhaps a little too much impressed with the views of the various Royal Commissions and Surgeon General's Reports. We do not feel as certain as they do that a really cast-iron case has been made out for the causation of coronary heart disease, or even lung cancer, by cigarette smoking; in this respect therefore our position is closer to that of Burch than of Cederlöf.

However, we do not feel that it is possible to be dogmatic on these issues, one way or the other; there clearly are genetic and constitutional determinants of disease and smoking, and these must be taken into account in any proper research plan. This should not lead us to deny the possible existence of environmental causes, such as smoking, of these various diseases; the existing evidence does not conclusively prove that these factors have any decisive influence, but equally well it does not disprove such a possibility. Clearly what is needed is a larger body of research, and better research, than is available at the present time. The weaknesses of the research supporting the orthodox position have been pointed out in the last chapter; it will be clear from what has been said in this chapter that while there is a good deal of evidence in favour of the constitutional hypothesis, and while much of this evidence supports some such more detailed theory as outlined in this chapter, nevertheless the scale on which this work has been done, and the many gaps still open, make it impossible to claim that the proof for the theory is anything like sufficient. What is clear is that all future research must bear in mind the existence of many diverse and interacting factors in the causation of any of the disorders here discussed; the questions involved are quantitative rather than qualitative, and can only be solved by reference to much more complex and intricate research designs than have been used hitherto. Fisher's genetic hypothesis is beginning to take on some of the accoutrements of a testable scientific theory; this theory can only be tested in conjunction with the various environmental theories discussed in the last chapter. Heredity and environment are two sides of the same coin, and to imagine that one can be studied without the other is clearly inadmissible. We will discuss in the next chapter the kind of model which incorporates genetic and environmental factors, as well as their interactions; only by proceeding along the lines dictated by that model are we likely to reach a satisfactory conclusion in this very difficult field.

The likelihood that such a model will actually be used, and that proper research designs will be adopted in the future, is not increased by dogmatic statements such as that made by a former British Minister of Health and Social Security who blandly assured his listeners that 50,000 deaths a year could be avoided if only Britons gave up smoking. In a similar vein, American medical authorities have given estimates of the kind that 200,000 deaths in the USA could be avoided by the abolition of cigarette smoking. Joseph A. Califano, the US Secretary of Health, Education and Welfare, has now publicly given estimates of 320,000 lives to be saved by abstention from smoking. In a similar vein, *The Lancet* has given publicity to estimates stating that some 90 per cent of cancers are due to environmental factors and thus could be prevented. Burch (1978a) has shown how unfounded such an assertion is in the face of present knowledge — and ignorance. All these estimates present leaps from surmise into prophecy which are unsupported by scientific evidence, and which make it less rather than more likely that we shall ever discover the true network of causal factors involved in lung cancer, coronary heart disease, and the other disorders putatively linked with smoking. If the answer were already known, then why should we finance and carry out the large-scale, complex and time-consuming sort of research here advocated? The irresponsibility of such pronouncements is matched by the messianic certainty with which the results of doubtful and often ill-designed research programmes are used as propaganda material in the war against smoking.

Summary

It is a fact that some diseases are found to be positively correlated with smoking (lung cancer, coronary heart disease, suicide), so that smokers are more frequently found among the victims; other diseases are found to be negatively correlated with smoking (Parkinsonism, diabetes, trigeminal neuralgia), so that smokers are less frequently found among the victims. *These epidemiological correlations cannot be used as proof of causation;* at best they are suggestive of areas where proper medical and scientific research may begin to throw light on the obscure causal relations that may be responsible for the observed relationships.

It has been suggested that cigarette smoking is directly responsible for an alleged large increase in lung cancer over the past fifty years. This may be so, but there are many difficulties in accepting such a conclusion. (1) The correlation between smoking and lung cancer over countries is very weak. (2) Secular changes in deaths do not parallel similar changes in smoking. (3) Patterns of sex distribution in lung cancer have not changed since the nineteenth century, when cigarette smoking was insignificant. (4) Diagnosis of lung cancer was so poor at the beginning of the century that no statistical basis can be furnished from published data to indicate a rise in frequency over time. (5) Diagnosis of lung cancer is so unreliable now that epidemiological data are unable to furnish us with a valid basis for correlation or comparison. (6) Racial differences are very pronounced in sex ratios of lung cancer, ranging from 13 : 1 to 1 : 1! (7) There is an alarming failure to find dose-response relationships. (8) Inhaling has not been found to lead to a greater incidence of lung cancer, and may even be found correlated with a lesser incidence. (9) Effects of giving up smoking have been inappropriately analysed, and do not support the view that giving it up protects against lung cancer.

It has been suggested that cigarette smoking is directly responsible for coronary heart disease. This may be so, but there are many difficulties in accepting such a conclusion. (1) There are tremendous racial differences between whites, blacks, and mongol races in heart response to smoking. (2) Angina pectoris is no more frequent in smoking MZ twins than in discordant non-smoking MZ twins. (3) Pipe smokers often have lower death rates than non-smokers. (4) Dose-response relations are inconsistent. (5) Inhalation effects are puzzling and do not indicate the expected worsening of health status. (6) Ex-smokers seem to be safer than non-smokers. (7) No statistical connection is found in some countries.

When these specific points are taken together with the poor experimental control characteristic of most of the studies reported in the literature, the poor statistical treatment given the data, the general low quality of the original data, the failure to take into account alternative hypotheses, and the over-readiness to interpret inconclusive data in line with establishment expectations, we must conclude that no definitive verdict can be arrived at concerning the responsibility of cigarette smoking for lung cancer or coronary heart disease. To say this is not to absolve cigarette smoking from causing bodily harm; it is simply to say that this is a very complex and intractable problem for which at the moment there does not exist a conclusive answer, acceptable to scientists working in this field. It is only for purposes of propaganda that firm assumptions can be publicized about the frightening number of people dying each year as a consequence of smoking cigarettes; there is no basis in fact concerning these estimates.

An alternative theory to that which asserts that the observed correlations between smoking and disease are indicative of a causal relation (smoking causes disease) is the *constitutional hypothesis* which states that the correlations observed in the studies mentioned come about as a consequence of genetic and constitutional factors which predispose people to disease and to smoking, or which make people adopt a style of life which leads to less resistance to disease, and of which smoking is but one of many indicators; drinking, womanizing, and other 'live-it-up' behaviours being additional

parts of this life style. Such an hypothesis acquires credibility from a number of empirical findings. (1) Lung cancer, and many other cancers linked epidemiologically with smoking, have been shown to have a genetic basis. (2) Coronary heart disease too has been shown to have a genetic basis. (3) Smoking, as we shall show in the next Part of this book, is maintained in part by genetic factors. (4) Smoking is related to personality traits, which in turn have been demonstrated to have a genetic basis. (5) Smoking is related to morphology (body-build), which in turn is related to personality and social behaviour. (6) Personality is related to lung cancer, and probably to other types of cancer as well. (7) Personality is related to coronary heart disease. (8) Personality is indicative of a style of life, in which smoking plays a part, but in which it is only one of many indicators, drinking, womanizing, etc. being other indicators.

It is not suggested that these facts as yet make it possible to put forward a proper theory of smoking and disease; so far we only have suggestive findings which in due course may be fitted together to produce such a theory. All the research money over the past thirty years has effectively gone into trying to prove the orthodox, smoking-causes-disease theory; the alternative theory has been almost completely neglected and cold-shouldered. Under these circumstances it is not surprising that the available data are scant, uncoordinated, and often not properly replicated. It is only when a determined effort is made to carry out research which effectively pits one theory against the other, and attempts to make deductions from both which are contradictory, so that unambiguous results favouring one or the other may be obtained, that we are likely to get a better understanding of the situation. It is of course perfectly possible that both theories are partly right, and complement rather than oppose each other. Sufficient knowledge is simply not available at present to come to any definitive conclusion about the rival merits of these two theories. Until such knowledge is available, no premature conclusions should be drawn on the basis of the insufficient evidence so far gathered.

PART TWO

The Genetics of Smoking

By L. J. Eaves and H. J. Eysenck

CHAPTER 3

The Inheritance of Smoking: Evidence from Twin Studies

L. J. EAVES AND H. J. EYSENCK

Before we report the findings of our own study we consider the background from other studies. These have been based chiefly on the twin methodology (Galton, 1876) which compares the similarity (or 'concordance') in the smoking habits of identical and non-identical twins. Since identical twins are genetically identical whereas non-identical twins are no more or less alike genetically than brothers or sisters it is commonly assumed that the increased similarity between identical twins for indices of behaviour is indicative of partial genetical determination for the measured traits.

The simple appeal of the twin method does not leave it beyond criticism. Bulmer (1970, Chapter 3) for example, has reviewed the extensive literature concerning the cause and outcome of twin pregnancy and post-natal development. Here it suffices to observe that twins are atypical in a great many aspects. They display lower birthweights than singletons even when allowance is made for their shorter gestation period. The stillbirth rate in twins is twice that of single births and early post-natal mortality is considerably higher. Twin pregnancies and deliveries are subject to more complications. As far as post-natal development is concerned there are certain established persistent differences between twins and singletons. Some physical deficits may, like that in average height of twins, reflect the long-term effects of retarded foetal growth. Behavioural differences have also been established, however. The average IQ of twin pairs, for example, is about five points less than that of singletons. Bulmer suggests 'that the increased frequency of gross mental retardation in twins is due to their retarded foetal growth, but that the slightly lower intelligence of normal twins is due to differences in their upbringing'. Some support for the latter is given by Record et al. (1970) who show that surviving singletons of those births in which one twin died do not show the normal IQ deficit.

Obviously it does not require great ingenuity to invent alternative explanations of twin differences and similarities, involving, for example, the greater similarity in the treatment of identical twins compared with fraternal (non-identical) twins. However, since the difference would be predicted from known genetical theory for any inherited trait, the twin study makes a convenient starting point for the examination of inherited factors. Whilst the twin study cannot confirm a genetical theory, it can certainly falsify it for a given trait if there is no measured concordance between the habits of twins or if the concordance for DZ twins is no less than that for MZ twins. Thus, although the twin method cannot be definitive it can play a significant role in the preliminary analysis of human differences.

One of the most ardent advocates of a genetical basis for individual variation in the smoking habit was the late Sir Ronald Fisher. The scientific rationale of Fisher's position is summarized in the sceptical position that '*post hoc* is not the same as *propter hoc,* or in other words—as it would be put in the early years of our century, when statisticians had had perhaps ten years' experience of the correlation coefficient as a means of research—that correlation is not causation' (Fisher, 1958a). The ethical basis of his position is expressed as follows: 'Before one interferes with the peace of mind and habits of others, it seems to me that the scientific evidence—the exact weight of the evidence free from emotion—should be rather carefully examined' (ibid, p. 152).

It was thus Fisher (1958b) who reported the first evidence which had direct bearing on the genetical basis of smoking habits. He argues:

It seemed to me that although the importance of this [i. e. genotypic] factor had been overlooked. . . it was well within the capacity of human genetics, in its current state, to examine whether the smoking classes to which human beings assign themselves, such as non-smokers, cigarette smokers. . . etc., were in fact genotypically differentiated, to a demonstrable extent, or whether, on the contrary, they appeared to be genotypically homogeneous. . . . The method of enquiry by which such differentiation can be recognized is the same as that by which the congenital factor has been demonstrated for several types of disease, namely, the comparison of the similarities between monozygotic (one-egg) and dizygotic (two-egg) twins respectively; for any recognizably greater resemblance of the former may be confidently ascribed to the identity of the genotypes in these cases.

The data he presents relate to twins ascertained in Berlin by von Verschuer, consisting of 51 monozygotic and 31 dizygotic twin pairs. Of the 51 MZ pairs Fisher states that 33 pairs are 'wholly alike qualitatively'. Six pairs 'though closely alike, show some differences in the record'. Twelve pairs, 'less than one quarter of the whole, show distinct differences'. 'By contrast,' Fisher claims, 'of the dizygotic pairs, only eleven can be classed as wholly alike, while sixteen out of thirty-one are distinctly different, this being 51 per cent as against 24 per cent among the monozygotics.' According to Fisher, rearranging the data using different procedures of classification leads to little overall change in the pattern. In conclusion, Fisher states: 'There can therefore be little doubt that the genotype exercises a considerable influence on smoking, and on the particular habit of smoking adopted, and that a study of twins on a comparatively small scale is competent to demonstrate the rather considerable differences which must exist between the different groups who classify themselves as non-smokers or the different classes of smokers.'

A subsequent letter to *Nature* in the same year (Fisher, 1958c) begins: 'The curious associations with lung cancer found in relation to smoking habits do not, in the minds of some of us, lend themselves easily to the simple conclusion that the products of combustion reaching the surface of the bronchus induce, though after a long interval, the development of cancer.' The letter continues: 'Such results suggest that an error has been made of an old kind, in arguing from correlation to causation, and that the possibility should be explored that the different smoking classes. . .have adopted their habits partly by reason of their personal temperaments and dispositions and are not lightly to be assumed equivalent in their genotypic constitution.'

He then cites further borrowed data, this time from Dr Eliot Slater of the Maudsley Hospital. Since these data include twins separated at birth they are likely to have originated as part of that set accumulated and subsequently reported in great detail by the late James Shields (Shields, 1962). Fisher only considers female twins of the set, presumably to complement the findings of his examination of von Verschuer's data which were based only on male twins. The overall sample of Shields, however, consists of both male and female twins. Pooling over sexes, the sample consisted of 42 pairs of MZ twins separated since birth, 42 pairs of unseparated MZ twins and 20 pairs of DZ twins. The twins completed a questionnaire on which they were asked, 'How many cigarettes do you smoke in a day?' The responses of most of the MZ twins were subsequently checked by interview. Subjects' responses were classified by the amount smoked as follows: nonsmokers; 1-5 per day; 6-10; 11-15; 16 plus. Occasional pipe smokers had their tobacco consumption converted to the equivalent number of cigarettes. Pairs in which both twins fell into the same category were classified as closely similar, those which fell into neighbouring groups as 'fairly similar' and those which were less alike as 'dissimilar'. Obviously such data may be summarized in several ways, but the simplest method is to present the numbers of pairs of each type which fall into the various similarity groupings (Table 6). It is clear that the identical twins are more alike than non-identical twins in their smoking habits and that, if anything, separated twins are more alike than non-separated twins although the latter difference is hardly significant statistically. The data are thus consistent with the role of inherited factors in the determination of the smoking habit. The fact that the separated twins are not significantly less alike than the unseparated twins suggests that there are no overwhelming influences of the home environment on the amount of tobacco consumption reported by the twins, since twins reared together would tend to be more alike in their smoking habits if the family environments they had shared had exercised a strong influence in their development. Separated twins, however, who would have had relatively dissimilar home backgrounds, would be expected to be less alike if the family environment were really important in the determination of smoking. Such studies

TABLE 6

Concordance in the smoking habits of twins: the data of Shields (1962) on the number of twin pairs similar on cigarette consumption (percentages in parentheses)

Rating of similarity	Twin type		
	Monozygotic		Dizygotic
	Separated	Unseparated	
Closely similar	28(67)	21(50)	7(35)
Fairly similar	8(19)	13(31)	7(35)
Dissimilar	6(14)	8(19)	6(30)
Total number of pairs	42	42	20

of separated twins are rare, and provide a unique opportunity to assess the role of non-genetic family influences on development. No study is beyond criticism, and it is a tribute to the great care with which Shields documented his data that it is possible to reconstruct from his published twin records the individual case histories of his separated twins. Many of these knew little of one another's existence, though some were reared by relatives and occasionally members of a pair had met with one another. This means that the influences of the common family environment may not have been completely separated from inherited similarity in the separated twins if, in spite of physical separation, the twins were placed in similar homes. Several authors (e.g. Kamin, 1974) have attempted to undermine confidence in Shields' data on grounds similar to these. It is not our intention to rake over the same territory. Other authors have responded to these criticisms and found some of them to be lacking in substance (e.g. Fulker, 1975).

As in the case of the von Verschuer study, reclassification of the responses does not lead to any substantial change in conclusion. Dividing the respondents into smokers and non-smokers, for example, yields a similar interpretation. Overall, 63 of the 84 MZ pairs (74 per cent) are concordant in their smoking habits, whilst only 10 out of 20 DZ pairs (50 per cent) are concordant. Such differences in concordance, or larger differences, could only arise in 0.1 per cent or less of studies just by chance, which suggests that the data are consistent with a partly inherited basis for the smoking habit.

The last word on this study resides once more with Fisher (1958a) who considers only the females in the sample. 'So far there is only a clear confirmation of the conclusion from the German data that the monozygotics are much more alike than the dizygotes in their smoking habits. The peculiar value of these data, however, lies in the subdivision of the monozygotic pairs into those separated at birth and those brought up together. . . . It would appear that the small proportion unlike among these 53 monozygotic pairs is not to be ascribed to mutual influence.' Elsewhere he states: 'If it could be assumed as known facts (a) that twins greatly influence each other's smoking habits and (b) that this influence is much stronger between monozygotic than between dizygotic twins, then an alternative explanation would be afforded for the result [i.e. von Verschuer's findings] I have emphasised. The assumptions can be supported by eloquence, but they should, for scientific purposes, be supported by verifiable observations.' The analysis of the separated twins, albeit of a small sample, suggests that the mutual influence of twins is not as great as many critics have supposed.

In 1959 Todd and Mason reported the findings of a larger compilation of data on German twins, including many of those studied by von Verschuer, to which were added twins from Tubingen and the Frankfurt area. A questionnaire, devised by Fisher, was mailed to a total of 44 male MZ pairs and 46 male DZ pairs. Zygosity was established primarily on the basis of morphological characteristics, although when blood grouping data were available 'in all cases complete similarity was found between the blood groups of twins identified as monozygotic on the basis of morphological characteristics' (Todd & Mason, 1959, p. 419). These findings foresee the results of later studies on the alternative methods of zygosity diagnosis in twins (Nichols & Bilbro, 1966; Cederlöf et al., 1961; Kasriel & Eaves, 1976; Martin & Martin, 1975). Of the 90 pairs to whom questionnaires were sent, 68 pairs produced complete data. Thirty-three of these pairs also contributed to the data analysed by Fisher in his consideration of von Verschuer's data.

Broadly, the data give a picture consistent with the inheritance of the smoking habit. Division of the respondents into smokers and non-smokers, for example, produced 43 concordant MZ pairs out of 52 MZ respondent pairs whilst only 19 out of a total of 32 DZ pairs were concordant. The degree of concordance in DZ pairs falls marginally if smokers who 'smoke occasionally' are grouped with non-smokers, but that of MZ pairs is unchanged. A striking exception to this pattern, however, is revealed when the division of the sample is made into those who have 'smoked sometimes' and those who have 'never smoked'. The concordance for MZ twins is raised slightly to 45 concordant pairs but the most striking change is in the concordance of DZ twins, for which 25 pairs are now concordant. The difference between the concordance rates of the two twin groups is thus much reduced by this reclassification of the twins' responses. This suggests that the influence of non-hereditary factors on twin similarity is much greater for this variable. We may speculate that this is due to the influence of shared environmental effects in the onset of smoking, such as the influences of peers on the initial experience of the habit, which are subsequently dissipated when individuals develop their final smoking habit with advancing maturity.

In this study the authors attempted to consider the influence of physical proximity on similarities of smoking. They conclude 'proximity of residence of the members of a pair of twins does not appear to exercise any marked influence in leading them both to be smokers or both to be non-smokers. On the other hand, if both members of the pair do in fact smoke, there is more frequent concordance in respect of the types of product smoked between the members of pairs resident at the same address and in the same town than between the members of pairs resident in different towns'. The implication is clear, that whilst hereditary factors may influence the development of the smoking habit, the precise form of the habit which is adopted is influenced more by the environment to which individual twins happen to be exposed.

In this, as in every study employing volunteers, there is the possibility of biased ascertainment, that is, that the sample who respond to the questionnaire and cooperate in the study are not truly representative of the population. The authors consider various sources of sampling bias and conclude that they have no striking evidence for their significance in their study. They claim, 'We can therefore see no reason for doubting the reality of the definitely more frequent occurrence of concordance of smoking habits in monozygotic than in dizygotic twins'.

In the same year as the publication of the Todd & Mason study, Friberg, Kaij, Dencker & Jonsson (1959) published the results of a study of the smoking habits of Swedish twins. Fifty-nine monozygotic and 59 dizygotic twin pairs were selected for study, the groups being matched for age and sex. Zygosity was established by use of information on placentation—monochorionic twins being classified as monozygotic—and by anthropometric investigation supplemented by grouping of blood and serum according to ten systems. Two methods were employed to assess twin similarity in smoking. In the first, individuals were divided on the basis of their smoking habits into four groups: regular smokers; sporadic smokers (less than one cigarette per day); former smokers; and other non-smokers. In the second method the twin pairs were rated for similarity of smoking habits by forty adjudicators (described as 'public health officers, medical students and a few laboratory assistants') on an eleven-point scale of similarity, without prior knowledge of zygosity. Analysis of both types of classification confirmed that identical twins resemble one another significantly more than dizygotic twins for overall characteristics of the smoking habit. The authors comment on their findings as follows:

> How far may the results be said to indicate the importance of the genotype in relation to smoking? According to the conventional interpretation they imply that smoking habits are definitely influenced by constitutional factors. In recent years, however, this interpretation of investigations on twins has to some extent been challenged by writers . . . who pointed out that the environment of monozygotic twins may be more uniform than that of dizygotic twins. If this is true it must be particularly prominent as a source of error concerning factors which *a priori* can be classed as highly susceptible to the environment. On the other hand one may object that, as a rule, smoking habits are formed after the twins have passed the years of maximum unity. To what extent our results apply to other twin populations we have no certain knowledge. . . Fisher reported some preliminary observations on German twins . . . the tendencies in the results were identical with ours.

In their brief discussion of their data the authors cover several pertinent problems of such studies. We have already noted their reservation that MZ twins may receive more similar environments than non-identical twins, although, as these authors indicate in a footnote, the result Fisher quotes for the separated twins 'contradicts the theory of mutual influence between the twins as a major cause of concordance and supports the view of genotrophic influence on smoking habits'. They also indicate that there is no reason in principle why the same results should be obtained in different populations since these may differ in the genes which segregate and in the extent of environmental heterogeneity which might influence variation in smoking habits. Obviously, particular cultures may succeed in restricting access to particular types of tobacco, or make a more profound effort to influence the habits of their members by propaganda and advertising. In some cultures the influence of the family environment may predominate, whilst in others it may be the influence of peers or the chance encounters of those who are encouraged to 'do their own thing'.

In 1962 Conteno and Chiarelli reported a similar investigation of Italian twins. Their sample comprised 77 pairs of male twins from Parma, Pavia and Florence. In this case the sample was restricted to twins over twenty years of age, and the twins were interviewed separately using a standard form of questionnaire. Thirty-four pairs were finally classified as monozygous and 43 as dizygous. Zygosity diagnosis was based on a variety of considerations, including some blood groups and anthropometric measurements, although several twins refused to give blood and in nine cases the final decision about zygosity was based on the evaluation of resemblance using photographs and finger-prints. The concordance for smoking versus non-smoking was significantly different between the two types of twin, with monozygotic twins showing the expected greater resemblance than DZ twins. The concordance for the Italian DZ twins is somewhat larger than for the German DZ pairs; this small difference might reflect differences in procedure or genuine differences in the relative importance of cultural factors in the two populations. Division of the sample into regular and irregular smokers did not change the results significantly, though classification by the quantity of smoked products according to identical or non-identical code number revealed the most striking difference in concordance between the two types of twin, with 26 of the 34 MZ pairs being concordant compared with only 14 out of the 43 DZ pairs (X_1^2=12.92 P< 0.001). It was found, further, that the degree of concordance for consumption of tobacco products did not differ significantly between pairs who lived at the same address compared with those who lived at different addresses. The authors concluded that 'concerning smoking habits, there is no difference between the behaviour of the observed pairs in relation to their proximity of residence'. These authors also considered certain aspects of alcohol consumption and concluded that the effects of zygosity on concordance were in the same direction but not statistically significant.

Although all these studies give good reason to suppose that MZ twins are more alike in their smoking habits than DZ twins, the samples used have all been very small. One early exception to this rule is the Danish study carried out by Elisabeth Raaschou-Nielsen (1960). A sample of 1,240 pairs of twins was selected from a register of 4,700 twin pairs. The sample excluded pairs of unlike sex, pairs with at least one member dead or in which at least one member was known to be uncooperative. Altogether, data were obtained on the smoking habits of both partners of 894 pairs. Thus, although the author states that hers was an 'unselected' sample, we must be careful to understand exactly what 'unselected' means in this and similar contexts, including our own subsequently. It means that there was no systematic attempt to ascertain twins who were chosen for particular clinical or demographic reasons. It does not mean that the twins could necessarily and without further proof be regarded as a random sample of the population of genetical and environmental influences. Personality factors which influence cooperativeness, for example, could be related to the characteristics under study and thus lead to biased ascertainment. We shall see subsequently that the tendency to smoke is significantly associated with the 'psychotic' dimension of personality. If psychoticism is also related to uncooperativeness this could lead to an excess of non-smokers in the sample. On the other hand, an excess of smokers could result if smokers displayed a relatively greater than average interest in the causes of their own behaviour. Raaschou-Nielsen attempted to assess the reliability of her respondents by interviewing a subset of her twins and she reported 'good correspondence . . . between the information obtained by questionnaire and by personal visit'. The representativeness of her sample was checked against a non-twin sample collected seven years earlier by Hamtoft & Lindhardt (1956). The twin sample corresponded reasonably well with the earlier sample, although there was a substantially greater number of female smokers which Raaschou-Nielsen attributes to the fact 'that smoking has become more common among women in the last seven years'.

In this study the smoking habits were mainly summarized by dividing individuals into five groups: non-smokers; occasional smokers; former smokers; regular smokers; heavy smokers. For the purpose of assessing concordance, 'heavy smokers' and 'regular smokers' were assigned to the same group, and concordant pairs were defined as all those pairs in which members fell into identical groups.

Employing this definition of concordance the total numbers of concordant pairs is as follows:

	Male	Female
DZ/Total	39.4% (223)	55.7% (328)
MZ/Total	57.2% (147)	69.4% (196)

An alternative grouping of subjects into smokers and non-smokers
showed how the concordance in twins is generally greater than might
be expected by chance alone, and that MZ twins are, on average, more
similar than DZ twins.

A second large sample, of male twins, was studied in Finland by
Partanen et al. (1966). Of 198 male MZ pairs, 75.3 per cent were
concordant with respect to smoking or non-smoking whereas a significantly ($X_1^2=6.33$) smaller proportion (65.5 per cent) of the 640
DZ pairs in their sample were concordant. Twins were also asked to
estimate their daily tobacco consumption. The consumption of
tobacco *for those pairs concordant for smoking* was transformed to
grams and it was shown even for this highly selected sample that
intrapair differences in consumption were greater for DZ than MZ
twins.

The general finding of all these twin studies, therefore, agrees in
outline that there are factors, conceivably genetic, which make
identical twins more alike in their smoking habits than non-identical
twins and thus give some substance to Fisher's initial reservations
about the basis of the causal association between smoking and cancer,
or more specifically, give some legitimate reason to doubt that the
association did not depend wholly or in part upon a third common
basis in inherited temperamental differences.

Clearly none of the twin research entirely escapes criticism. The
basic concept of the twin study has been challenged often, although
this challenge has usually not been substantiated. The definitions
of the smoking habit employed in calculating concordance in the
different studies have been arbitrary and inconsistent across studies,
which means that we cannot compare the studies on different populations as we might like. The statistical methods employed in the
analysis of the data are often inefficient and involve throwing away
information which a more perfect analysis might retain. The chief

weakness in this respect has been the reduction of the number of categories of twin pairs from a large number (based on the contingency tables for the raw responses of twins) to only two, namely concordant and discordant. This highly conservative procedure precludes any test of the underlying scale of smoking behaviour, which would be of great interest in detailed study. Consider, for example, the study of Raaschou-Nielsen who identifies 'former smokers'. What is the genetic relationship, if any, between 'former smoking' and 'occasional smoking'? Is this relationship different in degree or kind from the relationship between non-smoking and former smoking?

Such information is contained in the contingency tables reported by the authors of such studies but discarded in the analysis by the arbitrary division into 'concordant' and 'discordant' pairs. Is the ranking of smoking behaviour into non-smoking, occasional smoking, regular smoking and heavy smoking, for example, justified by the data? Are non-smokers really furthest away biologically from heavy smokers? Or are they entirely different from all types of smoker? Such questions require more stringent quantitative methods for their resolution. Some of these will be discussed subsequently in this book (Chapter 4).

The second feature that all these studies have in common is the deliberate omission from the study of twin pairs of unlike sex. It is far from clear what dictated this policy since it leads to a general weakening of the scientific value of the twin study. It appears that the designers of these early twin studies must have been conditioned by the view that whatever factors determined individual differences must have been so inconsistent over sexes as to leave no need to test for their consistency. Yet what more important first vindication of the generality of any theory of individual differences is there than the demonstration that it generalizes at the very least across sexes? The omission from these studies, and from many other twin studies, of unlike-sex pairs throws away the simplest opportunity to test the generality of the causes of variation by comparing the results for like-sex twins with those for unlike-sex twins. If pairs of unlike-sex are significantly less concordant than pairs of like-sex, then we have every reason to doubt a simple genotype-environmental explanation of variation. If on the other hand the concordance of DZ twins is consistent no matter what the sex composition of the pairs, we have a very strong basis for the more general theory that the causes of variation are consistent over sexes. Comparing the results for male and female like-sex pairs is only half the story, since the sexes might be consistent in their concordance but the concordance may be brought about by entirely different genetical and cultural factors. The way in which unlike-sex pairs permit some simple sex interactions to be detected will be considered subsequently.

The third and, in this context, most damaging criticism of the early twin work is the absence of any direct bearing on the cause of the association between smoking and disease, for although the twin studies indeed establish a case for the involvement of genetical differences in variation in smoking, the twin data do not elucidate any correlated genetic effects on disease.

This weakness of the early twin studies has been appreciated nowhere more powerfully than in the Swedish studies of smoking in relation to morbidity and mortality undertaken by Cederlöf, Friberg & Lundman (1977). They have established the twin method as a powerful tool for scientific epidemiology. In particular, their work illustrates how the twin method may be used to help establish the environmental basis of an association between disease and such behavioural factors as smoking habits. Their strategy, which they term the NET ('non-exposed twin') analysis, may be conceptualized simply as follows. Consider, for example, identical twins. We select from our total sample of twins those pairs of whom at least one member does not smoke. In the case of discordant pairs one twin is automatically designated as the 'non-exposed twin', that is the twin who does not smoke. Of pairs which are concordant non-smokers, one twin is selected at random and designated the 'non-exposed twin'. We now divide the non-exposed twins into two groups: the first group consists of those twins whose co-twins smoke (i.e. the non-exposed twins of discordant pairs); the second group comprises those twins designated as non-exposed twins from the pairs in which neither member of the twin smokes. Thus one group of non-exposed twins have partners who smoke, the other group have partners who do not. The NET analysis then considers the incidence of disease (for example, cancer) in the two groups of non-exposed twins. On a simple environmental hypothesis of the relationship between smoking and disease both groups of non-exposed twins should show the same reduced incidence of the disease, since the mere fact that the twin had not smoked should provide the necessary environmental protection.

On a Fisherian hypothesis, however, in which genetical factors are partly responsible for the common basis of smoking and disease, the non-exposed partners of smoking co-twins will display an increased incidence of the disease because, although they do not smoke themselves, they share identical genes with a co-twin who *does* smoke. If these genes are also responsible for the development of disease there should be a significant proportion of non-exposed twins who develop the disease, because the presence of smoking in their co-twin acts as a kind of genetic marker for the presence of genes which predispose to disease. On the other hand, the non-exposed partners of non-smoking twins are expected to have a lower genetical predisposition to the disease and so to show a reduced incidence compared with the non-exposed partners of smoking twins.

As the authors themselves indicate, the real situation is unlikely to be so simple, since 'the likelihood of finding a complete verification of either hypothesis is small for several reasons. For many exposure factors, it may be reasonable to assume that *both* constitution *and* the factor, each *per se* or in interaction, may have a true effect on the disease or mortality entity. The problem is a quantitative rather than a qualitative one.'

Cederlöf and his colleagues examine two large bodies of twin data. The first consists of an older sample of Swedish twins, the second of a younger cohort of Swedish twins. The structure of their sample, which

TABLE 7

Sample structure in the Swedish studies

	Number of complete pairs			
	Dizygotic		*Monozygotic*	
Cohort	*Male*	*Female*	*Male*	*Female*
(Year of birth)				
1886-1925	2,984	3,868	1,649	2,007
1926-1958	3,703	4,170	2,292	2,733
Total	6,687	8,038	3,941	4,740

involves 23,406 twin pairs, is summarized in Table 7. Zygosity was established by questionnaire and all the pairs tabulated provided completed responses to a questionnaire concerning smoking habits and other background sociological variables. The authors themselves document more fully the history of the study and such factors as response rate. This large sample confirms the findings of previous studies about the increased similarity of the smoking habits of MZ twins. The authors report that 'with one single exception all sex and age groups have significantly increased ratios for observed over expected coincidence rates. It has also been shown that the quotients are significantly higher for monozygotic than for dizygotic twins which may be interpreted as evidence of a genetic component or of a stronger environmental pressure for conformity'. The study of Cederlöf et al. also reports similar findings for alcohol consumption, drug consumption and other aspects of behaviour including 'instability', 'extravertness', 'sleeping difficulties', 'stress', and 'divorce' in female twins though not in males.

As we have already suggested, however, the principal advance of the work of Cederlöf's group has been the attempt to relate the causes of variation in smoking to those responsible for morbidity, and in particular to provide a test of the hypothesis of genetical association between smoking and disease which could result in the disease even in the absence of smoking. The twin data as a whole, analysed as a conventional population sample, demonstrate all the established relationships between smoking and disease. As far as respiratory symptoms were concerned, the authors found that the symptoms defined as 'cough' and 'prolonged cough' showed a marked association with smoking in both of the Swedish studies and in a large additional sample of American twins. The authors observe: 'Independent of sex, age and country both symptoms are clearly related to the number of cigarettes smoked among present smokers. The gradient is consistently steeper for the symptom 'prolonged cough' in comparison to 'cough', although the prevalence is lower. The values for former smokers are lower than those for present smokers throughout but in many subgroups somewhat above unity.' The non-exposed twin analysis is revealing, however. Classifying the non-smoking twins according to the smoking behaviour of their partners reveals that even the non-smoking partner of an MZ twin who smokes reports a variety of symptoms more frequently than the non-smoking partner of a non-smoking twin. Thus, for example, the non-smoking partner of a monozygotic twin who currently smokes cigarettes is 2.71 times as likely to report a 'cough' as an individual selected at random from the population. Similar, though less significant, findings are reported for pains in the chest and shortness of breath. The non-smoking partners of DZ twins, however, do not show such associations. Other diseases show the same basic pattern, including migraine, back disorders and stomach disorders. All of these show that the non-smoking partner of an MZ twin who presently smokes cigarettes reports these disorders more frequently than a non-smoking twin who does not smoke. In the case of back disorders and migraine the effect is restricted to monozygotic twins. It was also found that the non-smoking partners of cigarette-smoking MZ twins reported long periods of sick leave (greater than three months in a row) one and a half times more frequently than individuals in the population at large.

When we turn to examine the relationship between smoking and mortality the study confirms that smokers, and especially comparatively heavy cigarette smokers, die sooner than non-smokers. Thus, of individuals born in the period 1901 to 1910 the death rate among males is 2.2 times as great among smokers of more than ten cigarettes per day as among non-smokers for deaths up to and including June 1975. The rate for female smokers is similar. Essentially the same findings are reported for other age groups, and the results are similar though less striking among smokers who smoke rather less. The study also attempts to provide more specific data on the causes of death. Some of their findings may be summarized for the group of subjects who report smoking more than ten cigarettes per day. The most striking increase is in mortality from cancer of the lung. The effect is most marked among individuals born in the period 1901 to 1910 (since these are the oldest in the sample). Among males the death rate from lung cancer is nearly twenty-five times that of non-smokers, and it is thirteen times as great among females. For other types of cancer, however, the sample does not show such elevated risk. Other causes of death are also associated significantly with smoking. The well-known association with coronary heart disease is replicated in the Cederlöf study. Also it is found that deaths from suicide, especially among the younger twins in the sample (i.e. those born between 1911 and 1925), are eight times more frequent in females who smoke more than ten cigarettes per day and nearly three times more frequent in males who smoke. In fact, in terms of actual deaths (rather than in terms of relative frequencies for the different groups), suicide is responsible for more deaths among smokers born between 1911 and 1925 than cancer of the lung. There is also some support for the view that smokers are more prone to accidental death than non-smokers.

The data of Cederlöf and his associates, therefore, confirm many of the well-known broad features of the association between smoking and mortality. Can the data elucidate the nature of the association? The answer is 'ideally yes' but unfortunately 'practically no'. In spite of the enormous number of twins enrolled in the study, the actual number of deaths reported is comparatively small, resulting in very small numbers available for the critical non-exposed twin analysis. However, significant associations were still detected between mortality of non-smoking twins and the smoking status of their partners, though these were not replicated across all zygosity and sex groups. Averaging over sexes and zygosity, there is a significantly inflated gross mortality among the non-smoking partners of twins who smoke. Dividing causes of death into coronary heart disease and cancer shows that the overall mortality from heart disease is significantly higher among the male non-smoking partners of twins who smoke and that the non-smoking partners of smoking twins are also at a generally higher risk of death from cancer. As far as individual twin groups are concerned, the significant effects appear to be confined to dizygotic rather than monozygotic twins. This is not what we would normally expect but may be attributed to the smaller numbers available in the MZ groups. Unfortunately, the numbers become far too small to permit the examination of the causes of the association for more specific diseases of interest.

What then can be learned from the Swedish study? The widespread association between smoking and morbidity and mortality is confirmed. The effects are not confined to cancer of the lung but extend to other diseases and states which are indicative of stress and for which smoking may be a palliative rather than a cause. The association with suicide provides one such example. The NET analysis suggests that a great many of the symptoms associated with smoking arise in the non-smoking partners of twins who smoke and that this association is more marked among monozygotic twin pairs. This finding could quite legitimately be interpreted in genetical terms as indicating the genetical basis for the association between smoking and disease and suggests that smoking should be regarded as one symptom, rather than the cause, of a more generalized inherited predisposition to develop physiological disorders whose origin could even be psychosomatic. The fact that the most significant associations are confined to monozygotic pairs, in spite of the comparatively small numbers involved, argues against a simple-minded interpretation in social terms, since the family environment is expected to contribute to the similarity of both types of twin. It is conceivable that monozygotic twins display their own unique social conditions which could result in the behaviour of one twin exercising an effect on the other. If, for example, the physical proximity of monozygotic twins were consistently greater than that of DZ twins then the results could indicate that even people who are closely associated with smokers for a long period are at a significantly higher risk for certain respiratory and behavioural symptoms. Such an interpretation of the findings, however, which relies on MZ twins sharing the same smoke-filled environment more closely than DZ twins, requires a new principle which is not clearly demonstrated to affect DZ twins more than monozygotes.

This reservation apart, therefore, the study of Cederlöf argues for a genetic basis for the association between disease and smoking, although it must be recognized that the evidence on the causal nature of the association between smoking and death from lung cancer specifically is too slight to be convincing either way. The data suggest that cancer of the lung is only part of a wide spectrum of disorder and disability which is associated with smoking.

CHAPTER 4

New Approaches to the Analysis of Twin Data and their Application to Smoking Behaviour

L. J. EAVES AND H. J. EYSENCK

As we can see from the previous chapter, two themes have characterized most research on the inheritance of the smoking habit. The first has been the emphasis on the twin study as the principal strategy for genetical investigation. The second has been reliance on the method of concordance as the basic device for statistical interpretation. Although this approach yields important *prima facie* evidence for the inheritance of the tendency to smoke, it leads neither to a more refined understanding if its causes nor to any test of whether the findings for twins can be applied to the much wider population of non-twins.

The generality of twin results

The twin design has intrinsic appeal because of the ease with which twins can be ascertained and because, superficially at least, twins offer the most clear-cut method of controlling for the influence of the family environment. We have already mentioned (Chapter 3) the many challenges which have been offered to the validity of the twin method. There is no general answer to the question of whether the results for twins can be used as if they were estimates of population parameters. The matter is one for specific investigation. Later (Chapter 5) we shall attempt to compare the findings on twins with those for other types of relationship. Such comparisons do not merely test the validity of the twin method for a particular behavioural trait; they yield far greater information about the principal sources of genetical and environmental variation. Frequently, it may be that models derived from twin data do not have the generality we would like, but in such cases a combination of the classical twin study with data from other sources can yield novel findings about the origin of the differences in question.

Concordance and scaling

Just as the twin method is conceptually, if deceptively, simple, so too is the method of concordance. The chief advantage of analyses based on tables of concordance is that they make no assumptions about the scale of measurement, nor about the nature and number of any genetical effects responsible for observed differences. If we accept the basic premise of the twin method, the analysis of concordance yields a simple and compelling test for the importance of genetical factors for any trait, even though we may have no information apart from an (arbitrary) recognition that some individuals display a characteristic which others do not.

The fact that the method of concordance avoids questionable speculations about scales of measurement might make it deceptively attractive at first sight. Whatever appeal the method might have for a single twin study is rapidly dissipated once we begin to ask more detailed quantitative questions about, for example, the influence of the family environment or the causes of similarity between parents and offspring. Such questions cannot be answered adequately until we are committed, however tentatively, to a particular scale of measurement and to a more precise theory about the causes of variation underlying the observed response categories. The genetical and environmental theory underlying the method of concordance is very weak, in the sense that it makes few assumptions. It is not a bold theory, so it is difficult to falsify in practice. Conversely, such a theory provides few precise quantitative predictions about the findings in non-twins. Having once demonstrated that MZ twins are more alike than DZ twins, the method of concordance applied to twins has 'shot its bolt'.

In a specifically statistical context, Fisher observed (1960), 'an erroneous assumption of ignorance is not innocuous'. A price is paid whenever we sacrifice assumptions about the scale of measurement. Information is lost, and we are thus restricting our capacity to make and test predictions.

Before we can begin any analysis we are thus faced with the problem of scaling. Clearly, there are several possible ways of scaling subjects' statements about their smoking habits. At the very simplest level we can assume that there is, indeed, a legitimate ordering of the categories such that an individual who does not smoke at all is regarded as more extreme in one direction than an individual who smokes a little, whereas individuals who smoke excessively are treated, for the purposes of analysis, as more extreme in the opposite direction. Thus, we regard the categories of smoking behaviour as an ordered sequence reflecting the severity of the smoking habit. For analytical purposes we then assign ordered numerical values to each of the classes to reflect our belief, or hypothesis, about the relevant scale on which tobacco consumption and its correlates are to be measured. In the first instance we may assign integer values to the categories, but subsequently we shall assign values which assume that underlying the observed categories there is a continuous and normal distribution of smoking behaviour in the population sampled. For simple purposes this distinction may not make a great deal of difference to the interpretation of the data, but the latter approximates better our perception of the arbitrariness of the categories and may help in constructing more adequate tests of significance.

We should, however, stress that the assignment of order to the subjects' responses is a scaling assumption and may be proved wrong subsequently. We shall consider later in this chapter how the validity of the scaling may be tested. For now we observe that the validity of a scale is judged only by its ability to support reliable inferences.

In the context of psychological measurement such a position is not new. Lord & Novick (1968), for example, comment as follows:

> If we construct a test score by counting up correct responses (zero-one scoring) and treating the resulting scale as having interval properties, the procedure may or may not produce a good predictor of some criterion. To the extent that this scaling produces a good empirical predictor the stipulated interval scaling is justified. . . . If a particular interval scale is shown empirically to provide the

basis of an accurately predictive and usefully descriptive model, then it is a good scale and further theoretical developments might profitably be based on it. Thus measurement (or scaling) is a fundamental part of the process of theory construction.

A remarkably similar stance is found among biometrical geneticists who argue (Mather & Jinks, 1971, p. 63):

The scales of the instruments which we employ in measuring our plants and animals are those which experience has shown to be convenient to us. We have no reason to suppose that they are specifically appropriate to the representation of the characters of a living organism for the purposes of genetical analysis. Nor have we any reason to believe that a single scale can reflect equally the idiosyncrasies of all the genes affecting a single character.... The scale on which the measurements are expressed for the purposes of genetical analysis must therefore be reached by empirical means. Obviously it should be one which facilitates both the analysis of the data and the interpretation and use of the resulting statistics.

These authors agree that virtually any scale employed in psychology or biology is arbitrary. The units are chosen primarily for convenience rather than because we necessarily believe that they represent with any particular accuracy an underlying biological or psychological process. The most we can expect from a scale is that it does not lose any of the information which might be recovered from the original observations and that it leads to valid and useful predictions. The dichotomous scales chosen to represent much of the data on smoking lose information because they do not represent clinicians' perceptions of the heterogeneity of the smoking habit in terms of the amount or type of tobacco product consumed. They are also poor because they do not enable any precise predictions to be made about the degree of resemblance between other types of relatives under alternative hypotheses about the causes of variability.

The analysis of a simple scale for twins' responses: data summary and statistical model

Our initial approach to the analysis of twin data is best described by reference to our own data. The structure and collection of the sample is described in Appendix A, which also contains the smoking questionnaire used. Langford (1976) conducted a preliminary study of the twin sample and examined the age of onset of smoking of the five groups of twins: female and male monozygotics; female, male and unlike-sex dizygotic twins. She assigned scores to represent the age of onset of smoking as given in Tables 8-9. On the basis of these scores it can be seen (Table 10) that females begin smoking later and are somewhat less variable in their age of onset than males. The

TABLE 8

Raw weights assigned to age of onset of smoking

		Number of subjects	
Age of onset (years)	*Code*	*Male*	*Female*
< 14	1	53	35
14 – 15	2	67	72
16 – 17	3	52	114
18 – 20	4	37	153
20 – 25	5	9	67
26 +	6	2	21
Never smoked	7	98	310

TABLE 9

Raw weights assigned to average daily consumption of cigarettes

		Number of subjects	
No. / day	*Code*	*Male*	*Female*
Nil	0	164	453
< 1	1	29	75
1 – 4	2	16	45
5 – 9	3	15	34
10 – 14	4	23	67
15 – 19	5	30	52
20 – 29	6	30	34
30 +	7	11	12

critical question, however, is, what factors are responsible for the variation in age of onset within the populations of like-sex individuals? Langford summarized the twin data by computing the mean squares (using her category weights) between and within pairs. These are reproduced in Table 11. No correction has been made for age

TABLE 10

Means and variances for raw twin data

		Age of onset		Average consumption	
		Male	*Female*	*Male*	*Female*
N	Full sample	318	772	318	772
Mean		3.88	4.88	1.90	1.40
Variance		5.34	3.98	5.72	4.18
N	Omitting 'non-smokers'	220	462	154	319
Mean		2.49	3.45	3.93	3.40
Variance		1.43	1.58	3.85	3.36

TABLE 11

Mean squares for twin pairs for raw scores (Langford)

Twin type	*Item*	*d.f.*	mean square	
			Age of onset	*Average cigarette consumption*
MZ female	Between pairs	235	5.38	6.77
	Within pairs	236	2.13	1.74
MZ male	Between pairs	79	7.90	8.44
	Within pairs	80	3.49	3.27
DZ female	Between pairs	120	5.73	5.77
	Within pairs	121	2.81	2.21
DZ male	Between pairs	49	6.24	6.15
	Within pairs	50	2.78	5.11
DZ male-female	Between pairs	57	5.65	5.91
	Within pairs	58	4.38	4.18

or sex in computing these mean squares. The contribution of such factors will be considered later.

The mean squares of Table 11 constitute the raw data summary. The only assumptions they embody are the statistical ones that such a data summary is adequate for the chosen scale of measurement. For a given group of twins we may represent the mean squares in terms of a statistical model which specifies the contribution of variation within twin pairs and between the true means of twin pairs. If the pair means were known exactly their variance could be represented by σ_b^2. For each type of twin family we could define different $\sigma_b^{2'}$ s : σ_{bmzf}^2; σ_{bmzm}^2; σ_{bdzf}^2; etc., to represent the variation between the true means of pairs of monozygotic male, dizygotic female twin pairs, etc. Since twin pairs only supply two measurements, however, and since these are subject to error, the variance of the pair means is expected to be not simply σ_b^2 but σ_b^2 plus a contribution due to the variation of individual measurements, σ_w^2, divided by the number of individuals contributing to the observed mean (i.e. two, in the case of twins). The variance of the means of MZ female twins, therefore, in terms of the statistical components of variance is expected to be $\sigma_{bmzf}^2 + \frac{1}{2}\sigma_{wmzf}^2$.

The analysis of variance of twin data, however, normally yields mean squares calculated on the basis of individual twins rather than on the means of twin pairs, so the mean square between twin pairs is twice the variance of the pair means. Hence the expectation of the mean square between MZ female twin pairs is $2\sigma_{bmzf}^2 + \sigma_{wmzf}^2$. The within-pair item of each analysis, on the other hand, is an estimate of σ_w^2 since it reflects the variation of individual twins around their corresponding pair means. Thus, for monozygotic female twins, the within-pair mean square is expected to be σ_{wmzf}^2. Similarly, expectations for all the other mean squares in the analysis may be defined (see Table 12). If the component of variance between twin pairs is zero (i.e. if twin pairs do not differ from one another on average) then the mean square betweeen pairs will not be significantly greater than the corresponding within-pair mean square and the ratio of the two means squares (the 'F-ratio') will not be significantly greater than unity. In the particular example given, F-ratio tests confirm the presence of significant variation between twin pairs in four out of the five twin groups. No significant between-pair variation was detected in the unlike-sex pairs. This could be due simply to chance or possibly to a real feature of the determination of age of onset

TABLE 12

**Contributions of components of variation within and
between twin pairs to the mean squares from the analysis
of variance of monozygotic and dizygotic twins**

Twin type	# of pairs	Item	d.f.	Expected mean square
Monozygotic (MZ)	n	Between pairs	n-1	$\sigma_{wmz}^2 + 2\sigma_{bmz}^2$
		Within pairs	n	σ_{wmz}^2
Dizygotic (DZ)	m	Between pairs	m-1	$\sigma_{wdz}^2 + 2\sigma_{bdz}^2$
		Within pairs	m	σ_{bds}^2

$\sigma_{wmz}^2 =$ component of variance within MZ pairs
$\sigma_{wdz}^2 =$ component of variance within DZ pairs
$\sigma_{bmz}^2 =$ variance of *true* means of MZ pairs
$\sigma_{bdz}^2 =$ variance of *true* means of DZ pairs

of smoking. We shall consider the possibilities in greater detail subsequently. The details of the analysis of variance of method are only outlined here. Fuller details are given in, e.g., Snedecor & Cochran (1967).

Testing causal hypotheses

Merely to have summarized the variation in this form, however, tells us little about the factors responsible for its creation and maintenance. Mather (1967) observed, 'We might, for example, measure the thickness of a thousand banana leaves without learning any more than the thicknesses of this particular sample of leaves'. Our task is to consider whether these data give us good reason to limit the range of hypotheses which might be advanced to explain the variation we observe, perhaps to the point where we are left with a few simple possibilities to become the basis for further study.

Twin data provide us with an opportunity to rule out certain possibilities at an early stage of an investigation as those which cannot even explain the elementary observations of the twin study. At least one hypothesis will fit the data perfectly: we could assume that every mean square (or variance component) in the twin data should be represented by a unique parameter reflecting causes of variation unique to that particular statistic. Such a hypothesis would explain everything about the data perfectly but would predict nothing. Merely to invoke a separate principle to explain every difference in the data would yield no expectations for the statistics which might be found in subsequent twin studies or in the examination of data on other types of relatives. A hypothesis of this type is not very informative because it cannot be distinguished from the hypothesis that every observation is unique and must be interpreted uniquely. A more informative hypothesis not only explains the available data economically but leads us to predictions about the findings in subsequent studies.

We employ two basic principles in the analysis and interpretation of data. These are the criteria of 'fit' and 'parsimony'. The first criterion requires that any model advanced should predict the main features of the data to a degree of imprecision comparable with that to be expected from sampling variation alone. A model which fails to predict adequately salient features of the data is a poor model and would be rejected. The criterion of parsimony stipulates that simpler hypotheses are more informative. So, if faced with alternatives both of which satisfy the test of goodness of fit, we select the simpler hypothesis. The history of the criterion of parsimony can be traced to the well-known 'Razor' formulated by William of Occam: *pluritas non est ponenda sine necessitate;* but the appeal of parsimony is less arbitrary than might appear from a reference to mediaeval philosophy, since economical hypotheses have two important advantages over their more diffuse alternatives. Firstly, economical hypotheses lead to more precise and general predictions and there is, therefore, a bonus in generalizing correctly from a parsimonious theory. Secondly, since the predictions of a simple model are more precise they can be more easily falsified in the light of subsequent developments if indeed the model is incorrect.

We know well that there will be occasions, especially in the study of traits which are subject to sampling variation, on which we shall mistakenly adopt the wrong hypothesis or an hypothesis which is unduly simple, but the important feature of the approach we adopted is that it is ultimately self-correcting in that any sweeping errors of inference will become apparent with the incorporation of new data into the study. Indeed, as we shall show, one of the issues raised by our analysis is the validity of generalizing from the causes of smoking in twins to those in the population as a whole.

We now examine how these principles are applied in practice in the interpretation of the ten mean squares for the age of onset of smoking. One simple hypothesis, which may be advanced for the sake of argument, is embodied in an assumption that all the variation in the observed trait, for males and females, can be attributed solely to the influence of environmental experiences unique to individual twins. That is, a simple model might assume that there are no environmental experiences affecting the onset of smoking which are shared by members of a twin pair except those which happen to arise by a coincidence of chance events. Furthermore, a simple hypothesis might assume that such environmental effects as influence the trait contribute no more nor less to variation in males than in females. Such a model would assume that the effects of parents and peers, in so far as they contribute jointly to members of a pair, would have little influence on the adoption of the smoking habit.

Mere examination of the data should rule out such a simple hypothesis since we have already seen that there is significant variation between the true means of the twin pairs. This could not be the case if all the environmental influences depended on random events unique to each individual. Secondly, we have already seen that male twins display greater variation in the age at which they first smoke. This again cannot be the case on the simple model which attempts to reduce all the ten mean squares to a single causal principle. Therefore, we are forced by the data to modify the simple hypothesis. However, in the interests of our ensuing treatment we pursue this trivial hypothesis further and ask whether (i) we can obtain an estimate of the contribution of our hypothesized environmental factors to the observed variation, and (ii) whether the ability of the model to encompass the observations (in this case the mean squares chosen to summarize the raw data) can be quantified.

For any set of parameter values under a given specific hypothesis it is possible to compute the likelihood of obtaining the observations. The likelihood is proportional to the probability of obtaining the given set of observations under particular hypotheses. Its numerical value will depend on considerations which are directly under examination in the given study, for example, the causes of variation and their relative contributions to the measured variation, but will also depend on considerations which are not directly under examination, such as the statistical assumptions made in the analysis. For a given hypothesis, parameter estimates can be found which maximize the likelihood of obtaining the observed data set. Such maximum likelihood estimates have many desirable properties, especially in large samples. In large samples ML estimates are normally distributed and unbiased. They also exhaust all the information the data can yield about a parameter — no further analysis can possibly give additional information about the statistic in question. The large-sample property of normality is attractive because it simplifies the task of specifying the range of values within which particular effects may lie. Unfortunately we are unable to say at this stage exactly how large the sample must be for these properties to apply since each case must be decided on its merits either by mathematical analysis or by simulation. It is our impression from the simulation of related problems (see e.g. Martin et al., 1978) that the assumption of normality and lack of bias for the estimates for samples of the size we have may not be unjustified, given that the original data are normal. In general we have tried to secure scales which come as close as possible to satisfying this criterion. We note, however, that this is done for statistical rather than genetical reasons and that there is no particular reason why the distribution of genetical and environmental effects should be normal for a given measurement.

It may be seen intuitively that comparison of the likelihoods obtained under different hypotheses yields a quantitative basis for deciding whether one model is to be preferred to another. Generally the difference between the logarithms of the two likelihoods under competing hypotheses is taken as the basis of a statistical test of the preferred alternative, since it is undesirable to increase the complexity of a model unless the data provide clear justification for such a step by a demonstrable jump in the ability of the more complex model to explain the anomalies beyond the scope of a simpler hypothesis. Edwards poses the question thus (1972, p. 200): 'How much simplicity are we prepared to lose for a given increase in the excellence of the fit?', and indicates that there can be no rigid rules for such decisions but that the conventional 5 per cent significance levels may be insufficiently stringent for secure inference in some areas. He observes, 'It is one thing to say "we will not even bother to think of an alternative hypothesis until we can obtain an increase of at least 2 units of support from it" and quite another to say "we will adopt an alternative hypothesis as soon as it will increase the support by two units"'. For most applications we could as well read 'improvement in fit significant at the 5 per cent level' for 'increase of two units of support'. Statistical inference does not preclude entirely the exercise of good judgement but provides a rational basis on which the consequences of such decisions can be assessed.

In the causal analysis of behaviour, therefore, the problem becomes one of formulating alternative hypotheses in quantitative terms, obtaining estimates of the parameters of a given model (or series of models), and comparing the values of the likelihood so obtained to arrive at a model which combines economy with a sufficiently precise explanation of the observations.

Testing the most basic model

Before any parameters can be estimated the model must be formulated precisely. In the case of the trivial hypothesis described above this is simple. Every component of variance within twin pairs is expected to reflect the contribution of specific environmental influences and every component of variance between pairs to be zero. Letting E_1 represent the expected contribution of environmental factors to variation within families of twins gives, for the expected components of variance:

$$\sigma_w^2 = E_1$$
$$\sigma_b^2 = 0$$

These expectations of variance components may be translated into expectations of mean squares by recognizing that the expected value of a mean square within pairs is equal to the corresponding component of variance, whereas the expected mean square between pairs is twice the corresponding between-pairs component of variance plus the contribution due to the within-pair variance component. In terms of the basic model, therefore, all the observed mean squares are expected to be equal to E_1, the contribution of within-family environmental factors. Thus, the model predicts that any variation between the mean squares from different groups of twins and any differences among the mean squares between pairs and within pairs could be explicable purely on the basis of chance departures of observed mean squares from their values expected on the basis of the model.

The problem now reduces to obtaining the maximum-likelihood

estimate of E_1 and comparing the observed mean squares with those predicted from a knowledge of the most likely value of the parameter.

If the observed mean squares were known with equal precision, and if they were normally distributed around their expected values, the classical procedures of least squares, familiar through its common-place application in regression analysis, would yield the maximum likelihood estimates of the parameters, given linear models for the observed statistics. However, we know that the former is not the case since the mean squares are all based on different numbers of d.f. and the variance of a mean square is proportional to the square of its expected value (Kendall & Stuart, 1961, Vol. I). That is, the larger the mean square the smaller the precision with which it is known for a given d.f. Secondly, mean squares follow the gamma distribution which only approximates to the normal distribution satisfactorily when the d.f. are large. It turns out that the approximation is adequate for many practical applications of our type. Since the mean squares are not known with equal precision, however, it is necessary to allow for this inequality in computing the estimates of the parameters and in testing the adequacy of the model. It makes intuitive sense to allow those parts of the data which are known more precisely to have a relatively greater role in fixing the final solution. In terms of our data, the mean squares based on female twins should contribute more to the final interpretation of the data since these are based on larger numbers of twins.

The least squares procedure may be modified, therefore, to reflect the differing precision of the component statistics by introducing a weighting factor for each mean square which is equal to the inverse of the variance of the corresponding mean square. Thus, for each mean square we employ as weight the factor:

$$w_i = \frac{d_i}{2\epsilon x_i^2}$$

where ϵx_i is the expected value of the mean square, based on d_i, d.f. given normality in the original observations. The maximum likelihood estimates of the parameters of the model are obtained by minimizing the weighted sum of the squared deviations of the observed mean squares (ten in number in the example) from their values expected on the basis of the parameters of the model. Since the weights depend not on the observed values of the mean squares but on their values expected under the hypothesis under test, these cannot be determined finally until the expected values are known. An iterative procedure has to be adopted, therefore, in which trial values are chosen for the weights to yield approximations for the parameter values which can be used to generate closer approximations to the true weights by substitution in the above formula. This procedure is implemented easily on a computer. The observed mean squares are represented by the vector $\underset{\sim}{x}$, and the model by a matrix of coefficients $\underset{\sim}{A}$ by which the estimated parameter values $\hat{\underset{\sim}{\theta}}$ must be multiplied to yield the expectations for $\underset{\sim}{x}$, $\epsilon\underset{\sim}{x}$. We require the $\hat{\underset{\sim}{\theta}}$ which minimizes:

$$S^2 = \left(\underset{\sim}{x} - \epsilon \underset{\sim}{x}\right)' \underset{\sim}{W} \left(\underset{\sim}{x} - \epsilon \underset{\sim}{x}\right)$$

where $\underset{\sim}{W}$ is a matrix of weights. In this application, since the mean squares are independent, the weight matrix will be diagonal consisting of the amounts of information w_i about each statistic. For a given set of weights, the weighted least squares estimates of the parameters are given by the solution, $\hat{\underset{\sim}{\theta}}$, of the equations:

$$\hat{\underset{\sim}{\theta}} = (A' \underset{\sim}{W} A)^{-1} A' \underset{\sim}{W} \underset{\sim}{x}$$

The expected values of the mean squares are then given by

$$\epsilon\underset{\sim}{x} = \underset{\sim}{A} \hat{\underset{\sim}{\theta}}$$

These values can be used to generate further weights and the process repeated until successive estimates of the parameter values and the residual sum of squares, S^2, differ by less than a given amount.

The procedure is sufficiently simple to be practical on a desk machine provided there are few observed statistics and the number of parameters in the model is small. The magnitude of S^2 can be used as a guide to the adequacy of the model since, when the model fits, S^2 is approximately distributed as chi-square with k-p d.f., k being the number of statistics (mean squares) constituting the data summary, and p being the number of parameters estimated from the data. In practice, if the model is adequate, relatively few iterations are required to secure convergence and the trial values of the weights will yield solutions close to the final ones since the observed mean squares will then be close to their expected values. Similarly, if the chosen model fails disastrously the failure will be apparent almost at once, since after the first cycle the deviations of observed from expected will be so gross as to yield a value of S^2 so unacceptable as to improve but little on subsequent cycles.

Nelder (see Nelder, 1975, and Nelder & Wedderburn, 1972) has implemented essentially the above procedure in a more general form in the computer package for Generalised Linear Interactive Modelling (GLIM) with modifications to the iterative procedure to allow for non-normality of the summary statistics and to yield a likelihood ratio test which compares the hypothesis implicit in the fitted model with the more general (and consequently less informative) hypothesis that each data point is represented by its own value. The advantage of this approach is that it does not depend, as the above weighted least squares does, upon the assumption of normality for the observed mean squares and therefore yields maximum likelihood estimates of the parameters even when the mean squares are based on small d.f. For our application, we have not come across instances in which the classical weighted least squares procedure leads to markedly different estimates or inferences from the more exact procedure of Nelder and Wedderburn and we suspect that the results do not differ greatly in our area for any sample sizes for which practical decisions are possible. However, for convenience of interpretation we have adopted the results obtained using the strict maximum likelihood procedure as implemented in Nelder's package. Instead of s^2, the log-likelihood ratio

$$g^2 = \sum_i d_i \, l_n \left(\frac{\epsilon x_i}{x_i} \right)$$

is maximized with respect to variation in θ. The likelihood ratio, g^2, is approximately distributed as $\frac{1}{2}\chi^2$, for k-p d.f. as before. Provided the model is adequate the inverse of the matrix of second partial derivatives of the log-likelihood with respect to the unknown parameters, $\hat{\theta}$ is the covariance matrix of the parameter estimates and employed to give an indication of the sampling variation attached to the estimates.

Employing the likelihood ratio test we find that the E_1 hypothesis is very much less likely to yield the observed statistics than the most likely (though least informative) hypothesis which invokes a separate causal principle to explain each of the ten mean squares. Twice the difference between the log-likelihood under the competing hypotheses is

$$2g^2 = 98.02$$

The probability of obtaining such a large χ^2_9 by chance is very small, confirming that the data are not consistent with the hypothesis that all the observed variation on the age of onset of smoking as assessed by this questionnaire can be attributed to chance experiences of individual twins. Although the maximum likelihood estimate of E_1 turns out to be 4.39, the failure of the model precludes our attaching any significance to this value. The data have already suggested that there is variation between families in the trait not simply due to coincidence, and there is every indication that males are more variable than females. It is now necessary to consider the ways in which the initial and disproven hypothesis might be modified to include some of these further possibilities.

Including the family environment

Twins rarely grow up in isolation. Separated identical twins are exceptionally rare (e.g. Shields, 1962) and even those who are separated at birth share a common uterine environment. In addition, most pairs of twins studied live in the same family, share the same social environment and often attend the same school where they may well share the same friends. Certain mothers may make a special point of dressing their twins alike, especially if the twins are identical. All of these factors tend to produce correlations between the environments of members of the same family. Usually we would expect such correlation of environment in a family to be positive, that is, members of the same family are more likely to receive the same environmental treatment than unrelated individuals reared in different families. There are, however, some instances in which this need not be the case. Eaves (1976a), for example, has shown how the existence of competitive effects could yield a negative correlation between the environments of members of the same family. More recently (e.g. Corey et al., 1976) attention has been focused on the possibility of intrauterine interaction between twins due to vascular anastomosis.

The fact that the relatively untutored eye can discern apparent associations between treatments within a family (social class is one example) should not lead to the conclusion that such an association is contributing to the development of any positive association between twin measurements of a particular behavioural trait. No more should we assume that the fact that identical twins are identical for every identifiable genetic locus is indicative of a genetic influence in the development of a particular trait for which we have measurements. The presence of social heterogeneity, whatever its ultimate cause, leads us to include the family environment as one of the range of possibilities for the determination of a particular trait. Similarly the ubiquity of genetical variation among living organisms renders it foolish to discount the possibility of genetical influences upon human behaviour. Our task is to decide between these alternatives, if alternatives they be, and to discern and quantify such influences, genetic or environmental, which contribute to variation in the particular trait of interest.

As far as twins are concerned, all factors which tend to produce environmental similarity for twin pairs will contribute to the variation between pair means, σ_b^2. This will be true for maternal effects, cultural effects, effects of the social and educational environment and any non-hereditary effects of the parental phenotype whenever these are shared by members of a twin pair. Without additional data, for example on parents and adoptees, it is not possible to decide which of these many possibilities is responsible for the observed environmental similarity. It is, however, possible to specify the effects of such similarity in the model, and, under some circumstances, detect and estimate its contribution to the variation between families. Jinks & Fulker (1970), employing the notation of biometrical genetics, introduce the component E_2 into the range of models for collateral relatives of the twin and sibling type to specify the contribution of environmental differences between families as distinct from that within families (E_1). In the absence of genetical effects and of environmental treatment differences which depend on genetical differences, E_2 is expected to be the same for MZ and DZ twins and to contribute to σ_b^2 for each type of twin. Our model for the variance components is thus

$$\sigma_w^2 = E_1$$
$$\sigma_b^2 = E_2$$

giving for each of the five twin groups, expected mean squares E_1 and $E_1 + 2E_2$ for the mean squares within and between pairs respectively. Formulated in this way the model embodies many assumptions which we desire to test. We have included no facility for the causes of variation to depend on sex or zygosity. The same environmental components are specified for male and female twins and for identical and non-identical twins. The question is, 'does this model represent a significant improvement on our previous attempt and how well does it predict the form of the mean squares we have calculated?'

Using the GLIM package the likelihood ratio test for the goodness of fit of the new model gave: $\chi_8^2 = 21.82$ and estimates of 2.78 and 1.58 for E_1 and E_2 respectively. The chi-square is still significant beyond the 1% level, suggesting that our model is a poor predictor of the observed pattern of variation in the twins. This does not by itself mean the E_2 is zero, but that we would be presumptuous to interpret the parameter values as they stand since there remains room for significant improvement in our model. However, addition of one parameter, E_2, has produced a very large change in the likelihood ratio, corresponding to a change in the chi-square from 98.01 for the E_1 model to 21.82 for the E_1, E_2 model. The difference between these two chi-squares is itself a chi-square for 1 d.f. which can be used as a guide to the improvement achieved as a result of fitting the additional parameters. Clearly the gain in support is highly significant, but the inadequacy of the modified hypothesis compels the search for alternatives which might yield a more substantial improvement in the quality of our predictions.

Introducing genetical effects

Subsequently we shall see how the environmental model may be modified to incorporate additional parameters. Before we consider extensions of the environmental model, however, we consider an alternative which does not increase the complexity of the model but alters its form radically. We consider the contribution of genetical effects to variation in a quantitative trait and, in particular, the contribution of such effects to variation within and between pairs of twins.

Genetical theory leads to quite different predictions about the degree of similarity between relatives. The exact degree of resemblance, even in a trait which is completely heritable, will obviously depend on the degree of relationship, more distant relatives being expected to be less similar, but the resemblance will also depend on more subtle aspects of the genetical system such as the mating system and the type of gene action (additive, dominant, epistatic, etc.). Fisher (1918) provided the classical extension of Mendelian theory to the case of multiple loci, in a form which has survived at the heart of human quantitative genetics today. Fisher also showed how the resemblance between relatives would be generally reduced if there were environmental influences unique to members of the family. In the human population, of course, individuals are not scattered at random over the whole environment but tend to live with their parents and siblings. This raises the possibility that environments may not be unique to individuals but may be shared by members of a family and thus superimpose environmental similarity upon similarity due to biological inheritance. This is not a novel statement. Several authors, including Newman, Freeman & Holzinger (1937), Wright (1934), Cattell (1960), Shields (1962), Jinks & Fulker (1970), Cavalli-Sforza & Feldman (1973), Morton (1974) and Eaves (1976a), have considered various ways in which environmental similarity may be confounded partly or completely with genetical similarity. Except in the simplest cases, some form of adoption data may be required to disentangle fully the biological and cultural aspects of familial similarity. Our problem thus reduces to that of explaining the variation between individuals and the similarity between biological and non-biological relatives.

Often, though by no means exclusively, the effects of genes on a trait can be shown to be additive. That is, the effect of one allele at a locus is not influenced by another homologous allele at the same locus nor by alleles at other loci. If there is interaction between the different alleles at a locus there is said to be dominance. If the expression at one locus is altered by changes in the alleles at other loci there is said to be non-allelic interaction or epistasis.

These properties can be represented in terms of a simple model for gene effects. Since each individual has two representatives of each gene locus we consider the effects of pairs of alleles and we imagine a population in which there are just two main alleles A and a at a given locus. There are three possible genotypes with respect to the A locus: denoted by AA, Aa and aa. The phenotypes of these individuals will depend on the effects of the component loci. Following Mather (1949) and Mather & Jinks (1971) we consider firstly the two homozygotes AA and aa, and define a scale of measurement for which the individuals of the two genotypes differ. We may represent the scale by the line AA-aa below.

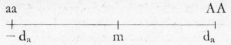

The point m represents the midpoint of the scale between AA and aa. The distance m-aa is $-d_a$ and the distance m-AA is d_a, ('d' for 'deviation'). We have so far only included the homozygotes (AA and aa) on the scale. The heterozygous (Aa) individuals will also lie somewhere on this scale, generally between aa and AA, at a point h_a units from m. The deviation of the heterozygote from m, (h_a) may be positive, i.e. Aa is more like AA than aa, in which case there is said to be dominance for increasing expression of the trait; zero (i.e. Aa coincides with m on the scale) in which case there is said to be no dominance; or Aa may resemble aa rather than AA when dominance is for decreasing trait expression. Similar scales could be defined for the effects of other loci (B, b; C, c, etc.) each having its own additive deviation d_b, d_c and dominance deviation h_b, h_c.

There is no particular reason why the effects at the different loci should be equal, nor is there any reason, on any scale chosen for measurement, why all the dominance deviations should be consistent in sign. The fundamental scale in biology is that of reproductive fitness and there is growing evidence to suggest that dominance deviations measured on such a scale will be uniform in sign, the expression of genes themselves having been altered during the evolution of the species to optimize the expression of the phenotype in a given environment. Thus the action and interaction of loci responsible for variation in a trait will be modified under selection to produce the most favourable range of phenotypes. Thus we may expect non-additive genetic effects to be uniform in the direction of increasing fitness, i.e. all the h's will be positive. This conception of genetic architecture was formulated by Mather (1943) and subsequently greatly developed (e.g. Mather, 1966).

In principle any scale of measurement could be related to fitness, though in practice the determination of the form of such a relationship is likely to be difficult as short-term fluctuations may obscure long-term evolutionary trends. In so far as the trait we measure is a component with a linear relationship to fitness, it may be expected to show directional dominance and other directional interactions between loci which produce similar effects at the phenotypic level.

On the other hand, if the trait measured has no obvious relationship to fitness or if such relationship is basically non-linear it may be expected that the dominance deviations are small, or not uniform in direction. In the case of dominance which varies in direction it is usual to speak of ambi-directional dominance.

The possibility of a relationship between the type of gene expression and the biological significance of a trait is exciting since it provides one ray of hope to those who try to infer the adaptive significance of behavioural traits. In practice, however, with man the subtleties of gene action are much more difficult to tease out because of the possible confounding of hereditary and cultural factors and because it is impossible to ensure experimental matings of a type which would be most efficient for the purpose.

Having thus defined the gene effects on an appropriate scale, we may now specify their contribution to the variance in the population. To do this we require the frequencies of the increasing and decreasing alleles in the population. Let the frequency of the increasing allele (A) be u_a, and that of the decreasing allele (a) be $v_a = 1-u_a$. In a randomly mating population in Hardy-Weinberg equilibrium, the contribution of the A locus to the genetic variation is:

$$\sigma_A^2 = u_a^2\, d_a^2 + 2u_a v_a h_a^2 + v_a^2 d_a^2 - [d_a(u_a^2 - v_a^2) - 2u_a v_a h_a]^2$$

which simplifies to:

$$\sigma_A^2 = 2u_a v_a [d_a + h_a(v_a - u_a)]^2 + 4u_a^2 v_a^2 h_a^2$$

provided the population is in linkage equilibrium and the loci act independently, the contribution to the phenotypic variance of the individual loci can be added together to represent the total genetic variance thus:

$$\sigma_G^2 = 2 \sum_a u_a v_a [d_a + h_a(v_a - u_a)]^2 + 4 \sum_a u_a^2 v_a^2 h_a^2$$

or, following Mather & Jinks (1971) and letting

$$D_R = 4 \sum_a u_a v_a [d_a + h_a (v_a - u_a)]^2$$

$$H_R = 16 \sum_a u_a^2 v_a^2 h_a^2$$

we may put:
$$\text{and}$$
$$\sigma_G^2 = \tfrac{1}{2} D_R + \tfrac{1}{4} H_R$$

Mather (1974) gives a similar expectation for the much more tedious case of randomly mating populations when there is also epistatic gene action, that is for traits in which the effect of a substitution at one locus depends on the alleles at other loci. The resolution of epistatic effects requires very large and carefully designed studies in experimental organisms for which the degree of control is much greater. In randomly mating populations, although studies might be designed which could resolve epistasis in theory, the practical resolution of epistasis from other sources of non-additivity in man (such as dominance and certain types of genotype-environmental interaction) is a virtual impossibility, when the effects of environment and the mating system are also included in the model.

The covariances of relatives

Still retaining, for simplicity, the assumption of random mating and independent gene effects, we may now write the expected contributions of D_R and H_R to various covariances derived from data on relatives. Mather & Jinks show how this can be done (1971) and Falconer, though employing a somewhat different notation, presents essentially the same conclusions (1964). Since the results are standard it suffices merely to present an example to illustrate one approach to the algebra. Consider the covariance of pairs of monozygotic twins. We begin as before by specifying the effects for a single locus A, a. In a population in which A is segregating, there will be three types of monozygotic twin pair present in frequencies approximated by the Hardy-Weinberg equilibrium if mating is random. We may tabulate the possible types of pair (Table 13). The expected contribution of the locus to the covariance of MZ twins is now obtained by multiplying the product of each pair of gene effects by the frequency of the pair, summing over all three types of twin pair, and correcting for the mean thus:

$$C_{MZ_A} = 2u_a v_a [d_a + h_a(v_a - u_a)]^2 + 4 u_a^2 v_a^2 h_a^2$$

As before, we assume that the contributions of genes are independent, so to obtain the contribution of many gene loci to the covariance of MZ twins we simply sum the contributions of the individual loci. Thus, the expected genetical covariance between MZ twins is

$$C_{GMZ} = \tfrac{1}{2}D_R + \tfrac{1}{4}H_R$$

TABLE 13

Population frequencies of twin genotypes at single dimorphic locus under Hardy-Weinberg equilibrium

Frequency of genotype pairs

Pair type	Equal allele frequences		Unequal allele frequencies	
	MZ pairs	DZ pairs	MZ pairs	DZ pairs
AA, AA	$\frac{1}{4}$	9/64	u_a^2	$u_a^4 + u_a^3 v_a + \frac{1}{4}u_a^2 v_a^2$
AA, Aa	—	3/32	—	$u_a^3 v_a + \frac{1}{2}u_a^2 v_a^2$
AA, aa	—	1/64	—	$\frac{1}{4}u_a^2 v_a^2$
Aa, AA	—	3/32	—	$u_a^3 v_a + \frac{1}{2}u_a^2 v_a^2$
Aa, Aa	$\frac{1}{2}$	5/16	$2u_a v_a$	$u_a^3 v_a + 3u_a^2 v_a^2 + u_a v_a^3$
Aa, aa	—	3/32	—	$\frac{1}{2}u_a^2 v_a^2 + u_a v_a^3$
aa, AA	—	1/64	—	$\frac{1}{4}u_a^2 v_a^2$
aa, Aa	—	3/32	—	$\frac{1}{2}u_a^2 v_a^2 + u_a v_a^3$
aa, aa	$\frac{1}{4}$	9/64	v_a^2	$\frac{1}{4}u_a^2 v_a^2 + u_a v_a^3 + v_a^4$

That is, the genetical covariance of MZ twins is identical to the genetic variance of the population from which the twins were obtained. This is obvious, since a pair of twins is merely obtained by sampling a genotype from the population and replicating the same genotype. Of course, if twins do not represent a random sample of the population as far as the genes affecting a given trait are concerned, both the total variance of twins and their covariance will differ from the variance of the population.

Turning to DZ twins, the algebra for the expectations is somewhat more tedious because the individuals of a pair are no longer identical, with the result that there are now nine types of twin pair (allowing e.g. AA, aa and aa, AA pairs to represent different types). The types of twin pair will be present in frequencies which will depend on the frequencies of the different types of parental pair and the expected proportion of the different pairs within a family of given parents. In a randomly mating population, proportion u_a^4 of parental pairs will be of type AA x AA. Such pairs will, in the absence of mutation, yield DZ twin pairs of one type only, namely AA, AA. Table 13 gives the expected frequencies of DZ twin pair types for a single dimorphic locus in a randomly mating population. The corresponding frequencies are also presented for MZ twins for comparison. To simplify the reader's task in verifying some of the algebraic conclusions the frequencies are also given on the assumption that $u = v = \frac{1}{2}$, which special case yields essentially the same coefficients for D and H in the expectations but with much simpler expectations for the variance components themselves. The covariance of DZ twins is obtained in exactly the same way, but since members of a pair are often different in genotype the covariance is less than that for MZ twins, although still greater than zero since DZ twins are more alike genetically than unrelated individuals. The result is well known, namely:

$$C_{GDZ} = \tfrac{1}{4}D_R + \tfrac{1}{16}H_R$$

It can easily be verified that since the overall genotype frequencies still satisfy Hardy-Weinberg the total variance of DZ twins is simply that of the population, i.e $\sigma_G^2 = \tfrac{1}{2}D_R + \tfrac{1}{4}H_R$.

For purposes of statistical simplicity we have chosen to summarize the twin data by analysis of variance, rather than by computing variances and covariances. This was done because the mean squares of the analysis of variance are independent. Although there is no insuperable problem in the analysis of variances and covariances, the numerical procedures for handling independent observations are much easier to perform without a computer. Furthermore, whatever starting point is chosen for analysis, the answer should be the same, provided no information has been lost in summarizing the data and provided the method makes the most efficient use of the information available in the data summary.

Normally, the use of analysis of variance as a starting point for model fitting of the type we consider will not be seriously misleading, provided that there are no systematic differences between first- and second-born twins in either mean or variance. Differences in mean can be extracted as an item in the analysis of variance. To a large extent, differences in variance can be accommodated by including additional parameters in the model, as may be seen in the subsequent analyses. Given that these assumptions are not violated, the between-pairs components of variance are simply equal to the corresponding expected covariances thus:

$$\sigma_{bGDZ}^2 = \tfrac{1}{4}D_R + \tfrac{1}{16}H_R$$

$$\sigma_{bGMZ}^2 = \tfrac{1}{2}D_R + \tfrac{1}{4}H_R$$

and the within-pair covariances are expected to be equal to the expected total variance, less the contribution from the pair covariance, i.e.

$$\sigma^2_{GWMZ} = \sigma^2_G - C_{GMZ} \quad 0$$

$$\sigma^2_{GWDZ} = \sigma^2_G - C_{GDZ} = \tfrac{1}{4}D_R + \tfrac{3}{16}H_R$$

It has been pointed out several times that the detection of dominance in twin data is virtually impossible because the contribution of dominance is almost completely confounded in any estimate of the additive genetical variance obtained for twin data on the assumption that dominance is absent. We thus proceed on the assumption of no dominance, in the knowledge that if dominance were present it would almost certainly remain undetected with our sample sizes and would contribute substantially to bias in the estimate of the additive genetical variance.

In the absence of dominance, and other sources of genetical non-additivity, and given that mating is random, we may write the contribution of the additive genetical variance (represented by D_R) to the variance components as follows:

$$\sigma^2_{BMZ} = \tfrac{1}{2}D_R; \; \sigma^2_{WMZ} = E_1; \; \sigma^2_{BDZ} = \tfrac{1}{4}D_R; \; \sigma^2_{WDZ} = \tfrac{1}{4}D_R + E_1$$

Where appropriate, the contribution of within-family environmental factors (E_1) has been added to the expectations, so the model, like the E_1, E_2 model above, involves two parameters. The contribution of E_2 could be specified as well, if desired, by adding the parameter to the expectations of the between-family variance components. The expected mean squares are thus:

$$\epsilon MS_{BMZ} = D_R + 2E_2 + E_1 \qquad \epsilon MS_{WMZ} = E_1$$

$$\epsilon MS_{BDZ} = \tfrac{3}{4}D_R + 2E_2 + E_1 \qquad \epsilon MS_{WDZ} = \tfrac{1}{4}D_R + E_1$$

The model thus predicts different relationships between the magnitudes of the observed mean squares from those predicted by the previous model which did not include genetical effects. These are chiefly that the variation within DZ pairs is now expected to exceed that within MZ pairs and that between MZ pairs is expected to exceed that between DZ pairs. The extent to which such predictions might be violated purely by chance is the basis of our test of the model. Any model involving genetical effects is going to predict greater intrapair variation for DZ twins (as indeed will some models involving treatment effects). This is the basis of all tests of genetic components in twin data, including the method of concordance and the comparison of twin correlations. Notice, however, that the prediction is more precise than that. If we assume only additive gene action and environmental variation *within* families (i.e. E_2 being excluded from the model) we expect the total variances for MZ and DZ twins to be equal (i.e. $\frac{1}{2}D_R + E_1$). Furthermore, the value of $\sigma^2_{BMZ} - 2\sigma^2_{BdZ}$ is not expected to differ from zero except by chance. Thus the model includes quantitative as well as qualitative predictions about the relationships between the components of the data. Of course, the capacity of the experiment to falsify these predictions in practice may be slight, especially if the study is small, since it may be difficult to show that the departures observed could be due to anything other than chance. The extent to which a given study is capable of rejecting a false hypothesis is the 'power' of the study. The power of the twin study has been the subject of detailed consideration by Martin et al. (1978). Such work makes us cautious about the power of our study, or indeed of any studies based on less than several hundred twin pairs. We should, however, be able to determine the gross features of the variation in the measured behaviour using our study.

When the D_R, E_1 model is fitted the chi-square test comparing the model with the perfect fit solution yields $\chi^2_8 = 18.96$ which fits marginally better than the E_1, E_2 model, but is still far from satisfactory. Looked at objectively, the data give us every reason to prefer both models to the simple E_1 model, but give us little reason to distinguish between either. Both leave much to explain.

The joint effects of genes and the family environment

The above genetical model makes strong assumptions which, although they are often empirically justified with other traits, have clearly been shown to be wanting in the case of the age of onset of smoking. Before attempting to modify these assumptions, however, it is appropriate to ask whether the inclusion of E_2 in the above model would explain the inadequacy of our $D_R E_1$ model. Fitting such a three-parameter model yields the following estimates:

$$\hat{E}_1 = 2.52$$
$$\hat{D}_R = 2.50$$
$$\hat{E}_2 = 0.61$$

The chi-square test of goodness of fit gives $\chi_7^2 = 17.74$, indicating that deviations of the same or greater magnitude would only occur in 1-2% of samples of this structure. The fit of the model remains poor. Comparing this value for chi-square with the value obtained for the fit of the D_R, E_1 model gives $\chi_1^2 = 1.22$ which clearly indicates that inclusion of the effects of the family environment do not significantly improve the ability of the model to predict the given mean squares. Notice, in passing, that the three-parameter model does lead to a somewhat greater (though still hardly significant) improvement in fit over the model which includes only environmental factors within and between families (E_1, E_2). Such an improvement may give some weight to the inclusion of genetical factors in the model but is unlikely to be very convincing, especially when we remember that the fit of the three-parameter model is still far from adequate.

The effect of assortative mating

The coefficients applied in the above genetical models assumed that mating is random for the determinants of the trait in question. If this were not the case, and there were to be some degree of genetical similarity between spouses as a result of assortative mating, there would be a tendency for alleles of like effect to become associated in families, leading to an increase in the additive genetic variance in the population. The effect of such association on the components of variance in siblings and twins is the same. In both cases the additional genetic variance due to assortative mating, to a very good approximation for a polygenic trait, affects only the additive component of genetic variance and contributes solely to differences between families of siblings and twins. In the absence of parental data, or of adoption data which would permit the finer resolution of environmental differences between families, the effect of assortative mating on the genetical composition of the population is formally inseparable in twin data from the estimated contribution of the family environment (E_2). This means that our estimate of E_2 in the above analysis will contain any unresolved genetical contribution arising as a result of assortative mating. If E_2 were detected, therefore, we would be unable to decide without additional data whether the effects of the family environment were confounded with those of assortative mating. On the other hand, if we are justified in omitting E_2 from our model, because its inclusion does not improve our ability to predict the observed mean squares, then we are equally justified, within the resolution of our study, in assuming that there are no detectable genetical effects of assortative mating. Of course, both of these conclusions are provisional and bound by the power of the particular study. Hence they may be modified in the light of subsequent data and we might well choose to estimate their contribution in any case if we have prior data suggesting their importance.

The effect of dominance

If there is dominance the genetic similarity between dizygotic twins will be less than half that between identical twins. Inclusion of dominance in the model would yield the expectations in Table 14 on the

TABLE 14

Contributions of additive and dominance genetic effects, and environmental effects within and between families to statistics derived from monozygotic and dizygotic twins in randomly mating populations*

		Statistic	
Twin type	Source	Variance component	Mean square
Monozygotic	Between pairs	$\frac{1}{2}D_R + \frac{1}{4}H_R + E_2$	$D_R + \frac{1}{2}H_R + E_1 + 2E_2$
	Within pairs	E_1	E_1
	Total	$\frac{1}{2}D_R + \frac{1}{4}H_R + E_1 + E_2$	
Dizygotic	Between pairs	$\frac{1}{4}D_R + \frac{1}{16}H_R + E_2$	$\frac{3}{4}D_R + \frac{5}{16}H_R + E_1 + 2E_2$
	Within pairs	$\frac{1}{4}D_R + \frac{3}{16}H_R + E_1$	$\frac{1}{4}D_R + \frac{3}{16}H_R + E_1$
	Total	$\frac{1}{2}D_R + \frac{1}{4}H_R + E_1 + E_2$	

*For parameter definitions, see text.

assumption of random mating. Two things should be noted. Firstly, the coefficients of the dominance parameter (H_R) in the model follow very closely those of D_R, the additive genetic variance. This means that the separation of additive and dominance variation in data of this type is very difficult since any tendency to over-estimate the contribution of additive factors by chance will lead to an almost exactly opposite tendency to under-estimate the contribution of dominance and vice versa. Martin et al. (1978) have shown further that the power of the test of even complete dominance, especially when this has no directional component, is likely to be very small in data of this kind. Secondly, it can be verified that, in the presence of family environmental effects and given that we have only data on twins reared together, there is no way in which we can estimate all four parameters, D_R, E_1, E_2 and H_R. In order to obtain any estimates of three of these four parameters the fourth has to be assumed arbitrarily to be zero. Such an assumption is untestable with these data, although it can be tested (and will be tested subsequently) with data on more extensive relationships. This means that no goodness-of-fit test nor comparison of likelihoods can ever distinguish between the adequacy of the D_R, H_R, E_1 model and that of the D_R, E_1, E_2 model, since both will yield equally likely solutions. Thus, although the test of the model may lead us to reject the simpler two-parameter models, it will not suggest directly which of the two three-parameter alternatives is the most viable. A consequence of this inability to separate the parameters of a more complex model is the fact that certain sets of parameter values might mimic those of a simpler model. Since E_2 tends to increase the similarity between siblings and dizygotic twins, whereas dominance tends to reduce their similarity, the two factors make opposing contributions to the variation. Indeed, it can be shown (Eaves, 1970) that if the contribution of the family environment to the variation is equal to one half of the total dominance variation, then the data will simulate precisely the effects to be expected in the presence of additive genetical effects in the absence of E_2 and dominance.

It is, however, instructive to obtain estimates of the parameters of the D_R, H_R, E_1 model since any very marked genetical non-additivity, including dominance, may still yield positive and significant values for H_R. In the event of there being significant E_2, however, fitting the D_R, H_R, E_1 model will frequently yield significant negative values of the dominance parameter. Thus, although the goodness-of-fit test cannot provide any basis for deciding between models involving dominance and those involving E_2, the actual values of the parameter estimates obtained for these models may lead to the exclusion of one of the alternatives because certain of the parameters (usually E_2 or H_R) take nonsense values.

Maximum likelihood estimates of D_R, H_R and E_1 are

$$\hat{D}_R = 6.16$$
$$\hat{H}_R = -4.88$$
$$\hat{E}_1 = 0.61$$

We have already seen how the introduction of the third parameter does not increase the likelihood to any significant degree and we can see that the estimate of H_R is numerically negative, confirming that the model involving dominance indeed yields nonsense values, and should be discounted on both biological and statistical grounds. This does not, of course, mean that dominance does not exist, merely that its contribution is too small to be detected and at the very least its effect is obscured by that of the family environment. Data on other types of relative will enable us to test this view more thoroughly.

In none of the cases so far have we cited standard errors for the parameters. So far we have not found a satisfactory model. This means that we cannot be sufficiently confident of our parameters to set viable limits to their magnitude. Indeed, if we were to compute standard errors, taking into account our uncertainty about the model which should be fitted at this stage, they would be very large.

Testing for the presence of sex interactions in gene expression

So far we have established that models which assume a common causal basis for variation in subjects' reported age of first smoking in the two sexes do not give a very satisfactory fit to the available twin data. We already know that males are more variable than females, and we would expect this fact to be reflected in the adequacy of our existing models. We now turn to modifications of the genotype-environmental models which take account of the possibility that the expression of genetical and environmental factors may depend significantly on sex.

We consider firstly a modification of our simple D_R, E_1 model to allow for the possibility that the magnitude of the effects of the genes depends on sex. Just as before, we defined the additive effects of a single locus as d_a, so now we let the increasing effect of the homozygote be d_{am} in males and d_{af} in females. Just as the additive genetical component, D_R, was defined in terms of the gene frequencies

TABLE 15

Additive model for male and female twin pairs, allowing for
dependence of causes of variation on sex

Twin type	Mean square	Expected mean square							
		E_{1m}	E_{1f}	D_{Rm}	D_{Rf}	D_{Rmf}	E_{2m}	E_{2f}	E_{2mf}
MZ_m	Between pairs	1	.	1	.	.	2	.	.
	Within pairs	1	.	.	.	.	.	.	.
MZ_f	Between pairs	.	1	.	1	.	.	2	.
	Within pairs	.	1	.	.	.	.	.	.
DZ_m	Between pairs	1	.	$\frac{3}{4}$	.	.	2	.	.
	Within pairs	1	.	$\frac{1}{4}$	.	.	.	.	.
DZ_f	Between pairs	.	1	.	$\frac{3}{4}$	.	.	2	.
	Within pairs	.	1	.	$\frac{1}{4}$	.	.	.	.
DZ_{mf}	Between pairs	$\frac{1}{2}$	$\frac{1}{2}$	$\frac{1}{4}$	$\frac{1}{4}$	$\frac{1}{4}$	$\frac{1}{2}$	$\frac{1}{2}$	1
	Within pairs	$\frac{1}{2}$	$\frac{1}{2}$	$\frac{1}{4}$	$\frac{1}{4}$	$\frac{1}{4}$	$\frac{1}{2}$	$\frac{1}{2}$	1

N.B. In the complete medel $\frac{1}{4}D_{Rmf}$ and E_{2mf} are completely
　　confounded

and gene effects, so we may define D_{Rm} and D_{Rf} to represent the
contribution of the gene effects to variation in males and females
respectively. The magnitude of D_{Rm} and D_{Rf} will only be the same
if the genes affecting the trait each have the same effect in the two
sexes. Otherwise there will be a difference in scale between the sexes
reflected in a difference in variance. Provided our analysis is restricted
to pairs of the same sex (i.e. if we omit male-female DZ pairs from
the analysis) then separate estimates of D_R for males and females
can be obtained and the results for the two sexes compared. There are
now only eight statistics. The model for like-sex twins is given in Table
15. It can be seen that the expectations of the mean squares for like-
sex twins are identical to those generated under the D_R, E_1 model
in which it is assumed that there are no sex interactions. We may
estimate the parameters of the D_R, E_1 model for the eight statistics
using maximum likelihood and we find that the likelihood ratio testing
the goodness of fit gives

$$\chi_6^2 = 16.60 \ (0.01 <p< 0.02)$$

Parameter estimates are:

$$\hat{D}_R = 2.38$$
$$\hat{E}_1 = 3.76$$

However, if we fit separate D_R additive genetical parameters to males and females (whilst keeping E_1 constant over sexes), thereby increasing the number of parameters by one, we obtain a chi-square of 13.04 for 5df $(0.02 < P < 0.05)$ which represents a reduction of 3.56 for 1df. This is barely significant, suggesting that some slight improvement might be achieved by allowing for sex differences in gene expression. Allowing for sex differences in E_1, however, led to a substantial improvement in fit, the addition of the extra parameter leading to a further reduction of 6.05 units in chi-square to $\chi^2_4 = 6.99$ $(.10 < P < 20)$ suggesting that credibility would be unduly stretched by the addition of further parameters.

The parameter estimates are now:

$$\hat{D}_{Rm} = 4.12 \pm 1.10$$
$$\hat{D}_{Rf} = 3.65 \pm 0.49$$
$$\hat{E}_{1m} = 3.13 \pm 0.46$$
$$\hat{E}_{1f} = 2.11 \pm 0.18$$

they show that the greater variance of female twins is due to more marked expression of both genetic and environmental factors.

This analysis has excluded unlike-sex pairs, because this is the procedure common in many twin analyses. Analysis of the like-sex twins may well detect differences in the *scale* of gene effects between males and females, but this is only part of the story. There is no particular reason why the trait that is being measured should represent the effects of the same genes in males and females. The estimate of D_R obtained for males would reflect the expression of quite different genes from those contributing to variation in females. We would, for example, be surprised if the genes contributing to variation in chest measurement in males were wholly the same as those contributing to the same measurement in females! The same could well be true of the smoking habit. The analysis of like-sex pairs, however, provides no indication of such sex-specific gene effects. For this reason, the pairs of unlike sex, which are so often excluded from twin analyses because of a desire to achieve uniformity of conditions, are so critical in testing the hypothesis which has to be assumed by default if the study consists only of like-sex twins.

We may extend our model for additive gene effects to consider their contribution to the similarity of unlike-sex DZ pairs as measured by their covariance. To simplify the algebra we assume the increasing and decreasing alleles are equally frequent, but this is not necessary for a more general treatment. The frequencies of the different types of DZ pairs for an autosomal locus have already been given (Table 13). These frequencies apply whatever the sex of the pair members and can be used, in conjunction with the gene effects in the basic model, to obtain the expected variances and covariances for unlike-sex twin pairs.

Multiplying the frequency of each type of pair by the product of the gene effects in the two sexes we obtain for the covariance:

$$C_{DZmf} = \tfrac{1}{4} \, d_{am} \, d_{af}$$

Relaxing the constraint that the allele effects should be equal simply redefines the parameter as follows:

$$C_{DZmf} = u_a \, v_a \, d_{am} \, d_{af}$$

Summing over the effects of man independent and additive loci we obtain:

$$C_{DZmf} = \tfrac{1}{4} D_{Rmf} = \sum_a u_a \, v_a \, d_{am} \, d_{af}$$

Similar definitions analogous to those above for D_R and H_R could be obtained for the situation in which there are dominance deviations. The critical point is that D_{Rmf} reflects the contribution of the products of male and female gene effects. It will only be positive if there is any net consistency of gene action between the sexes, that is, if the genes increasing trait expression in males also increase it in females. There could just as well be a net negative covariance between gene effects in males and females, or a zero covariance if the gene effects are not consistent in their direction over the two sexes or if a large proportion of the loci contributing to variation in one sex are not being expressed in the other. Thus, even though we may find significant similarity between like-sex pairs, the inclusion of pairs of unlike sex provides a critical test of the consistency of gene action over the two sexes.

To the expectations of mean squares for the like-sex twins may now be added the expected mean squares for the unlike-sex pairs (Table 15). These expectations assume that the mean effect of sexes has been extracted from the within-pair mean square for male–female pairs. This was not done, in fact, in Langford's summary of the data, but a correction will be made for the overall sex difference in a subsequent analysis.

The mean square between unlike DZ pairs is expected to be:

$$\tfrac{1}{4} D_{Rm} + \tfrac{1}{4} D_{Rf} + \tfrac{1}{4} D_{Rmf} + E_{1m} + E_{1f}$$

and that within pairs:

$$\tfrac{1}{4} D_{Rm} + \tfrac{1}{4} D_{Rf} - \tfrac{1}{4} D_{Rmf} + E_{1m} + E_{1f}$$

The covariance between the effects of loci in males and females can be rescaled thus:

$$r_{gmf} = D_{Rmf} \, / \, (D_{Rm} \, D_{Rf})^{\tfrac{1}{2}}$$

to yield the correlation between gene effects across sexes. This may be considered as a rough guide to the proportion of loci whose effects are common to both sexes. We should remember, also, that a zero correlation *could* result if all the loci were in fact contributing in an inconsistent way to variation in both sexes since the covariance is the sum of products of the effects of loci. Some of these may have increasing effects in both sexes whilst others may have increasing effects in one sex and decreasing effects in the other.

Assuming that the within-family environmental variation (E_1) is consistent over sexes, the model now has four parameters, E_1, D_{Rm}, D_{Rf} and D_{Rmf}, in the absence of family environmental effects and dominance. Maximum likelihood estimates of the parameters are:

$$\hat{D}_{Rm} = 5.26; \ \hat{D}_{Rf} = 3.33; \ \hat{D}_{Rmf} = 2.10; \ \hat{E}_1 = 2.40$$

and the likelihood ratio test of the goodness of fit gives $\chi^2_6 = 13.7$ ($2\% < P < 5\%$). The fit of this model is still not excellent, but shows a marginally significant improvement over the model which assumes gene action is consistent over sexes ($\chi^2_2 = 5.26 \ 5\% < P < 10\%$).

Allowing for different values of E_1 in males and females gives:

$$D_{Rm} = 4.28 \pm 1.09; \ D_{Rf} = 3.69 \pm 0.05; \ D_{Rmf} \ 2.17 \pm 2.40$$
$$E_{1m} = 3.17 \pm 0.05; \ E_{1f} = 2.12 \pm 0.02$$

The goodness of fit $\chi^2_5 = 7.42$ ($10\% < P < 20\%$) so there is no suggestion that the observed mean squares differ significantly from those predicted from the model. The covariance matrix of the estimates is obtained as the inverse of the matrix of second derivatives of the log-likelihood with respect to the parameters of the model. The square roots of the diagonal elements of the covariance matrix yield the standard errors.

Comparing the fit of this model with that of a reduced model which assumes equal environmental effects for males and females reveals that the latter is significantly poorer ($x_1^2 = 6.28$, $1\% < P < 2\%$) confirming that the assumption of equal environmental variances is not justified. Furthermore, the fit of the model which assumes equal genetic and environmental variances in the two sexes is even more significantly worse ($x_3^2 = 11.54$, $P < 1\%$) suggesting that the assumptions of equal environmental effects and equal genetical effects are both clearly violated by the observations.

On the basis of the estimates of the genetical parameters we may calculate the correlation between the effects of genes in males and females, giving a measure of the common determination of the age of onset of smoking in the two sexes. We find this correlation to be:

$$r_{gmf} = 2.17 / \sqrt{4.28 \times 3.69} = 0.55$$

suggesting that there is substantial specificity of gene action, though perhaps insufficient to make r_{gmf} significantly different from unity. Since this particular model assumes no common environmental effects there is, by definition, no environmental correlation between male and female siblings. Given the parameters of this model, we may obtain other statistics to summarize the variation for the trait measured on this particular scale. For each sex we may obtain, for example, the best estimate of the proportion of the total variation which is due to the additive effects of genes.

For males we have:

$$h^2 = 0.40$$

and for females:

$$h^2 = 0.47$$

Thus there is little reason to regard the genetic determination of the trait in males as substantially different in magnitude from that in females, although the correlation between the gene effects in the two sexes (0.55) does leave some room for speculation that different loci may be contributing to variation in each sex.

Although the twin data are consistent with these findings, and although we have shown several explanations with which the data are quite clearly inconsistent, we turn finally to consider whether the data might be explained equally well, if not better, by a non-genetic model if allowance is made for the possibility that environmental factors depend on sex.

We thus fit an environmental analogue of the above model which includes the effects of the family environment but which allows the E_2 to differ between sexes and which, furthermore, does not constrain to unity the correlation between the family environments of dizygotic pairs of unlike sex. The model resembles that given in Table 13 deleting the genetic parameters, and allows different values for the within-family environmental variance, since we have already shown this is needed to explain anomalies in the given mean squares. The likelihood ratio test shows that this model fits very well $\chi^2_5 = 5.31$ (indeed somewhat better than the genotype-environmental model considered above). It represents a slight but significant improvement over a model which forces the E_1's to be identical for males and females ($\chi^2_1 = 5.03$ 2% < P < 5%) but a most substantial gain over the E_1, E_2 model which assumes the same values for both parameters in both sexes ($\chi^2_3 = 16.51$ P < 0.1%)

We have deliberately pursued this illustrative analysis at length to introduce the rationale by which at least some explanations of the variation in a trait might be excluded even with twin data. The results of the model-fitting analysis are summarized in Table 16 which gives the values of the chi-squares obtained for likelihood ratio tests of the competing hypotheses considered above. Each model is compared with the 'perfect fit' solution, which represents the hypothesis that a separate parameter needs to be invoked for every mean square, and with a variety of reduced alternatives. From the results it is possible to summarize the findings in which we can have reasonable confidence.

1. There is clearly variation in the age of onset of smoking which depends on factors other than the unique environmental experiences to which individuals are exposed by chance. This finding follows from the significance of the between-family components of variance and can be inferred from the original analyses of variance, but is confirmed still more powerfully by the failure of the E_2 model to explain the full pattern of the mean squares when these are considered jointly.

2. There are sex differences in either the causes of variation or the magnitudes of their effects, when the age of onset of smoking is measured on the given scale. This could be inferred at the outset from the difference in variance between the sexes, but is confirmed more powerfully by the joint analysis of the mean squares since none of the models which assume equal genetic and environmental parameters for males and females are capable of explaining the observations satisfactorily.

TABLE 16

Comparison of alternative hypotheses for variation in age of onset of smoking in twins (raw scores)

Model		E_1	$E_1 D_R$	$E_1 E_2$	$E_1 E_2 D_R$	$E_1 D_{Rm}\ D_{Rf}\ D_{Rmf}$	$E_1 E_{2m}\ E_{2f}\ E_{2mf}$	'perfect fit'
E_1	χ^2	—	79.06	76.20	80.28	84.32	87.68	98.02
	df	—	1	1	2	3	3	9
	P%	—	<0.1	<0.1	<0.1	<0.1	<0.1	<0.1
$E_1 D_R$	χ^2	79.06	—	—	1.22	5.26	—	18.96
	df	1	—	—	1	2	—	8
	P%	< 0.1	—	—	20-30	5-10	—	1-2
$E_1 E_2$	χ^2	76.20	—	—	4.08	—	11.48	21.82
	df	1	—	—	1	—	2	8
	P%	< 0.1	—	—	2-5	—	<1	<1
$E_{1m} E_{1f}$ $D_{Rm} D_{Rf}$ D_{Rmf}	χ^2	90.6	11.54	1	—	6.28	—	7.42
	df	4	3	—	—	1	—	5
	P%	< 0.1	<1	—	—	1-2	—	10-20
$E_{1m} E_{1f}$ $E_{2m} E_{2f}$ E_{2mf}	χ^2	92.71	—	16.51	—	—	5.03	5.31
	df	5	—	3	—	—	1	5
	P%	< 0.1	—	<0.1	—	—	2-5	30-50
'perfect fit'	χ^2	98.02	18.96	21.82	17.74	13.70	10.34	—
	df	9	8	8	7	6	6	—
	P%	< 0.1	1-2	<1	1-2*	2-5	10-20	—

3. Some of the sex differences in variance can be attributed to the difference in within-family environmental variance for males and females, that within male twinships being about 50% greater than that within female twinships. The difference in E_1 components could be seen at the start because the variance within monozygotic male twin pairs exceeds that within female pairs. The finding is confirmed by model-fitting since models which assume equality of the E_1's are shown to be significantly less likely to yield the observed mean squares than those in which this assumption is relaxed.

Beyond this, however, the findings are more ambiguous. There is evidence that the mechanism of sex dependence in the components of variance involves other determinants of variation apart from the within-family environmental factors since mechanisms which assume no such dependence are significantly less likely to generate the data. At no point, however, are genotype-environmental models clearly superior in their predictive validity to environmental models of equivalent complexity when allowance is made for the interaction of the causes of variation with sex. Indeed, such unconvincing evidence as the twin data provide suggest that a straightforward interpretation in terms of the experiences specific to individual twins of a pair and shared by members of the same pair may be sufficient to explain our twin data. Returning to the original mean squares gives little reason to doubt this model for the onset of smoking since there is no obvious excess of variation within like-sex dizygotic pairs compared with that within monozygotic pairs. Thus it seems that one of the principal indicators of the effects of genetical segregation is absent from the data. Our twin data, then, leave us in a somewhat agnostic position about the causes of onset of smoking. There is little reason on internal evidence to prefer a partly genetic to a purely environmental interpretation, although identical twins show a slightly higher correlation than non-identical twins.

With the chosen scale of measurement, therefore, there is little to choose between explanations of twin similarity in the age at which smoking begins in terms of environmental factors (possibly the influence of peers) and those based on genetical factors.

Variation in reported average consumption in twins

Application of the same form of analysis to the mean squares for the amount of cigarette smoking reported by the twins reveals a pattern of determination broadly similar to that shown by the age of onset data. For the raw responses no model which assumes consistency of genetic or environmental factors across sexes comes anywhere near offering a satisfactory fit of the observed mean squares. The results of model-fitting are summarized in Table 17. Only two of the models fitted yield parameter values which could predict the data at all precisely, namely the two five-parameter models which include sex differences in the within-family environmental component in addition to either sex-dependent genetical effects or familial environmental effects which depend on sex. Of the two, the genotype-environmental model gives a somewhat more likely solution, but the difference is too small to

TABLE 17

Comparison of alternative hypotheses for variation in amount of cigarette smoking in twins (raw scores)

Model		E_1	E_1D_R	E_1E_2	$E_1E_2D_R$	$E_1D_{Rm}\ D_{Rf}\ D_{rmf}$	$E_1E_{2m}\ E_{2f}\ E_{2mf}$	'perfect fit'
E_1	x^2	—	128.2	111.9	128.2	134.7	121.81	158.5
	df	—	1	1	2	3	3	9
	P	—	<0.1	<0.1	<0.1	<0.1	<0.1	<0.1
E_1D_R	x^2	128.2	—	—	0.01	6.44	—	30.27
	df	1	—	—	1	2	—	8
	P	<0.1	—	—	>90	2-5	—	<0.1
E_1E_2	x^2	119.9	—	—	16.32	—	9.89	45.58
	df	1	—	—	1	—	2	8
	P	<0.1	—	—	<0.1	—	1-2	<1
$E_{1m}E_{1f}$ $D_{Rm}D_{Rf}$ D_{Rmf}	x^2	153.0	—	—	—	18.37	—	5.46
	df	4	—	—	—	1	—	5
	P	<0.1	—	—	—	<0.1	—	30·50
$E_{1m}E_{1f}$ $E_{2m}E_{2f}$ E_{2mf}	x^2	150.5	—	38.60	—	—	28.71	7.98
	df	4	—	3	—	—	1	5
	P	<0.1	—	<0.1	—	—	<0.1	10·20
'perfect fit'	x^2	158.5	30.27	46.58	30.26	23.83	36.69	—
	df	9	8	8	7	6	6	—
	P	0.1	0.1	<0.1	0.1	0.1	0.1	—

be considered reliable. If we concede that partial genetic determination is more likely, then the data are consistent with a heritability of 0.42 for males and 0.60 for females, the parameter values in Table 18 having been used for the calculation. The parameters of the genotype-environmental model imply a correlation of 0.69 between the effects of the genes in males and females and a correlation of 0.41 between the family environments of males and females if the alternative model is accepted as the basis for study. On the basis of the genetic model, therefore, we would argue that the causes of variation are quite consistent across sexes in their effects. The alternative hypothesis, however, suggests that the environmental influences leading to intrapair similarity in males must be different from those making female twins alike in their tobacco consumption.

TABLE 18

Average reported cigarette consumption: parameter estimates under alternative assumptions for variation in raw scores

| Parameter | Estimate | |
	Model I	Model II
D_{Rm}	4.85 ± 1.20	—
D_{Rf}	4.92 ± 0.52	—
D_{Rmf}	3.35 ± 2.53	—
E_{1m}	3.38 ± 0.49	3.99 ± 0.49
E_{1f}	1.66 ± 0.15	1.90 ± 0.14
E_{2m}	—	1.81 ± 0.52
E_{2f}	—	2.27 ± 0.25
E_{2mf}	—	0.84 ± 0.63
χ_5^2	5.46	7.98
P%	30-50	10-20

The effects of changing the scale.

The questionnaire method imposes many arbitrary constraints upon subjects' responses which seem to have little to do with the nature of the variation which, we suppose, may be expected to underlie them. This arbitrariness is reflected in the crude weights assigned to the responses given in reply to the questions concerning the age of onset of smoking and the average consumption of tobacco. It is worth considering, firstly, what changes, if any, are produced in our models for variation if we modify the scale of measurement to reflect more realistically the properties of a multifactorial mechanism for the traits underlying the observed response categories.

One simple method of rescaling the responses is to assume that there is a continuous normal scale of onset or consumption upon which the observed response categories are arbitrarily superimposed. Thus, for example, we imagine the categories of age of onset are approximately an ordered set superimposed upon a continuous variable (see Figure 15) with zero mean and unit variance. The boundaries between the categories, in terms of the continuous metric, will simply be the upper limits, z_i of the normal probability integrals which satisfy:

$$\int_{-\infty}^{z_i} \phi(x)\, dx = \sum_{j=1}^{j=i} p_j \text{ where } \phi(x) \text{ is the normal p. d. f.}$$

p_j is the proportion of individuals endorsing the jth response category. For a given set of p's, therefore, the z_i can be obtained from tables of the normal probability integral by finding the deviate which yields the corresponding cumulative probability of endorsement.

Having defined the category boundaries, the corresponding weight for subjects in a given category is the mean normal score of individuals whose scores would lead them to be classified in that category. Thus, the weight given to all individuals in class j (Figure 15) is:

$$\frac{1}{p_j} \int_{z_{j-1}}^{z_j} x\, \phi(x)\, dx$$

In view of the known differences in scale between males and females in the sample, the data for this study were standardized separately for males and females. The pooled frequencies of individuals in the categories, based on all twins of the same sex, were used to generate the category weights. Thus, although the data have been standardized by sex they have not been standardized by zygosity. Clearly, the application of a transformation of the normal type to twin data (where the members of a pair are independent) and to data where an independent variable such as age may be contributing to the variation is at best only an approximation. In conducting the transformation Langford assumed an underlying distribution with a standard deviation of 15. No correction was made for the small number of categories employed, so the observed total variance of the transformed scores is somewhat less than the 225 which would apply if a large number of subdivisions were included in the responses. The same type of transformation was employed for the age of onset and for the reported average consumption of cigarettes.

The twin mean squares for both sets of transformed scores are given in Table 19. The transformation should have removed the additional source of variation within unlike-sex dizygotic pairs because each sex was scaled around its own mean.

As we might expect, the results of the model-fitting analysis are much simpler for the transformed scores because one major source of complexity, the sex differences in variability, has been removed by the transformation. Considering first the results for the normalized and standardized scores for the age of onset of smoking we find

Figure 15: Parameters of the continuous metric model for response categories

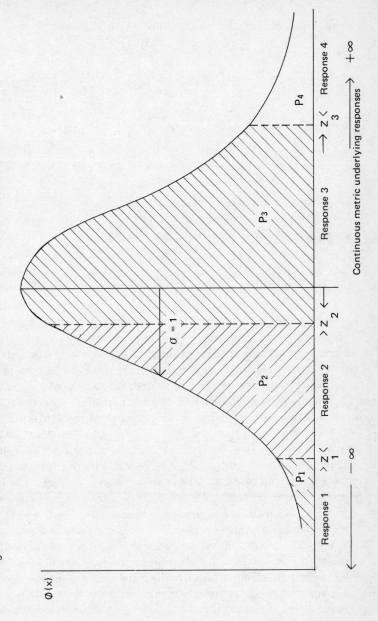

TABLE 19

Mean squares for normalized and standardized twin data (Langford)

Twin type	Item	d.f.	Mean square	
			Age of onset	Average consumption
MZ Female	Between pairs	235	255.64	265.09
	Within pairs	236	104.39	76.13
MZ Male	Between pairs	79	269.75	274.42
	Within pairs	80	123.21	109.51
DZ Female	Between pairs	120	238.14	241.38
	Within pairs	121	140.27	94.45
DZ Male	Between pairs	49	252.08	182.13
	Within pairs	50	109.46	157.02
DZ Male-female	Between pairs	57	254.88	200.51
	Within pairs	58	170.92	134.48

(Table 20) significant variation which cannot be attributed simply to chance environmental experiences (E_1). There are either cultural influences governing the age of onset (E_2 effects) or genetical influences. As is expected, allowing any of the causes of variation to depend on sex leads to very little improvement in the fit of any model. Thus, no environmental model fits significantly better than the original E_1, E_2 model and none of the genetical models tested fits any better than the D_R, E_1 model. There is one important pay-off in this finding since we can now conclude with reasonable confidence that there is no real reason to adopt the view that there are sex-specific effects in the determination of the age of onset. It seems that the correlation between genetical effects can be assumed to be unity since attempting to subdivide D_R into its components D_{Rm}, D_{Rf} and D_{Rmf} does not lead to any improvement, nor does the corresponding subdivision of E_2 achieve any significant change in fit. We would thus conclude that virtually all the apparent sex interaction found for the raw scores is a simple feature of the chosen scale of measurement; the same factors are apparently operating in both sexes but their scale of effect is greater in males than in females on the raw scale.

Do the results provide any further basis for preferring an envi-

TABLE 20

Comparison of alternative hypotheses for normalized and standardized age of onset of smoking in twins

Model		E_1	$E_1 D_R$	$E_1 E_2$	$E_1 E_2 D_R D_{Rf}$	$E_1 D_{Rm} D_{Rf} D_{Rmf}$	$E_1 E_{2m} E_{2f} E_{2mf}$	'perfect fit'
E_1	x^2	—	73.57	69.96	74.34	73.77	73.36	78.29
	df	—	1	1	2	3	3	9
	P%	—	<0.1	<0.1	<0.1	<0.1	<0.1	<0.1
$E_1 D_R$	x^2	73.57	—	—	0.77	0.20	—	4.72
	df	1	—	—	1	2	—	8
	P%	0.1	—	—	30-50	>90	—	50-70
$E_1 E_2$	x^2	69.96	—	—	4.38	—	3.40	8.33
	df	1	—	—	1	—	2	8
	P%	<0.1	—	—	2-5	—	10-20	30-50
$E_{1m} E_{1f} D_{Rm} D_{Rf} D_{Rmf}$	x^2	74.10	0.53	—	—	0.33	—	4.19
	df	4	3	—	—	1	—	5
	P%	<0.1	>90	—	—	50-70	—	50-70
$E_{1m} E_{1f} E_{2m} E_{2f} E_{2mf}$	x^2	73.36	—	3.43	—	—	0.02	4.91
	df	4	—	3	—	—	1	5
	P%	<0.01	—	30-50	—	—	80-90	30-50
'perfect fit'	x^2	78.29	4.72	8.33	3.95	4.52	4.93	—
	df	9	8	8	7	6	6	—
	P%	<0.1	50-70	30-50	70-80	50-70	50-70	—

ronmental model to one involving both genetical and environmental factors? The short answer is 'not much'. Although the D_R, E_1 model is somewhat more likely than the E_1, E_2 model there is no great reason to reject either. The D_R, E_1, E_2 model fits no better ($x_1^2 = 0.77$, $30\% < P < 50\%$) than the D_R, E_1 model, and scarcely better ($x_1^2 = 4.38$, $2\% < P < 5\%$) than the E_1, E_2 model. It would be foolish to base any decision on such unimpressive changes in fit. We must therefore retain the broad conclusions of the original analysis. Similarities in the age of onset of smoking in twins could almost as well be explained by the effects of the shared environment as by the effects of genetical segregation. The results do, however, strengthen our conviction that the same underlying causes of variation operate in both sexes when allowance is made for the scale of their effects.

Turning lastly to the analysis of cigarette consumption we find (Table 21) that the balance of evidence weighs more heavily in the direction of genetic determination superimposed upon variation due to chance and individual environmental experiences. As in every previous analysis we find that the E_1 model comes nowhere near explaining the observations but that marked improvement in fit is found with the inclusion of additional parameters. In this case, however, the fit of the E_1, E_2 model is far from adequate ($\chi^2_8 = 21.59$, P<1%) although the E_1, D_R model yields maximum likelihood parameter estimates which are able to predict the observed pattern of mean squares quite acceptably.

The three-parameter model including specific and family environmental effects (E_1 and E_2) in addition to the additive effects of genes is in no way superior to the simple D_R, E_1 model ($\chi^2_1 = 0.56$; 30% <P< 50%) whilst it is very substantially superior ($\chi^2_1 = 10.01$, P<1%) to the alternative E_1, E_2 model. The model fitting gives some weight, therefore, to the view that a model excluding the family environment is more likely to yield the given mean squares than a model excluding genetical factors. There remains, even in the standardized data for cigarette consumption, some evidence of sex differences in the magnitude of the within-families environmental components since models which permit this difference tend to fit somewhat better (at the 1-2% level) than models which do not. Any improvement due to relaxing similar constraints on the values of D_R or E_2, however, is too slight to be considered at all seriously. In Table 22 we summarize the results of fitting the basic models to the normalized data for the age at which smoking commences and for the average reported daily consumption of cigarettes. The results for three models are presented so that the reader can judge for himself the consequences of omitting either the additive genetic component (D_R) or the between-families environmental component (E_2) from the model. The actual parameter values are quoted, with their standard errors obtained from the covariance matrix of the estimates. In addition we give the proportional contribution of each hypothesized source to the total variation in the trait. Although we estimate D_R to represent the additive genetical component, its contribution to the total variation is actually only $\frac{1}{2}D_R$. Readers better acquainted with the notation of the Edinburgh school (Falconer, 1964) will recognize that V_A in Falconer's

Comparison of alternative models for variation in normalized and standardized amount of cigarette smoking

Model		E_1	$E_1 D_R$	$E_1 E_2$	$E_1 E_2 D_R$	$E_1 D_{Rm}$ D_{Rf} D_{Rmf}	$E_1 E_{2m}$ E_{2f} E_{2mf}	'perfect fit'
E_1	x^2	—	119.8	110.31	120.32	120.0	115.34	131.9
	df	—	1	1	2	3	3	9
	P%	—	<0.1	<0.1	<0.1	<0.1	<0.1	<0.1
$E_1 D_R$	x^2	119.8	—	—	0.56	0.24	—	12.14
	df	1	1	—	1	2	—	8
	P%	<0.1	—	—	30-50	80-90	—	10-20
$E_1 E_2$	x^2	110.31	—	—	10.01	—	5.03	21.59
	df	1	—	—	1	—	2	8
	P%	<0.1	—	—	<1	—	5-10	<1
$E_{1m} E_{1f}$ $D_{Rm} D_{Rf}$ D_{Rmf}	x^2	126.34	6.58	—	—	6.31	—	5.56
	df	4	3	—	—	1	—	5
	P%	<0.1	5-10	—	—	1-2	—	30-50
$E_{1m} E_{1f}$ $E_{2m} E_{2f}$ E_{2mf}	x^2	125.03	—	14.72	—	—	9.69	6.87
	df	4	—	3	—	—	1	5
	P%	<0.1	—	<1	—	—	<1	20-30
'perfect fit'	x^2	131.9	12.14	21.59	11.58	11.90	16.56	—
	df	9	8	8	7	6	6	—
	P%	<0.1	10-20	<1	10-20	5-10	1-2	—

TABLE 22

Estimated parameter values under most likely simple hypotheses for variation in reported age of commencement of smoking and reported average daily cigarette consumption (normalized and standardized scores)

Parameter	Age of onset			Average consumption		
Model	$D_R E_1$	$E_1 E_2$	$D_R E_1 E_2$	D_R, E_1	E_1, E_2	$D_R E_1 E_2$
$\hat{D}_R \pm$ s.e.	160 ± 20	—	114 ± 56	179 ± 18	—	145 ± 48
$\hat{E}_1 \pm$ s.e.	108 ± 8	123 ± 7	110 ± 8	83 ± 6	99 ± 6	84 ± 4
$\hat{E}_2 \pm$ s.e.	—	65 ± 9	21 ± 24	—	74 ± 8	16 ± 21
χ^2	4.72	8.34	3.95	12.14	21.59	11.58
df	8	8	7	8	8	7
P						
$\frac{1}{2}\hat{D}_R$ %	43	—	30	52	—	42
$\hat{E}_1$ %	57	65	59	48	57	48
$\hat{E}_2$ %	—	35	11	—	43	10
$\frac{1}{2}\hat{D}_R + \hat{E}_1 + \hat{E}_2$	188	188	188	172	173	173

notation is exactly the same as $\frac{1}{2}D_R$ in the notation of the Biometrical Genetical school which is adopted in this treatment.

Considering the age of onset first, the major contribution to the observed variation comes from the individual's unique environmental experiences which are reflected in E_1. Approximately 60 per cent of the variation arises from this source and this estimate is fairly stable over different models. The reason for this stability is that E_1 is estimated directly and powerfully from the intrapair variation for monozygotic twins. It is a feature of the twin design that by far the greater part of the experimental effort is devoted to the estimation of what, for many purposes, might be construed as 'noise'. Of course, any unreliability of measurement will generally tend to inflate the estimate of E_1 but taken at its face value the substantial within-family environmental component suggests that chance rather than any particular developmental or social factors plays the greater role in deciding when people begin to smoke. When allowance is made for the possible contribution of the family environment (as in fitting the three-parameter model) it is estimated that about 30 per cent of the variance in the age of onset may be attributable to the additive effects of genes segregating in the population, though it will be noted that D_R is known with nothing like the precision of E_1. The relatively slight involvement of hereditary factors suggests that further detailed understanding of the genetics of smoking may require additional refinement of measurement or further speculation about the physiological processes involved in the acquisition of this form of behaviour. The estimate of the family environmental contribution will be an underestimate if there is much genetical non-additivity, since the estimate of E_2 is actually $E_2 - \frac{1}{8}H_R$ in the presence of undetected dominance (Eaves, 1970). Taking it at its face value, however, suggests that only about 11 per cent of the total variation in the age of onset of smoking can be attributed to the shared environment of twins. This implies that the influence of parents and peers is not tending to encourage or discourage smoking in any systematic or substantial way amongst the twins in the sample. Even if we are prepared to discount genetical factors entirely, a view which is at least defensible in the light of the adequacy of the E_1, E_2 model, we should notice that such cultural factors, along with other features of the shared environment of twins, can at the very most contribute only 35 per cent to the total variation in the age of onset of smoking. The message then seems fairly clear that attempts to generalize from properties of family and social groups rather than their individual members and their unique environment is not very likely to be a productive strategy in understanding why people begin to smoke when they do.

Turning to subjects' reported average daily consumption of cigarettes, we see that the discrimination between the two-parameter models is rather easier because of the somewhat lower within-pair environmental component, accounting for nearer 50 per cent than the 60 per cent found for age of onset. As we observed above, the inclusion of the additive genetical component leads to a marked improvement in the ability of the E_1, E_2 model to predict the pattern of variation among the ten mean squares. Considering the three-parameter model in which E_2 takes a positive but statistically not significant value, we find that additive genetical factors contribute an estimated 42 per cent to the observed variation in cigarette consumption. This value is known somewhat more precisely than the corresponding value for age of onset because of the smaller contribution of intrapair environmental factors. The apparently small contribution of the family environment may seem remarkable. Certainly, if twins lived together at the time of testing they might be likely to pool their resources and be uncommonly similar in their smoking habits. Here we have little evidence of such cooperation (or competition) in regard to the available resources of tobacco! It seems again, therefore, for the amount of tobacco consumed as much as for the stage at which smoking begins, that the key to understanding the observed variation lies in the individual, with his unique experiences and his unique genetical make-up, rather than in any generalizations about the features of his social environment.

Do the data justify the chosen scale?

In assigning normal weights to the response categories, two kinds of assumption have been made. First, it has been assumed that the categories form an ordered set. In the case of age onset it is assumed, perhaps with some justification, that the group which starts to smoke very early is closer psychologically and biologically to other relatively early smokers than to those who first smoke late in life, or do not smoke at all. Some weak support for this view is provided for the general linearity of the relationships between smoking and personality to be discussed in Chapter 6. Similarly, it is assumed that very heavy smokers resemble moderate smokers more than they do light smokers or non-smokers. Secondly, it has been assumed that the distribution underlying the observed arbitrary categories is continuous and normal, as might be expected under certain simple hypotheses of multifactorial determination.

As long as the data consist of unrelated individuals we can only test the assumption of order very weakly by reference to other external criteria. Any set of ordered categories can be transformed into a quasi-normal scale by assigning normal weights as we have done. However, once the data consist of relatives it is possible to obtain a test of the internal consistency of the scale of measurement and determine whether the ordering chosen for the categories could reflect the scale on which the primary biological determinants are expressed.

Persistence in the smoking habit

Table 23 presents data which may be used to illustrate the principle. The twins' replies to the questionnaire were grouped into three categories: 'never smoked'; 'used to smoke but doesn't now'; 'still smokes'. The raw data consist of contingency tables containing the numbers of two pairs whose joint responses fall into each of the nine possible categories of response pairs. For example, Table 23 shows that there were six pairs in which the first male MZ twin 'never smokes' and the second twin 'still smokes'.

The model we wish to test assumes that there is an underlying normal distribution of predisposition to smoke which is arbitrarily divided into the three categories, and that the 'used to smoke' category represents intermediate predispositions. The model is thus the same as that shown diagrammatically in Figure 15. However, the responses of twin pairs may be additionally conceived as derived by the arbitrary division of an underlying bivariate normal distribution of twin predispositions correlated to an extent which depends on the relative magnitudes of different causes of variation. Figure 16 presents the problem diagrammatically. Assuming that the continuous scale has zero mean and unit variance, the proportion of twin pairs in which the first and second twins endorse categories i and j respectively is expected to be:

$$P_{ij} = \int_{t_{1i}}^{t_{2i}} \int_{t_{1j}}^{t_{2j}} \phi\,(x, y, \rho)\, dy\,dx \qquad \ldots . (1)$$

where t_{1i} and t_{1j} are the upper and lower thresholds or boundaries between the categories in standard measure and ρ is the correlation between the particular class of twin for the hypothesized underlying

TABLE 23

Contingency tables of twins' responses relating to persistence in smoking

		Observed Twin 2			*Expected* Twin 2		
		Never	*Once*	*Still*	*Never*	*Once*	*Still*
MZ$_{male}$							
	Never	19	7	6	13.8	5.8	4.3
Twin 1	Once	5	7	7	5.8	5.6	7.4
MZ$_{female}$	Still	5	3	21	4.3	7.4	26.6
	Never	67	25	11	65.6	20.3	8.0
Twin 1	Once	14	25	15	20.3	21.6	19.0
	Still	10	11	58	8.0	19.0	54.4
DZ$_{male}$							
	Never	5	3	3	6.4	3.7	4.9
Twin 1	Once	1	3	5	3.7	2.9	5.2
	Still	4	11	15	4.9	5.2	13.3
DZ$_{female}$							
	Never	28	10	9	25.7	11.9	10.5
Twin 1	Once	15	14	13	11.9	8.6	10.7
	Still	7	5	22	10.5	10.7	20.5
DZ$_{male/female}$		*Female twin*			*Female twin*		
Male twin	Never	8	3	11	8.3	5.6	9.2
	Once	3	4	6	4.4	3.6	7.0
	Still	4	6	13	4.7	4.5	10.8

*under hypothesis assuming additive gene action, with sex-dependent thresholds and gene effects.

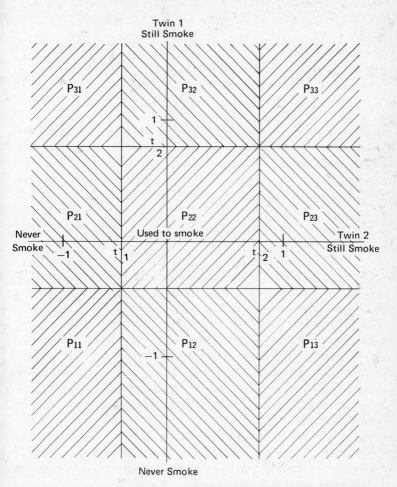

Figure 16: Diagrammatic representation of the threshold model for twin pairs scored on a discontinuous variable with three categories

scale. If the scale were divided into only two categories, this correlation would be termed the 'tetrachoric correlation' (Pearson, 1900), but the conception is more general. ϕ (x, y, ρ) is the standard bivariate normal distribution function for correlation ρ.

Following Tallis (1962), who considered the general problem of estimating correlations for tables like these, we recall that the log-likelihood of obtaining the given contingency table is:

$$L = \sum_{ij} n_{ij} \ln p_{ij} + C \qquad \qquad \dots (2)$$

where p_{ij} is the expected proportion of twin pairs whose joint responses fall into the categories i and j, n_{ij} is the corresponding observed number of pairs in the category.

For a sample consisting of only one type of twin the problem would then reduce to the estimation of those values of t_1 t_2 and ρ which maximize L. The whole point of the twin design, however, is not merely to estimate the correlations but to ask whether these correlations are consistent with a particular underlying causal hypothesis. Thus, the log-likelihoods for each twin group under a given hypothesis may be added and maximized jointly with respect to the thresholds, t_1 and t_2 and the correlations ρ_{MZ} , etc. Under the most restricted model it is assumed that all twin groups have the same threshold values and that the correlations can be simplified, irrespective of sex, such that $\rho_{MZ} = 2\rho_{DZ} = V_A$, where V_A is the proportion of the total variation due to additive genetical differences i.e. $\frac{1}{2}D_R$. The relative contributions of V_A to the MZ and DZ correlations assume random mating. The initial model is identical to that proposed on page 182 for the genetical variation in the age of onset of smoking and the reported consumption of cigarettes. Thus, the simple model for persistence in smoking has three parameters: two thresholds which are assumed to be the same for all types of twin and one parameter to represent the degree of similarity between twins due to the additive genetical components of individual differences.

In order to maximize the likelihood an iterative procedure was adopted in which the expected proportions of twin pairs in each category were obtained by evaluating (1) for given parameter values and substituting the expectations in (2) to obtain the likelihood for these values. Successive improvements in the parameter values were sought, using the first and second derivatives of the likelihood function to indicate the direction of departure from the maximum and the shape of the likelihood surface at a given set of parameter values.

In practice,—L was minimized using a computer programme incorporating the Numerical Algorithms Group subroutine for numerical optimization, E04HAF (Numerical Algorithms Group, 1977), and employing numerical methods to obtain the derivatives. The method selected was based on the Newton–Raphson procedure. For this method to converge reliably, reasonable trial values are required for the parameter estimates. In our experience this becomes more critical as the number of parameters increases. For this model it was sufficient to generate trial values from the contingency table obtained by pooling over all groups of twins, irrespective of sex or zygosity. A trial value for V_A was the correlation between twins obtained by assigning the weights 1, 2 and 3 to the ordered response categories. The cumulative marginal proportions were employed to generate starting values for t_1 and t_2 by recognizing that the intervals of the standard normal distribution can be approximated quite acceptably by multiplying those of the cumulative logistic distribution by 1.7 (Hayley, 1952). Thus, if the proportion of individuals in the 'never smoke' category is p, a reasonable approximation to t_1 would be 0.59 $\ln\left(\dfrac{p}{1-p}\right)$ given that the assumption about ordering is correct.

The simplest model fitted to the data assumed that the thresholds between the response categories were the same for males and females, i.e. $t_{1m} = t_{1f}$ and $t_{2m} = t_{2f}$, and that the same genetic effects were being expressed in both sexes. The model thus involved three parameters t_1, t_2 and V_A, where $V_A = V_{AM} = V_{AF} = V_{AMF}$. The maximum likelihood parameter estimates are given in Table 24, under the heading 'Model I'. There is no perfect test of goodness of fit but an approximate test is given by the value of

$$\Sigma \, (n_{ij1} - e_{ij1})^2 / e_{ij1}$$

The d.f. of this chi-square are equal to $K(p^2 - 1) - k$, where K is the number of tables, p the number of categories and k the number of parameters estimated. The observed and expected entries in the ith row, jth column of Table 1 are n_{ij1} and e_{ij1} respectively. In this example the chi-square has $5 \, (9\text{-}1) - 3 - 37$d.f. The numerical value of the chi-square under this hypothesis is $\chi^2_{37} = 56.54$, $(P \simeq 0.02)$ suggesting that the fit is not good. In the light of our experience of the other scale, it is likely that a major weakness of the model is the assumption that the thresholds are identical for males and females, so this constraint was relaxed and the model refitted, allowing the thresholds to take different values in males and females but still assuming that

TABLE 24

Persistence in smoking: threshold analysis of twin data

Parameter	Model			
	I	II	III	IV
t_{1M}	−0.335	−0.518	−0.513	−0.529
t_{1F}	−0.335	−0.261	−0.261	−0.259
t_{2M}	0.305	0.079	0.082	0.084
t_{2F}	0.305	0.405	0.405	0.400
V_{AM}	0.683	0.680	0.571	0.602
V_{AF}	0.683	0.680	0.571	0.711
V_{AMF}	0.683	0.680	0.571	0.357
E_2	−	−	0.102	−
Goodness of fit*				
x^2	56.535	42.288	42.133	39.691
df	37	35	34	33
P	2%	19%	16%	20%
Improvement†				
x^2	−	12.546	0.378	2.46
df	−	2	1	2
P	−	<1%	>50%	>20%
Log L	−1114.595	−1108.321	−1108.132	1107.191

*Based on observed and expected frequencies
†Based on log-likelihood ratios

the same genetic effects were expressed in both sexes. This model will account for differences in the mean persistence of males and females and absorb any sex differences in the category widths. The addition of two parameters to the model reduces the chi-square to 42.29 for 35d.f. (P ≃ 0.19) suggesting that the change of scale is sufficient to explain the departures from expectation under the previous model. The log-likelihood increases under this hypothesis from −1114.60 to −1108.32, corresponding to a highly significant x_1^2 of 12.55. This change confirms that there is considerable support for the hypothesis that threshold values differ for males and females as far as the transition from non-smoker to persistent smoker is concerned. The parameter values are given in column II of Table 24.

It is apparent that, under this hypothesis which fits the facts available, approximately 68 per cent of the variation underlying subjects' persistence in the smoking habit is genetically determined. Furthermore, these data give us no reason to suppose that the scale of persistence in smoking is anything other than unidimensional, with individuals who have succeeded in giving up smoking being intermediate between those who have never smoked and those who persist in smoking. Put in another way, *there are indeed quantitative genetical differences between those who give up smoking and those who persist in smoking, and these differences are of the same quality as those which differentiate smokers from non-smokers.*

The robustness of this conclusion can be examined by looking at the consequences of changes in the model. We considered two changes which are like those applied in the analysis of the age of onset and the average consumption discussed earlier. Firstly, we added a family environment parameter (E_2) to the model to absorb effects of the shared environment together with any genetical effects of assortative mating. Secondly, we permitted the additive genetic parameter, V_A, to take different values in male and female twins and in unlike-sex pairs. This change allows the consistency of gene expression to be examined across sexes. The results of fitting these two models are given in columns III and IV of Table 24. In both cases the chi-square measuring the improvement in fit reveals that neither model is significantly better supported than the simple model of column II. Adding E_2 causes the estimate of V_A to drop to 0.571, suggesting that even when allowance is made for the family environment the contribution of inherited factors explains an estimated 57 per cent of the variation underlying persistence in the smoking habit. Apparently only 10 per cent of the variance can be attributed to the influence of environmental factors for which twin pairs differ from one another. That is, *whatever shared environmental factors may lead to the initiation of smoking are apparently dissipated when we consider the long-term persistence of the habit.*[1]

The model-fitting suggests that there is also very little additional

[1] There are few existing studies on reasons for starting and continuing to smoke which would be relevant to the discussion of our genetic data. The only exception is a study currently being conducted at the University of Southern Florida by C. Spielberger; this is still in progress and only preliminary results are available, covering over 400 male and female smokers and non-smokers. Items like 'Because most of my friends smoke' and 'Because it made me feel more relaxed around my

support for the view that the genetic determination of persistence differs between males and females. Although our maximum-likelihood estimate of the correlation between gene expression in males and females is only

$$r_{gMF} = 0.357/(0.602 \times 0.711)^{\frac{1}{2}} \simeq 0.55$$

the increase in likelihood associated with the relaxation of the constraint that $r_{gMF} = 1$ is too small to be taken seriously. We are thus tempted to conclude that the same genes contribute to persistence in smoking in both sexes.

Age of onset of smoking

The analysis of persistence in smoking suggests that the approach we have outlined does offer a means of testing some of the assumptions implicit in the analysis of categorical scales. We now employ the same method to examine more closely the twin data on age of onset. The raw categories are too numerous to yield reliable estimates of the cell frequencies for this variable since attempts to fit models to the larger tables produce values which are too unstable to permit a reliable search for the maximum likelihood estimates. We have thus reduced the number of categories to the point at which there are sufficient observations in each cell for effective analysis. This was achieved by collapsing the seven categories of the original scale (Table 8) to five by including all those who smoked for the first time after the age of eighteen in the same category. That is, categories 4, 5 and 6 of Table 8 were combined. The reduced contingency tables for the five types of twin pairs are given in Table 25.

friends' were much the most important influences cited by current smokers and also by ex-smokers in relation to their starting to smoke. In relation to factors determining their continuance of smoking, reference to friends dropped to a very low level. This finding strongly supports our emphasis on peer groups as determinants of starting to smoke, but not affecting continuation of smoking.

References to parents and siblings were only made in a very small proportion of cases, both by current smokers and by ex-smokers, and in relation to both starting and continuing. The major reasons for continuing were enjoyment, boredom, relaxation, and stimulation.

The influence of television, newspaper advertisements and other media was almost non-existent in any of the groups studied, both for starting and for continuing. Thus these preliminary data concur with our analysis, in so far as relevant comparisons can be made.

TABLE 25

Age of onset of smoking: contingency tables of twins' responses

Twin type	Age of onset	Age of onset: males Twin 2					Age of onset: females Twin 2				
		<14	14-15	16-17	18+	Never	<14	14-15	16-17	18+	Never
MZ	<14	4	3	0	0	3	3	1	0	3	4
	14-15	2	7	7	1	2	7	6	3	0	3
Twin 1	16-17	0	2	4	0	3	0	2	12	3	7
	18+	0	1	1	5	3	2	3	11	44	11
	Never	4	4	2	3	19	2	5	8	21	67
DZ	<14	4	2	3	0	0	2	1	1	2	3
	14-15	2	4	1	0	2	0	7	2	3	2
Twin 1	16-17	1	3	1	4	2	0	3	5	4	3
	18+	3	2	2	2	1	2	1	9	14	14
	Never	1	0	5	0	5	1	4	6	8	23
DZos	<14	2	0	0	0	1					
	14-15	2	0	1	1	3					
Female twin	16-17	3	3	2	4	1					
	18+	3	5	1	2	2					
	Never	3	3	2	6	8					

Male twin

TABLE 26

Age of onset of smoking: threshold analysis of twin data

Parameter	I	II	III	IV	V
			Model		
t_{1M}	-1.341 ⎱	-1.343 ⎱	-0.948	-0.952	-0.955
t_{1F}	-1.341 ⎰	-1.343 ⎰	-1.590	-1.590	-1.585
t_{2M}	-0.771 ⎱	-0.775 ⎱	-0.299	-0.305	-0.302
t_{2F}	-0.771 ⎰	-0.775 ⎰	-1.029	-1.030	-1.026
t_{3M}	-0.329 ⎱	-0.333 ⎱	0.115	0.108	0.116
t_{3F}	-0.329 ⎰	-0.333 ⎰	-0.535	-0.538	-0.534
t_{4M}	0.317 ⎱	0.312 ⎱	0.510	0.502	0.514
t_{4F}	0.317 ⎰	0.312 ⎰	0.235	0.232	0.234
V_{AM}	0.554 ⎫	0.323 ⎫	0.533 ⎫	0.306 ⎫	0.499
V_{AF}	0.554 ⎬	0.323 ⎬	0.533 ⎬	0.306 ⎬	0.549
V_{AMF}	0.554 ⎭	0.323 ⎭	0.533 ⎭	0.306 ⎭	0.472
E_2	—	0.210	—	0.207	—
Goodness of fit					
χ^2	297.62	290.20	204.29	200.99	202.53
df	115	114	111	110	109
P	$<10^{-4}$	$<10^{-4}$	$<10^{-4}$	$<10^{-4}$	$<10^{-4}$
Improvement					
χ^2	—	2.14	69.82	1.98	0.28
df	—	1	4	1	2
P	—	$>10\%$	$<10^{-4}$	$>10\%$	$>80\%$
Log L	-1548.53	-1547.46	-1513.62	-1512.63	-1513.48

Exactly the same model as that in Table 24 (I) was fitted to the data on age of onset except that, having five response categories, there are now four threshold values to be estimated. Assuming only additive gene action and the same thresholds and gene effects for males and females yields the parameter estimates of Table 26 (I). The most striking finding is the enormously significant chi-square for testing the deviations of observed from expected cell frequencies, which suggests that the model is radically wrong. Inclusion of E_2 to allow for the effects of the environments shared by pair members leads to an increase of only 1.07 units in the log-likelihood ($\chi_1^2 = 2.14$, $P > 0.05$) suggesting that the principal fault does not lie in the assumption that the family environment is unimportant, although we observe that the contribution of the family environment is estimated to be over 20 per cent of the total variance, approximately twice the figure obtained for persistence in smoking, and much more comparable with the estimated contribution of additive genetical factors. This figure is similar to that obtained by model-fitting to the mean squares derived from the normalized data earlier (Table 23). Although the chi-square testing the model is approximate because many of the expected cell numbers are very small, we think it is highly improbable that improving the properties of the test of significance could make much impact on the very large residuals $(x^2_{114} = 290.20)$ so we must seek a further change in the model which yields a far better agreement between the observed and predicted cell frequencies. We may try fitting separate threshold values to the frequencies for males and females. The results assuming gene action alone, and additive gene action supplemented by the family environment, are given in columns III and IV of Table 26.

There is a clear and highly significant increase in the likelihood $(x^2_1 = 69.82, P < 10^{-4})$ associated with the change to thresholds which depend on sex. The addition of a family environmental component (E_2), however, does not increase the likelihood at all significantly, although the shared environment contributes an estimated 21 per cent of the total variability in twins.

Modifying the model still further, to represent the dependence of gene expression on sex, leads to an increase of 0.14 units in log-likelihood compared with the model which assumes a common genetic basis in the two sexes. The estimates (Table 26, column V) are consistent with a consistency (correlation in gene expression) of 0.90 across sexes, suggesting that there is very little evidence of sex-specific gene action once allowance is made for differing thresholds on males and females. In spite of the significant improvement obtained by fitting different thresholds to the tables for males and females, the overall fit of the model is bad, suggesting that there is a more fundamental problem with the scale of age of onset. There are several possibilities which we are forced to consider. The ordering of the responses may be different from that presupposed in the model assumed or, indeed, any ordering of the responses along a single dimension may be insufficient to represent the genetic and environmental components for which twin pairs differ. One approach to this problem will be considered subsequently (p. 218 ff).

Average reported cigarette consumption

A similar analysis to that for age of onset was also conducted for average consumption, employing the data summary in Table 27. Once again the number of classes was reduced to five by combining cells in the full table in order to secure sufficiently large numbers in individual cells to provide parameter estimates stable enough for the numerical algorithms. Table 28 summarizes the results of the model fitting for this trait, and these resemble those for age of onset quite closely, except that the estimated additive genetic component is slightly larger and that of the family environment is comparably smaller. As in both the previous examples of the threshold analysis, it is essential to allow for sex differences in the category boundaries and it is quite clear that none of the simple models proposed could explain the distribution of the subjects' responses over the categories. Allowing for sex differences in the additive genetic component does lead to a significant ($P \simeq 2\%$) increase in the likelihood (Table 28, column V), but the correlation between the gene effects in males and females does not differ significantly from unity ($r_{gmf} = 1.02$), suggesting that the difference between sexes is a matter of scale rather than causal mechanism. Indeed, this is the conclusion supported by the analysis of the normalized mean squares, for there it was shown (Table 21) that the difference in the environmental components within twin pairs was significant for this trait. The analysis of the contingency tables supports this finding, since the parameter estimates under model V leave over 47 per cent of variance in age of onset of males to the effects of intrapair differences in environment (E_1) whereas in females the figure is closer to 39 per cent.

However, in spite of the modification made to the model for the contingency tables, the discrepancy between observed and expected proportions is still very large. In the light of this finding we are compelled to examine our assumptions underlying our choice of scale in more detail.

The dimensions of twin similarity: another approach

The analysis of the contingency tables for the twins' responses confirmed that the response patterns of the twin pairs were consistent with a very simple unidimensional scale of genotypic predisposition to

TABLE 27

Average daily cigarette consumption: contingency tables of twins' responses

Twin type		Twin 2 *Average consumption: males*					Twin 2 *Average consumption: females*				
		Nil	<1	1–9	10–19	19+	Nil	<1	1–9	10–19	19+
MZ	Nil	37	3	1	0	4	111	10	6	7	5
	<1	2	1	0	0	0	10	8	3	2	0
Twin 1	1–9	2	1	2	2	1	7	3	7	7	0
	10–19	4	1	1	6	0	6	0	5	19	4
	19+	4	1	1	1	5	4	0	1	6	5
DZ	Nil	8	4	3	2	3	52	5	9	6	1
	<1	2	1	1	0	1	7	6	2	1	0
Twin 1	1–9	1	2	0	1	0	1	2	1	3	0
	10–19	6	0	2	2	1	5	1	6	3	1
	19+	1	2	1	1	2	3	0	1	2	3

		Male twin				
		Nil	<1	1–9	10–19	19+
DZos	Nil	21	1	1	10	2
	<1	0	1	0	0	0
Female twin	1–9	3	2	1	1	0
	10–19	4	1	2	3	2
	19+	1	0	0	1	1

persist in the smoking habit. The substantial differences between observed and expected cell frequencies for age of onset and average reported cigarette consumption argue against such a monolithic interpretation of these aspects of smoking behaviour. Certainly, a unidimensional scale *may* be constructed to represent both aspects

TABLE 28

Average cigarette consumption: threshold analysis of twin data

| | | | *Model* | | |
Parameter	I	II	III	IV	V
t_{1M}	0.168	0.168	0.120	0.129	0.038
t_{1F}	0.168	0.168	0.188	0.185	0.222
t_{2M}	0.423	0.423	0.321	0.329	0.278
t_{2F}	0.423	0.423	0.467	0.464	0.485
t_{3M}	0.718	0.717	0.588	0.594	0.522
t_{3F}	0.718	0.717	0.778	0.774	0.808
t_{4M}	1.390	1.388	1.141	1.145	1.111
t_{4F}	1.390	1.388	1.527	1.522	1.546
V_{AM}	0.648	0.474	0.648	0.485	0.525
V_{AF}	0.648	0.474	0.648	0.485	0.689
V_{AMF}	0.648	0.474	0.648	0.485	0.612
E_2	—	0.164	—	0.155	—
Goodness of fit					
x^2	194.96	192.33	172.31		163.96
df	115	114	111	110	109
P	$<10^{-4}$	10^{-4}	10^{-4}		10^{-3}
Improvement					
x^2	—	1.00	11.82	0.92	7.80
df	—	1	4	1	2
P	—	30%	<2%	30%	2%
Log L	−1320.30	−1319.80	−1314.39	−1313.97	−1310.49

of smoking, and these scales subjected to analysis in terms of their genetic and environmental components, but it is also clear that such simple scales do not exhaust all the information contained in the twins' responses. We now consider a simple approach which can help visualize the response categories in a more systematic fashion and explore what other dimensions, if any, can be detected in the twins' replies.

Consider one of the contingency tables above, for example, that relating to the age of onset in female monozygotic twins (Table 25). The cell *frequencies* may be denoted by the square matrix $\underset{\sim}{P}$. We require a set of weights to apply to the response categories to generate a scale which gives a better effective summary of the data than that we have assumed previously. What criterion might be adopted in choosing the weights? Since we intend to examine the causes of twin similarity, one obvious possibility would be to select those weights which maximize the twin correlations, ρ, on the grounds that these would reflect the maximum contribution of reliable familial components of variation.

Writing $\underset{\sim}{s}$ for the vector of weights, the scale mean is

$$\bar{s} = \underset{\sim}{r}\,\underset{\sim}{s}$$

where $\underset{\sim}{r}$ is a row vector of the individual response frequencies, i.e.

$$r_i = \sum_j (P_{ij} + P_{ji})/2$$

If we make $\underset{\sim}{R}$ a matrix consisting of n identical rows, $\underset{\sim}{r}$, the weights may be expressed as deviations from the scale mean thus:

$$\underset{\sim}{\delta} = (I - \underset{\sim}{R})\,\underset{\sim}{S}$$

where I is the n x n identity matrix.

The twin covariance is thus:

$$w = \underset{\sim}{s}'\,(I - \underset{\sim}{R})'\,\underset{\sim}{P}\,(I - \underset{\sim}{R})\,\underset{\sim}{s} \qquad \ldots(3)$$

which is equal to the twin correlation, ρ, when $\underset{\sim}{s}$ is chosen to constrain the total variance to unity, i.e.

$$\sigma^2 = \underset{\sim}{s}'\,(I - \underset{\sim}{R})'\,\underset{\sim}{\Delta}\,(I - \underset{\sim}{R})\,\underset{\sim}{s} = 1$$

where $\underset{\sim}{\Delta}$ is a diagonal matrix such that $\Delta_{ii} = r_i$.
We thus require the $\underset{\sim}{s}$ to maximize w, subject to the constraint that σ^2 is unity. Since $\underset{\sim}{R}$, $\underset{\sim}{P}$ and $\underset{\sim}{\Delta}$ are all functions of $\underset{\sim}{P}$ and independent of $\underset{\sim}{s}$ it is convenient to write.

$$\underset{\sim}{Z} = (I - \underset{\sim}{R})'\,\underset{\sim}{P}\,(I - \underset{\sim}{R})$$

$$\underset{\sim}{W} = (I - \underset{\sim}{R})'\,\underset{\sim}{\Delta}\,(I - \underset{\sim}{R})$$

The weights are chosen to satisfy the equations

$$\frac{\partial}{\partial \underset{\sim}{s}}\,\underset{\sim}{s}'\,\underset{\sim}{Z}\,\underset{\sim}{s} = 0$$

subject to

$$\underset{\sim}{s}'\,\underset{\sim}{W}\,\underset{\sim}{s} = 1$$

The constraint may be handled by introducing the Lagrange multiplier, λ. and requiring that

$$\frac{\partial}{\partial \underset{\sim}{s}}\,[\underset{\sim}{s}'\,\underset{\sim}{Z}\,\underset{\sim}{s} + \lambda\,(1 - \underset{\sim}{s}'\,\underset{\sim}{W}\,\underset{\sim}{s})] = \underset{\sim}{0}$$

In many respects, the derivation follows that of principal components, canonical variates and canonical correlations (e.g. Morrison, 1967). Differentiating we obtain the equations:

$$(\underset{\sim}{Z} - \lambda \underset{\sim}{W}) \underset{\sim}{s} = \underset{\sim}{0} \qquad \ldots\ldots(4)$$

which, indeed, are recognizable as those employed in the more conventional canonical analysis. It would appear, therefore, that λ is the dominant eigenvalue of $\underset{\sim}{Z} \, \underset{\sim}{W}^{-1}$ and $\underset{\sim}{s}$ is the corresponding eigenvector.

Unfortunately, $\underset{\sim}{W}$ is singular because the frequencies in the population sum to unity. The rank $\underset{\sim}{W}$ is thus $k = n - 1$. To remove the singularity we set one of the elements of $\underset{\sim}{s}$ (for example, the last) to zero, and delete the corresponding column of $\underset{\sim}{R}$. The dimensions of $\underset{\sim}{W}$ and $\underset{\sim}{Z}$ are thus reduced to k, and the $\underset{\sim}{W}$ is now of full rank. Since $\underset{\sim}{Z}W^{-1}$ is of rank k, there are an additional $k - 1$ solutions for $\underset{\sim}{s}$ which satisfy (4) above. These are given by the eigenvectors corresponding to the other $k - 1$ eigenvalues of ZW^{-1}. The eigenvalues, λ , are the correlations generated by applying the weights to the frequencies as in (3) above. In principle, vectors corresponding to λs not significantly greater than zero do not reflect any real pattern of the responses. However, we are not aware of any statistical treatment of this approach.

As an example, we analyse the data on age of onset in female MZ twins. The raw numbers given in Table 25 yield the following (symmetric) matrix of cell frequencies:

```
0.013158  0.017544  0         0.010965  0.013158
          0.026316  0.010965  0.006579  0.017544
                    0.052632  0.030702  0.032895
     symmetric:               0.192982  0.070175
                                        0.293860
```

Since the matrix is symmetric only the upper triangle is given. The elements of the diagonal matrix of category frequencies are thus:

$$\underset{\sim}{\triangle} = \begin{matrix} 0.054825 & . & . & . & . \\ . & 0.078947 & . & . & . \\ . & . & 0.127193 & . & . \\ . & . & . & 0.311404 & . \\ . & . & . & . & 0.427632 \end{matrix}$$

The matrix $(\underset{\sim}{I} - \underset{\sim}{R})$ is (after deletion of the last column):

$$0.945175 \quad -0.078947 \quad -0.127193 \quad -0.311404$$
$$-0.054825 \quad 0.921053 \quad -0.127193 \quad -0.311404$$
$$-0.054825 \quad -0.078947 \quad 0.872807 \quad -0.311404$$
$$-0.054825 \quad -0.078947 \quad -0.127193 \quad 0.688596$$
$$-0.054825 \quad -0.078947 \quad -0.127193 \quad -0.311404$$

Evaluating $\underset{\sim}{Z} = (\underset{\sim}{I} - \underset{\sim}{R})' \underset{\sim}{P} (\underset{\sim}{I} - \underset{\sim}{R})$ yields the symmetric matrix

$$\underset{\sim}{Z} = \begin{array}{rrrr} 0.010152 & 0.013216 & -0.006973 & -0.006108 \\ & 0.020083 & 0.000923 & -0.018006 \\ & & 0.036454 & -0.008907 \\ & & & 0.096010 \end{array}$$

and $\underset{\sim}{W} = (\underset{\sim}{I} - \underset{\sim}{R})' \underset{\sim}{\Delta} (\underset{\sim}{I} - \underset{\sim}{R})$ is also symmetric:

$$\underset{\sim}{W} = \begin{array}{rrrr} 0.051819 & -0.004328 & -0.006973 & -0.017073 \\ & 0.072715 & -0.010042 & -0.024585 \\ & & 0.111015 & -0.039608 \\ & & & 0.214431 \end{array}$$

The eigenvalues and eigenvectors of $\underset{\sim}{Z}\underset{\sim}{W}^{-1}$ were extracted on the University of Manchester CDC 7600 computer using the Numerical Algorithms Group FORTRAN subroutine FO2AEF for solution of eigenvalue problems of the type $\underset{\sim}{A} = \lambda \underset{\sim}{B}$. In descending order, the eigenvalues are 0.498984, 0.456744, 0.341634 and -0.003338. These correspond to the four possible maximum independent values of the correlation, ρ, between female MZ twins.

The eigenvectors corresponding to the first three eigenvalues (we shall ignore the fourth since it is close to zero) are the category weights which should be applied to the responses to generate the corresponding set of correlations. These are scaled to constrain $\underset{\sim}{S}' \underset{\sim}{W} \underset{\sim}{S} = I$, where $\underset{\sim}{S}$ is the matrix of eigenvectors (weights). That is, they are scaled to generate scores with unit total variance. The eigenvectors are:

$$\underset{\sim}{s}_1 = (\quad 2.20556 \quad 2.35354 \quad -0.22283 \quad -0.96533)$$
$$\underset{\sim}{s}_2 = (-2.17185 \quad -2.09402 \quad -1.58726 \quad -2.10266)$$
$$\underset{\sim}{s}_3 = (\quad 0.95868 \quad -0.34078 \quad -2.69237 \quad 0.41498)$$

These correspond to the weights for the *first four* response categories; the weight for the fifth, the 'never smokes' category, was arbitrarily fixed to zero, so an additional zero element must be appended to each row to give the complete data summary. All the categories are thus scaled relative to the last. It is probably more convenient to rescale each vector around the scale mean to generate 'deviation' vectors.

The scale means are obtained by post-multiplying, $\underset{\sim}{r}$, the vector containing the category frequencies by the vectors of category weights.

$$\bar{s}_i = \underset{\sim}{r} \, \underset{\sim}{s}_j.$$

The means for the first three scales are thus:

$$\bar{s}_1 = -0.02222;$$
$$\bar{s}_2 = -1.14105;$$
$$\bar{s}_3 = -0.18757.$$

Subtracting the appropriate scale mean from the elements (including the arbitrary zero) of each weight vector gives

$$\delta_{ij} = s_{ij} - \bar{s}_i.$$

For the first three dimensions of discrimination between the twin pairs we have, to two decimal places:

$$\underset{\sim}{\delta_1} = (\ \ \ 2.23, \ \ \ 2.38, \ -0.20, \ -0.94, \ \ \ \ 0.02)$$
$$\underset{\sim}{\delta_2} = (-1.03, \ -0.95, \ -0.45, \ -0.96, \ -1.14)$$
$$\underset{\sim}{\delta_3} = (\ \ \ 1.14, \ -0.15, \ -2.50, \ \ \ \ 0.60, \ \ \ \ 0.19)$$

A convenient method of representing the results is to plot the δ's pair-wise as coordinates in two dimensions. Figure 17 gives the two-dimensional plot of the first two principal axes of discrimination between pairs.

Examination of the figure suggests why the simple threshold model for age of onset probably failed to represent the observations even after allowance was made for sex differences in the scale of measurement. The similarity between twins is not confined to a unidimensional scale on which non-smokers are merely the far extreme of late onset. Categories 1 and 2 coincide, suggesting that there is little reason to discriminate causally among individuals who begin smoking before the age of 15 years. Those who begin at 16-17 years, however, are more distinct, though less extreme on the first dimension than the 18 + category. The striking feature, however, is the fact that the non-smokers (category 5) do not fall along the line which joins the other four categories. Non-smokers lie 'out on a limb' which differentiates them quite clearly from smokers. The figure implies that the smoking partner of a non-smoking twin is not predisposed to begin smoking any later, on average, than the smoking partner of a smoking twin. That is, given that a person is going to smoke, his age of onset will depend on quite different factors from those which decide whether he begins or not.

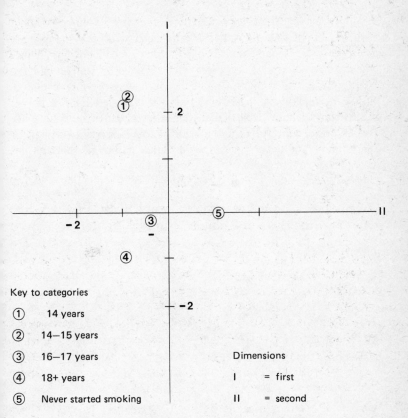

Key to categories

①   14 years
②   14—15 years
③   16—17 years
④   18+ years   Dimensions
⑤   Never started smoking   I   = first
                                 II   = second

Figure 17: The first two dimensions of interpair differences for age of
               onset of smoking in female monozygotic twins

The identical computations for the other like-sex twin groups yield the correlations and weights of Table 29. The first two dimensions of intrapair similarity for age of onset in each group are represented graphically in Figure 18.

Unfortunately, the picture which emerges from Figure 17 is not replicated over twin groups. In the female DZ twins, for example, the two most widely separated classes in the first two dimensions (Figure 18), i.e. classes 1 and 2, are those which are closest in MZ females. Furthermore, the configuration of the five categories in two dimensions is quite different between the four twin groups. Even when we recall that the signs of a particular weight vector can be reflected without altering the interpretation, there is no obvious way in which the four figures could be superimposed. Thus, although this analysis

TABLE 29

Age of onset of smoking: correlations and category weights for first three dimensions of intrapair differences

Twin type	Dimen-sion	Corre-lation	Weight				
			< 14 yrs	14—15	16—17	18+	Never
MZ male	I	0.53	0.53	0.98	1.04	−2.03	−0.51
	II	0.46	−1.60	0.57	1.19	1.38	−0.67
	III	0.29	−1.74	−0.49	0.81	−1.16	0.90
MZ female	I	0.50	2.23	2.38	−0.20	−0.94	0.02
	II	0.46	−1.03	−0.95	−0.45	−0.96	1.14
	III	0.34	1.15	−0.15	−2.50	0.60	0.19
DZ male	I	0.45	1.11	0.69	−0.28	0.40	−1.71
	II	0.24	−0.34	1.71	−0.41	−1.46	0.25
	III	0.16	1.62	−0.75	−0.34	−1.31	0.54
DZ female	I	0.42	0.54	−2.55	−0.34	0.37	0.59
	II	0.26	1.14	−0.56	1.07	0.90	−1.12
	III	0.25	3.79	0.37	−0.91	−0.35	−0.05

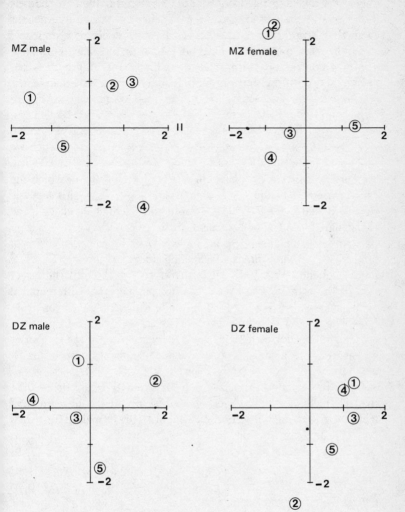

Figure 18: First two dimensions of intrapair similarity for age of onset
of smoking in twins

implies the multidimensionality of age of onset in twins and confirms the results of the previous analysis, it gives little additional insight about the nature or form of the scale. In the absence of a statistical theory for the approach we have adopted it is possible to stipulate how much of the apparent inconsistency between twin groups is due to sampling error and how much to genuine causal discrepancies.

Average consumption

Similar inconsistencies appear in the analysis of average reported daily cigarette consumption (Table 30 and Figure 19), although the results for females are somewhat more consistent. In both MZ and DZ female twins the non-smokers (category I) occupy one quadrant (bottom left of Figures 19ii and 19iv) with the four categories of progressively more intensive smoking forming an approximately linear sequence. In female twins, therefore, which form the larger part of the sample, it is clear that non-smokers are differentiated biologically and/or culturally along quite a distant dimension from those who acknowledge even a very limited consumption of cigarettes.

The findings for male twins are not consistent. All the categories appear well separated in the first two dimensions of intrapair similarity but there is no eye-catching order of the 2, 3, 4, 5 categories as there was in both the female groups. It is tempting to conclude that the relatively heavy smokers (group 5) might be differentiated from the rest along the second axis (Figure 18i) in males, but this is not replicated convincingly in the less powerful group of male DZ twins.

Persistence in smoking

By contrast with age of onset and average consumption, the analysis of intrapair similarity for persistence in smoking (Table 31) shows remarkably consistent results. Since there are only three categories there are just two possible dimensions of intrapair similarity. In every case, the first dimension yields twin correlations which are substantially higher than the second, so the latter could perhaps be regarded as a residual component. For all four groups of like-sex twins the pattern of weights for the first component locates the subjects who used to smoke approximately midway on the vector joining those who have never smoked to those who still smoke. That is, persistence in smoking can be regarded as on ordinal scale with approximately equal intervals between the categories. The numerical values of the weights are also remarkably consistent between groups, especially between the larger samples of female twins.

TABLE 30

Average consumption: correlations and category weights for first three dimensions of intrapair differences

Twin type	Dimension	Correlation		Nil	<1	1–9	10–19	19+
MZ male	I	0.59	−0.63	0.03	1.21	2.21	−0.13	
	II	0.40	0.48	0.02	−0.80	0.74	−2.31	
	III	0.20	0.10	−1.87	−2.52	1.05	0.92	
MZ female	I	0.61	−0.69	−0.51	0.76	1.78	1.48	
	II	0.38	−0.41	2.18	1.61	−0.04	−1.80	
	III	0.22	−0.25	2.01	−1.17	−0.55	2.52	
DZ male	I	0.25	0.40	−1.24	0.12	1.35	−1.58	
	II	0.11	0.48	1.24	0.58	−1.07	−1.71	
	III	−0.00	1.06	−0.67	−1.88	−0.75	0.34	
DZ female	I	0.46	−0.41	−0.93	0.37	0.89	3.43	
	II	0.35	−0.74	1.95	1.03	0.80	−0.41	
	III	0.23	0.04	1.51	−1.27	−1.52	2.06	

It was demonstrated above (page 212) that these data were consistent with a unidimensional genotypic model for twin similarity. The analysis of the dimensions of pair similarity, using this somewhat

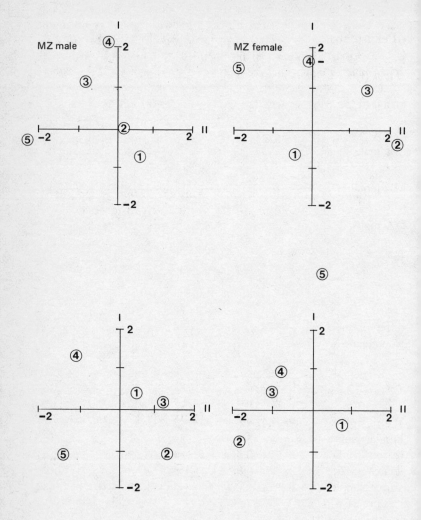

Figure 19: Average daily consumption: first two dimensions of intrapair similarity in twins

TABLE 31

**Persistence in smoking: correlations and category weights
for the two dimensions of intrapair differences**

Twin type	Dimension	Correlation	Weight		
			Never smoked	*Used to smoke*	*Still smoke*
MZ male	I	0.47	1.06	0.28	−1.19
	II	0.21	−0.71	1.83	−0.36
MZ female	I	0.59	0.98	0.22	−1.31
	II	0.25	−0.69	1.75	−0.41
DZ male	I	0.34	1.91	−0.43	−0.56
	II	−0.07	−0.11	1.63	−0.75
DZ female	I	0.38	0.98	0.23	−1.38
	II	0.14	−0.80	1.54	−0.45

different approach, adds further convincing support to the conclusion reached earlier by model-fitting methods.

Discussion and summary

We regard the twin study as a valuable opportunity to take preliminary soundings about the causes of variation in a trait. Attached to this study there is an area of uncertainty reflecting legitimate doubts about the quality of data, the design of the study and the size of samples. Scales of measurement are inevitably crude and since it is not easy to observe actual 'behaviour' there is always the possibility that the subjects may not be 'telling the truth'. This is no new problem in studies of personality through self-report and we can offer no more than the usual checks through the use of 'lie' scales. The relationship between one such scale and the reported smoking behaviour of our subjects will be the object of further analysis subsequently (Chapter 6). The twins, like all the subjects in our study, are volunteers. This is reflected in the bias in favour of females and monozygotic twins in the study. The sample is under-representative of the lower socio-economic status groups and consists of a disproportionate number of younger twins.

It is known that the twin study cannot resolve certain factors of potential importance. For example, we know that the consequences of assortative mating for the similarity between twins cannot be separated from the effects of the family environment. If the family environment depends on the genotype of the parents of the twins the resultant genotype-environmental covariance will also be inseparable from the effects of the family environment (Eaves et al., 1977). The effects of dominance and the family environment (or any factors confounded with the family environment) are known to oppose one another in their effects on twin data even to the point of cancelling one another out under certain conditions (Martin et al., 1978). Such cautions do not add up to a damning critique of the twin study but they do suggest that the twin study cannot be exhaustive and self-contained.

On the other hand, the twin study can yield powerful initial tests of many factors of great importance. We have seen how it can detect the dependence of genetical and environmental factors on sex (though the twin study is not exclusive in this respect). The data have not forced us to consider the influence of cooperative and competitive factors on the development of smoking behaviour, but Eaves (1976a) has shown how such effects might first be detected in twin data if they have any genetical basis. Any overwhelming effects of the family environment would usually be detected by the twin study, and consequently certain types of genotype-environmental covariance might also be excluded, given that E_2 effects are negligible.

A cynic might argue that methods based on comparison of concordance rates and correlations are likely to yield about as much as may be inferred reliably from twin studies: that identical twins are (or are not) more alike than non-identical twins. There is some substance to this view since larger samples are needed to make more subtle distinctions about the causes of variation even in twin studies. Martin et al. (1978) considered the power of the classical twin study for the discrimination of quite simple hypotheses about the causes of variation. They generated tables of the sample sizes needed to be really confident (95 per cent certain) that one explanation of variation was to be preferred to another on statistical grounds, using samples of identical and fraternal twins reared together. In particular, they considered the analysis of randomly mating populations in which there were differing amounts of heritable and non-heritable variation with the environmental variation variously divided between influences specific to individuals within families ('E_1') and effects shared by members of a twin pair because they lived in the same place, received similar education and so on ('E_2'). Considering only samples in which monozygotic and dizygotic twins were represented with equal frequency (Martin et al. consider other situations too), it may be shown, for example, how likely it is that an investigator would actually reject one explanation in favour of another and how big a survey would be required to achieve this discrimination with a given degree of reliability. As an illustration we reproduce from Martin et al.'s paper part of a table showing the sample sizes required to be 95 per cent certain of rejecting either the D_R, E_1 model or the E_1, E_2 model when in reality the contributions of the three sources of variation are approximately equal (Table 32). In our study we are unable, especially in the case of the normalized age of onset of smoking, to discriminate between the two models involving two parameters. This inability may indicate that our situation is similar to that illustrated in Martin et al.'s simulation, i.e. all three sources of variability are contributing in roughly comparable proportions to the observed variation.

Although our twin study is larger than many it still falls short of the numbers required to distinguish any but the grossest determi-

TABLE 32

Sample sizes required to reject false explanations at the 5% significance level in 95% of twin samples of equal numbers of MZ and DZ pairs from a population in which additive genetic, between-family and within-family environmental effects contribute to the total variance

			Total number of twin pairs to reject false models		
			E_1	E_1, E_2	E_1, D_R
True contributions (%)					
$\frac{1}{2}D_R$	E_2	E_1			
0.4	0.3	0.3	47	466	966
0.4	0.1	0.5	101	940	11458
0.2	0.3	0.5	84	3268	1233

(After Martin et al., 1978)

nants of variation. This partly explains why some of the findings are ambiguous, in particular why the resolution of the family environment and additive genetic effects is not entirely convincing. As a result of simulation studies, however, we know that if either of the competing models were false our study would have a reasonably high probability of rejecting the incorrect hypothesis.

It is our view that, in spite of the many limitations of twin studies in general and our data in particular, the work has revealed that the study of twins is a fertile ground for evaluating many basic assumptions underlying the analysis of smoking. We hope that our analysis of the twin data has gone beyond the mere reporting of concordance and the application of the conventional methods of quantitative genetics into a more rigorous analysis of the causes of variation, and considers the legitimacy of applying these techniques to scales created out of discontinuous categories. It is quite clear from the threshold analysis that the unidimensional multifactorial model of quantitative genetics is perfectly adequate to distinguish those who have never smoked from those who persist in smoking, and that those who once began smoking but have subsequently relinquished the habit are, on the scale of genotypic predisposition, between the extremes of non-smoking and persistent smoking. Furthermore, we have shown that the distribution of twins' responses over the categories is quite consistent with a model which assumes that this dimension of predisposition is inherited rather than cultural, since the inclusion of a family environmental effect in the model for twin similarity neither increases the likelihood significantly nor leads to a substantial change in the parameter values.

When we turn to the factors which determine the age of onset of smoking or the reported average daily consumption of cigarettes, however, the story is not so simple. The raw tables of twin concordance and the simple unidimensional ordering of the responses obscure differences which are not exposed in more conventional analysis. First, even if we accept the basic assumption that non-smokers are distinct only quantitatively from different categories of smoker, or that non-smokers differ only quantitatively from those who begin smoking relatively late, the causes of differences on scales constructed on this assumption are more ambiguous. It is fairly clear that there are genetical differences which affect the age of onset and average consumption, but these are expressed in addition to other non-genetic familial effects. With the samples available, it is not possible to resolve the additive genetic effects and the family environmental effects with complete reliability, but it may be shown that this inability probably reflects the joint contribution of both factors to the differences we observe.

For both age of onset and average consumption the attempt to reduce the pattern of twins' responses to a unidimensional ordered scale of genetic and cultural predisposition does not succeed. Examination of the dimensions of intrapair similarity, using a modified form of canonical analysis, suggested that the difficulty was one of dimensionality as well as category order. Twins were apparently correlated for more than one independent dimension of smoking behaviour. Unfortunately, in the absence of a statistical theory for this approach to the analysis of the data, it is difficult to assess how much of the variation along additional dimensions is real and how much due to chance. Also it is impossible to say with any conviction whether the apparent inconsistencies in the findings for different zygosity and sex groups are a feature of sampling error or a reflection of real causal differences. It is fairly clear, however, that *non-smokers are differentiated genetically from smokers along quite a distinct dimension from that which discriminates between the different degrees of cigarette consumption among smokers.* Here, apparently, is an area for further theoretical and empirical study with larger numbers of less highly selected subjects.

CHAPTER 5

Are Twins Enough? The Analysis of Family and Adoption Data

L. J. EAVES AND H. J. EYSENCK

Our analysis of the twin data led us to question some of the assumptions underlying the application of the twin method to the analysis of smoking. By and large, however, the data were consistent with a fairly simple basis for the causes of variation in the age of onset, the amount of tobacco consumed, and the factors which determine persistance in the smoking habit given that we were prepared to assume the scale was unidimensional. In spite of reservations about the choice of scale and concerning the validity of the chosen categories for twins' responses, the twin data lend some support to Fisher's original view that smokers and non-smokers are not genetically equivalent. Although a simple genotype-environmental model was sufficient to account for the overall pattern of variation in the responses of twins, there was some evidence that environmental factors common to twin pairs were partly responsible for deciding the age at which smoking was first tried and that the causal factors affecting age of onset might be different at different stages of development.

The conceptual simplicity of the twin method gives it much of the obvious appeal of the scientific experiment. But, just as the results of laboratory studies do not always predict what happens in less closely controlled quarters of nature, so any model resulting from the twin study needs to be tested against data from a variety of additional relationships before it can be used more widely with any confidence.

The selection of twins as our primary subjects leads the study in the direction of detecting genetical effects for several reasons. Given that variation is inherited, the comparison of monozygotic and dizygotic twins does provide one of the most controlled and powerful tests of genetical effects, but the fact that twins are always measured at the same age can lead to local support for genetical models which might not predict the findings for other relatives at all well if the expression of the loci controlling the measured behaviour depends in any marked way on age. Furthermore, it is possible that twins share more similar environments than non-twins, because they are more likely to have identical educational, uterine and social environments than non-twins. In order to test the general validity of the twin study, therefore, two principal types of family were sought in addition to twins from the twin register. The first type were 'normal' families, encompassing as many individuals as were of sufficient age and willing to participate. Often the families were small, consisting only of a parent and one or two offspring; occasionally the families were large including grandparents, cousins, uncles, aunts and even on some occasions great-uncles/aunts and cousins once removed. The second type of family was ascertained through an appeal for adults who had been adopted in childhood. The ascertainment of this part of the sample is outlined in Appendix A. As many as possible of their cooperative foster relatives as could be traced were included in the family cluster. Taking the adopted families and the normal pedigrees together, a total of 1,359 subjects yielded satisfactory responses from this part of the appeal, which together with the twins gave a total of 2,469 individuals who supplied suitably complete questionnaires for both the smoking/drinking study and the personality study.

Summarizing the family data

The twin study has great appeal for the ease with which twin data can be summarized. Because twins almost without exception come in pairs, and because more than one set of twins in the same family is a fairly infrequent occurrence, the analysis of variance within and between pairs provides a convenient and simple starting point for data analysis. Pairs are independent and the family size is constant.

When we turn to the highly unbalanced pedigree and adoption data, however, nothing could be further from the case. The family sizes range between one individual (in the case of isolated adoptees) and twenty in the case of some of the larger families. Such data yield a wide variety of relationships. Furthermore, the same individual may enter into a large number of relationships with different individuals in the pedigree. A father may be the father of many children and a child may have many siblings. With such data the conventional analysis of variance is out of the question because there is no uniform structure to the data and the various relational pairings which might be found are far from independent. In the past, such shortcomings of family data have not been allowed to obtrude into the problems of data analysis, so much so that the degree of overlap between the individuals entering into reported correlations between relatives has never been questioned even though it may affect the power of the analysis.

With such heterogeneous sets of data it is difficult to visualize the structure of the sample. For this reason we have tabulated (Table 33)

TABLE 33

Frequencies of different types of correlational pairing in full data set

Relationship	*Number of pairs*
spouse	156
parent	545
grandparent	57
uncle/aunt	314
sibling	418
DZ twin	229
MZ twin	316
first cousin	113
foster parent	230
foster child/natural child	36
foster child/foster child	22
Total number of individuals	2,469
Total number of fostered individuals	340

the data structure in a convenient form by counting all the possible pairs of individuals of each biological and adopting relationship in the entire sample. This means that a family with three siblings yields three possible sibling pairs, a father with four children yields four father-offspring pairs, and so on. This is merely a psychological aid to grasping the relative contributions of the different kinds of relationship to the final solution and does not reflect the way the data are analysed subsequently. Especially in the case of the commoner family relationships (parents and offspring, siblings, etc.) many pairs will involve the same individual in different relationships.

Before undertaking any analysis of the smoking behaviour of these individuals the entire data on the 2,469 subjects were rescaled by sex for the age of onset and the average consumption of cigarettes. Normal scores were assigned as before in Langford's analysis of the twin data, the only difference being that the total variance of the underlying scale was constrained to be unity rather than 225 as in Langford's analysis. No age correction was performed at this stage because the analysis of age effects was to be treated as an integral part of the subsequent investigation.

All the possible pairs of the various main types of biological and foster relationships were extracted from the pedigree data and correlation coefficients were computed for age of onset and the average consumption of cigarettes. These are in Tables 34 and 35. The resulting coefficients, especially those for parents and offspring and siblings, are therefore to be treated with caution. In particular, it is not known what weight should be given to significance tests based on the reported sample sizes, since the pairs entering the correlations are by no means independent. Ideally the approach of maximum likelihood (see pp. 244) might be used to obtain estimates of the correlations for the unbalanced data, but since the number of pedigrees is large and the number of possible correlations substantial this is impracticable with present computer resources. There are several things to notice about the summary statistics. We use the correlation merely as a guide to give some initial feel for the kind of results to be expected from a more formal analysis. Examination of the correlations will give a gross picture of the consistency of the data. Also, they give an indication of the varying amounts of information which the data provide about different types of relationship. For example, sibling and parent-offspring pairs are well represented whereas pairs of foster siblings are relatively infrequent.

TABLE 34

Correlations between relatives for age of onset of smoking

Relationship	MM		MF		FM		FF	
	r	N	r	N	r	N	r	N
MZ twin	.371	80	— — —		— — —		.414	236
DZ twin	.392	50	.029	30	.273	28	.333	121
spouse	— — —		.209	34	.191	122	— — —	
parent/offspring	.042	88	.027	110	.149	148	.135	199
sibling	−.006	72	.115	86	.298	109	.102	151
grandparent/ grandchild	.254	12	−.494	10	.165	12	−.244	23
uncle/ nephew etc.	.090	57	.200	65	.165	87	.215	105
first cousin	.002	18	.091	27	.211	29	.276	39
foster child/ foster parent	−.243	18	−.187	27	−.114	75	.117	110
foster child/ natural child	— — —		.386	5	.023	15	−.046	16
foster child/ foster child	— — —		.852	6	.337	8	.254	8

Sex of pair (younger individual first)

In Tables 34 and 35 raw correlations are presented for same-sex and opposite-sex pairs separately. Within a relationship (e.g. MZ twins, DZ twins, etc.) the correlations have been tested for homogeneity (Snedecor & Cochran, 1967) and pooled where appropriate to give a single estimate for each type of relationship. The pooled correlations are given for both traits in Table 36. Those for MZ and DZ twins are based entirely on independent pairs as are many of the correlations for which the numbers of observations are small.

Examination of the correlations in Table 36 confirms some of the previous trends and suggests others. As far as age of onset is concerned, the correlation for DZ twins is not significantly less ($p \simeq 0.30$) than that for MZ twins. This finding translates into another statistical test the difficulty of detecting significant genetical variation in the earlier twin analysis, and suggests that the effects of the family environment may be acting along with genetic effects in

Table 35

Correlations between relatives for average reported cigarette consumption

Relationship	Sex*							
	MM		MF		FM		FF	
	r	N	r	N	r	N	r	N
MZ twin	.449	80	— —		— —		.543	236
DZ twin	.064	50	.186	30	.160	28	.440	121
spouse	— —		−.130	34	.183	121	— —	
parent/offspring	.009	88	.180	110	.273	148	.250	199
sibling	.025	72	.123	86	.144	109	.111	151
grandparent/ grandchild	.375	12	−.480	10	.177	12	.105	23
uncle/ nephew etc.	.095	57	.256	65	−.058	87	.056	105
first cousin	.432	18	.112	27	−.010	29	.009	39
foster child/ foster parent	−.049	18	.118	27	−.124	75	.031	110
foster child/ natural child	— —		.141	5	−.199	15	.006	16
foster child/ foster child	— —		−.406	6	.742	8	.200	8

*The sex of the younger partner is given first

the determination of twin differences in the age at which smoking commences. The difference in twin correlations is much more marked ($p \simeq 0.01$) for the average cigarette consumption, confirming the findings of our more detailed model-fitting analysis that a genetical explanation for twin similarity was somewhat more likely than a purely environmental explanation. There are certain other notable trends which suggest that the twin data do not constitute the 'last word' on the inheritance of the smoking habit. In particular, the correlation between siblings is substantially lower than that between DZ twins. The difference is especially marked in the case of cigarette consump-

TABLE 36

Pooled correlations between relatives for smoking

Relationship	N (d.f.)	Age of onset	Average consumption
MZ twin	310	.403	.521
DZ twin	217	.304	.303
sibling	406	.139	.108
spouse	150	.195	.117
parent/offspring	533	.103	.205
grandparent/ grandchild	45	−.109	.080
avuncular	302	.176	.073
first cousin	101	.176	.096
foster parent/ foster child	218	−.018	−.016
foster child/ natural child	27 ⎫	.018 ⎫	−.097 ⎫
	⎬ 40	⎬ 0.181	⎬ 0.047
foster child/ foster child	13 ⎭	.483 ⎭	.333 ⎭

tion (p ≃ 0.05) suggesting that twins are something of a special case, either because of exceptional similarity in their environments or because of the interaction of genetical differences with age. Twins will tend to be alike in their gene expression since members of a pair are measured at a similar stage of development; they may also be more alike in their environments. Siblings, on the other hand, developed in somewhat different environments and have been measured at different ages with the result that age differences in gene expression contributing to the similarity of twins will contribute partly to the dissimilarity of siblings. Furthermore, the raw scores employed in the computation of these correlations have not yet been corrected for the straightforward population trend of behaviour with age. Such effects will contribute entirely to the similarity of twins but only partly to the similarity between sibs and other pairs.

A comparison of great interest is between the correlation of parents with their natural children and that between parents and their foster children. If the correlation for natural parent-offspring pairs exceeds that for adopting parents and their adopted children the presence of some hereditary influence is indicated. The fact that the difference is slight for the age of onset suggests that hereditary influences on this aspect of smoking are relatively slight. Indeed, we can go further than this. The fact that the estimate of the foster-parent/foster-child correlation is so close to zero implies there is no suggestion whatever that having a parent who began smoking early is going to lead to a family environment which will promote early smoking in offspring. This does not, of course, preclude the possibility that other independent factors in parental behaviour, such as their personality, may exercise a greater influence on the environment in which offspring develop. The slight but significant correlation for natural parent and natural child suggests that some familial influence may be operating on the age of onset. This effect could be hereditary in view of the excess of the natural parental correlation over the foster-parental correlation, but the difference is not large enough to be statistically significant. The pattern is somewhat different for the average daily consumption of cigarettes. Once more the foster-parent/foster-child correlation is so close to zero as to preclude any environmental connection between the consumption of cigarettes in parents and in offspring. The correlation of 0.205 between natural parent and offspring is significantly different from zero on a conventional test and also exceeds the foster-parent/adopted child correlation, suggesting once more that hereditary factors play a more significant part in the determination of the continuing smoking habit. Indeed, with the exception of the abnormally low sibling correlation, all the data for cigarette consumption fit quite neatly into the picture to be expected for a trait which is partly heritable but for which unique environmental experiences (E_1 in the notation of the previous chapter) play a major role in the determination of variation. Both adopted correlations, that between parent and offspring and that between unrelated individuals reared together, are consistent with there being neither cultural influence of parents on the smoking habits of their children nor of the import of other shared environmental influences on the similarity of members of the same family. The sample size for unrelated individuals reared together is very small; indeed, so small as to make the correlation consistent with almost any hypothesis which the data might reasonably suggest. The small avuncular, cousin and grandparental correlations are also consistent with a relatively small contribution from hereditary and cultural factors.

With these preliminary considerations in mind, our analysis of the full data concentrates on certain basic substantive issues:

(a) What are the best estimates of parameters of the various models for variation in the two normalized traits based on the entire sample?

(b) To what extent are the results of the twin study substantiated by the data on pedigrees and adopting families?

(c) To what extent do the findings of the twin study require modification in the light of the wider body of data?

Model fitting to unbalanced data

Since the family structures are so highly unbalanced, none of the conventional summaries of family data (analysis of variance, correlations, etc.) is satisfactory as a starting point for further analysis. We are, thus, forced to return to the raw data and to estimate the parameters of our model directly by the method of maximum likelihood. The application of the method to family data has been explained by Lange et al. in a series of recent papers (1975, 1976a, b) but since it is likely to be unfamiliar to many readers and less accessible than most methods we give an outline of their approach here.

It is assumed in writing the likelihood function that the distribution of the trait in pedigrees is multivariate normal. For a pedigree of k individuals we define the vector $\underset{\sim}{\mu}$ for the expected values of the individuals in the pedigree and the matrix $\underset{\sim}{\Sigma}$ to represent their expected covariance matrix. For a given $\underset{\sim}{\mu}$ and $\underset{\sim}{\Sigma}$ the log-likelihood of observing the particular vector of actual scores $\underset{\sim}{x}$ is

$$L = -\tfrac{1}{2}|n|\underset{\sim}{\Sigma}| - \tfrac{1}{2}(\underset{\sim}{x} - \underset{\sim}{\mu})'\underset{\sim}{\Sigma}^{-1}(\underset{\sim}{x} - \underset{\sim}{\mu}) + \text{constant}$$
$$\text{(Lange et al., 1976b).}$$

Similar expressions may be written for each of the pedigrees in the sample. The values of $\underset{\sim}{\mu}$ will depend on the model assumed for the means of the groups of individuals in the sample and the elements of $\underset{\sim}{\Sigma}$ will depend on the model for the covariation between relatives. Consider, for example, a pair of MZ twins. When mating is random, gene action is additive and there are no family environmental effects, we may write (see pp 179):

$$\underset{\sim}{\Sigma} \simeq \begin{pmatrix} \tfrac{1}{2}D_R + E_1 & \tfrac{1}{2}D_R \\ \tfrac{1}{2}D_R & \tfrac{1}{2}D_R + E_1 \end{pmatrix}$$

where D_R is the additive genetical component of variation and E_1 is the within-family environmental component of variance. For the log-likelihood to be defined $\underset{\sim}{\Sigma}$ must be positive definite. For family data and a sensible model this must be the case and will usually be ensured (as Lange et al. point out) when $E_1 > 0$. This will always be the case in practice since the quantitative trait is still to be found which is *completely* heritable and measured without error. The log-likelihood of obtaining all pedigrees given a particular hypothesis is the sum of the log-likelihoods of obtaining the individual pedigrees.

The estimation problem consists in finding values of parameters for which L is maximized. In practice it is convenient to minimize $-L$. Lange et al. advocate a method based on Fisher's scoring technique which requires the first and second partial derivatives of the log-likelihood. For models in which the covariances between relatives are linear functions of covariance components, the algebraic evaluation of these derivatives is not too prohibitive. Lange et al. give derivatives for many such models. However, a general approach may require models for covariance components which are not linear (e.g. path models, models involving genotype-environmental interactions and covariance, assortative mating, etc.). Algebraic differentiation is then tedious. In many applications it is found that numerical differentiation can yield solutions as accurate and as quick as algebraic differentiation, so the latter is often unnecessary. This makes the approach far more practicable for those with little aptitude for heavy algebra or with little practice in computer programming. In our applications we were able to employ a flexible and robust routine for numerical optimization written by the Numerical Algorithms Group (NAG) which provide a variety of possible algorithms and permit the incorporation of constraints on the parameters if desired. The NAG routine E04HAF (Numerical Algorithms Group, 1977) provides the facility for numerical differentiation if required whilst permitting the user to supply his own (algebraic) derivatives if preferred. Minimization may employ a technique requiring second derivatives (as in Fisher's scoring method) or may proceed with first partial derivatives only, or indeed without any explicit information from derivatives at all.

As far as elapsed time was concerned there seemed to be little to choose between the methods for analyses of the type discussed here. Methods which employed no derivatives seemed more likely to lead to violation of the constraint that the expected covariance matrix should be positive definite. Provided reasonable trial values are chosen (the analysis of twin data or correlations using more conventional methods is one way of providing 'reasonable' trial values), the methods based on the information from both second and first derivatives, evaluated numerically, usually lead to a rapid convergence.

Even with a very powerful computer (we conducted our analysis on the University of Manchester CDC 7600) the minimization procedure takes considerable time with a large number of unbalanced pedigrees since restrictions on core size mean that the pedigrees had to be reconstructed each time the likelihood was evaluated for new parameter values. There are few systematic patterns in the different pedigrees which can be used to reduce the number of stages in evaluating the likelihood. Small increases in the number of parameters did not appear to affect the computation time very greatly, though the time taken to evaluate initial values for the second derivatives may make the estimation of large numbers of parameters prohibitive in data like ours.

A disadvantage of this approach, compared with the approach through the use of balanced pedigrees such as twins or families of uniform structure (see e.g. Young et al., 1980, for an example of the approach to balanced pedigrees), is that there is no straightforward test of the goodness of fit of a given model. In principle it would be possible to construct some type of test by introducing additional parameters to remove constraints implicit in simpler models just as we relaxed the constraint of consistent gene action over sexes in our earlier analysis of twin data. Ideally, we might estimate separate covariances for each type of relationship recognizable in the structure of the given families providing a practical upper limit to the likelihood under the assumption of multivariate normality. Such an approach was attempted with these data but proved impracticable because the problem required the estimation of an unreasonably large number of parameters given the already substantial numerical problem stemming from the need to reconstruct so many pedigrees individually during the evaluation of the likelihood for given parameter values.

We have to be content, therefore, with comparisons of alternative hypotheses using the likelihood ratio test to decide whether additional parameters need to be included in the model. This is undesirable but the additional information obtainable from the variety of new relationships will go far to offsetting any lack of an overall test of our model.

Specifying the structure of pedigrees

The key to the analysis of pedigrees is an efficient method of coding the relationships. We chose a system of coding for our analysis which employed as its starting point the principle of graph theory (Maruyama & Yasuda, 1970) which states, in effect, that all the information about the relationships between individuals in a pedigree can be reconstituted from a knowledge of the parents of each individual. In our initial coding of the family data, therefore, we reconstructed the pedigree of cooperative subjects to the point that all the individuals in a given family were traceable through a common ancestor, even though that ancestor and certain intermediate relatives had not actually participated actively in the survey. An example of such a pedigree is given in Figure 20. Males are represented by squares, females by circles. Participants for whom data are available are repre-

Figure 20: A typical pedigree

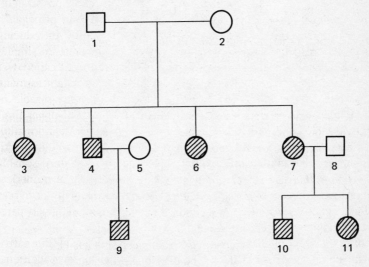

Squares denote males. Circles denote females.
Cooperative individuals are shaded.

sented by black symbols, non-cooperating relatives (included simply for relational data) are represented by open symbols. The original coding (see Table 37) would note for each individual in the pedigree just the individual number and the number of the male and female parents.

TABLE 37

Matrix representation of pedigree

Column	1	2	3	4	5	6	7	8	9	10	11
Row											
1	0	0	0	0	0	0	0	0	0	0	0
2	0	0	0	0	0	0	0	0	0	0	0
3	1	1	0	0	0	0	0	0	0	0	0
4	1	1	0	0	0	0	0	0	0	0	0
5	0	0	0	0	0	0	0	0	0	0	0
6	1	1	0	0	0	0	0	0	0	0	0
7	1	1	0	0	0	0	0	0	0	0	0
8	0	0	0	0	0	0	0	0	0	0	0
9	0	0	0	1	1	0	0	0	0	0	0
10	0	0	0	0	0	0	1	1	0	0	0
11	0	0	0	0	0	0	1	1	0	0	0

A '1' denotes that the individual in the designated row is a child of the individual in the intersecting column. Thus '3' is the child of '1' and '2'.

If we restrict our analysis to individuals of a single sex, twin data provide four summary statistics which are relevant to the analysis of intra-sex variation: the mean squares within and between pairs of monozygotic and dizygotic twins. In principle, therefore, there are only four independent parameters that can be estimated, so many more subtle causes of variation will remain confounded in twin data. Twin data may lead us to reject some models which assume a very simple genetical or environmental basis for the observed differences, but in the event of our rejecting, for example, a simple additive model with no cultural effects it may be difficult, provided the analysis is restricted to twin data, to decide more precisely upon the nature of the factors which contribute to failure of this model.

When we turn to the whole body of data we discern a great many possible variances and covariances between biological and non-biological relatives, all of which are capable of supplying some information about the causes of variation (Table 38). Many more parameters can now be estimated in theory, although the practical difficulties of estimating large numbers of parameters with such highly unbalanced data are

TABLE 38

Example coding of pedigree to specify relationships for model-fitting

Individual

	Column	1	2	3	4	5	6	7	8	9	10	11
Row												
	1	0	20	21	21	0	21	21	0	24	24	24
	2		0	21	21	0	21	21	0	24	24	24
	3			2	23	0	23	23	0	25	25	25
	4				1	20	23	23	0	21	25	25
	5					0	0	0	0	0	0	0
Individual	6						2	23	0	25	25	25
	7							2	20	25	21	21
	8								0	0	21	21
	9									1	26	26
	10										1	23
	11											2

Key-	0	no data
diagonals:	1	male
	2	female
off-diagonals :	0	no biological relationship
	20	spouse
	21	parent/offspring
	23	sibling
	24	grandparental
	25	avuncular
	26	first cousin

prohibitive. Furthermore, there is no simple test of the model any more. We can only compare alternative hypotheses for the observed data and consider what alterations of the model, if any, lead to substantial increase in the support.

In the light of the analysis of twin data we begin by examining the consequences for the whole body of data assuming that variation is due entirely to the additive effects of genes in a randomly mating population with all environmental influences being attributed to environmental differences within families, i.e. due to the unique experiences of particular individuals within the family. Classical genetical theory yields the expectations in Table 39 for the total variance of

TABLE 39

Contributions of additive genetic variance to the variance and covariance of relatives on the assumption of no familial environment

Relationship	Expected covariance
MZ twin	$\frac{1}{2}D_R$
DZ twin	$\frac{1}{4}D_R$
sibling	$\frac{1}{4}D_R$
spouse	0
parent/offspring	$\frac{1}{4}D_R$
grandparent/grandchild	$\frac{1}{8}D_R$
avuncular	$\frac{1}{8}D_R$
first cousin	$\frac{1}{16}D_R$
foster parent/foster child	0
unrelated reared together	0
Total variance	$\frac{1}{2}D_R + E_1$

$\frac{1}{2}D_R$ = additive genetic component
E_1 = environmental variation within families
Expected *correlations* are obtained by dividing each covariance by the total expected variance

individuals in the population and for the covariances between biological relatives of different degrees. Since there is assumed to be no influence of the family environment in such a system there is expected to be no covariation between individuals with no common biological ancestry.

Employing the method of pedigree analysis outlined above we find maximum-likelihood parameter estimates are as follows:

	Age of onset	Average consumption
$\mu_m = $	−0.011	−0.025
$\mu_f = $	−0.013	−0.013
$D_R = $	0.71	0.80
$E_1 = $	0.53	0.38

The log-likelihoods of obtaining the observed data sets under this hypothesis are −1035.5 and −842.5 respectively. There is no direct test of the model, although the correlations observed (with no allowance for the overlap between different pairs) differ quite considerably from those which would be predicted on the basis of the parameter estimates obtained above (Table 40). In particular, the predicted correlations for twins are somewhat lower than those actually observed, whereas the above estimates for non-twins are generally lower (at least for the first-degree relatives, for whom the greatest information is available) than those predicted. Is this difference between twins and non-twins significant?

One simple way of deciding whether the two major subdivisions of the data are heterogeneous is to fit the same model to the twin data and the family and adoption data separately, and obtain for each data set separate parameter values and log-likelihood values. When this is done we find:

	Age of onset		Average consumption	
	Twin data	*Family data*	*Twin data*	*Family data*
L =	−419.3	−598.4	−264.2	−560.3
$\mu_m = $	0.812	−0.793	−0.021	0.055
$\mu_f = $	0.127	−0.118	−0.079	0.078
$D_R = $	0.75	0.43	0.68	0.67
$E_1 = $	0.48	0.67	0.32	0.52

Clearly, the parameter values differ quite markedly between the groups. The contribution of genetical factors appears to be greater in

TABLE 40

Observed and expected correlations compared under purely additive genetic system with random mating in the absence of family environmental effects

Relationship	Age of onset		Average consumption	
	Observed	*Expected*	*Observed*	*Expected*
MZ twin	0.40	0.40	0.52	0.51
DZ twin	0.30	0.20	0.30	0.26
sibling	0.14	0.20	0.11	0.26
spouse	0.19	0.	0.12	0.
parent/offspring	0.10	0.20	0.21	0.26
grandparent/ grandchild	−0.11	0.10	0.08	0.13
avuncular	0.18	0.10	0.07	0.13
first cousin	0.18	0.05	0.10	0.06
foster parent/ foster child	−0.02	0.	−0.02	0.
unrelated, reared together	0.18	0.	0.05	0.

Expectations are obtained using the ML estimates of D_R and E_1 combined according to the expectations of variance and covariance in Table 39.

twins than in the rest of the data. Also, there are substantial differences between the means of the two groups. Considered jointly, are these differences in mean and in the components of variation statistically significant? Fitting the same four parameters to the whole data set yields a log-likelihood for age of onset of −1035.5. Allowing the parameters to take separate values in the two bodies of data gives a total log-likelihood of −1017.7. This is the sum of the log-likelihoods for the separate sets of data. By fitting separate parameters to the two sets of data the number of estimated parameters has been increased from four to eight. The gain in support achieved at the expense of fitting four additional parameters is inferred from the difference between the support for the four-parameter model and that for the eight-parameter model. For the age of onset this difference is 17.8 units, corresponding to a χ_4^2 of 35.6, $P < 0.1\%$. For average consumption the difference turns out to be 18.0 units, or the χ^2 measuring improvement in fit is 36.0, $P < 0.1\%$. Thus in both cases the data lend substantial support for the view that different parameter values need to be assumed for the two major divisions of the data. We are thus compelled to re-examine our model for obvious discrepancies. Clearly the simple additive model, which assumes that genes and environment act additively and independently without modification with age and without correlation due to assortative mating, cannot encompass the observations satisfactorily. This finding raises more questions than it answers directly since the estimates of D_R and E_1 obtained from the two sets of data contain different biases if the model fails and the difference between the means of the two principal groups may reflect quite simple demographic factors such as the age structure of the sub-samples. Consider, for example, the possibility of non-additive genetic variation such as dominance. In twin data, the greater part of the information about genetical differences arises from the comparison of the intrapair variances for monozygotic and dizygotic twins. In the absence of dominance this difference is a powerful estimator of $\frac{1}{4}D_R$. If dominance is present, however, the difference will contain, in addition to $\frac{1}{4}D_R$, three-quarters of the dominance variance, or $\frac{3}{16}H_R$. It is known that the twin study is a very inefficient design for the separation of additive and dominance variation (Eaves, 1969; Martin et al. 1978), so that even a large amount of genetical non-additivity may remain undetected and therefore lead to an incorrectly inflated estimate of the additive genetical variance. Although the argument has been couched in terms of dominance variation, the same considerations will generally apply in the case of epistasis. In the case of the family and adoption data, however, the reverse is true. If anything, we have precise estimates of the contribution of additive genetical variance from relationships in which dominance does not contribute to the covariance (parents and offspring, uncles and nephews, etc.) or in which the contribution of dominance is relatively small as in the case of the covariance between siblings. In such data the omission of dominance from the model will lead to inflated estimates of the environmental variation but will have relatively little effect on the estimated additive genetical variation. The pattern of components obtained from the separate analyses of the two subsets of data is consistent with that to be expected from biases due to undetected dominance or other genetical non-additivity.

It is one thing to say that the difference *could* be due to dominance, but quite another to assert that it must be so. In this study, each twin was tested at the same age as his co-twin, although twin pairs differed in their ages at the time of testing. There is, therefore, no opportunity for age differences in the expression of genetical and cultural effects to contribute to intrapair differences. The covariance between twins, therefore, is a covariance between individuals measured at identical stages in development. Any estimate of genetical variation which is based on the comparison between MZ and DZ covariances, therefore, is automatically corrected for age interaction and the estimate of D_R will reflect the contribution of genes which are expressed at an identical stage of development. Under most conceivable models of development this is the strategy most likely to yield significant estimates of genetical variation, but there is no guarantee that they will generalize to relatives measured at different stages of development.

Except in the most extensive longitudinal study, it is almost certain that other types of relatives will be measured at quite different environmental stages of development, and even the best study cannot overcome the long-term changes in the simultaneous measurement of parents and offspring culture for example; this will ensure that they are separated by about twenty years in development and a generation in culture. A similar problem will occur even with siblings on account of parity differences. For a great many behavioural traits, which are less provocative issues than smoking, it may well be that the influence of age and fashion does little to affect the similarity between relatives.

The fact that social pressure is often regarded as modifying people's habits, however, may lead us to suppose that in the case of smoking the contribution of developmental factors and interaction of genetical differences with age may prove a significant component in the transmissibility or otherwise of the smoking habit.

Although we shall consider a quantitative model for such influences subsequently, it suffices to mention in this context that the consequences of such age-dependence of gene expression will be remarkably similar to those of dominance in the present data. That is, the interaction of genetical differences with age will tend to reduce the similarity between relatives measured at different ages compared with that found in the case of twins, who are studied at virtually identical chronological ages.

Our discussion so far has centred primarily upon the issue of non-additivity because the parameter estimates for the simple model display many of the characteristics associated with undetected non-additivity. However, it is noted that we have considered neither the contribution of environmental factors to the similarity between relatives nor the effects of assortative mating. Although sample sizes were small, especially in the case of adopted siblings, it is suspected that the data give little reason to suppose that the family environment is contributing significantly to the similarity between relatives. With a fair degree of certainty we can assert that the smoking behaviour of parents has little environmental influence on the development of smoking in offspring. We can be less certain, on the basis of the correlations quoted above, that all sorts of shared environment are trivial in their effect since we have neither a large number of unrelated individuals reared together nor a great number of measurements on the family environment. The contribution of dominance to the hypothesized genetical variation may be specified on the assumption of effective random mating by adding the contributions of H_R given in Table 41. H_R is defined by Mather & Jinks (1971) as $\sum_a 16u_a^2 v_a^2 h_a^2$ and is equivalent to $4V_D$ in the notation of Falconer and the Edinburgh school. Thus, although we estimate H_R, following the convention of the biometrical genetical school, the actual contribution of dominance to the genetical variation in the population is given by $\frac{1}{4}H_R$.

Fitting three variance components (D_R, H_R, and E_1) and two means to the full data set yields log-likelihood values and parameter estimates as follows:

	Age of onset	*Average consumption*
L	-1033.0	-841.0
μ_m	-0.130	0.022
μ_f	-0.153	0.013
D_R	0.44	0.62
H_R	0.72	0.47
E_1	0.48	0.35

For the data considered as a whole the addition of dominance to the model increases the support by only 2.5 units for age of onset and by a mere 1.5 units for the average consumption; this, even though the estimates of genetical non-additive variation are numerically large. On the basis of a conventional significance test the improvement as a result of estimating dominance is significant in the case of age of onset ($\chi_1^2 = 5.0$, $P < 0.05$) but barely so in the case of average consumption. Although this may indicate some form of non-additivity it would be premature to jump to this conclusion until alternative explanations have been considered, for, as we have hinted above, a variety of other 'non-additive' factors including certain types of genotype-environmental interaction may simulate the effects of dominance in transgenerational data. The estimate of H_R for age of onset is especially large and would imply, in addition to very large individual dominance deviations, substantial inequality in the fre-

TABLE 41

The contribution of dominance to the covariance of relatives when mating is random

Relationship	Expectation	Correlations			
		Age of onset		Average consumption	
		Observed	Expected	Observed	Expected
MZ twin	$\frac{1}{2}D_R + \frac{1}{4}H_R$	0.40	0.45	0.52	0.55
DZ twin	$\frac{1}{4}D_R + \frac{1}{16}H_R$	0.30	0.18	0.30	0.24
sibling	$\frac{1}{4}D_R + \frac{1}{16}H_R$	0.14	0.18	0.11	0.24
spouse	—	0.19	0.	0.12	0.
parent/ offspring	$\frac{1}{4}D_R$	0.10	0.12	0.21	0.20
grandparent/ grandchild	$\frac{1}{8}D_R$	−0.11	0.06	0.08	0.10
avuncular	$\frac{1}{8}D_R$	0.18	0.06	0.07	0.10
first cousin	$\frac{1}{16}D_R$	0.18	0.03	0.10	0.05
foster parent/ foster child	—	−0.02	0.	−0.02	0.
unrelated, reared together	—	0.18	0.	0.05	0.
Total variance	$\frac{1}{2}D_R + \frac{1}{4}H_R + E_1$	—	—	—	—

quencies of increasing and decreasing alleles, if it were finally accepted as a genuine estimate of dominance rather than as an artefact of some other form of non-additivity. It is possible to obtain separate parameter estimates of the above model for the two data sets, since there are sufficient underlying covariances and variances to allow this. This results are as follows:

		Age of onset		Average consumption	
		Twin data	*Family data*	*Twin data*	*Family data*
L	=	−418.3	−598.3	−264.0	−559.7
$\hat{\mu}m$	=	0.087	−0.078	−0.022	0.056
$\hat{\mu}f$	=	0.130	−0.117	−0.079	0.079
$\hat{D}_R$	=	1.31	0.40	0.91	0.73
$\hat{H}_R$	=	−1.19	0.27	−0.48	−0.87
$\hat{E}_1$	=	0.49	0.62	0.33	0.70

Compared with the estimates for the pooled data set, the above estimates seem very bizarre, although they are in fact by no means atypical of the results to be expected from attempting to fit a dominance parameter to restricted subsets of data for which dominance is unlikely to be a 'true' component of variance. The negative estimate of dominance for both twin sets of data comes as no surprise. We already know that there is a very marked negative correlation between estimates of D_R and H_R obtained from twin data in the absence of E_2 effects (correlations close to unity are fairly typical). The result is that additive and dominance effects are almost inseparable in twin data except when the effects of dominance are very marked and the sample sizes are enormous (Martin et al., 1978). Hence, slight over-estimation of D_R by chance or because of other undetected effects will lead to a correlated decrease in the estimate of H_R. Furthermore, we had already reserved judgment about the contribution of family environmental effects in the twin data, observing that the twin data, considered separately, were consistent with a contribution of more than 10% from variation due to such factors. If such a contribution exceeds in magnitude even one-eighth of the true value of H_R then any attempt to ignore the effects of E_2 in explaining twin data will yield negative (sometimes even significantly and non-sensically negative) estimates of H_R.

The large negative dominance parameter from the family data on cigarette consumption does require brief comment, however, and is attributable to the excess of the parent-offspring correlation over that reported for siblings. The latter, together with the other ancestral and collateral correlations for cigarette consumption all suggest a fairly small and additive contribution from genetical factors. The parent-offspring correlation, however, suggests a somewhat larger contribution which in the absence of cultural effects implied by the non-significant correlation between adopted child and adopting parent would normally be attributable to additive genetical factors. If mating is random then the sibling correlation may exceed the parent-offspring correlation by $\frac{1}{16}H_R$, but if sampling or other factors lead to an excess of the parental correlation over the sibling correlation then unjustified attempts to estimate dominance may yield large negative estimates of H_R such as that obtained here for consumption of cigarettes.

The above discussion should not be interpreted as giving premature significance to the nonsense values of the dominance parameter, any more than credibility attaches to the quite reasonable estimates obtained for the pooled data or from the family data for the age of onset of smoking. In only one case, namely that of the pooled age of onset data, is there any indication that the inclusion of dominance is leading to any significant improvement in the likelihood of obtaining the observed data set. The fact that this finding is not supported by comparable evidence from either of the two data sets considered separately must lend some support to the view that the apparent non-additivity detected on the pooled data should be attributed to factors other than dominance.

The effects of the shared environment

The absence of any significant similarity between foster parents and their adopted children implies that any effects of the common environment of individuals reared together depend on factors other than the direct influence of parental smoking behaviour. This may be hardly surprising in the case of the age at which individuals begin to smoke, since it may be envisaged that other factors in the shared environment of twins may be more significant in bringing about initiation in the practice of smoking. The influence of peers, for example, could be a significant factor, as might other facets of parental behaviour which are quite independent of parents' own smoking habits. Even parents who do not smoke might well provide an environment in which offspring are encouraged to try for themselves. Initiation, therefore, might be quite independent of the factors which influence the establishment of the adult smoking habit. This facet of smoking behaviour will be examined subsequently. At this point we consider whether there is any evidence on the basis of our data for an overall shared environmental effect for those who are reared together, whether they be siblings, twins, or in the case of adopted children, unrelated individuals reared together. Only if there is convincing evidence for such an effect are measurements made on the family environment considered as a unit likely to prove fruitful in the subsequent analysis of the smoking habit.

At this stage we consider whether the addition of a fourth parameter, E_2, can lead to a marked improvement in the ability of our model to predict the observations. The model we wish to test is simple. We assume that, in addition to the sources of variation already considered, there may be a contribution to the covariance of individuals reared together which is due to features of their shared environment. The precise nature of these factors is of no immediate concern; we are merely attempting to *infer* their presence from their consequences for the similarity between related and unrelated individuals reared together. It may, of course, be argued that such a model is unrealistic in its simplicity. It may equally be argued that a model which is not at some stage unrealistic in its simplicity will lead to little development in understanding of the problem.

The expectations of the variances and covariances are given in Table 42. No environmental similarity is postulated between parent and offspring at this stage, neither is there assumed to be any environmental similarity between more distant relatives. We know already that it is no longer possible to separate all the four effects with twin data alone, so we have to be content with estimates obtained on the basis of the pooled data, and the family data alone. The latter will

TABLE 42

The contribution of random shared environmental effects to the covariances of relatives

Relationship	Expected covariance	Correlations			
		Observed	Expected	Observed	Expected
MZ twin	$\frac{1}{2}D_R + \frac{1}{4}H_R + E_2$	0.40	0.44	0.52	0.56
DZ twin	$\frac{1}{4}D_R + \frac{1}{16}H_R + E_2$	0.30	0.21	0.30	0.22
siblings	$\frac{1}{4}D_R + \frac{1}{16}H_R + E_2$	0.14	0.21	0.11	0.22
spouse	—	0.19	0	0.12	0
parent/ offspring	$\frac{1}{4}D_R$	0.10	0.10	0.21	0.20

Relationship	Expected covariance	Correlations			
		Observed	Expected	Observed	Expected
grandparent/ grandchild	$\frac{1}{8}D_R$	−0.11	0.05	0.08	0.10
avuncular	$\frac{1}{8}D_R$	0.18	0.05	0.07	0.10
first cousin	$\frac{1}{16}D_R$	0.18	0.03	0.10	0.05
foster parent/ foster child		−0.02	0	−0.02	0
unrelated, reared together	E_2	0.18	0.07	0.05	−0.02
Total variance	$\frac{1}{2}D_R + \frac{1}{4}H_R + E_1 + E_2$	—		—	

be very unreliable because there are few pairs of unrelated individuals reared together. The estimates of H_R and E_2 would thus be very highly correlated because they would both rely on comparison of ancestral and distant collateral correlations with the correlation for siblings. As far as the twins alone are concerned, D_R, H_R, E_1, and E_2 cannot be separated. Only simplifying assumptions can be made.

Adding the single parameter, E_2, to represent the shared environment of twins, siblings and unrelated individuals reared together (Table 42) yields the following for the two traits under consideration:

		Age of onset	Average consumption
L	=	−1032.2	−840.9
μ_m	=	−0.010	0.023
μ_f	=	−0.014	0.014
D_R	=	0.37	0.64
H_R	=	0.59	0.53
E_1	=	0.50	0.35
E_2	=	0.06	−0.02

In both cases the change in the likelihood is so slight as to lend very little support to the view that a simple family environmental component of the type specified need be included in the model. Furthermore, the actual estimates of E_2 are numerically small, confirming the earlier conclusion that the data are not really consistent with the presence of a large family environmental effect.

What then are the gross conclusions to emerge from the analysis so far? The first and most striking conclusion is that our twin data are remarkably and significantly different from the family data in their picture of the causes of variation in smoking as we have measured it. This is seen from the very outset in the clear heterogeneity of the sets of data with respect to the estimates of the simple additive genetic within-family environment (D_R, E_1) model. Furthermore, very little of this heterogeneity can be explained by simple modifications of the model for the components of variance which assume that the genetical and environmental effects are comparable for all types of relationship. So, although there may be some evidence of genetical non-additivity, reflected in the changes found after fitting a dominance parameter, this is hardly sufficient to explain the inadequacy of the simpler model. In addition, it seems that invoking a general effect of the family environment which does not depend on the parents for its creation leads to only the most trivial change in the ability of the model to encompass the data.

The effect of age and genotype x age interaction

We are thus compelled to consider hypotheses which do not constrain the causes of variation in the two major divisions of our data to be identical. At this point, therefore, we introduce the consideration of the differences in the mean and variance for age within our two subsamples. Reference to Table 64 shows that the twin sample is younger and more uniform in age than the sample of non-twins. In so far as the measures under study show a relationship with age this may be reflected in differences in mean and variance between the two subsamples. This is especially likely in the case of the age of onset, since younger subjects will not have had all the opportunity to develop the smoking habit of their older contemporaries.

The population age trends

There are several ways in which the age structure of the population studied might influence the pattern of variation for a measured trait. The simplest, and that which is considered most regularly, is a population trend in behaviour with age, which is resolved by representing an individual's behaviour as a deviation from the mean performance of all individuals measured at the same age. This procedure underlies most attempts to correct psychometric scores for the effects of age, and assumes that the underlying population trend is appropriate for all individuals.

Assuming for the moment that this model is appropriate, and that the general age trend is linear, we may incorporate the linear regression of score on age as part of our model, modifying our expectations for each subject's score, y_i, to be

$$\hat{y}_i = c + bx_i$$

for subjects of age x_i, where the constant, c, and regression coefficient b are to be estimated along with the components of variance in our genotype-environmental model.

The numerical problem of estimation is simplified by removing some of the redundant variance components from the model first. Though this is not essential, it leads to a substantial reduction in computer time. Initially, therefore, we deleted the dominance (H_R) and family environment (E_2) terms, so fitting D_R, E_1, with the regression coefficient b and two constants, one each for males and females. Although the population means were arbitrarily standardized to zero for sexes separately, we retained these differences to reflect differences in mean age of the samples of males and females. The model thus assumes that the age trends are similar in all subsets of the data.

Fitting this modified model to the entire population gave a significant increase in support corresponding to a chi-square of more than 30 for the age of onset and of 8.6 for average consumption, when the model including the age trend is compared with the D_R, E_1, model which omits the age correction. This finding offers small comfort in our attempts to explain the difference between the twins and the rest of the population, however, since fitting the age trend with D_R and E_1 to the separate data sets reveals the existence of great residual heterogeneity. Indeed, it might be argued that the age correction has unmasked further heterogeneity in the data relating to average consumption because the sharp change in the log-likelihood associated with the inclusion of an age trend for the family and adoption date is not matched by any marked decrease in the likelihood for the pooled data. The findings for the age-corrected data are summarized in Tables 43 and 44.

As far as the age of onset is concerned, the two data sets retain

TABLE 43

Parameter estimates before and after age correction: age of onset

Parameter	Before age correction			After age correction		
	Full data	Twins	Families	Full data	Twins	Families
L	−1035.5	−419.3	−598.4	−1019.7	−416.5	−577.6
$\hat{c}_m$	−0.011	0.812	−0.793	−0.268	−0.086	−0.486
$\hat{c}_f$	−0.013	0.127	−0.118	−0.257	−0.067	−0.474
$\hat{b}$	—	—	—	0.0068	0.0057	0.0095
$\hat{D}_R$	0.71	0.75	0.43	0.70	0.74	0.40
$\hat{E}_1$	0.53	0.48	0.67	0.53	0.48	0.66

TABLE 44

Parameter estimates before and after age correction: average consumption

Parameter	Before age correction			After age correction		
	Full data	Twins	Families	Full data	Twins	Families
L	−842.5	−264.2	−560.3	−838.2	−262.9	−548.5
$\hat{c}_m$	−0.025	−0.021	0.055	0.152	−0.126	0.350
$\hat{c}_f$	−0.013	−0.079	0.078	0.133	−0.201	0.531
$\hat{b}$	—	—	—	−0.0033	0.0036	−0.0069
$\hat{D}_R$	0.80	0.68	0.67	0.80	0.67	0.61
$\hat{E}_1$	0.38	0.32	0.52	0.38	0.32	0.53

their different parameter values after age correction although the correction leads to a significant improvement in fit in all cases and the regression coefficients do not differ markedly between the two groups. Despite the despondency often expressed by critics of analyses based on scores with no correction for age, the striking fact is that the correction for the population age trend makes only the slightest difference to the values obtained for the variance components. These differences are certainly well within the sampling error attached to the estimates and are probably almost within the numerical accuracy of the algorithms! This is a recurrent observation in a wide range of behaviour-genetics applications.

The extraction of a linear component for age may not be the whole story, as seen in the corresponding analysis for average consumption. Although there is, once more, striking evidence of an age trend, this is confined substantially to the family data in which average consumption declines with increasing age, although with apparently little effect on the magnitudes on the variance components D_R and E_1, compared with their estimates obtained without age correction. The age effect in the twins, for which the mean age and age range are less than the families, we find the regression actually *opposite* in sign to the estimate obtained from the families. Although there is little justification for any age correction in the twin sample (since the increase in support from fitting the age regression is slight) this might indicate an overall non-linear trend of smoking with age such that there is an early increase followed by a later decline in cigarette consumption.

The model of age trends incorporated so far, whilst that most commonly employed in attempts to correct populations of heterogeneous age structure for the effects of age, leaves much to be desired. Relating individuals to the mean of their age group is only legitimate in so far as every individual in the same group displays the same characteristic ageing pattern and provided chronological age is an adequate guide to the individual's stage of development. Clearly there is no reason why this should be the case and there are many reasons why it should not.

The interaction of gene expression with age

During development, different genes are expressed at different times and different environmental influences are significant at different stages. If individuals differ in the times at which particular genetic effects are expressed, then the interaction of gene expression with age will lead to non-additivity (a kind of genotype-environment interaction) which cannot be explained simply from a knowledge of the population trends with age. Indeed, it is conceivable that a population may show no overall age trend yet remain riddled with age effects due to the interaction of genetical and environmental differences with age.

The only definitive way of analysing such interactions is through a longitudinal study in which the same individuals are studied at different stages. The problem of age dependence of gene expression then reduces to that of studying the covariation between individuals' scores at different developmental stages. Such studies are difficult but in default of longitudinal information we may attempt to extract from our, albeit unsatisfactory, data some guide to the importance of age interactions by examining the similarities and differences between related individuals measured at different stages, to see whether individuals of a given degree of relatedness display greater or lesser similarity with increasing dissimilarity in their ages. This sounds fine in principle, though it may be fraught with interpretational problems in practice because we can never guarantee that parents and offspring, for example, would have shared the same experiences had they been reared at similar times. It is none the less the best that can be done with short-term data such as ours.

On the basis of genetical theory we can write expectations for the covariances between relatives of various degrees. These expectations are those employed in calculating the likelihood for the above models. In fact, the approach to be outlined does not specifically depend on there being genetical effects at all; it could equally be adopted where there are age-dependent cultural effects in an appropriately designed study.

For simplicity we shall assume that the total genetic variance is constant over age, though this is not essential for the formulation of the model. Ignoring other sources of genotype-environmental interaction, therefore, we write the expected covariance between two related individuals measured at the same age as

$$w_0 = cD_R$$

where c is the coefficient of D_R appropriate for the degree of relationship under consideration. This will be $\frac{1}{2}$ for MZ twins, $\frac{1}{4}$ for siblings, etc. if mating is random, but the important feature is the expected covariance between individuals measured at identical ages. For a given relationship the covariance expected between individuals measured at different ages will be a function of the above and the age difference between them. Clearly, in the absence of genotype x age interaction the covariance is expected to be the same no matter how great the age difference. In other cases, however, we might expect the covariance to decline with increasing age difference, t years. One plausible form of the decline would be to put

$$w_t = e^{-kt}w_0 \quad ....(5.1)$$

where k is a constant to be determined, i.e. to let the similarity decline exponentially as a function of increasing age difference. Other, more complex functions might be postulated, but our concern here is with the basic idea rather than with the resolution of alternative refinements which may be well beyond the power of the existing data. Our data provide us with the opportunity to explore such trends crudely because we have a range of individuals of the same degree of genetical relatedness but which have been measured at variously different stages of development. Thus we have dizygotic twins who have been measured at the same age, siblings who are separated by at least one year and frequently more, and parents and offspring who are separated by a generation, yet all, on the simple additive model of gene action under conditions of random mating, display the same degree of genetical similarity.

Because twins provide a convenient anchor-point for this analysis, having the unique characteristic of being measured at the same age, the analysis is conducted on the whole body of data. Indeed, although it would be possible to estimate the decay coefficient, k, with the family data alone, there is no way in which it could be estimated from the twins separately because twins are not separated in age. We thus employ the whole body of data, whilst recognizing that other, environmental, factors might lead to a greater similarity between twins apart from the strict developmental synchrony ensured by measuring individuals at identical ages.

We thus recast our original D_R, E_1 model in a form which permitted the expected covariance between individuals to be a function of the absolute age difference between them, as in equation 5:1 above. The linear trend of expected behaviour with age was retained in the model, so we now estimated six parameters, the constants for males and females (c_m and c_f), the common regression of smoking behaviour on age (b), the additive genetical parameter (D_R), the within family environmental component (E_1) and the genotype x age interaction parameter, k. The parameter estimates obtained when this model is fitted to the data for both traits are given in Table 45.

The change in support is highly significant ($x_1^2 = 7.8$) for the age of onset data, but barely so for average consumption, suggesting that genotype x age interaction is at least a possible explanation of the greater similarity in the age of onset of smoking in twins compared with non-twin siblings and parents and offspring. The original tabulated correlations concur with this explanation since the correlations for fraternal twins, siblings and parents and offspring agree with the ranking to be expected on the hypothesis that the observed correlation between subjects of identical genotypic similarity is a function of the age difference between them.

The maximum likelihood estimates of k (Table 45) are -0.028 for age of onset and -0.011 for average consumption; these values imply that the similarity between relatives of given degree declines with increasing difference in their ages. As a guide to the magnitude of the effect we may calculate the expected degree of similarity between individuals separated by a ten-year age gap compared with that expected for individuals measured at identical ages. We thus evaluate e^{-10k}, which for age of onset is approximately 0.75 and for average consumption approximately 0.9. The data thus suggest that a ten-year age gap between siblings, for example, would result in the similarity falling to an estimated 75 per cent of its 'true' value predicted on the basis of genetical theory applied to individuals of uniform age. Average consumption, on the other hand, does not show such a marked trend since the predicted similarity for individuals differing by ten years in age is still 90 per cent of that expected for individuals measured at the same age. An age gap of twenty-five years would apparently be required to reduce the correlation in the consumption of tobacco to as much as 75 per cent of the correlation based on subjects of uniform age.

This model assumes that all the similarity between relatives is genetic, and that all the decay of similarity with increasing age difference is thus due to changes with time of gene expression. This could in principle be one explanation of the fact that the raw correlation of DZ twins in age of onset exceeds that for siblings, which in turn is greater than the parent-offspring similarity. Although this might be true qualitatively, the estimates above predict nothing

TABLE 45

The effect of age difference on the similarity of relatives

	Age of onset	Average consumption
L	−1015.8	−836.8
$\hat{c}_m$	−0.275	0.157
$\hat{c}_f$	−0.268	0.141
$\hat{b}$	0.0070	−0.0035
$\hat{D}_R$	0.77	0.84
$\hat{E}_1$	0.48	0.36
$\hat{k}$	−0.028	−0.011
Improvement χ_1^2	7.8	2.8
P%	<1	≃10

like the large difference in similarity between DZ twins and siblings. Even a ten-year gap, which must surely be greater than the typical gap between siblings, would only lead to a sibling correlation which is 75 per cent of the DZ correlation. The observed difference, however, is much greater, the average sibling correlation being under 50 per cent of the corresponding twin correlation. Thus, although the data are sufficient to yield a significant estimate of k, at least for age of onset, we should not assume that the decay of similarity between DZ twins and siblings can be attributed simply to the type of interaction postulated in the model.

So far, then, the data support the view that twins are a special case in the sense that the same model cannot be applied to both twins and non-twins. The apparent differences cannot be attributed to simple genetical factors such as dominance, nor to the interaction of additive genetical differences with age. It follows, therefore, that the explanation must be sought in terms of either some other environmental mechanism or a different type of genotype-environmental interaction. We consider the first of these possibilities, namely that twins, as far as smoking is concerned, are subjected to environmental influences which are substantially more similar than those experienced either by siblings or by unrelated individuals reared together.

Returning to the D_R, H_R, E_1, E_2 model, it will be recalled that the family environmental parameter, E_2 was applied to all individuals reared together, however they were related and irrespective of the age difference between them. It is possible that the total environmental variation in the onset of smoking and in the consumption of cigarettes is constant throughout the population, but distributed differently between individuals depending on the temporal similarity of their experiences. Thus, although twins may be subjected to an environment which is no more or less heterogeneous than that of siblings or other children, it is conceivable that the degree of similarity between the environments experienced by twins is greater than that of siblings simply because the latter are exposed to the same range of influences at different times. This effect may be specified simply by writing three environmental parameters for the total environmental variation. V_E.

We write $V_E = E_1 + E_2' + E_T$

As in all the previous examples, E_1 represents the contribution of environmental effects which are uncorrelated within the family. We now recognize two degrees of environmental correlation between offspring reared in the same family, depending on whether the offspring are twins or not. Offspring which are not twins (i.e. siblings and unrelated individuals reared together) share a proportion E_2'/V_E of their environmental effects. Twins, on the other hand, being born at the same time and therefore exposed to environments which may be more similar still than siblings, have an additional component of their environmental effects in common, represented by E_T, so that the environmental correlation between twins is $(E_2'+E_T)/V_E$. The model now implied by these environmental components, in conjunction with additive genetical effects, is given in Table 46. It may be argued that such a model is still an over-simplification, and that some compromise which expresses the environmental correlation as a function of age difference (just as before we expressed the correlation between gene effects as a function of age difference) is desirable. Before attempting such refinements, however, we will fit the crude model to determine whether there is any substance in the claim that twins are subject to significantly more similar environments than non-twins reared together.

In the model actually fitted, we allowed different means for twins and non-twins as before and incorporated a linear age regression in our expectations. The contribution of dominance was retained in the model, to assess the effects of inclusion of the twin environment on the estimate of dominance. The parameter estimates are given in Table 47. The new model turns out to be as capable of producing the observations for the age of onset as the model which fitted different D_R's, E_1's, means and age regressions to the two data groups separately. On the latter model (see Table 43) the joint likelihood is

TABLE 46

**Observed and expected correlations under
additive model when allowance is made
for the twin environment**

Relationship	Expected covariance	*Correlations*			
		Age of onset		*Average consumption*	
		Observed	*Expected*	*Observed*	*Expected**
MZ twin	$\frac{1}{2}D_R + E_2' + E_T$	0.40	0.41	0.52	0.56
DZ twin	$\frac{1}{4}D_R + E_2' + E_T$	0.30	0.29	0.30	0.35
sibling	$\frac{1}{4}D_R + E_2'$	0.14	0.14	0.11	0.14
spouse	—	0.19	0.	0.12	0.
parent/ offspring	$\frac{1}{2}D_R$	0.10	0.11	0.21	0.19
grandparent/ grandchild	$\frac{1}{8}D_R$	−0.11	0.05	0.08	0.09
avuncular	$\frac{1}{8}D_R$	0.18	0.05	0.07	0.09
first cousin	$\frac{1}{16}D_R$	0.18	0.03	0.10	0.05
foster parent/ foster child	—	−0.02	0.	−0.02	0.
unrelated, reared together	E_2'	0.18	0.02	0.05	−0.05
Total variance	$\frac{1}{2}D_R + E_1 + E_2' + E_T$	—		—	

*calculated to include a small negative component, E_2'

Table 47

The effect of the 'twin environment'

Parameter	Age of onset	Average consumption
L	−994.03	−825.47
$\hat{c}_m$	−0.162	0.102
$\hat{c}_f$	−0.157	0.066
$\hat{c}'_m$	−0.442	0.238
$\hat{c}'_f$	−0.438	0.240
$\hat{b}$	0.0084	−0.0043
$\hat{D}_R$	0.37	0.58
$\hat{H}_R$	0.07	0.06
$\hat{E}_1$	0.50	0.34
$\hat{E}_2$	0.02	−0.04
$\hat{E}_T$	0.13	0.16

$-416.5 - 577.6 = -994.1$ which is virtually the same as the value of -994.03 obtained under the current model, and considerably better than other models which have tried to account for the inconsistency between twins and other types of relatives.

The average consumption data are less consistent with the 'twin environment' hypothesis, as judged by the much better fit obtained when fitting different D_R's and E_1's, etc., to twins and non-twins (Table 41). It is possible that much of this disparity might be attributable to the inconsistency of the age trends in the two sub-populations. Leaving this consideration aside, however, the results for the two traits are broadly similar and quite convincing. We notice particularly that inclusion of the twin environment reduces the estimated contribution of dominance (measured by $\frac{1}{4}H_R$) to virtually zero. This would not have been so with these data unless the substantial apparent non-additivity reflected in the estimate of H_R earlier had been an artefact of the much greater twin correlations which would receive considerable weight in the analysis.

Estimates of the twin environmental component are positive and large, accounting for approximately 16 per cent of the total variance in twins for age of onset and about 20 per cent of the variance in average consumption. This finding may be interpreted in several ways. One interpretation is that the twin situation is qualitatively unique as far as smoking is concerned, that twins may cooperate in their smoking habits simply because they are twins. Such cooperative effects, whether they are based on genetic or environmental differences, will tend to create an E_2 effect in twins (Eaves, 1976a) but will lead to detectable differences in variance between twins and, for example, singletons. There is very little to suggest that twins are more variable than non-twins in these data. An alternative interpretation, which is more attractive because it has greater generality, is that the similarity between twins is largely due to the effects of peers, school friends, colleagues, etc., on whose influence the pattern of smoking may depend in part. Twins, simply because they are twins irrespective of zygosity, share environments which are no more nor less variable than those of other individuals but which are more highly correlated than for other relatives. If this is the correct interpretation then the similarity of twins is an important guide to one significant environmental source of variability in the smoking habit.

It will be recalled that our analysis of the twin data in the previous chapter provided slight but by no means conclusive evidence of a family environmental effect, which we termed E_2 in that context, accounting for about 10 per cent of the variance. Our analysis of the entire body of data now suggest that this E_2 effect could be explained entirely by the specific correlation of twin environments rather than by the long-term environmental similarity between all types of offspring in the family. Our analysis suggests that the role of the latter effects is slight, there being little reason to retain a 'non-twin' shared environment (E_2) in our model. It may thus be argued that the environmental influences which lead to the development of the smoking habit, both in onset and duration, have little to do with the family and are only correlated in twins as a result of the coincidence of their birthdays. *By far the greater part of the environmental influences contributing to variation in the smoking habit come from outside the family,* are not shared by members of the family who do not belong by virtue of their age to the same peer group, do not depend on the smoking behaviour of parents and are, in short, largely specific to individuals in their location and effect.

By far the greatest contribution resides in E_1, the within-family environmental variation. The estimates in Table 47 confirm that approximately 60 per cent of the variation in age of onset of smoking is attributable to such unique environmental influences and approximately 40 per cent of the variation in consumption of cigarettes is due to similar factors. Apart from the long-term causal effects of individual experiences and hazards, the magnitude of E_1' will often reflect any short-term fluctuations in behaviour or reported behaviour. Thus, individuals' errors of memory in the case of age of onset may contribute to E_1, individual fluctuations in consumption may also contribute to the individual-specific environmental variation assessed by self-report on one particular occasion. It could turn out, on a more detailed study, that such fluctuations themselves have a partly inherited basis, but the only clear way of examining such changes is by studying the genetics of repeated measurements (e.g. Eaves & Eysenck, 1976; Eaves et al., 1978).

As far as we can tell, the contribution of genetical effects to the onset of smoking and the consumption of cigarettes is additive. When allowance is made for the effects of the twin environment the estimates of dominance are numerically very small and are certainly not significant, ranking with the contribution from the correlation between the environments of 'non-twin' siblings. In the model above, which assumes mating is random, the narrow heritability is estimated from

$$\tfrac{1}{2}\hat{D}_R \ / \ (\tfrac{1}{2}\hat{D}_R + \tfrac{1}{4}\hat{H}_R + \hat{E}_1 + \hat{E}_2' + \hat{E}_T)$$

Employing the actual numerical estimates of the parameters (including the small negative estimate of E_2') for average consumption yields narrow heritability estimates of 0.22 for age of onset and 0.38 for average consumption. These are maximum likelihood estimates and include information from all the different relationships in the study. Each type of relationship contributes in proportion to the frequency with which it is represented in the population and the degree of genetical similarity implied in the degree of relationship. In this sense, therefore, these are 'best' estimates. In this case, as in every other case, however, the ultimate acceptability of the estimates depends on the validity of the model assumed at the outset. The imbalance of the data set does not enable us to offer a rigorous general test of the model because the possibilities for overfitting are virtually endless and difficult to explore exhaustively with unbalanced data. It is none the less possible to show that certain simpler explanations are ruled out because they give significantly smaller values for the log-likelihood. We also know that complications, such as the specification of the family environment (E_2) or dominance, are not required by the data. We know from the previous chapter that the model which includes genetical effects and environmental correlation between members of a twin pair is adequate, suggesting that certain types of sex interaction are not major components of variation in smoking, although this does not contradict the existence of sex differences in average behaviour, nor does it preclude the extension of the model to specify such effects should subsequent more adequate data reveal their presence.

This significant but modest role for genetical factors is fairly typical for a wide variety of human traits in the personality and attitude domain though substantially less than those normally implied by data on abilities and morphological traits.

Certain features of the data are not predicted by the model. Foremost among these is the significant correlation between spouses for age of onset and average cigarette consumption. Subsidiary anomalies are the large avuncular and cousin correlations for age of onset and the fact that the parent-offspring correlation exceeds the sibling correlation for average consumption. In the case of the former it is conceivable that biases of ascertainment are greater in more distant relationships. It may be far easier to ascertain 'pet uncles and favourite cousins' than it is to secure the cooperation of 'black sheep'. The raw correlations for average consumption appear generally more tidy than those for age of onset.

The number of observations is tantalizingly small in some parts of the data. The number of foster-parent/foster-child pairs is presentable, but the fact that we could only ascertain a total of forty unrelated pairs reared together is disappointing because it is from these that much of the most direct information about the family environment of siblings would arise. Most people are likely to be more convinced by a zero correlation based on a large number of adoptions than by a variance component inferred at the end of a tortuous analysis. It suffices to say that the data taken as a whole, which include such adoption data as we have, are consistent with there being a relatively slight contribution from the shared environment for individuals other than twins.

Similarity between spouses

In all the above models, the contribution of additive genetic effects to the variation in smoking behaviour has been computed on the assumption of random mating. That is, it has been assumed that a person's phenotype with respect to smoking does not influence his choice of spouse. The fact that there is a slight correlation between spouses both for the age of onset of smoking and for the average consumption of cigarettes suggests that this assumption is false. It is possible that the correlation between spouses is a reflection of the same types of peer effect that were thought to contribute to twin similarity, in which case it will not affect the genetic contribution to the similarity between relatives. Indeed, even if this is not the case and the correlation between spouses does reflect an element of choice in the selection of mate, the combination of a comparatively small marital correlation with a trait of fairly low heritability will contribute little additional genetic variation to the population as far as smoking is concerned, given that spouse selection is based on phenotype with respect to the smoking habit. For the sake of completeness, however, we consider the effect of such assortative mating on the parameter estimates obtained for the age of onset and average consumption of cigarettes. In doing this, we follow in a very simple fashion the approach of Fisher (1918) who first obtained expectations for the genetical correlations between relatives under assortative mating. This work has been the subject of an illuminating commentary by Moran & Smith (1966) and more recently by Vetta & Smith (1974) who clarify further critical steps in Fisher's argument. Fisher obtains expectations for the contribution of linkage disequilibrium to the additive genetical variance in a population which is in equilibrium under assortative mating. He shows that when the parental phenotype exercises no environmental influence on the phenotype of offspring, the contribution of assortative mating increases the total additive genetic variance in the population from $\frac{1}{2}D_R$ to $\frac{1}{2}D_R (A/1-A)$, at equilibrium, where A is the correlation between the additive genetic deviations of spouse. Fisher considers several bases for assortative mating, including mating based primarily on the phenotype which produces a secondary correlation between the genotypes of spouses, but also outlines the treatment of assortative mating when the phenotypic correlation is merely a secondary consequence of mating based on the genotype. Our treatment will be restricted to the former. Following Fisher (1918) we obtain the expectations of the covariances of relatives in the population given in Table 48. The expectations assume that the genetical system is entirely additive and that there are no effects of the family environment. Initially, we discounted the effects of the twin environment, but retained the linear age trend and the separate constants for the two data groups, whilst fitting a constant D_R, and E_1 to the whole data set.

The estimates obtained under the assumption that assortative mating is based on the phenotype and that the population is in equi-

TABLE 48

Observed and expected correlations under additive model when allowance is made for phenotypic assortative mating

Relationship	Expected covariance*	Correlations			
		Age of onset		Average consumption	
		Observed	Expected	Observed	Expected
MZ twin	A_1	0.40	0.36	0.52	0.51
DZ twin	$A_1 A_2$	0.30	0.19	0.30	0.26
Sibling	$A_1 A_2$	0.14	0.19	0.11	0.26
spouse	$\mu(A_1 + E_1)$	0.19	0.15	0.12	0.05
parent/ offspring	$\frac{1}{2}A_1(1 + \mu)$	0.10	0.21	0.21	0.27
grandparent/ grandchild	$A_1 A_2^2(1 + \mu)$	−0.11	0.12	0.08	0.14
avuncular	$A_1 A_2^2$	0.18	0.10	0.07	0.13
first cousin	$A_1 A_2^3$	0.18	0.05	0.10	0.07
foster parent/ foster child	0	−0.02	0	−0.02	0
unrelated, reared together	0	0.18	0	0.05	0
Total variance	$A_1 + E_1$	.	.	.	.

*Assuming no environmental correlation, following Fisher (1918). The following substitutions have been made for convenience:

$$\mu = A\left(1 + \frac{E_1}{A_1}\right)$$
$$A_1 = \frac{1}{2}\left(\frac{1}{1-A}\right)D_R$$
$$A_2 = \left(\frac{1+A}{2}\right)$$

Table 49

The genetical consequences of assortative mating, on the assumption that mating is based on the smoking phenotype

Parameter	Age of onset	Average consumption
L	−997.78	−830.19
$\hat{c}_m$	−0.160	0.098
$\hat{c}_f$	−0.153	0.058
$\hat{c}'_m$	−0.454	0.245
$\hat{c}'_f$	−0.434	0.235
$\hat{b}$	.0083	−0.0041
$\hat{D}_R$	0.593	0.767
$\hat{E}_1$	0.545	0.381
$\hat{A}$	0.053	0.023

librium are given in Table 49. In both cases it can be seen that the estimate of A is numerically close to zero, confirming our original intuition that the genetical effect of assortative mating is too small to be detectable for traits with such low heritability. Since, under conditions of equilibrium, Fisher's model predicts that $A = h^2{}_\mu$ we can use our estimates of D_R E_1 and A to give predicted values of the marital correlation, μ, which can then be compared with the observed values as a guide to the adequacy of assortative mating equilibrium as an explanation of the similarity between spouses. For the age of onset the narrow heritability is estimated to be:

$$h_n^2 \; \tfrac{1}{2}D_R\left(\frac{1}{1-A}\right)\Big/\left[\tfrac{1}{2}D_R\left(\frac{1}{1-A}\right)+E_1\right] = 0.3649$$

giving $\hat{\mu} \simeq 0.053/0.3649$
$$\simeq 0.145$$

Similar calculations for average consumption yield:
$$\hat{\mu} = 0.045$$

In both cases these estimated marital correlations are less than the corresponding values obtained for the sample (see Table 36), suggesting that the observed degree of phenotypic assortative mating is not consistent with genetical equilibrium for the alleles which affect the traits in question, nor with the assumption of straightforward pheno-

TABLE 50

The consequences of assortative mating with a shared twin environment

	Age of onset	*Average consumption*
L	−992.47	−825.22
$\hat{c}_m$	−0.159	.099
$\hat{c}_f$	−0.155	.062
$\hat{c}'_m$	−0.455	.242
$\hat{c}'_f$	−0.433	.236
$\hat{b}$	0.0084	−.0042
$\hat{D}_R$	0.357	.510
$\hat{E}_1$	0.504	.353
$\hat{E}_T$	0.167	.153
A	0.046	.040

typic assortative mating.

Modifying the expectations to include the effect of the added similarity in twin environments leads to an increase of approximately 5 units in the log-likelihood ($p \simeq 0.1\%$) for both age of onset and average consumption (Table 50) and to a marked improvement in the goodness of fit, as assessed by a visual inspection of the differences between observed and expected correlations (Table 51). We should, perhaps, be not too excited by this since by far the greater part of the information in these analyses comes from the twins and first-degree relatives. This means that these relationships play a far greater role in the determination of the outcome and are thus expected to be more closely approximated by whatever set of parameter estimates are deemed most satisfactory. However, it is cheering that the discrepancy between observed and expected marital correlations is largely removed when allowance is made for phenotypic assortative mating and the twin environment. It is unjustified to see this simply as support for the particular model assumed for assortative mating. It is little more than a demonstration of the simple fact that spouses are cor-

TABLE 51

Observed and expected correlations under additive model when allowance is made for phenotypic assortative mating and the twin environment

Relationship	Expected covariance*	Correlations					
		Age of onset		Average consumption			
		Observed	Expected	Observed	Expected		
MZ twin	$A_1 + E_T$	0.40	0.41	0.52	0.54		
DZ twin	$A_1A_2 + E_T$	0.30	0.31	0.30	0.38		
sibling	A_1A_2	0.14	0.11	0.11	0.18		
spouse	$\mu (A_1 + E_1 + E_T)$	0.19	0.21	0.12	0.12		
parent/offspring	$\frac{1}{2}A_1 (1 + \mu)$	0.10	0.11	0.21	0.18		
grandparent/ grandchild	$A_1A_2^2 (1 + \mu)$	-0.11	0.06	0.08	0.10		
avuncular	$A_1A_2^2$	0.18	0.06	0.07	0.09		
first cousin	$A_1A_2^3$	0.18	0.03	0.10	0.05		
foster parent/ foster child	0	-0.02	0.	-0.02	0.		
unrelated, reared together	0	0.18	0.	0.05	0.		
Total variance	$A_1 + E_1 + E_T$	—	—	—	—		

*Same substitutions as those in Table 45, except that $\mu = A \left(1 + \dfrac{E_1 + E_T}{A_1} \right)$ assuming no environmental correlation between non-twins.

related for their age of onset and average consumption of cigarettes. Since the heritability is relatively small for both traits, about 0.22 for age of onset and 0.34 for average consumption under this model, the allowance for assortative mating will have very little effect on the correlations apart from that between spouses, given that relatively more of the information about the additive genetic component (D_R) now comes from first-degree relatives and rather less from twins once allowance is made for the twin environment. The principal discrepancies in the observations are in the more distant relatives (uncles and cousins, etc.) for age of onset, whereas the sibling and DZ twin correlations are somewhat lower than expected for average consumption. It might be argued that this is due to a greater peer effect for MZ twins, but there are dangers in explaining away every new anomaly in the absence of proper replication. The agreement between observed and predicted correlations for distant relatives is somewhat better for consumption than for age of onset.

Is there a lesson from family studies?

Throughout we have been cautious about reading too much into, or out of, data collected on subjects for whom sampling biases are difficult to assess, but in view of the substantial investment in twin research in relation to smoking and disease it is appropriate to consider whether, in the light of our tentative findings, twin methodology is likely to yield a convincing solution to the aetiology of smoking and to the causal basis of its association with disease.

Our data do make us question the simple-minded exploitation of the twin design and its conventional genetic interpretation in relation to smoking. In particular, although we agree that dizygotic twins are less alike than monozygotics in aspects of the smoking habit, we are not so sure that the similarity of twins for onset and consumption of tobacco is purely genetic. This is particularly critical when we are tempted to assert that the increased risk of non-smoking partners of smoking twins is due to genetic communality of smoking and disease. The non-metric methods which have been employed in the conventional pursuit of a smoking genotype do not, in our view, seriously examine the possibility that part of the similarity of twins is a reflection of environmental similarity. In the case of onset and average consumption of cigarettes, it is likely that about 20 per cent of the measured variation in these traits could be attributed to peer effects for which twins are alike. In the case of age of onset, this amounts to half the total variation between monozygotic twin pairs. It is thus on a par with the estimated contribution of inherited factors. *If this is true for the smoking habit itself, then we cannot discount, on the basis of available twin data alone, the view that shared environmental factors, as well as common genetic factors, may account for some of the increased incidence of certain diseases in the non-smoking partners of smoking twins.*

The consideration of age-dependent gene expression also raises questions for advocates of twin methodology in the area of genetic epidemiology. We have argued that the twin study has much in common with a laboratory study because many extraneous factors are excluded by the constraint that individuals within a pair be studied at the same stage of development. Whether we see this as a desirable position or otherwise will depend on our view of development and must ultimately depend on data rather than on discussion of principle. The twin study can certainly reveal the effects of genes on aspects of behaviour and disease, but what view is taken of these effects will depend to a large degree on their stability during development and across heterogeneous environments. If gene expression can be shown to vary widely across the range of environments represented in a particular population then the demonstration that a trait is heritable in the controlled conditions of the twin study is largely academic and attention might be better focused on those aspects of the environment, material or psychological, in which certain genotypes develop the smoking habit whilst others do not. At the present stage of knowledge this is just a pious hope! Our data do little more than suggest that such interactions could be important and point objectively to the influence of peers as one domain in which environmental differences might arise. On the other hand, such adoption data as are available suggest that the direct environmental influence of parents on their offspring is slight, or at least that these influences do not correlate directly with the smoking behaviour of parents. It may be that the provision of more or less coercive environments by parents, irrespective of their smoking habits, might exercise an effect which would not be detected in parent-offspring similarity although it might still contribute to the similarity of siblings, both natural and fostered. Unfortunately, our sample of foster-siblings is too small to be convincing on this issue, and more data are clearly desirable.

CHAPTER 6

The Relationship between Smoking and Personality

L. J. Eaves and H. J. Eysenck

The evidence reviewed in the last three chapters has suggested a slight but significant contribution of genetical factors to characteristics of the smoking habit. The most striking contribution of inherited factors, as judged by the twin data, was to differentiate non-smokers from persistent smokers. The genetic contribution to age of onset of smoking and average reported cigarette consumption was substantially less, and it was suggested that about half the similarity between twins for the smoking habit could be attributed to non-genetic effects such as the environmental influence of peers.

In this chapter we examine the proposition that part of the genetic variation in the smoking habit is mediated through inherited differences which affect other more general aspects of behaviour, particularly individual differences in personality.

There have been many twin studies of personality, which suggest in general the partial determination of personality traits. In England, Eaves & Eysenck (1975, 1976, 1977) have reported biometrical genetical analyses of twin data relating to the three principal dimensions of adult personality of Eysenck's theory: Psychoticism, Extraversion and Neuroticism. In each case the twin data suggested a fairly simple basis for the determination of differences in these three dimensions. It seems as if gene action is fairly straightforward, being predominantly additive. The mating system is effectively random, there being little suggestion that spouses choose one another on the basis of measurable dimensions of personality. Effects of the environment are largely confined to the unique experiences of individual twins rather than to the shared environmental effects common to twin pairs. In general, the contribution of genetical effects to these dimensions of behaviour is intermediate, with a significant proportion of the apparent environmental variation being due to such short-lived factors as measurement errors. Indeed, in the case of psychoticism (Eaves & Eysenck, 1977) as much as 75 per cent of what passes for environmental variation may well be due to random variation in subjects' responses.

In summarizing the results of one of the largest twin studies of personality, Loehlin & Nichols (1976, p. 91) confirm the suggestion that variation in personality is affected but little by the shared environments of twins. They observe, 'As far as personality and interests are concerned, then, it would appear that the relevant environments of a pair of twins are no more alike than those of two members of the population paired at random'.

As in the case of smoking, twin studies therefore suggest a deceptively simple mechanism for the determination of differences in adult personality. Recently, Eaves et al. (1978) have attempted to extend the analysis of personality beyond the twin study by consideration of family and adoption data. There is some evidence that the consistent and simple findings with twins do not generalize very readily to the non-twin population. Although there is little to suggest assortative mating, and little to imply the importance of the family environment, there are indications that the assumption of genetic additivity is not generally supported. Also, as Young et al. (1980) have shown, there is significant inconsistency between the mechanism of determination of personality variation in juveniles and adults. Apart from neuroticism, in which the long-term consistency of the trait is reasonably clear, the other traits display substantial differences in determination between adults and juveniles. In the case of extraversion and psychoticism, for example, it is necessary to invoke either substantial genetic non-additivity to explain the pattern of family similarity or to argue that markedly different gene effects are expressed at different stages of development. In the case of the EPQ lie scale, there is evidence that an entirely different mechanism operates in adults and juveniles. In adults the trait is partly inherited, whereas in juveniles the trait is almost exclusively environmental, with the greater part of the environmental similarity between twins depending directly on the lie scores of the parents and on the interaction between members of a twin pair.

So far we have claimed a partial genetic basis for aspects of the smoking habit and we have postulated that some such genetic effects may reflect the genetical differences in more stable personality dimensions. Before we examine this suggestion in detail it is helpful to consider whether there is any support for the idea that personality and smoking are related phenotypically in our sample.

The phenotypic relationship between smoking and personality

How do personality characteristics differentiate aspects of the smoking habit we have studied so far? All the individuals who completed the smoking questionnaire also answered the Eysenck Personality Questionnaire (EPQ) and scores were extracted on the three principal scales, Psychoticism (P), Extraversion (E), and Neuroticism (N). In addition, subjects' responses to the so-called 'Lie' scale were summarized to give a 'Lie score' (L). The raw scales of the EPQ have error variances which vary between different parts of the scale. This heteroscedasscicity can be removed by transformation. The square-root transformation was employed for the P scale and the angular transformation for E, N and L. These four transformed scales formed the basis for the analysis of the relationship between smoking and personality.

Personality differences between smokers and non-smokers

The problem of summarizing the relationship between smoking and personality was first approached by asking, 'What combination of personality measurements discriminate best between the different classes of smoking behaviour?' Discriminant functions were computed which gave the linear combination of the four EPQ scales, P, E, N and L, which maximized the differences between response categories relating to persistence in smoking, age of onset of smoking, and reported average cigarette consumption. The analysis was performed using the DISCRIMINANT procedure of the Statistical Package for the Social Sciences. The analysis was performed separately for males and females and the results are summarized in Table 52 and Figure 21.

TABLE 52

Personality and smoking: discriminant function analysis

Response	Sex	Coefficients				Correlation	x^2	df	P%
		P	E	N	L				
Age of onset	Males	−0.62	0.12	−0.23	0.58	0.233	63.70	24	< 0.1
	Females	−0.60	−0.24	−0.29	0.56	0.278	149.44	24	< 0.1
Average consumption	Males	−0.80	−0.05	−0.31	0.25	0.170	37.86	28	10.0
	Females	−0.68	−0.35	−0.39	0.31	0.250	133.38	28	< 0.1
Persistence	Males	−0.60	−0.07	−0.43	0.46	0.216	38.40	8	< 0.1
	Females	−0.57	−0.37	−0.36	0.49	0.266	134.48	8	< 0.1

Key

Group   Age of onset

1   14yrs
2   14—15
3   16—17
4   18—20
5   21—25
6   26+
7   Never

Average consumption

1   Nil
2   1
3   1—4
4   5—9
5   10—14
6   15—19
7   20—29
8   30+

Persistence

1   Never
2   Once
3   Still

Age of onset

Males: 342, 5, 1, 6, 7, 6   (scale −0.5, 0, +0.5)

Females: 1, 2, 6, 345, 2, 7, 1   (scale −0.5, 0, +0.5)

Average consumption

Males: 84, 637, 2, 5, 1   (scale −0.5, 0, +0.5)

Females: 73, 6, 85, 24, 1   (scale −0.5, 0, +0.5)

Persistence

Males: 3, 2, 1   (scale −0.5, 0, +0.5)

Females: 2, 3', 2, 1   (scale −0.5, 0, +0.5)

The table gives the coefficients which must be applied to the personality scores to generate combined personality measures which discriminate most between the response categories on the smoking questionnaire. A discriminant function analysis generates as many dimensions of discrimination between the categories as possible, the number being equal to the number of variables employed in the discrimination of one less than the number of categories, whichever is the smaller. It is hoped that some of the dimensions will supply no reliable information about group differences and may be ignored. In this analysis, the first dimension was nearly always highly significant (the only exception being the analysis of average consumption in males, for which the first dimension of variation between response groups was significant only at the 10 per cent level), and subsequent dimensions added very little to understanding the group differences (persistence in females being the only exception to this rule). The significance of the discriminant functions can be assessed by a chi-square test, and their substantive contribution to group differences can be judged by computing the canonical correlation which is the proportion of variation of the combined variate associated with differences between groups. The discriminant function analysis generates that combination of the personality variables which maximizes this correlation.

In every case, the results of Table 52 confirm the major factor contributing to differences between response categories in the combination of a high 'P' score with a low 'L' score. That is, socialization and social desirability are apparently the most significant joint discriminators between the phenotypic categories into which smokers and non-smokers sort themselves. This result is consistent over all three variables and both sexes.

The raw responses can be transformed to yield scores which can be plotted on the discriminant function scale in order to describe the category differences more effectively. In Figure 21 the means of the different categories of smoking behaviour are plotted on the scale defined by the first discriminant function which is the composite of the four personality scores shown to be sufficient to describe the differences between the group of smokers and non-smokers. The results are easiest to interpret for the measure of persistence in the smoking habit, since subjects who used to smoke are quite clearly intermediate, on average, in personality between those who never smoked and those who still smoke. This result is consistent over sexes, and confirms the apparent simplicity of the scale demonstrated by analysis of the twin similarity in Chapter 4.

Is the phenotypic relationship consistent throughout the scale?

The various attempts to derive a satisfactory scale of smoking in Chapter 4 lead us to question whether the relationship between smoking and personality implied in the discriminant function analysis is confined principally to the distinction between smokers and non-smokers or whether the difference would persist even if the individuals who never smoked were excluded from the analysis. In other words, 'Do the same psychological variables which differentiate smokers from non-smokers also discriminate between different grades of the smoking habit among smokers?'

The discriminant function analysis was repeated for the measures of onset and consumption, but individuals who claimed never to have smoked were omitted. The results (Table 53) have much in common with those for the complete sample although the canonical correlations and their significance levels are somewhat lower than for the full sample. The pattern of weights for the four personality measures is similar in the two analyses, although the weights given to psychoticism are somewhat larger in the sub-sample than in the population as a whole, and the contribution of the lie scale to the discrimination between the grades of smoking behaviour is somewhat reduced. That for extraversion is inflated in males. Although we have no tests of significance for these trends, the data may support the hypothesis of qualitative as well as quantitative differences between those who have never smoked at all and those who have smoked at least once. The lie scores of the EPQ show the biggest difference, suggesting either that subjects are not telling the truth when they claim they have never smoked, or that the same traits of social desirability and conformity expressed in responses to the lie scale contribute to subjects' adoption of the smoking habit.

The marked reduction in the significance of the differences in the second analysis suggests that the measured personality traits contribute most to the determination of whether people begin to smoke at all rather than to the level of indulgence once the habit is started.

The canonical correlations in the table reflect the contribution of measurable personality dimensions to aspects of the smoking habit.

TABLE 53

The relationship between smoking and personality among subjects who report experience of smoking—discriminant analysis

Response	Sex	Coefficients				Correlations	χ^2	df	P%
		P	E	N	L				
Age of onset	Males	−0.73	0.52	0.37	0.42	0.177	31.48	20	5
	Females	−0.82	−0.04	−0.13	0.36	0.170	42.46	20	<1
Average consumption	Males	0.82	0.39	−0.38	0.27	0.191	19.97	24	70
	Females	−0.94	−0.16	−0.25	−0.04	0.182	45.92	24	<1

Although the contribution is statistically significant, the comparatively small numerical values of the correlations suggest that many factors affecting smoking do not contribute to more generalized aspects of behaviour and vice versa.

The examination of phenotypic associations without any attempt to assess their causal basis may be misleading, for several reasons. Firstly, such associations do not usually distinguish the long-term inherited and environmental causes of variation from those which are due to comparatively transient influences. The practice of many psychologists of correcting correlations for unreliability of measurement is one crude approach to the separation of short- and long-term effects. The analysis of twin data, however, permits us to examine the relative contributions of inherited and environmental factors to the association between traits. Indeed, it was the possibility of exploiting the twin method in this way which led Cederlöf and his associates to propose their 'NET' analysis of the association between smoking and morbidity (see Chapter 3). Underlying this analysis is the concept of genetic correlation—the idea that an association between traits may have a genetic as well as a causal environmental basis. The attraction of the NET analysis is its compelling simplicity and conservatism. It combines the simplicity of an analysis of concordance with the conservatism which does not make a commitment to any particular model of gene action or environmental involvement. By restricting the analysis to discordant pairs the interpretation of the data is unambiguous (given that the basic premises of the twin method are endorsed) although somewhat wasteful of data since concordant pairs make no contribution to the analysis. The NET analysis can reject the simple-minded causal model of the association between traits. The increased incidence of morbidity in the non-smoking partner of a smoking co-twin would constitute an impressive rejection of the most thoroughgoing environmental hypothesis that the entire association between smoking and disease is due to the environmental effects of the smoking habit on the body's tissues. The difficulty remains, however, that the rejection of one simple hypothesis still leaves the alternative a matter for debate. Is the increased incidence of disease in the non-smoking co-twin a result of genetic or environmental similarity between twins? This question can only be answered at all by a more rigorous comparison of the full data on concordant and discordant twins. Unfortunately, our study does not incorporate the data on disease which could enable us to examine the approach in greater detail in a clinical context, but the existence of data on smoking and personality between which there is a demonstrable phenotypic association does enable us to tackle the question of its causal basis as an illustration.

Genetic and environmental correlations: a simple model

In our earlier treatment (Chapter 4) we began by specifying the effects of alleles at a single locus upon a given trait. Now we consider a like locus, A/a, but represent the effects which the locus might have upon a pair of traits of which one, for concreteness, is a personality trait (trait 'p') and the other an aspect of the smoking habit (trait 's'). We may write:

Genotype at A/a locus

	AA	Aa	aa
Effect on 'p'	$m_p + d_{ap}$	$m_p + h_{ap}$	$m_p - d_{ap}$
Effect on 's'	$m_s + d_{as}$	$m_s + h_{as}$	$m_s - d_{as}$

When the frequency of the A allele is u_a, and that of the a allele is v_a, we may define the contribution of the a locus to the genetic variance of 'p' and 's' for a randomly mating population and, following Mather & Jinks (1971), add the effects of many independent loci, in the absence of epistasis, to give:

$$\text{the genetic variance in 'p'} = \tfrac{1}{2}D_{Rp} + \tfrac{1}{4}H_{Rp}$$
$$\text{the genetic variance in 's'} = \tfrac{1}{2}D_{Rs} + \tfrac{1}{4}H_{Rs}$$

where D_{Rp}, D_{Rs}, H_{Rp} and H_{Rs} are used to represent the additive and dominance variance components for traits p and s. Since there are now two traits, however, it is possible to conceive of the genetic *covariance* between them due to the fact that some of the loci may affect both traits in a systematic way. Following Eaves & Gale (1974) we put the genetic covariance between 'p' and 's':

$$C_{gps} = \tfrac{1}{2}D_{Rps} + \tfrac{1}{4}H_{Rps}$$
$$\text{where} \quad D_{Rps} = \sum_a 4u_a v_a [d_{as} + h_{as}(v_a - u_a)][d_{ap} + h_{ap}(v_a - u_a)]$$
$$H_{Rps} = 16\sum_a u_a^2 v_a^2 h_{ap} h_{as}$$

It is a little easier to see the form of the covariance term if we consider the simpler case of additive gene action and equal gene frequencies since the additive genetic components are simplified to

$$D_p = \sum_a d_{ap}^2, \; D_s = \sum_a d_{as}^2 \text{ and } D_{ps} = \sum_a d_{ap} \, d_{as}$$

Since the variance components D_p and D_s always involve the square of the gene effects (e.g. d_{ap}^2 and d_{as}^2) they will inevitably be positive. The covariance term D_{ps}, however, involves the cross products of gene effects on p and s. Since there is no necessary reason for the genes which increase p to increase s and vice versa, some of the product terms could be negative. Further, if certain genes are trait-specific in their action, so that a gene affecting p has no effect on s, or vice versa, the product $d_p d_s$ will be zero. Thus, although the variances reflect all the genetic effects on a trait, the covariance represents only the *net* effect of loci on the traits and will not bear any relationship to the proportion of genes affecting p which also influence s except under very artificial assumptions about the consistency of gene action over traits (Eaves & Gale, 1974).

For convenience we define the additive genetic correlation

$$r_{Dps} = D_{Rps}/\sqrt{D_{Rp} \cdot D_{Rs}}$$

There is no simple interpretation of the genetic correlation in terms of gene effects and the numbers of loci, since each term in the expression on the right-hand side is itself the sum of the effects of a large number of loci which may have variable effects and allele frequencies.

The model is very simple. Like all models in the previous chapters it assumes that the genes are independent in their effect and that alleles are uncorrelated in their distribution. The chief purpose of such models lies in helping us to decide what considerations are most likely to be relevant in the analysis of the variation with which we are concerned.

The model outlined only applies to the genetic component of individual differences in correlated traits and assumes random mating. Similar expectations could be derived for the contributions of the environment. We may define variance components E_{1p} and E_{1s} to represent the contribution of unique environmental experiences to the two traits. A covariance component, E_{1ps}, may also be defined to represent the common effects of the within-family environment on the two traits. Similarly, if we regard the between-family environment as important, we may define further variance and covariance components E_{2p}, E_{2s} and E_{2ps}. The model may be extended almost without bounds but the possibilities for hypothesis-testing are very restricted with twins so we will work within essentially the same framework that we explored for the separate smoking variables in Chapter 4.

Summarizing the data

It is possible, in principle, to apply the maximum-likelihood methods of Chapter 6 to the unsummarized data and fit components of variance and covariance to the unreduced observations on pairs of variables. Such an approach is expensive of computer time, however, and does not yield a simple test of any model. Where possible we have chosen the simpler expedient of analysing the summarized twin data by the method of weighted least squares (Eaves & Gale, 1974).

To some extent it is a matter of personal preference which data summary is chosen as the starting point subject to all the considerations outlined at the start of Chapter 4. It is important to preserve the information in the total variances of the different twin groups, so we avoid correlations. However, since we are prepared to assume that the early effects of birth order do not persist into adult behaviour there is little point in maintaining the distinction between first- and second-born twins in our study. In this instance, therefore, there are compelling reasons for adopting the analysis of variance model and extending it to include the covariances between traits.

Just as the data summaries of Chapter 4 consisted of mean squares within and between twin pairs, so now we obtained the corresponding cross products between and within pairs for every pair of measurements, thus generating mean squares for individual traits and mean products of analogous form for each trait pair. Twin pairs of unlike sex were omitted from this part of the analysis since the sacrifice of these data made the subsequent model-fitting more straightforward in the presence of sex differences in the parameter estimates. The age-corrected personality scores for the four EPQ scales and the normalized scores for the persistence, onset and consumption scales of smoking were entered jointly into the analysis to yield the mean squares and mean products between and within pairs given in Tables 54 and 55.

Expected mean squares and products

For each variable separately the mean squares (the diagonal ele-

TABLE 54

Mean squares and products between and within male twin pairs for personality and smoking*

Monozygotics (80 pairs)

Between pairs

	P	E	N	L	S1	S2	S3
P	.052	.002	.024	-.016	.085	-.042	-.059
E		.154	.011	-.009	-.012	.082	.027
N			.102	-.016	.095	-.096	.070
L				.069	-.054	.076	-.030
S1					1.299	-1.003	.975
S2						1.358	-.663
S3							1.121

Within pairs

	P	E	N	L	S1	S2	S3
P	.014	.001	.000	-.005	.014	-.021	.003
E		.089	-.004	-.002	-.024	.060	-.026
N			.034	-.007	.023	-.021	.012
L				.026	-.008	.010	-.016
S1					.462	-.379	.265
S2						.622	-.239
S3							.438

Dizygotic (50 pairs)

Between pairs

	P	E	N	L	S1	S2	S3
P	.034	.013	-.002	-.006	.017	-.059	.042
E		.136	-.020	.009	-.008	-.006	-.072
N			.054	-.004	-.019	.031	.013
L				.036	-.030	.028	-.023
S1					.922	-.752	.571
S2						1.232	-.623
S3							.740

Within pairs

	P	E	N	L	S1	S2	S3
P	.017	-.006	.005	-.003	-.015	.018	.009
E		.080	.005	-.007	.043	-.014	.055
N			.060	-.006	-.036	.042	-.021
L				.022	-.006	-.012	-.020
S1					.565	-.208	.376
S2						.537	-.050
S3							.651

*Key in Table 55

TABLE 55

Mean squares and products between and within male twin pairs for personality and smoking

Monozygotics (233) pairs

Between pairs

	P	E	N	L	S1	S2	S3
P	.035	.004	.013	−.017	.047	−.042	.043
E		.131	−.058	.005	.049	.028	.032
N			.127	−.002	.031	−.003	.015
L				.080	−.071	.061	−.070
S1					1.247	−.835	.952
S2						1.059	−.532
S3							.975

Within pairs

	P	E	N	L	S1	S2	S3
P	.015	.003	.000	−.001	.009	−.008	.006
E		.063	−.009	−.000	−.012	.001	−.015
N			.051	−.000	−.001	.002	−.003
L				.032	.004	−.004	.002
S1					.339	−.248	.226
S2						.440	−.096
S3							.289

Dizygotics (121 pairs)

Between pairs

	P	E	N	L	S1	S2	S3
P	.036	−.000	.008	−.017	.039	−.061	.034
E		.138	−.015	−.022	.028	.030	.033
N			.092	−.004	.012	.000	.035
L				.068	−.042	.036	−.032
S1					1.030	−.846	.772
S2						1.184	−.642
S3							.910

Within pairs

	P	E	N	L	S1	S2	S3
P	.022	.005	.003	−.001	.022	−.021	.013
E		.071	−.022	.004	.008	−.040	−.003
N			.089	−.801	−.002	.037	.001
L				−.034	.000	−.004	−.003
S1					.470	−.336	.264
S2						.593	−.199
S3							.358

Key to variable labels:

P — EPQ Psychoticism
E — " Extraversion
N — EPQ Neuroticism
L — " Lie scale
S1 — Persistence in smoking
S2 — Age of onset of smoking
S3 — Average consumption of cigarettes

ments of the matrices in the tables) have expectations in terms of the components of variance of a genotype-environmental model such as that given in Table 12. Similarly, the expectations may be extended to include the covariance parameters for a pair of variables as in Table 56. In the table the expectations are given for the mean products of the analysis of the personality variable 'p' and the smoking variable 's'. It can be seen that the expectations of the mean products are exactly analogous to those of the mean squares for the identical model.

How may such a model be fitted? Although the distinct matrices within and between pairs are independent, the individual mean squares and mean products are not, since the same observations enter into the mean products with each of the other variables. An expression could be written for the likelihood of obtaining the observed matrices which could then be maximized with respect to all the components of variance and covariance, but the optimization problem is substantial when so many parameters are involved. A simpler alternative is to adapt the method of weighted least squares to the more general case in which the component observations are not independent. This is the procedure adopted by Eaves & Gale (1974) and outlined in Mather & Jinks (1971). The approach is very much quicker and seems to work adequately as long as sensible models are fitted. It has been our experience that convergence may not be achieved when hopelessly inadequate models are fitted, with models which specify large numbers of redundant parameters, or when correlations between the traits are high. In view of the high correlations between the three smoking measures, persistence, onset and consumption, these were analysed separately, but all four personality measures were entered simultaneously into the analysis. Thus, in any one analysis we have eight 5 x 5 matrices of mean squares and mean products each involving the selected smoking variable and the four personality measures, P, E, N and L.

Beginning with a very simple model for the joint variation between the traits, we assumed additive gene action, random mating, and no family environmental effects. Furthermore, it was assumed that the magnitude of the variance and covariance components was consistent over sexes. That is, the same genetic and environmental components were fitted to males and females. Each mean-product matrix has 15 unique statistics, giving a total of 8 x 15=120 d.f. The simplest model involved 30 parameters. There were five within-family

TABLE 56

Expected mean squares and mean product for a personality variable (P) and smoking variable (S) assuming additive gene action, random mating, and environmental variation within and between families*

Twin type	Source	Personality	Smoking	Personality and smoking
		Expected mean square	Expected mean square	Expected mean product
Monozygotic	between pairs	$D_{RP} + E_{1P} + 2E_{2P}$	$D_{RS} + E_{1S} + 2E_{2S}$	$D_{RPS} + E_{1PS} + 2E_{2PS}$
	within pairs	E_{1P}	E_{1S}	E_{1PS}
Dizygotic	between pairs	$\frac{3}{4}D_{RP} + E_{1P} + 2E_{2P}$	$\frac{3}{4}D_{RS} + E_{1S} + 2E_{2P}$	$\frac{3}{4}D_{RPS} + E_{1PS} + 2E_{2PS}$
	within pairs	$\frac{1}{4}D_{RP} + E_{1P}$	$\frac{1}{4}D_{RS} + E_{1S}$	$\frac{1}{4}D_{RPS} + E_{1PS}$

*For definition of parameters, see text

TABLE 57

Summary statistics for model fitting to smoking and personality in twins: testing simple additive model

Smoking trait

	Persistence			Onset			Consumption		
	X	df	P%	X^2	df	P%	X^2	df	P%
Sexes pooled	116.8	90	3	137.5	90	<1	126.6	90	<1
Males only	40.2	30	10	44.9	30	3	34.8	30	25
Females only	32.0	30	37	41.3	30	8	35.1	30	24
Heterogeneity	44.6	30	3	51.3	30	<1	56.7	30	<1

environmental variance components and ten within-family environmental covariances. Similarly, the additive genetic variation was represented by five variance components and ten components of covariance. The chi-square for assessing the goodness of fit thus has 90 d.f. When the parameters are constrained to take the same values in males and females the residual chi-squares are all significant (see Table 57) suggesting that some alternative model must be found, especially for age of onset and average consumption, in which the failure is extreme. The fit of the model is much improved if the same model is fitted to each of the sexes separately, thus allowing the parameters to take different values in males and females. If we write X^2_m and X^2_f for the two X^2's for testing the fit of the model to males and females separately, and X^2_{mf} for that testing the joint model for both sexes, then the difference $X^2_{mf} - X^2_m - X^2_f$ is also a X^2 for 30 d.f. which may be used to test for heterogeneity of the parameter estimates across sexes. The component chi-squares, and the chi-square for testing the heterogeneity of parameters over sexes are given in Table 56. It is fairly clear that the bulk of the failure of the model to explain the pooled data can be attributed to the inconsistency over sexes of the estimates of the variance and covariance components.

In view of the detectable heterogeneity of the estimates over sexes, the findings of this analysis are summarized separately for males and females in Tables 58 and 59. Since the difference in variance between the measures is arbitrary, the results are presented in terms

TABLE 58

The relationship between smoking and personality in males: an additive model assuming no family environment (see note to Table 59 for explanation)

| | | Personality | | | | Smoking | |
		P	E	N	L	Persistence	Onset	Consumption
Personality	P	0.55***	0.11	0.32*	−0.21	0.23	−0.12	0.34*
	E	−0.02	0.28***	0.06	0.01	0.05	−0.02	−0.12
	N	0.01	−0.05	0.44***	−0.13	0.10	−0.10	−0.21
	L	−0.23*	−0.07	−0.21*	0.41***	−0.24	0.30	−0.09
Smoking	Persistence	0.09	−0.04	0.07	−0.06	0.46***	—	—
	Onset	−0.15	0.18	−0.04	0.03	—	0.40***	—
	Consumption	0.03	−0.04	0.02	0.16	—	—	0.39***

* significant at the 5% level
*** significant at the 0.1% level

TABLE 59

The relationship between smoking and personality in females: an additive model†

		Personality				Persistence	Smoking Onset	Consumption
		P	E	N	L			
Personality	P	0.41***	−0.01	0.34**	−0.51***	0.27**	−0.33**	0.28**
	E	0.10	0.38***	0.01	−0.05	0.21*	−0.05	0.21*
	N	−0.01	−0.21***	0.39***	−0.03	0.10	−0.02	0.11
	L	−0.03	0.00	−0.02	0.43***	−0.33***	0.32**	−0.33***
Smoking	Persistence	0.14*	−0.07	−0.01	0.06	0.57***	—	—
	Onset	−0.11	−0.02	0.05	−0.08	—	0.44***	—
	Consumption	0.09	−0.10	−0.01	0.03	—	—	0.56***

* significant at the 5% level
** significant at the 1% level
*** significant at the 0.1% level
† The model assumes no family environmental effects and random mating. The diagonal elements are heritability estimates. Additive genetic correlations are given in the upper triangle. Within-family environmental correlations are in the lower triangle.

of genetic and environmental correlations in the upper and lower triangles respectively. The genetic correlations are obtained by dividing the weighted least squares estimates of the genetical covariance by the square root of the product of the corresponding genetical variances. The environmental correlation (which reflects intrapair environmental differences only) is obtained by applying the same procedure to the environmental components. The estimates of heritability are given on the diagonals of the matrices, and obtained for each variable according to the formula given for the simple model in Chapter 4, i.e. $h^2 = \frac{1}{2}\hat{D}_R/(\frac{1}{2}\hat{D}_R + \hat{E}_1)$.

In the tables we give estimates of the heritability of the component measures, together with estimated genetic and environmental correlations obtained as described above. Standard errors are computed on the assumption that the simple additive model fits and employed to test the components of variance and covariance as a guide to their relative importance. Although the analysis does not give any strong suggestion that the assumptions are inadequate we warn that the test of the model is not very powerful. The univariate analysis of the standardized twin data led us to suggest that family environmental effects might be contributing to twin similarity. The analysis of the pedigree data confirmed that both identical and non-identical twins were likely to be similar for non-genetic reasons. In interpreting the tables, therefore, we should think of the figures as representing upper limits, computed on the assumption that a simple model is appropriate. Some of what passes for genetic effects in the tables may be attributable to the effects of the environment. On the other hand, we may be very confident that what is estimated as the effects of the within-family environment do indeed reflect such influences, given that we are prepared to accept reliable zygosity diagnosis. The significance levels applied, therefore, do not take into account our genuine uncertainty about the final validity of the model.

The figures as they stand confirm the common finding that personality measures have a significant basis in inherited variation, but that at least half of the measurable variation in personality is apparently due to environmental differences operating within the family, including those variables over which we have little control such as errors of measurement. The diagonal elements of Tables 58 and 59 are the heritability estimates obtained under the assumption of random mating, additive gene action and no familial environmental effects. How well these assumptions are justified in a wider context cannot be the subject for detailed discussion here. We have reason to suppose that there is some assortative mating for psychoticism, though not enough to have profound effects on the distribution of genetical differences in the population. Eaves et al. (1978) have suggested that the assumption of additivity might not be justified for neuroticism. Any further relaxation of the strong assumptions made here, however, would result in standard errors which were too large to suggest anything more specific than a general familial component to the covariance between traits. We thus accept provisionally the findings of the test of goodness of fit, and for the purposes of interpretation commit ourselves to the additive model. If such a step still yields estimates of the genetic correlations which are inconsistent or not significant then we would be forced to assert that there is no support whatever for the hypothesis that smoking and personality are related genetically. If on the other hand we do detect significant associations which the model assigns to genetic effects, then we would be justified in the collection of more powerful data.

Associations between personality dimensions

Considering, firstly, the inter-relationships of the personality measurements, we find, for the most part, that the effects of environmental differences within families do not exercise correlated effects on personality. The correlations in the lower triangles of Tables 58 and 59 are the within-family environmental correlations between the traits and these are mostly small. The only environmental association to which any real confidence could be attached is the negative one (−0.21) between extraversion and neuroticism in females (Table 59), suggesting that some of the environmental factors contributing to high neuroticism scores in females also contribute to low extraversion scores. Such factors will probably be largely specific to individuals, however, reflecting accidental influences, day-to-day fluctuations, and correlated errors of measurement. In males the lie scale apparently shows similar associations with the N and P scales, but a conservative approach would require more than a 5 per cent significance level for individual elements of a table involving so many entries.

As far as genetic associations are concerned, the results are more consistent, although the larger standard errors associated with genetic correlations mean that the effects in males are not statistically significant. There is a highly significant genetic correlation between neuroticism and P, consistent in direction and value across sexes. At the very least, this correlation indicates that there is a reliable association between the N and P scales of the EPQ. If the assumptions of our model are justified it further implies that the association reflects hereditary influences. It would be a mistake to jump to the conclusion that there are common genes affecting both psychoticism and neuroticism. Apart from the simple appealing hypothesis of pleiotrop there are several alternative causes of association between even physically unlinked genes which could account for the correlation. We recognize that associations can reflect little more than the structure of the population, its mating system or history of selection. Under these circumstances the association could be broken by changing any of those influences responsible for its maintenance. This argument is not true just for personality, but for any pair of traits for which an inherited familial association is detected. Although it is tempting to argue that an association between, for example, smoking and disease might have a common genetical basis, this proves little that can be exploited in finding the actual mechanism underlying the association even if we can bring twin data to support a genetic interpretation. The causal chain linking together two associated genetic disorders may not lead directly to biochemistry, but through the tortuous pathways of population and evolutionary genetics.

In addition to the genetic correlation between P and N, there is a substantial correlation between genetic effects on P and L in females, which is mirrored by the smaller, non-significant association in males. Taken together with the correlation of N and P, we have some evidence that the psychoticism scale of the EPQ is not unitary from a genetical standpoint. Whatever the ultimate causes of these genetic relationships between traits, it is clear that the simple model of unitary independent scales is not adequate to explain the genetic relationships between the four scales of the EPQ. The genetic correlation between P and L is consistent with the view that P is partly concerned with the measurement of antisocial tendencies. High lie scores imply unwillingness to admit to mildly antisocial practices. Individuals who are genetically predisposed to make such admissions are also likely to give more 'P' responses on the P scale. It has been reported elsewhere (Eaves & Eysenck, 1974) that measures of toughmindedness and emphasis on scales of social attitudes show a significant genetic association with P scores. Such findings support an interpretation of P as an inherited lack of socializability.

The fact that neuroticism also has a significant genetic association with P, however, whilst itself remaining independent of the lie scale, suggests that there is a further genetic component in the P scale. As it stands, about 38 per cent of the genetical variation in P could be explained from a knowledge of genetic factors in N and L, in the females sampled in this study. The comparable figure for males is approximately 15 per cent. These figures are subject to considerable error and are only given to illustrate the degree of genetic commonality between the personality scales. Such figures depend on the genetic structure of the population.

Relationships between smoking and personality

The contribution of genetic factors to the association between personality and smoking is apparently more significant in the statistical sense for females than for males, although some of the trends are replicated across sexes. The principal relationship is identical to that obtained in discriminant function analysis of the phenotypic association, but the twin analysis shows that the association is more likely to be due to genetical factors than to the transient influences of environmental differences within families. It must be stressed again, however, that the interpretation of the association in strictly genetical terms does not make any allowance for sources of environmental variation between twin pairs which we believe could be a contributory factor to twin similarity. The personality profile of the 'early onset, persistent, heavy smoker' as being higher on the P scale and lower on the L is strongly suggested by the genetic analysis, especially of the female twins for whom more data are available. It is difficult to give a proper perspective to such correlations. Consider, for example, the relationship between P and L and persistence in females, which appears very striking at first sight, since the genetic correlations between the scales are quite large. Extracting only these three variables, and allowing for the fairly large genetic correlation (-0.51) between the two personality scales, leads to an estimate of the multiple genetic correlation between persistence and personality of approximately 0.35 which in turn implies that the *genetic* variation in persistence in smoking would only be reduced by about 12 per cent even if there were no genetic variation in P and L. When we recall that genetic factors explain only 57 per cent of the phenotypic variation in persistence in smoking (given that our model is adequate) then we must conclude that only about 7 per cent of the phenotypic variation in this aspect of the smoking habit is predictable in principle from genetic variation in these two components of personality. Similar calculations yield comparable figures for the other components of the smoking habit.

All the above computations depend on our assumption of a simple additive model for the genetic component of individual differences and on the notion that environmental differences act only to make members of a twin pair different from one another. We claimed that the model gives a reasonably good fit, but we can add parameters to represent the family environment (or peer effects) just as we did in the univariate analyses in Chapter 4. The analysis was repeated for the separate sexes adding a further set of parameters (five for variance components and ten covariance components) to specify the contribution of the shared environment (E_2) to the covariances.

The summary statistics for the analysis of the three smoking variables are given in Table 60 in the form of chi-square values for testing the fit of the full model for each sex. In every case the full model gives a good fit to the observed mean squares and mean products. The main issue is whether this represents a significant improvement over the model which assumed no family environmental effects. The bottom line, labelled 'E_2 improvement', is obtained by subtracting the residuals from the full model from those obtained when the 15 common environmental components are eliminated from the model. Assuming that these can be regarded as chi-squares for 15df, we can see that the addition of components to specify the shared environment does not, in general, improve the fit of the model significantly, although the borderline significance of the improvement in some of the cases may encourage some to suggest that the modified hypothesis is not without foundation. On the other hand, excluding the additive genetic components from the model and fitting only 'E_1' and 'E_2' effects (Table 60, line 3) leads to somewhat larger residuals which would yield a significant improvement (Table 60, line 4) if genetic effects were added to the model, in most cases. On balance, there is support for an interpretation in terms of a comparatively simple model including genetic effects but leaving out the family

TABLE 60

Comparing the contributions of genes and family environment to smoking and personality

Model	Males						Females					
	Persistence		Onset		Consumption		Persistence		Onset		Consumption	
	x^2	df	x^2	df	x^2	df	x^2	df	x^2	df	x^2	df
D_R, E_1, E_2	21.0	15	22.7†	15	14.0	15	10.7	15	14.7	15	11.5	15
D_R, E_1	40.2†	30	44.9*	30	34.8	30	32.0	30	41.3†	30	35.1	30
E_1, E_2	44.1*	30	48.9*	30	41.8†	30	43.6*	30	47.2*	30	40.7†	30
D_R improvement	31.1†	15	26.2*	15	27.8*	15	32.9**	15	32.5**	15	29.2*	15
E_2 improvement	19.2	15	22.2†	15	20.8	15	21.3	15	26.6*	15	23.6†	15

Approximate significance levels

† significant at the 10% level
* significant at the 5% level
** significant at the 1% level

D_R — additive genetic component
E_1 — within family environmental component
E_2 — between family environmental component

environment, although the conclusions are ambiguous.

In this respect, the analysis of the multiple variables echoes our findings for the individual smoking traits in Chapter 4. A partially genetic hypothesis receives some support, but we were not sure that the shared environment can be excluded.

We do not give parameter estimates for the full D_R, E_1, E_2 model since the individual parameter values are too ill-determined to be of any real use. Clearly, if we are prepared to be completely undecided in the light of the tests of the various models, then we are forced into virtual agnosticism about the relative contributions of heredity and environment to the inter-relations of smoking and personality although we are sure that a reliable relationship exists. Obviously our data are suggestive, but not definitive.

The relationship in adoption and family data

The joint analysis of the multiple variables can be conducted fairly easily with the twins for the same reason that univariate analysis of twin data is easy—the balanced structure of the data allow us to work from a convenient data summary. When we turn to examine the consistency of the relationship and its hypothesized causes in the family and adoption data, however, we are faced with the problems of imbalance which made the univariate analysis of these data so tedious. It is practically impossible with the method we used to fit the more complex models that we have exploited in Chapter 5 for the multiple measures. Instead we have to be content with obtaining parameter estimates for the very simple hypothesis of additive gene action and within-family environmental variation (i.e. D_R and E_1) for the trait variation and covariation. Furthermore, it is practically impossible to obtain estimates for all the traits simultaneously, as we did for the twins. Instead we take pairwise combinations of smoking traits with the personality variables and estimate the means, and components of variance and covariance for each pair of traits in turn by the approach of maximum-likelihood outlined in Chapter 5. Because of the difficulty of separating sexes in the analysis, the same covariance components were fitted to males and females. In general, it has been found that genetic models for personality in twins are consistent over sexes, so it is likely that any errors are confined chiefly to the smoking variables.

Parameter estimates were obtained only for age of onset and average consumption in view of the large amount of computer time required and because it seemed too far-fetched to apply the ML procedure to the persistence scale with only three categories. The results for the two smoking variables in relation to all four personality variables are in Table 61. In virtually every case the correlation between the

TABLE 61

The relationship between onset of smoking, cigarette consumption and personality in family and adoption data

Personality scale	Smoking				
	Age of onset		*Average consumption*		
	r_g	r_e	r_g	r_e	h^2
P	−0.26	−0.15	0.30	0.05	0.26
E	−0.39	−0.05	0.14	0.04	0.40
N	−0.32	−0.08	0.56	−0.01	0.12
L	0.33	0.18	−0.15	−0.05	0.20
h^2	0.24		0.39		—

within-family environmental effects ('r_e') is slight, confirming the finding for twins. We see that the estimates of the heritability of the smoking variables is smaller for the families than for twins, confirming the findings of the more detailed analysis of Chapter 5 that there are either special environmental effects in twins or that gene expression is age-dependent. With the exception of extraversion, the findings are similar for the personality scales, i.e. genetic variation apparently explains less of the similarity between relatives than might be predicted from the twin data alone. In view of the apparent inconsistency of twin and family data, it is perhaps not surprising that the genetic correlations ('r_g') do not confirm the values obtained in twins although the values are subject to larger errors in the family data. The results for average consumption roughly reflect those obtained with twins with the exception of the very large estimate of the genetic correlation with neuroticism (0.56). This value is expected to have a very large standard error because it related smoking to a trait for which there is very little detectable genetic variation in non-twin data. Taken at its face value, the correlation implies that approximately 12 per cent of the variation in average consumption of cigarettes might be predicted from the inherited/familial component of neuroticism.

As far as age of onset is concerned, the estimates obtained for the genetic correlation are somewhat higher for extraversion and neuroticism than those given for twins. That for the lie scale is similar to the twin value.

Conclusion

There is a significant phenotypic relationship between questionnaire measurements of personality and aspects of the smoking habit. Smoking is associated with higher scores on Eysenck's P scale and with low scores on the lie scale of the EPQ. Although the association does not depend much on the individual environmental experiences of subjects, it is difficult to discriminate between genetic and environmental explanations of the familial component of the correlation. The results for twin and family data are not very consistent, but it could be argued that hereditary factors in antisocial behaviour explain a small part of the variation in the smoking habit. The greater part of the variation in smoking cannot be predicted from personality measures, though how much this is a reflection of measurement error has still to be determined.

Summary

A great many authors have now produced large bodies of twin data which show that twins are similar for several facets of the smoking habit. This work has been reviewed in Chapter 3. Such studies have also shown that the resemblance is greater for identical twins. These findings constitute a *prima facie* case for the involvement of hereditary factors in the determination of aspects of the smoking habit. The early studies, however, offered very little more than what must, to many psychologists and geneticists, be so fundamental as to be trivial—that wherever there is variation it is likely that its cause is partly genetic. Because these studies were primarily concerned with differences in concordance there has been little attempt to translate the figures into any more comprehensible summary of the substantive significance of the statistical tests. In the analyses of Chapter 4 we have attempted, for our own twin data, to supply a quantitative estimate of the relative importance of genetic and environmental factors on the assumption that the traits we have studied represent arbitrary divisions of underlying continuous scales of liability. In general the contribution of inherited factors has not exceeded that clearly assignable to the effects of the environment.

A second major weakness of the earlier work on twin concordance has been the failure to test any of the broader assumptions which are equally critical to any general evaluation of the nature of genetic and environmental influences on smoking. In particular, although the difference between the concordances of identical and non-identical twins may be taken as indicating partial genetic determination of the variables in question, attention has been almost entirely diverted from consideration of the causes of twin *similarity* in which the effects of genes and environment are partly confounded. The model-fitting approach we have adopted enables us to test very simple hypotheses about variation between twin pairs. We are not deluding ourselves that the results are foolproof, but they are at least suggestive that not all the similarity of identical and fraternal twins can be explained by genotype alone. Although the results fall tantalizingly short of statistical significance when we consider the twin data alone, there is a suggestion that environmental factors are comparable with genetic factors as far as the causes of twin similarity are concerned.

The absence of any testable assumptions about underlying scales of variation is also a problem in many studies of twin concordance. In our twin analysis we have suggested that many of the aspects of the smoking habit studied by ourselves and others cannot easily be represented by points on a unidimensional scale of variation. Although we argued that degree of persistence in smoking could be regarded as a unidimensional scale, generated by an underlying continuous normal variable, there is striking evidence that this is not the case for consumption of cigarettes and for age of onset. Differences among smokers are probably caused by quite different inherited and environmental factors from those which lead to the initial separation of smokers from non-smokers. There is some additional support for this view from the examination of the personality variables in Chapter 6.

In Chapter 5 we examined in greater detail the validity of the results of the twin method by comparing these with data on adopted individuals and normal non-twin families. We showed that non-twin siblings are less alike than non-identical twins, and that parents and offspring are not as alike as might be expected on the basis of the analysis of twin data. We argued that this may be due to the greater environmental similarity of twins compared with siblings, or because of the interaction of genetical differences with age. Both of these effects are confounded in our cross-sectional data, though correction for the effects of the special environmental similarity of twins does lead to a significant improvement in the compatibility of data and theory.

The data support the hypothesis that the age of onset of smoking, and the average consumption of cigarettes are both partly governed by the environmental influences of peers. This is at least a plausible explanation of the additional similarity of twins who are more likely to experience identical social environments than non-twins. Whatever environmental factors contribute to the similarity of twins and siblings, it is fairly clear that they do not depend on the smoking habits of parents. Although we recognize that larger adoption studies are desirable, the fact that the correlations between the smoking habits of foster parents and their adopted children are so close to zero must rule out an overwhelming environmental effect of parental habits on the development of their children's smoking habits. We could argue, though with the number of subjects available to us we would not push the point, that the similarity between parent and biological offspring, although quite small, is largely genetic rather than social.

It is tempting to dismiss the significant similarity of spouses as purely social. Either way, even if it had a genetic component, its contribution to genetical variation between offspring families would be very slight.

There are significant sex differences in mean and raw variance for aspects of the smoking habit. These are examined in some detail in Chapter 4 when the twin data are discussed. There is not much evidence, however, that these differences reflect any underlying sex differences in the mechanism by which the smoking habit develops. The overall data are insufficiently precise, however, to permit a more detailed examination of this issue. Males and females clearly differ in their smoking habits, and we have assumed that these differences are a matter of scale rather than kind. Subsequent more detailed investigations may falsify this assumption.

All in all, therefore, the picture emerges from the whole body of data that the onset of smoking and the consumption of cigarettes are governed by both genetical and environmental factors. The overriding single component is the unique environmental experiences of individuals. In these we must include chance day-to-day fluctuations, errors of memory and reporting, most of which will contribute systematically to their unsystematic environmental effects. Approximately half the remaining variation is apparently due to inherited factors which may remain stable with age. What is left seems due to social factors for which twins are more alike than non-twins. For this reason we suggest tentatively that the influence of peers may be of primary interest. An alternative hypothesis would simply dismiss the inconsistency of twin and family data as a reflection of the inherent lack of stability of gene expression with age.

Chapter 6 considers the linear and additive relationships between measures of personality and aspects of smoking. Although we demonstrated significant phenotypic correlations between smoking and personality, it proved difficult to decompose this relationship into its genetic and environmental components. At the phenotypic level, the major single factor discriminating smokers from non-smokers was the combination of the P and L scales of the EPQ. Smokers were found to obtain higher P (Psychoticism) scores and lower L (Lie) scores. A significant component in the determination of the difference between smokers and non-smokers, therefore, seems to be the greater overall 'social desirability' of non-smokers. Smokers clearly give much more toughminded responses on personality questionnaires than non-smokers. Even in a permissive age, it seems that smoking is regarded as a scurrilous habit! Once we examine the personality correlates of the smoking habit among smokers, the relationship with the L scale is slightly reduced, although P still contributes to differences between 'light' and 'heavy' smokers and between 'early' and 'late' onset smokers.

Analysis of the causal basis for the association in the twin data reveals that these effects are almost entirely familial, since the environmental differences within families do little to bring about an association between smoking and personality. The results of an attempt to resolve the familial association into its genetic and environmental components, however, were ambiguous. The assumption that the relationship is genetic gave marginally better agreement between observations and theory, but explanations involving the joint influences of genes and social factors are likely to be necessary. The relationship between extraversion and smoking, so often assumed to be of paramount importance, does not emerge in our data. It seems likely that the addition of P to E and N as a major dimension of personality has led to the incorporation in P of some of the elements of E which previously mediated the correlation with smoking; if this were to prove a correct hypothesis, then most of what was said in the text about E would now apply to P.

There is also little evidence that neuroticism makes any overall contribution to differences between smokers and non-smokers, although it is quite clear (Appendix B) that anxiety and its correlates do affect smokers' beliefs about the consequences of their actions. The lie scale, presumably related to self-deception, is also shown to be a significant correlate of subjects' beliefs about the consequences of their actions.

APPENDICES

APPENDIX A

The Sample: Its Structure, Rationale and Ascertainment

JUDITH KASRIEL

Rationale

The work described in this book is part of an attack on the broader issue of causes of human variation in behaviour, including the study of personality, social attitudes, attitudes to sex, together with a preliminary study of tobacco and alcohol consumption and its behavioural correlates. By far, the majority of research hitherto has concentrated on one or other of a few basic types of family, in order to obtain an indication of the primary causes of variation. For ease of ascertainment, nuclear families have often been favoured, providing parents and offspring which can, under certain very restricted assumptions, provide estimates of the inherited component of variation for particular traits. It is, however, these assumptions which make the nuclear family very unattractive for testing hypotheses about the likely genetic basis of behavioural traits. Although such studies can indeed demonstrate the familial aggregation of behavioural patterns they are virtually powerless to do more than demonstrate the presence of parental influence on the similarity of siblings. The simple family study, consisting of relatives who have shared, not merely common genes, but an unspecified degree of environmental communality can do little to identify and quantify the causal basis, hereditary or environmental, of the similarity between relatives. For this reason many workers have adopted a second strategy, that of the twin study. The employment of identical and fraternal twins provides a greater degree of control over the family environment by incorporating two degrees of genetical similarity in the experimental design whilst having only one (presumed) degree of environmental similarity. The weaknesses of the twin method are discussed elsewhere (Chapter 4) but may be summarized under three primary headings. (1) The environmental similarity is assumed to be the same for identical and fraternal twins. (2) The effects of genes assayed in the classical twin study are always measured at the same stage of development for each individual of a twin pair. Even after correction for the overall population trends of behaviour with time and age, any idiosyncratic age effects of genetical origin will lead to enhancement of the estimated genetic parameters from the twin study. Prediction and counselling, however, have to recognize that such factors are imperfectly controlled in the population at large and it is desirable for their contribution to be assessed at the outset. The twin study, unless it is longitudinal, cannot provide this information. (3) When twins are, or have been, reared together, which is the rule to which very few exceptions are known, it is impossible to separate the effects of the post-natal familial environment from the genetical consequences of assortative mating among the twins' parents.

The third strategy is the study of families in which individuals have been reared by unrelated foster parents and in the presence of siblings who are not related biologically. Under such circumstances, and in the absence of spurious correlations due to placement, the study of foster families can yield estimates of the contribution of environmental similarity between family members and helps us to discriminate between environmental similarity which is primarily parental in origin from that which does not depend directly on the measured phenotype of the parents. The chief disadvantage of the foster study is practical, in that it is extremely difficult to ascertain fostered individuals on a population basis because of the justifiable confidentiality surrounding adoptions. In addition, the foster study by itself, whilst concentrating effort into the assessment of the familial environment, is virtually useless as a means of discriminating between the effects of genetic segregation and the substantial non-familial environmental component which depends on those experiences and accidents of development and living which are unique to every individual.

Considered separately, each strategy has its own attractions and its own limitations for the study of behavioural traits about which little is already known or can be deduced *a priori*. At the outset of our study, therefore, it was apparent that any analysis required the synthesis of data from all three sources. Family data would provide the backbone of population parameters concerning familial transmission; twin data would provide the greatest degree of environmental control possible; adoption data would yield insight about the importance of non-genetic familial factors in the determination of individual differences for the traits in question. It is hoped that each group will provide the necessary controls for the other. The philosophy, explicit in our methodology, lies in the attempt to explain the entire data set by reference to the same few causal principles. If this can be done, then the individual criticisms and difficulties of the component studies may be discounted as relatively unimportant. If, on the other hand, the data defy such a parsimonious description, we have good reason to doubt some aspects of the data or model and will be in a far stronger position to suggest alternative hypotheses for subsequent enquiry.

The twin sample ascertainment

The three components of the study were conducted in an overlapping sequence beginning in the summer of 1971 with the collection of the twin data on smoking and personality, with the initial ascertainment of the adoptees and families shortly afterwards. The twin subjects were drawn from volunteers who had agreed to cooperate with the formation of the Volunteer Twin Register based in the Psychology Department of the Institute of Psychiatry. The register was established in 1969 with the aid of a grant from the Medical Research Council, initially under the direction of Dr John S. Price. A small number of pairs were drawn from subjects who had cooperated in earlier twin studies, but the first significant enhancement of the sample resulted from the opportunity to contact 155 pairs of identical twins who participated in a David Frost television programme broadcast by Rediffusion Ltd in March 1968. From these 155 pairs, 102 pairs subsequently completed and returned an early form of the

Eysenck Personality Inventory. Thus approximately two-thirds of the twin pairs contacted yielded complete sets of responses. At this point, with MRC support, efforts were immediately made to increase the number of cooperative twins by local and national appeals. A further 300 pairs, with ages ranging between two months and eighty-seven years, were recruited following publicity in the *Daily Mail*. Subsequent appeals and publicity in the press and on radio and television had secured a total of 1,261 pairs by June 1971. The structure of the register at this point is given in Table 62. Inevitably, in long-term research, the maintenance of a register of twins is a continuous process with new pairs being recruited to take the place of those who fail to return questionnaires. In order to retain good will,

TABLE 62

Twins on the Institute of Psychiatry Twin Register in 1971

Children   *(under the age of 12 years)*

	MZ	DZ	Total
male	88	81	169
female	97	111	208
unlike sex	—	157	157
Total	185	349	534

Juniors   *(12 — 16 years)*

	MZ	DZ	Total
male	22	16	38
female	26	41	67
unlike sex	—	35	35
Total	48	92	140

Adults   *(16 years +)*

	MZ	DZ	Total
male	67	42	109
female	222	155	377
unlike sex	—	101	101
Total	289	298	587

Total 1,261

no pressure was brought to bear on twins who did not return questionnaires. This results in a fairly low response rate. As an example of the typical current cooperation rate among twins on the register we tabulate (Table 63) the frequencies of returns from the register in 1977. We see that approximately 50 per cent of pairs on the register yielded replies from both members.

A regular feature of volunteer samples of this type is the marked bias towards female participants, who are much more ready to co-operate in such studies than males, and are more readily accessible.

Also striking is the relative predominance of monozygotic twins in spite of their scarcity in comparison with dizygotic twins in the population at large. Bulmer (1970), for example, cites the frequency of monozygotic twin births as 3.6 per thousand in England and Wales compared with a rate of 8.9 per thousand for dizygotic twins. The most likely explanation for this bias is the greater intrinsic self-interest shown by identical twins and the conscious effort, in the early days of the register, to recruit MZ twins. It is quite clear that we have a highly selected sample. Clearly, a population-based sample would be a desirable second stage of this work, but since the administrative structure for such a sample is not currently established in the United Kingdom, we have to be content with demon-

TABLE 63

Cooperativeness* of twins on the Institute of Psychiatry Twin Register in 1977

Twin type	Cooperation of pair members			
	Both cooperate	One only cooperates	Neither cooperates	Total (pairs)
MZ female	244	66	104	414
DZ female	153	47	48	248
MZ male	94	33	50	177
DZ male	64	31	50	145
DZ male/female	97	28	94	219
Total	652	205	346	1,203

*Individuals over 16 years returning questionnaire mailed in 1976.

strating firstly the feasibility of the method in the hope that it will stimulate a more concentrated and systematic future effort.

Zygosity

A recurrent problem in large-scale twin research is that of zygosity diagnosis-deciding whether or not twins are genetically identical. No approach is absolutely foolproof, but by far the most reliable is to determine the genotype of each individual (and, ideally, his parents) for a large number of genetic loci. Usually blood groups prove the most convenient and reliable to assay. Any pair of twins in which the members differ even for one blood group is certainly dizygotic, apart from the very small chance of mutation. Although identity for all the loci studied might arise by chance, it is possible to calculate how much more likely it is that a pair of twins are identical than not, given that they are identical for a known selection of loci. Obviously, the more loci that are used and the greater the genetic variation for the loci concerned, the greater the relative probability that a given pair of twins, identical at all loci, is monozygotic. Bulmer (1970) gives a more detailed account of the method and its rationale.

This approach has great appeal for its objectivity and because the results, although not error-free, do permit the probability of error to be quantified. The difficulty lies in the need to obtain blood samples from twins and in having these typed in a laboratory specializing in the determination of genotype for large numbers of loci.

When twins can be studied individually, even if blood groups cannot be determined, it seems that careful observation is generally sufficient to establish zygosity with fair reliability, but when twins are not even interviewed, as in studies involving postal questionnaires, a simple but reliable criterion for zygosity diagnosis becomes important.

An approach which has become common, but for which there are conflicting reports, is to attempt zygosity diagnosis by questionnaire. Generally, when such methods have been compared with diagnosis based on blood groups the results have been quite satisfactory. Kasriel & Eaves (1976) summarize some of the claims made for this method and we tried to obtain data to check on the validity of the approach in our case.

Between March 1970 and September 1972 blood samples were

taken from 178 pairs of twins who visited the Institute of Psychiatry to participate in other experiments. The samples were tested initially with 18 antisera at the MRC Blood Unit at the Lister Institute, and in doubtful cases a further five antisera were used. The details are given in Kasriel & Eaves (1976). Prior to this study, the twins had individually completed questionnaires which included the two questions relating to similarity:

1. 'In childhood, were you frequently mistaken by people who knew you?'
2. 'Do you differ markedly in physical appearance and colouring?'

Twins were subsequently classified by their responses to these questions. It was found (see Table 64) that twins classified as likely to be monozygotic on the blood tests almost always agreed that they

TABLE 64

Agreement of MZ and DZ twins for responses to questionnaire concerning similarity in childhood

		MZ		DZ		
*Question 1**	*Question 2†*	*Female*	*Male*	*Female*	*Male*	*Total*
Both state	Both alike	36	56	1	4	97
confusion	Disagree	1	—	1	2	4
	Both unalike	—	—	3	2	5
Disagree	Both alike	1	—	2	1	4
	Disagree	—	—	2	4	6
	Both unalike	—	—	2	6	8
Neither states	Both alike	—	—	3	—	3
confusion	Disagree	—	—	2	3	5
	Both unalike	—	—	18	28	46
	Total	38	56	34	50	178

* 'In childhood were you frequently mistaken by people who knew you?'

† 'Do you differ markedly in physical appearance and colouring?'

were confused in childhood and were alike in physical appearance. Twins classified as dizygotic on the basis of blood groups, however, showed a wide range of responses. Altogether, adopting a criterion which classified as monozygotic all pairs who agreed they were mistaken for one another and were alike in appearance misclassified 5 per cent of DZ twins as MZ and 2.5 per cent of MZ twins as DZ. Of the 178 pairs, therefore, only seven (3.9 per cent) would be misclassified by adopting this criterion of zygosity diagnosis. Clearly, since the criterion has been generated by the data we may expect a somewhat poorer average performance on replication, but nevertheless the approach should give fairly good results when applied to the whole sample.

The frequencies of the different types of twin pair given in the tables of Chapter 4 are based on this criterion of zygosity.

It is commonly assumed that errors of zygosity diagnosis will reduce the apparent contribution of inherited factors. This will only be strictly true if the misclassification is random, or biased towards counting more similar MZ twins as DZ and less similar DZ twins as MZ. Our work, in common with that of others (e.g. Cederlöf et al. 1961; Nichols & Bilbro, 1966), suggests that misclassification is more frequent in DZ than in MZ twins. The consequences of this will depend on the causes of variation and on the reasons for misclassification. If only the most similar DZ twins are classified wrongly as MZ then this would tend to reduce the DZ correlation. The effect on the MZ correlation will depend on the intrapair differences of the misclassified DZ twins compared with those of the correctly diagnosed MZ pairs. Such errors may increase the apparent component, if they are systematic, though such biases are likely to be fairly small, provided the errors are relatively infrequent. Certainly, the gain from measurements on large numbers of subjects, even with a small error of diagnosis, may outweigh the disadvantages of only being able to ascertain and diagnose a fairly small sample of individuals by the more precise procedure of blood-typing.

In a recent Birmingham study, twins were interviewed on an individual basis. A preliminary impression has been formed that twins' understanding of the question relating to physical similarity is variable, especially in women. Occasionally it is clear that purely environmental factors such as hairstyle and dress were included as 'physical differences', and a certain amount of explanation is sometimes needed in order to clarify what is required. On the other hand, the question relating to childhood similarity seemed to accord quite well with the opinion of a panel of interviewers about the zygosity of the twins. It would seem wise, however, to retain some reservations about the questionnaire method of diagnosis.

Adoption sample

As with the twins, the adopted subjects were secured as volunteers by appeals through the same media and by the same methods as in the twin study. It is much more difficult, quite understandably, to obtain a population-based adoption sample because of the confidentiality surrounding the adoption process. Although it may be possible to secure juveniles in a more systematic way, there is little alternative but to seek volunteers for studies of adults.

Volunteers were requested who had been adopted in the early months of life. Altogether 349 adopted individuals agreed to complete questionnaires and in many cases it was possible to secure the cooperation of their adopting relatives. The types of relationship recoverable from the adoption study are given in Table 66. Among the adoptees, the age of adoption ranged from 0 to 180 months, with a modal value at 2 months and median of 3.4. We are unable to verify the facts of adoption, but the average age of adoption is sufficiently early to rule out much by way of post-natal environmental influence of biological parent on foster child as far as smoking is concerned. The majority of foster relatives who responded were foster parents, although a number of foster siblings agreed to take part, both natural children of the foster parents and additional fostered siblings. The number of unrelated individuals reared as foster siblings, however, was too small to make much impact on the final analysis of the data.

Normal families

The third component of the study, the 'normal' families, were obtained by (a) contacting students at local colleges and inviting themselves and members of their families to complete the relevant questionnaires; (b) advertising in newspapers and magazines for interested individuals to fill in questionnaires; (c) by personal contacts.

SUMMARY OF SAMPLE STRUCTURE:

Age structure of sample. Table 65 gives the age distribution of respondents by sex for each of the three principal groups in the sample. It should be noted that the 'adoption' sample does not just comprise adoptees but includes their families. A disproportionate number of respondents fall into the under-thirties group in all three samples. In the adoption and family studies there is a higher proportion of older respondents because of the generation gap between parents and children.

Social class distribution. On the basis of reported occupation respondents were grouped according to the Registrar General's social classification. The class structure of the sample is given for each

TABLE 65

Structure of sample by age in five-year cohorts.
Number of subjects

Cohort (Years)	Males			Females		
	Family	Adoption	Twins	Family	Adoption	Twins
< 20	22	5	55	75	21	73
20 − 24	62	15	85	95	67	175
25 − 29	35	22	74	49	116	128
30 − 34	12	17	31	25	52	83
35 − 39	16	6	23	21	28	64
40 − 44	20	3	10	30	20	40
45 − 49	20	3	19	37	27	61
50 − 54	37	14	4	41	30	56
55 − 59	34	13	4	22	19	46
60 − 64	21	18	7	31	40	21
65 − 69	9	23	4	17	25	6
70 − 74	6	12	2	4	7	8
75 − 79	4	2	0	9	0	4
> 79	3	1	0	1	1	0
Total	299	154	318	474	453	765

Number of missing observations = 6.

sex (Table 66). The sample is clearly biased in favour of respondents in classes I and II. This reflects the difficulty of securing the co-operation of individuals who fall into the other social groupings for whom the 'academic' aspect of the research has little appeal and who have probably got better things to do with their time than fill in questionnaires!

Finally, we give the actual questionnaire (Table 67) used in the investigation; all the genotype-environmental analyses are based on this.

Table 66

Distribution of respondents by sex and social class

	Sex		
	Male *1.*	*Female* *2.*	*Row* *Total*
Class 1 (higher managerial, administrative, or professional)	86	9	95
Class 2 (intermediate managerial, administrative or professional)	190	202	392
Class 3 (supervisory or clerical and junior managerial, administrative or professional)	198	567	765
Class 4 (skilled manual workers)	118	28	146
Class 5 (semi and unskilled manual workers)	29	90	119
Class 7 (housewives, unemployed, retired)	68	678	746
Class 8 (students and scholars)	84	121	205
Column Total	773	1696	2468

Table 67

NAME..........................

Smoking Questionnaire

Please answer each question by putting a circle around the answer you agree with

	YES	NO

HAVE YOU EVER SMOKED?
(If the answer is YES, answer ALL the following questions.)

AT WHAT AGE DID YOU START SMOKING?

Before 14	18-20
14-15	20-25
16-17	26 +

	YES	NO

DO YOU SMOKE NOW?

HOW MANY CIGARETTES DO YOU SMOKE EACH DAY,
ON THE AVERAGE?

Less than 1	15-19
1-4	20-29
5-9	30 +
10-14	

HOW MANY OUNCES OF PIPE TOBACCO DO YOU SMOKE
IN ONE WEEK?

Less than ½oz	4½-6
½-1	6½-8
1½-2	
2½-4	

HOW MANY CIGARS DO YOU SMOKE EACH DAY?

HOW MANY CIGARILLOS (SMALL CIGARS) DO YOU SMOKE
EACH DAY?

HAVE YOU EVER TRIED TO GIVE UP SMOKING COMPLETELY?	YES	NO	
WERE YOU SUCCESSFUL?	YES	NO	
DO YOU BELIEVE THAT SMOKING IS HARMFUL?	YES	NO	
DO YOU BELIEVE THAT SMOKING CAUSES LUNG CANCER?	YES	NO	
DO YOU BELIEVE THAT SMOKING CAUSES CORONARY (HEART) DISEASE?	YES	NO	
DID YOU SMOKE MORE IN THE LAST YEAR, LESS, OR ABOUT THE SAME (AS COMPARED WITH BEFORE)?	MORE	LESS	SAME
DO YOU SMOKE TO CALM YOUR NERVES?	NEVER	SOMETIMES	OFTEN
DO YOU SMOKE WHEN YOU ARE BORED?	NEVER	SOMETIMES	OFTEN
IS SMOKING SIMPLY A HABIT WITH YOU?	YES	PARTLY	NO
IF YOU SMOKE CIGARETTES, DO YOU INHALE? (DRAW ON THE CIGARETTE, THEN TAKE A BREATH IN, SO THAT THE SMOKE GOES DOWN INTO YOUR LUNGS)	NEVER SOMETIMES OFTEN	USUALLY ALWAYS	
HAVE YOU EVER SUFFERED FROM ANY OF THE FOLLOWING?			
REGULAR BOUTS OF COUGHING	YES	NO	
CHRONIC BRONCHITIS	YES	NO	
CHEST PAINS	YES	NO	
SHORTNESS OF BREATH	YES	NO	
HEART DISEASE	YES	NO	
CHRONIC STOMACH DISORDER	YES	NO	

APPENDIX B

Attitudes to Smoking

H. J. EYSENCK AND L. J. EAVES

In Chapter 2 a discussion was offered of the relation between smoking and personality, and a theory developed to account for the various facts emerging from the literature. In this appendix we propose to analyse some of the data from our own twin research, described in detail in Chapters 3 and 4; these data are concerned with various questions asked of the twins concerning their smoking behaviour. Our genetic analysis concentrated chiefly on scales which might discriminate between smokers and non-smokers. However, among smokers there is wide variation in attitudes to their behaviour and its consequences, and although we are not able to offer a genetic analysis of these attitudes it is worth reporting some of the principal characteristics of different types of smoker at the phenotypic level, especially as these relate to personality.

Reported changes in the smoking habit

Subjects were asked 'How much do you smoke compared with last year?' and to endorse either 'more', 'same' or 'less'. The mean EPQ scores of the different types of respondent are tabulated (Table 68). The scores have been transformed to remove heteroscedasticity, and age-corrected. The variance (σ^2) within response groups is given in the significance of the overall group differences, together with a test of non-linearity of relationships over the categories 'less', 'same', 'more'. There is a striking effect for Psychoticism in females, and for Neuroticism. Those who report smoking more are more 'psychotic' on the EPQ scale. Those who report any change in their habits in either direction are more neurotic. This is reflected in the highly significant non-linear component in the group differences.

TABLE 68

Personality related to recent change in smoking habit

Dimension	Sex	Amount smoked compared with last year				Significance (%)	
		Less	Same	More	σ^2	Over-all	Non-line-arity
P	M	0.013	0.008	0.060	0.0272	6	6
	F	0.002	0.018	0.069	0.0253	0	8
E	M	0.017	0.001	−0.002	0.1045	87	81
	F	0.023	0.018	0.025	0.0999	95	77
N	M	0.008	0.013	0.076	0.0719	19	23
	F	0.022	0.009	0.094	0.0856	0	1
L	M	−0.011	−0.014	−0.039	0.0479	68	59
	F	−0.031	−0.022	−0.054	0.0478	25	14
Cases	M	130	401	63			
	F	236	710	157			

Relinquishing the smoking habit and personality

Table 69 gives the personality scores of individuals grouped according to whether or not they had tried and succeeded in giving up smoking. There are some significant differences but these are all specific to females. Females who have *not* tried to give up smoking are more extraverted. Females who have not succeeded are more

TABLE 69

Personality and relinquishing the smoking habit

Personality dimension	Sex	Tried to give up?				Succeeded in giving up?			
		No	Yes	σ^2	Significance (%)	No	Yes	σ^2	Significance (%)
P	M	0.021	0.011	0.0273	40	0.027	−0.008	0.0269	5
	F	0.030	0.020	0.0258	40	0.041	0.002	0.0262	0
E	M	0.023	−0.001	0.1044	75	−0.005	0.056	0.1038	93
	F	0.078	0.003	0.0986	0	0.106	−0.009	0.0986	45
N	M	0.012	0.019	0.0721	94	0.031	0.003	0.0699	51
	F	0.006	0.029	0.0865	56	0.064	0.001	0.0842	0
L	M	−0.001	−0.020	0.0477	22	−0.030	−0.009	0.0466	18
	F	−0.026	−0.030	0.0479	47	−0.036	−0.026	0.0497	48
Cases	M	129	462	—	—	253	211		
	F	269	826	—	—	381	450		

'psychotic' and 'neurotic', as measured by the EPQ.

Beliefs about dangers of smoking

Table 70 shows that beliefs about the harm caused by smoking are related to EPQ neuroticism and lie scores. In general, neuroticism scores are higher among those who believe smoking is harmful, causes cancer or causes heart disease, than among those who do not. This finding is consistent over sexes and is to be expected since one of the components of more neurotic behaviour is greater concern over health. No less striking, in females at least, is the fact that those who do *not* believe smoking is harmful have higher lie scores than those who do. It is tempting to conclude that unwillingness to admit the truth about behaviour extends, in smokers at least, to an inability to admit that their actions may have dangerous consequences. On average, it will be recalled from an earlier chapter that smokers had lower than average lie scores in general. Even granted this population difference, therefore, it is clear that smokers are heterogeneous in their degree of self-awareness or truthfulness. A significant proportion of smokers are apparently unable to admit that their behaviour can have undesirable consequences.

Beliefs about consequences of smoking

There is a clear relationship between subjects' beliefs about the consequences of their smoking and their reported success in giving it up. Among those who have ever smoked it is found that by far the largest proportion of those who have relinquished the habit (Table 71) say they believe smoking to be harmful. This seems to be especially marked for belief in the more general statement that smoking is harmful, and least obvious for beliefs about the relationship between smoking and heart disease. It is not possible to analyse the cause of this association in more detail. We could see this as a victory either for anti-smoking propaganda or for ego defence mechanisms! People have either changed their behaviour in the light of the evidence or have adjusted their perception of the evidence to justify their behaviour.

TABLE 70

Personality and smokers' beliefs about the effects of smoking

Dimension	Sex	Harmful?				Causes cancer?				Causes heart disease?			
		No	Yes	NR	Significance (%)	No	Yes	NR	Significance (%)	No	Yes	NR	Significance (%)
P	M	0.047	0.012	0.023	41	0.052	0.005	0.013	2	0.040	0.003	0.013	4
	F	0.046	0.020	0.015	33	0.028	0.021	0.012	77	0.011	0.031	0.006	10
E	M	0.069	-0.000	-0.016	41	0.016	0.003	0.003	91	0.012	0.006	0.016	91
	F	-0.002	0.022	0.005	76	0.037	0.017	-0.016	52	0.039	0.012	-0.002	34
N	M	-0.082	0.027	-0.067	3	-0.050	0.037	-0.016	1	-0.027	0.040	0.014	2
	F	-0.018	0.029	-0.062	11	0.001	0.033	-0.055	7	-0.003	0.046	-0.039	1
L	M	0.105	-0.026	0.069	<1	0.012	-0.025	0.035	14	0.007	-0.027	-0.008	22
	F	0.035	-0.036	0.034	0	-0.005	-0.039	0.047	1	0.001	-0.049	-0.004	0
Cases	M	41	546	68	—	114	458	23	—	180	388	27	—
	F	88	994	26	—	226	839	43	—	383	652	73	—

TABLE 71

Beliefs about consequences and relinquishing the smoking habit

Sex	Harm?	Broken habit?	Causes cancer			Harmful			Heart disease		
			Never tried	Failed	Succeeded	Never tried	Failed	Succeeded	Never tried	Failed	Succeeded
Male	No		38	56	21	21	17	4	53	81	46
	Yes		88	186	181	106	233	204	71	162	153
Female	No		85	102	40	47	32	9	115	141	126
	Yes		181	264	390	220	344	427	139	221	290

TABLE 72

Reasons cited for smoking related to personality

Dimension	Sex	To calm nerves				When bored				Simply a habit			
		Never	Some-times	Often	Signifi-cance (%)	Never	Some-times	Often	Signifi-cance (%)	No	Partly	Yes	Signifi-cance (%)
P	M	-0.002	0.028	0.037	6	0.000	0.014	0.051	3	-0.003	0.018	0.038	3
	F	0.000	0.032	0.056	0	0.004	0.018	0.063	0	0.004	0.026	0.053	0
E	M	0.003	0.015	-0.054	40	0.010	0.026	-0.058	8	0.012	0.022	-0.023	41
	F	0.008	0.050	-0.039	0	-0.002	0.045	0.026	10	-0.000	0.055	0.026	5
N	M	-0.034	0.060	0.128	0	-0.027	0.025	0.120	0	0.005	0.016	0.042	37
	F	-0.041	0.033	0.202	0	-0.030	0.048	0.092	0	0.000	0.059	0.031	2
L	M	0.019	-0.047	-0.070	0	0.023	-0.033	-0.076	0	0.013	-0.039	-0.042	1
	F	-0.002	-0.052	-0.036	0	-0.007	-0.042	-0.051	1	-0.014	-0.041	-0.043	11
Cases	M	292	256	46	—	268	219	107	—	278	141	173	—
	F	465	495	145	—	493	360	250	—	541	292	273	—

Reasons cited for smoking

Table 72 summarizes the personality characteristics among smokers of those who give different reasons for their behaviour. Here there are many highly significant relationships in both sexes. Both males and females who say they smoke to calm their nerves, when they are bored, or simply habitually, are all significantly more neurotic on the EPQ neuroticism scale. Such individuals also have significantly lower lie scores. This implies that certain smokers see smoking to calm nerves, to relieve boredom or habitual smoking as undesirable aspects akin to petty theft, white lies, etc. Psychoticism scores are also significantly higher among those who often smoke to calm nerves or relieve boredom and who regard smoking as simply a habit. Relationships with extraversion scores are not very striking, though females who report they often smoke to calm their nerves are significantly more introvert than those who do not. The results are disappointing from the point of view of Eysenck's theory of the physiological basis of extraversion, which would have difficulties in accounting for the absence of any relationship between smoking, boredom and extraversion.

Inhalation

A highly significant positive linear relationship is found (Table 73) between reported frequency of inhalation and psychoticism. That is, there is a trend towards increasing P scores with increasing frequency of inhalation. Similarly, there is an equally significant negative trend for the lie scale scores. Those subjects who report that they 'never' inhale obtain higher average lie scores on the EPQ.

The results of these analyses demonstrate again the importance of personality as determining in various ways the attitudes and behaviours of smokers. High P scorers tend to increase their rate of smoking over time, particularly among the women; they fail to give up smoking, again particularly among the women; they inhale more; and they smoke to calm nerves, because they are bored, and from habit. High N scorers show similar reactions. They too show an increase in smoking over time when female, although they may also change in the opposite direction (i.e. there is a significant non-linear component in the regression). They do not succeed in giving

TABLE 73

Personality and inhalation of tobacco smoke

Dimen-sion	Sex	Reported frequency of inhalation						Significance (%)	
		Never	Some-times	Often	Usually	Always	2	Overall	Non-linearity
P	M	-0.0154	0.0309	0.0601	0.0332	0.0298	0.0267	1	24
	F	0.0004	0.0251	0.0359	0.0245	0.0565	0.0252	0	47
E	M	-0.002	-0.008	0.030	0.036	0.015	0.1057	89	90
	F	0.009	0.022	-0.022	0.030	0.036	0.1004	76	92
N	M	0.006	0.060	0.029	0.008	0.031	0.0741	73	67
	F	0.016	0.017	0.103	-0.004	0.053	0.0856	16	16
L	M	0.029	-0.046	-0.051	-0.027	-0.042	0.0468	<1	33
	F	-0.015	-0.024	-0.051	-0.009	-0.070	0.0474	1	10
Cases	M	223	41	27	84	189	564	—	—
	F	492	127	23	186	272	1100	—	—

up smoking, and they believe that smoking is harmful, causes cancer, and causes heart disease. Like high P scorers, they smoke to calm nerves, when they are bored, and out of habit. Extraverted women have not tried to give up smoking (meaning that introverted women have tried); similarly, introverted women smoke to calm nerves, but not extraverted ones.

The tendency for men and women (especially the latter) to smoke in order to calm their nerves is particularly strong among dysthymics, i.e. introverted neurotics; this is a conclusion which accords with common sense. So is the fact that high P and N scorers fail to give up smoking; they apparently need it more, and use smoking for more different reasons. It is not quite clear why the observed relations are stronger for the women than for the men; with respect to N this has been observed earlier. Clearly there is still much work to be done before we can be said to understand the interrelations between smoking and personality sufficiently to tie the observed facts up with an all-embracing theory.

APPENDIX C

The Effects of Giving up Smoking
H. J. Eysenck

There has been relatively little work done on studying the effects
of giving up smoking, or the personality traits of those who give up
smoking, as compared with continued smokers, non-smokers, and
people who tried to give up but failed (e.g. Thomas, 1978; Cherry &
Kiernan, 1978; Friedman et al. in press.). It is often assumed that people
who give up smoking put on weight, eat more sweets, etc., but there
is little evidence to support these hypotheses, however likely they
may seem. The present study was undertaken with two major hypotheses in mind. (1) With respect to personality, people who successfully give up smoking are more like non-smokers, and people who
try to give up smoking but fail are more like smokers. (2) Changes
in behaviour produced by giving up smoking will be similar regardless of whether the attempt is successful or results in failure; thus with
respect to these effects smokers and non-smokers will be contrasted
with smokers who have successfully or unsuccessfully tried to give
up smoking.

Our study used four groups, each consisting of 150 men and 150
women. (In the analyses of results to be presented later, the actual
numbers usually fall just short of 150 because isolated individuals
failed to complete one or other of the questionnaires. The actual numbers in each case have of course been taken into account in conducting

analyses of variance and tests of significance, but will not always be stated in detail.)

Group A consisted of medium to heavy smoking men and women who had given up smoking for two years or more, after smoking for at least three years at least 10 cigarettes a day. Group B consisted of medium to heavy smokers who had smoked at least 10 cigarettes a day for three years or over, and had not tried seriously to give up. Group C consisted of non-smokers, who had only smoked occasionally, if at all. Group D consisted of smokers as defined above (Group B) who had tried to give up several times and failed.

The survey was carried out by the Gallup Poll organization, and produced a quota sample of respondents, selected by age, location and socio-economic status. During the routine weekly interviews of adults carried out by the survey for their own purposes, interviewers enquired about smoking habits and then administered the questionnaires which constitute the basis of our study to people falling into the required categories.[1] As an incentive for taking part in the investigation, participants were offered a chance to win £100 as a result of a draw to be carried out on completion of the experiment. All available smokers and non-smokers were used until a given category was full.

Three questionnaires were used in this study. The first is the EPQ, or Eysenck Personality Questionnaire, which gives scores on the personality traits of P (psychoticism), E (extraversion-introversion) and N (neuroticism-stability), and a lie or dissimulation scale which, under the conditions of the experiment, is probably more realistically interpreted as a measure of conformity (Eysenck & Eysenck, 1976). This is a well standardized and widely used questionnaire, which gives reliable and valid data in experimental situations of the kind here encountered. For a detailed analysis of our results using the EPQ see Eysenck (1979).

The second questionnaire relates to possible changes that might have taken place during the last two years. This questionnaire was

[1] More precisely, the interviewers first enquired about smoking habits in order to identify the men and women belonging to the four groups of interest in the enquiry. Then, according to which group the respondent belonged to, the interviewer sought cooperation in getting the respondent to accept and to fill in at a later date and return to Gallup the appropriate questionnaire(s) for the group the respondent belonged to. Interviewers were instructed to recruit everybody in two waves of 1,000 interviews in whatever group, and then in subsequent waves to recruit only those groups that were still short of respondents.

specially constructed for the purpose on the basis of a good deal of preliminary interviewing and discussion, and is given below (Table 74). There are five possible answers for each of the 15 items, and these are scored 1 for the first, 2 for the second, 3 for the 'no change' answer, 4 for the fourth, and 5 for the fifth. When results are averaged, the score of 3 therefore means no change, scores below 3 mean a change in the direction of worse tempered, gaining a lot of weight, losing interest in sex, etc., whereas scores above 3 have the opposite meaning, i.e. an improvement in temper, a loss of weight, a gain of interest in sex, etc.

TABLE 74

Questionnaire

1. My temper is much worse. My temper is a little worse. No change. My temper has improved. My temper has improved a lot.
2. I gained a lot of weight. I gained a little weight. No change. I lost a little weight. I lost a lot of weight.
3. I lost interest in sex a lot. I lost interest in sex a little. No change. I got more interested in sex. I got much more interested in sex.
4. I eat a lot more sweets. I eat a few more sweets. No change. I eat somewhat fewer sweets. I eat many fewer sweets.
5. I have become much more sociable. I have become a little more sociable. No change. I have become somewhat less sociable. I have become a lot less sociable.
6. My health has improved a lot. My health has improved a little. No change. My health has got somewhat worse. My health has got a lot worse.
7. I take much more part in sport. I take somewhat more part in sport. No change. I take somewhat less part in sport. I gave up sport almost completely.
8. I drink a lot more. I drink a little more. No change. I drink a little less. I drink a lot less.
9. I watch TV a lot more. I watch a little more. No change. I watch a little less. I watch TV a lot less.
10. I read much more. I read a little more. No change. I read a little less. I read a lot less.

11. I go out much more.   I go out a little more.   No change.   I go out a little less.   I go out a lot less.
12. I do a lot more pleasure driving.   I do a little more driving. No change.   I do a little less driving.   I do a lot less pleasure driving.
13. I work a lot more on hobbies and activities that occupy my hands. I work a little more on such hobbies.   No change.   I work a little less on such hobbies.
14. I feel much more contented.   I feel a little more contented. No change.   I feel a little less contented.   I feel a lot less contented.
15. I am much more tense.   I am somewhat more tense.   No change.   I am somewhat less tense.   I am much less tense.

If there are any other changes that have taken place, not covered by any of these 15 statements, please write them down in your own words here.

Our third questionnaire enquired about occasions for smoking, and is given as Table 75. There are thirty-five statements, taken from our own past work and from the literature, and instructions are incorporated in the questionnaire.

Instructions in general had to be somewhat different for the different groups, of course. With respect to the statement in Table 74, instructions were as follows for group A: 'After giving up smoking did your behaviour, or your feelings, change in any way? Here are some ways in which you might have changed; please put a circle around the statements which would seem most correct for you. If there are ways in which you changed which we have not covered, please write in a description at the end of the questionnaire.' Group D received the same instructions as Group A. Groups B and C, however, received the following instructions: 'Many people experience changes over time, and we would be interested in any such changes you may have experienced during the past 2 or 3 years. Here are some ways in which you might have changed ... (continued as in instructions for Groups A and D).' The questionnaire given in Table 75 was of course only administered to the groups whose members were at the time,

TABLE 75

Occasions for smoking

Different people smoke on different types of occasion; we would like to know just when you are likely to light up. Here are 35 statements regarding situations when you might light a cigarette, or moods which might make you smoke. Please put a cross into column A if you would be *very* likely to smoke in that situation, in column B if you would be *quite* likely to smoke; in column C if you might or might not smoke; and in column D if you would very likely *not* smoke in that situation. Please be sure to put a cross after every statement!

	A *Very likely*	B *Quite likely*	C *Might*	D *Would not*
Situation:				

When you have just been informed of the death of a close friend.
When you feel uncomfortable.
When you have just heard the announcement of a train crash in which a close friend may have been involved.
When you are chatting with friends during a tea-break.
When you are worried.
When you feel frustrated.
When you simply become aware of the fact that you are not smoking.
When you are drinking alcohol.
When you are having an important interview for a job.
When you feel tired.
When you realize you are lighting a cigarette even though you just put one out.
When you feel impatient.
When you have just had a big meal.
When you are resting.
When you feel annoyed.
When you are having a restful evening

	A	B	C	D
alone reading a magazine.				

alone reading a magazine.
When you are overly excited.
When you have to drive at speed in heavy traffic.
When you want to relax.
When you realize that you may not be able to smoke for a while.
When you feel restless.
When you have to ask your boss for a raise at a time when he is known to be in a bad mood.
When you have to wait for your train home, which is very late.
When you find a cigarette in your mouth and don't remember having lit it.
When you feel embarrassed.
When you are speaking on the telephone.
When you are travelling on a train for several hours.
When you are feeling nervous.
When you feel angry.
When you want to take a break from work or some other activity
When you have to do some rapid arithmetic on your job.
When you are very tired and need to keep awake.
When you feel tense.
When you feel upset.
When you have just been making love.

or had previously been, smoking. Non-smokers were not administered this questionnaire.

Table 76 shows the results of the study as far as personality variables are concerned. Mean scores are given, for men and women separately, for P, E, N and L. Analysis of variance showed highly significant sex differences on P (men have higher scores), N (women have higher scores), and L (women have higher scores). These results are all above the P value of 0.0001, and are all in the expected direction, as found in previous studies. There are no significant differences

TABLE 76

Mean scores on personality variables, P, E, N and L for four smoking groups, for males and females separately

Men		P	E	N	L
A	Given up	3.69	11.43	9.88	7.95
B	Smokers	4.34	12.78	9.28	7.90
C	Non-smokers	3.70	12.30	9.51	7.26
D	Failed	4.11	13.75	10.50	7.26
Women					
A	Given up	1.65	12.25	12.36	9.67
B	Smokers	2.62	12.92	13.60	9.30
C	Non-smokers	2.48	12.58	12.31	8.76
D	Failed	2.76	13.02	14.38	9.47

on E, which is a little unusual as men tend to have slightly higher E scores.

Analysis of variance indicates that the smoking groups are differentiated on P ($p < .005$), E ($p < .002$), and N ($p < .002$); the results for L are insignificant ($p < .10$). There was no sex by group interaction.

It is apparent from the table that our hypothesis is borne out, i.e. that those who have successfully given up are similar to non-smokers, whereas those who have failed to give up are more similar to smokers. With respect to P, for instance, smokers are highest, with those who failed close to them; non-smokers and those who have given up smoking are low on P. This agrees with the finding mentioned in the body of the book that smokers tend to be higher on P than non-smokers. With respect to E, smokers and those who failed to give up have high scores, those who have given up and non-smokers have low scores. This again is in agreement with the usual finding that smokers of cigarettes tend to be more extraverted. With respect to N, those who fail to give up smoking have the highest scores, followed by continued smokers among the females, but not among the males. This is in agreement with the finding mentioned in the main body of the book that neuroticism correlates with smoking in women, but not in men.

We may conclude from this table that in so far as the results are comparable with previous data, they replicate earlier findings with considerable fidelity; this gives us faith in believing that in areas not previously explored the results too may be trusted. If that be so, then it is clear that those who have given up smoking successfully are temperamentally more like non-smokers, whereas those who have failed to give up smoking are temperamentally more like smokers. This is an important finding, which we hope will be replicated in future studies. It might be possible to argue that the personality traits may have been influenced by the successful or unsuccessful attempts to give up smoking, but we do not believe that this is a strong probability, in view of the very marked determination of these personality traits by genetic factors, and the lack of plausibility in linking changes in these particular variables with the personality traits in question. It is impossible to discount the possibility completely, as studies of smokers prior to their attempting to give up smoking are difficult to arrange. Had there been any such influence, we believe it would most likely have caused changes in the L score, interpreted in terms of conformity; having given up smoking could be interpreted as being a conformist act in the present climate of opinion, and should have led to an increase in these particular scores, whereas failure should have had the opposite effect. The lack of significance of the data for L suggests that this has not been so.

We next turn to Table 77, which gives the mean changes that have taken place for the four groups over time. Also given are the results of an analysis of variance done separately for the sexes for each of the 15 items. Items 10-13 inclusive (read more, go out more, more pleasure-driving, more hobbies) are quite insignificant as far as differentiating the groups are concerned and will not be discussed any further. It is quite important to have a number of items which fail to give significant results as otherwise one might have suspected that respondents were simply routinely reporting changes in order to please the interviewer, rather than because these had actually taken place. Failure of some items, and differences in significance of other items, suggests that this was not a powerful determinant of their responses.

For those items on which the analysis of variance showed significance, individual t tests were done comparing each group with each other, and each group with different combinations of all the other groups. Detailed analyses are available from the Institute of Psychiatry, but only the main results will be discussed here.

Item 1: temper worse. Clearly those who failed, and those who gave up smoking changed more in the direction of having a worse

TABLE 77

Change scores for the four smoking groups, for men and women separately on 15 items

	A) Given up smoking		B) Smokers		C) Non-smokers		D) Tried giving up		P<	
	F	M	F	M	F	M	F	M	F	M
1. Temper worse	2.78	2.87	2.89	3.21	3.12	3.16	2.05	2.34	.001	.001
2. Gained weight	2.09	2.30	2.85	2.61	2.72	2.56	2.13	2.43	.001	.05
3. Lost interest in sex	2.99	3.15	2.88	3.18	3.17	3.42	2.89	3.17	.01	.05
4. Ate more sweets	2.35	2.64	3.46	3.62	3.26	3.67	1.97	2.23	.001	.001
5. More sociable	2.89	2.87	2.46	2.54	2.39	2.44	3.21	2.99	.001	.001
6. Health improved	2.27	2.00	2.93	2.93	2.83	2.81	2.35	2.36	.001	.001
7. More sport	2.83	2.70	3.49	3.25	3.40	3.21	2.98	2.85	.001	.001
8. Drink more	2.88	2.98	3.07	3.03	2.87	2.93	2.73	2.67	.05	.05
9. Watched T. V. more	3.03	2.98	3.13	3.15	3.26	3.54	2.94	2.99	N.S.	.001
10. Read more	2.68	2.82	2.71	2.85	2.73	2.87	2.59	2.74	N.S.	N.S.
11. Go out more	2.96	2.95	2.71	2.87	2.75	2.69	2.88	2.79	N.S.	N.S.
12. More driving	2.88	2.95	2.78	2.91	2.71	2.83	2.95	2.90	.05	N.S.
13. More hobbies	2.48	2.67	2.85	2.77	2.60	2.81	2.38	2.55	.05	N.S.
14. More contented	2.59	2.44	2.47	2.31	2.19	2.44	3.40	3.08	.001	.001
15. More tense	2.89	3.14	3.11	3.25	3.31	3.14	2.15	2.50	.001	.001

temper than did smokers and non-smokers, who essentially did not change. For the males there is no significant difference between the changes in failures and in those who gave up; all other differences are fully significant. For the females, those who failed to give up are significantly worse than those who succeeded in giving up smoking.

Item 2: gain in weight. Those who gave up successfully and those who failed to give up successfully showed more gain in weight than did smokers and non-smokers. For both males and females there was no significant difference between groups A and D, or between groups B and C; all the significant differences are between these two sets.

Item 3: loss of interest in sex. Here the significance of the differences on the analysis of variance is less than in the preceding items, and there seems to be no regularity in the pattern. Consequently we shall not discuss this item any further; it seems to be unrelated to giving up smoking.

Item 4: eating more sweets. Here again we see that those who failed and those who succeeded in giving up show a greater change than smokers and non-smokers who continued in their way. Smokers and non-smokers are not significantly differentiated from each other, but failures are significantly more likely to eat more sweets than those who have succeeded in giving up.

Item 5: more sociable. Compared with smokers and non-smokers, those who tried and failed to give up, and to a lesser degree those who succeeded in giving up are less sociable. For the men there is no difference between groups A and D, or B and C; for the women this is true of groups B and C but A and D are significantly different at the $p < .01$ level.

Item 6: improvement in health. This is reported both by those who tried to give up and by those who succeeded in giving up, as compared with the other two groups. (Here as elsewhere, of course, it is important to realize that we only have the unsupported testimony of the respondents; no independent evidence of improved health is available.) Those who gave up smoking completely improved significantly more than those who did not as far as the males are concerned, but for the females there was no difference. No differences were apparent between groups 2 and 3, either for males or females.

Item 7: more sport. In males and females, groups A and D both reported engaging more in sport, whereas groups B and C reported engaging less in sport. Groups A and D show no significant difference in this, and groups B and C show no significant difference either.

Item 8: drink more. Here the significance of the result is very marginal for both men and women. But there is some slight evidence that those who gave up smoking, or tried and failed to give up smoking, drink more than smokers and non-smokers. Groups A and D differ significantly for the males, with those who tried and failed reporting more drinking than those who tried and succeeded; for the females the difference is not significant, and for neither sex is the difference between groups B and C significant.

Item 9: watch TV more. Here the difference is only significant for the males, with those who have given up smoking, or tried and failed to give up smoking, watching more. Groups A and D are not significantly differentiated, but groups B and C are, with non-smokers viewing less, as compared with previous years, than smokers. The trend for the women is in the same direction as for the men, i.e. for those who gave up smoking tending to view more than those who remained either smokers or non-smokers, but as the results are not significant they are obviously much weaker than for the males.

Item 14: more contented. Here the outstanding group seems to be those who tried to give up and failed; they seem to have shifted in the direction of less contentment. It is clear from the pattern of significances of individual t tests that whereas comparisons between group A and groups B and C are not significant, those involving group D are. It seems to follow that giving up smoking does not increase contentment, but failing in the attempt to give up smoking makes a person much more discontented.

Item 15: more tense. Here again the group that obviously stands out is that of the people who tried to give up and failed; they are showing a distinct change in the direction of being more tense. Group A is not significantly differentiated from groups B and C, except for the non-smoking women, where the significance level is $p < .001$. Group D is clearly differentiated from all the other groups.

We may summarize our data in terms of our original hypothesis. In most of the cases we find that indeed smokers who have given up, and smokers who have tried to give up and failed, show similar changes, as compared with smokers and non-smokers. The only clear-cut difference is in the last two items, where smokers who failed to give up are found to be less contented and more tense than in previous years; this is not true of smokers who succeeded in giving up smoking. This exception to our rule is, of course, quite intelligible, and indeed

might have been predicted. Otherwise our hypothesis is supported by the data.

We next turn to the results obtained from the analysis of the
questions contained in Table 75, i.e. the reason for smoking. The
items were intercorrelated for men and women separately, combining
the three groups in question, and the resulting matrix factor analysed.
There were four eigen-values above 1, and consequently four factors
were rotated by varimax and later by promax into oblique simple
structure. Only three of the factors could be interpreted. Loadings
for men and women separately are given in Tables 78 and 79. These
three factors which appear meaningful are clearly identifiable
as relaxation, nervousness, and automatic response, and all three
are similar to factors previously discovered in the literature.

The following items were used to score each of these scales. Scale 1
(Relaxation): 4, 13, 14, 16, 19, 30. Scale 2 (Nervousness): 1, 5, 9,
15, 22, 25, 28, 29, 33, 34. Scale 3 (Automatic): 7, 10, 11, 18, 24,

TABLE 78

**Factor loadings on four rotated figures for occasions to
smoke: men**

Row					
Row	1	.13	—.82	.11	.16
Row	2	.50	—.25	—.24	.16
Row	3	.36	—.62	—.02	.25
Row	4	.89	.15	.04	—.12
Row	5	.64	—.43	.19	.04
Row	6	.65	—.24	—.00	.15
Row	7	.24	.04	—.59	—.10
Row	8	.37	0.1	.14	—.59
Row	9	—.31	—.66	—.19	—.01
Row	10	.32	.03	—.49	.01
Row	11	.05	.01	—.76	—.01
Row	12	.53	—.23	—.24	.08
Row	13	.75	.18	.08	—.30
Row	14	.65	.23	—.25	—.07
Row	15	.11	—.62	.03	—.22
Row	16	.90	.22	—.03	—.06
Row	17	.43	—.27	—.16	.08
Row	18	—.08	—.03	—.53	.03
Row	19	.85	.15	—.04	.02
Row	20	.48	—.12	—.14	—.19

Row	21	.45	−.25	−.11	−.13
Row	22	−.44	−.72	−.19	−.30
Row	23	.14	−.27	−.01	−.50
Row	24	.10	.01	−.65	−.06
Row	25	−.25	−.69	−.10	−.29
Row	26	.01	−.13	−.18	−.53
Row	27	.53	−.08	.09	−.43
Row	28	.35	−.62	.17	−.12
Row	29	.09	−.70	.04	−.15
Row	30	.74	.07	.01	−.25
Row	31	.12	−.19	−.42	.00
Row	32	.53	−.03	−.24	.07
Row	33	.75	−.28	−.00	.22
Row	34	.26	−.66	.15	−.09
Row	35	−.07	−.04	−.04	−.66

31. The factors are quite highly correlated, with most of the correlations being in the 40s. This is the usual finding, meaning that people who tend to smoke in one situation also tend to smoke in all other situations. This fact must be taken into account in interpreting the results now to be reported.

Table 80 shows the mean scores, on the relaxation, nervousness, and automatic scales, of the three smoking groups, i.e. those who gave up successfully, those who continue smoking and those who tried and failed to give up. It is interesting to see that those who successfully gave up had the lowest scores on all three factors; in other words, their smoking apparently was less highly motivated, and consequently they found it easier to give up than other groups. Smokers and those who tried to give up and failed have very similar scores on all three scales, and are not therefore differentiated significantly. Overall analysis of variance indicates significant differences between the three groups on all three scales, at a $p < .0001$ level; this significance is exclusively due to the low scores of those who successfully gave up. This comparison therefore seems to bear out our hypothesis that those who failed to give up smoking would be found to be more similar to smokers, whereas those who gave up successfully would be found to be dissimilar to smokers.

Next we report the correlations between the four personality variables, and the scores on the 'occasions' factors (i.e. relaxation, nervousness, automatic), for the three groups (smokers, successful and unsuccessful attempts to give up smoking). Table 81 gives all the

TABLE 79

Factor loadings on four rotated factors for occasions to smoke: women

Row				
Row	1	.16	.80	—.10	—.16
Row	2	.53	.24	.23	—.16
Row	3	.39	.61	.02	—.26
Row	4	.89	—.16	—.03	.12
Row	5	.66	.41	—.18	—.04
Row	6	.67	.22	.00	—.14
Row	7	.25	—.05	.58	.12
Row	8	.34	—.03	—.14	.61
Row	9	—.30	.69	.21	—.02
Row	10	.33	—.03	.48	—.00
Row	11	.06	.00	.74	.03
Row	12	.56	.21	.23	—.07
Row	13	.74	—.19	—.08	.30
Row	14	.64	—.22	.25	.05
Row	15	.13	.59	—.04	.24
Row	16	.90	—.22	.03	.04
Row	17	.46	.25	.15	—.06
Row	18	—.08	.08	.53	—.07
Row	19	.86	—.15	.05	—.04
Row	20	.49	.09	.13	.22
Row	21	.47	.22	.10	.16
Row	22	—.44	.71	.19	.31
Row	23	—.13	.25	.01	.52
Row	24	.10	—.01	.63	.08
Row	25	—.25	.67	.10	.31
Row	26	—.00	.10	.16	.56
Row	27	.52	.07	—.09	.44
Row	28	.36	.59	—.17	.13
Row	29	.12	.67	—.04	.16
Row	30	.74	—.08	—.01	.25
Row	31	.13	.19	.41	—.01
Row	32	.54	.03	.24	—.06
Row	33	.78	.26	.00	—.22
Row	34	.28	.63	—.15	.11
Row	35	—.10	.04	.03	.68

T<small>ABLE</small> 80

**Mean scores on three 'occasions for smoking'
factors for three smoking groups**

	Relax		*Nervous*		*Automatic*	
	M	*F*	*M*	*F*	*M*	*F*
Given up:	11.89	11.00	20.75	21.06	8.95	7.59
Smokers:	19.20	18.90	27.56	30.04	11.33	11.61
Failed:	18.16	18.90	27.51	31.22	10.99	11.20

correlations in question, with those exceeding 0.10 being in italics. (For the size of the groups in question, the correlation would have to be 0.16 to be significant at the 0.05 level, and 0.21 to be significant at the 0.01 level.) Most of the correlations being quite low, only those will be taken seriously which are highly significant, or where there is congruence in the direction between the different groups.

The highest and most consistent correlations, as might have been expected, appear for the nervousness scale. Nervousness correlates positively, although only slightly, with P; negatively with E, particularly among women, and particularly highly with N, particularly among women. This again bears out the often noted relationship between femininity and smoking in order to relieve tension.

Automatic smoking seems to be associated with P, but only in the group that failed to give up smoking. There is some evidence of a negative correlation with E, but only slight. The correlation with N is quite strong, particularly again among women. The relaxation scale only has quite small correlations, the most consistent apparently being negatively with extraversion. These correlations are only just on the border line of significance, and should not be taken too seriously unless they can be replicated.

The major findings of this part of the study are that high N scorers, particularly among women, but also among men to a lesser extent, smoke in situations which are tense and produce nervousness, and also in situations characterized by automatic smoking. Nervous smoking is also negatively correlated with extraversion among women, but only very slightly among men. Thus dysthymic women (high N, low E), and to a lesser extent dysthymic men, smoke in situations which are tense, and which produce automatic responses.

So far, we have not analysed data in accord with socio-economic status (SES) and age. For personality, there is only a tenuous relation between SES and P, with the lowest social strata having the highest

TABLE 81

Correlations between: personality factors (P, E, N and L) and three 'occasions to smoke' scales (relaxation, nervousness, automatic)

	Relax P	Relax E	Relax N	Relax L	Nervous P	Nervous E	Nervous N	Nervous L	Auto. P	Auto. E	Auto. N	Auto. L
Men:												
Smokers: given up	08	00	00	00	04	−01	06	−08	09	06	04	−09
Smokers: continued	04	−16	−06	−18	−02	−04	12	−10	08	−14	17	−03
Smokers: failed	09	−16	09	−05	13	−03	17	−04	22	−02	19	−05
Women:												
Smokers: given up	−03	−12	15	−03	−11	−20	26	08	−05	−11	16	03
Smokers: continued	−04	−15	10	−02	−06	−14	18	−04	05	−13	28	−16
Smokers: failed	02	−03	03	−02	16	−10	18	03	22	00	18	00

TABLE 82

Mean socio-economic status of four smoking groups

Group	Males	Females
A (Given up)	3.38	3.45
B (Smokers)	3.87	3.86
C (Smokers)	3.46	3.53
D (Failures)	3.89	3.77
Significance	< .0001	< .003
Total group	3.65	3.65

P values; this relation, while statistically significant, is too slight to affect results.[1] As regards the four main groups of the study, results for SES are given in Table 82; analysis of variance demonstrates very high significance levels for both men and women. Non-smokers again line up with those who have given up successfully, both groups having relatively higher SES than those who smoke, or who have failed to give up. Results for the two sexes are remarkably congruent, with the mean SES of respondents of the two sexes being exactly equal.

Table 84 gives the information for age, and here again the differences are quite significant statistically. Those who have given up successfully, and those who are smokers, are older than those who are non-smokers, or who have failed to give up smoking. Here again there is congruity between the two sexes, so that it must be presumed that results are replicable; nevertheless, the differences in years are so small that one may doubt whether they are psychologically very meaningful. Possibly older men and women succeed in giving up smoking because there is a trend for age to correlate negatively with P, E and N; thus older persons would be lower on these personality variables which in turn are known to correlate with smoking. The difference between smokers and non-smokers might have arisen because of the propaganda drive against smoking which has changed to some extent the social acceptability of cigarette smoking.

SES is not connected with changes taking place after giving up smoking; all the scores are non-significant. As regards reasons for smoking (occasions), the results are given in Tables 85 to 87. It will be seen that results are significant for males on Relaxation only; the lower classes have higher scores. There is a trend in the same direction for the females, but this is not significant (Table 85). For Nervousness (Table 86) and Automatic smoking (Table 87), results

[1] Table 83 gives the correlations between Personality and SES and Age.

TABLE 83
Socio-economic status and age correlations with
personality scores

	S.E.S.		Age	
	M	F	M	F
P	.15	.13	−.21	−.23
E	.01	−.04	−.29	−.18
N	.04	.16	.01	−.06
L	.04	.08	.32	.32

are significant for the women, but not for the men, with lower-class women having higher scores in both factors. On Automatic smoking the men follow suit, although results are not significant, but on Nervousness there is no pattern at all for the men. None of the differences are at all large, and although statistically significant they have little psychological import.

The overall results of this study, even when taking into account the qualifications mentioned in the course of the text, are fairly clear-cut. People who give up smoking are in many ways more like non-smokers than smokers, whereas people who try to give up and fail are on the whole more like smokers than non-smokers. When smoking is given up, whether for good or only for relatively short periods, specific changes in behaviour, attitude and mood take place which on the whole are similar for smokers who succeed in giving up for good, and for smokers who resume smoking after giving it up for a time. The only exception to this rule is that smokers who fail to give up smoking become more tense and less contented, as compared with smokers who succeed in giving up the habit. On the whole our results are in close agreement with the conclusions of Friedman et al. (in press), who also find ex-smokers to differ markedly from smokers, even at a time when both groups are still smoking.

TABLE 84
Means of age variable for four smoking groups

Age	Males	Females
A	37.87	37.32
B	36.06	34.30
C	30.09	30.73
D	32.95	32.70
Significance	< .0001	< .0001
Total group	34.26	33.75

Table 85

Occasions for smoking scores for different S.E.S. groups: relaxation

S.E.S.	M	F
1	14.50	13.67
2	15.08	15.60
3	15.84	15.50
4	16.19	16.66
5	18.23	17.08
6	16.50	17.08
	$p < .01$	N.S.

Table 86

Occasions for smoking scores for different S.E.S. groups: nervousness

S.E.S.	M	F
1	27.17	17.60
2	25.34	27.15
3	24.45	26.71
4	24.75	27.51
5	27.00	29.14
6	24.00	28.67
	N.S.	$< .04$

Table 87

Occasions for smoking scores for different S.E.S. groups: automatic smoking

S.E.S.	M	F
1	10.67	8.00
2	10.24	9.22
3	9.85	9.57
4	10.52	10.24
5	11.14	11.14
6	11.20	11.33
	N.S.	$< .02$

References

Abse, D. W., Wilkins, M. M., Verton. D., Kirschner, L. G., Brown, R. S., Buxton, W. D., 1972. Self-frustration, nighttime smoking and lung cancer. *Psychosomatic Medicine*, **34**, 395-404.

Abse, D. W., Wilkins, M. M., Castle, R., Buxton, W. D., Demars, J., Brown, R. S. & Kirschner, L. G., 1974. Personality and behavioral characteristics of lung cancer patients. *Journal of Psychosomatic Research*, **18**, 101-113.

Achterberg, J. & Lawlis, G. F., 1979. A canonical analysis of blood chemistry variables related to psychological measures of cancer patients. *Multivariate Experimental Clinical Research*, **4**, 1-10.

Achterberg, J., Lawlis, G. F., Simonton, O. C. & Simonton, S. M., 1977. Psychological factors and blood chemistries as disease outcome predictors for cancer patients. *Multivariate Experimental Clinical Research*, **3**, 107-122.

Achterberg, J., Simonton, O. C. & Matthews-Simonton, S., 1976. *Stress, Psychological Factors and Cancer.* Fort Worth: New Medicine Press.

Adesso, V. & Glad, W., 1978. A behavioral test of a smoking typology. *Addictive Behaviors*, **3**, 35-38.

Adlersberg, D., Schaefer, L. E. & Steinberg, A., 1957. Studies in genetic and environmental control of serum cholesterol levels. *Circulation*, **16**, 487-488.

Anderson, D. E., 1978. Familial cancer and cancer families. *Seminars in Oncology*, **5**, 11-16.

Anderson, K., 1975. Effects of cigarette smoking on learning and retention. *Psychopharmacologia*, **41**, 1-5.

Anderson, K. & Post, B., 1974. Effects of cigarette smoking on verbal rate learning and psychological arousal. *Scandinavian Journal of Psychology*, **15**, 263-267.

Angst, J. & Maurer-Groeli, Y. A., 1974. Blutgruppe und Persön-lichkeit. *Archiv für Psychiatrie und Nerven Kraukheiten*, **218**, 291-300.

Armitage, A. K., Hall, G. H. & Sellers, C. M., 1969. Effects of nicotine on electrocortical activity and acetylcholine release from the cat cerebral cortex. *British Journal of Pharmacology*, **35**, 157-160.

Armitage, A. K., 1978. The role of nicotine in the tobacco smoking habit. In: R. E. Thornton (ed.), *Smoking Behaviour*. London: Churchill Livingstone.

Arnold-Krüger, M. A., 1973. Zur Persönlichkeit junger männlicher Raucher: I. Rauchen Extraversion und Neurotizismus. *Zeitschrift für Klinische Psychologie und Psychotherapie*, **1**, 72-80.

Ashton, H., Millman, J. E., Rawlins, M. D., Telford, R. & Thompson, J. W., 1975. The contingent negative variation: an objective electroencephalographic method for measuring the effects of centrally acting drugs on brain activity in man. *British Journal of Pharmacology*, **50**, 177-178.

Ashton, H., Millman, J. E., Rawlins, M. D., Telford, R. & Thompson, J. W., 1976. The use of event-related slow potentials of the brain in the analysis of effects of cigarette smoking and nicotine in humans. *Abstracts, International Workshop on the Behavioral Effects of Nicotine*. Zurich.

Ashton, H., Millman, J. E., Telford, R. & Thompson, J. W., 1973. Stimulant and depressant effects of cigarette smoking on brain activity in man. *British Journal of Pharmacology*, **48**, 715-717.

Ashton, H., Millman, J. E., Telford, R. & Thompson, J. W., 1974. The effects of caffeine, nitrazepam and cigarette smoking on the contingent negative variation in man. *Electroencephalography and Clinical Neurophysiology*, **37**, 59-71.

Ashton, H., Savage, R. D., Telford, R., Thompson, J. W. & Watson, D. W., 1972. The effects of cigarette smoking on the response to stress in a driving simulator. *British Journal of Pharmacology*, **45**, 546-556.

Ashton, H. & Watson, D. W., 1970. Puffing frequency and nicotine intake in cigarette smokers. *British Medical Journal*, 19 September, 679-681.

Bahnson, C. B. & Bahnson, M. B., 1964a. Cancer as an alternative to psychosis. In: D. M. Kissen & I. I. Le Shan (eds), *Psychosomatic Aspects of Neoplastic Disease*. Philadelphia: Lippincott.

Bahnson, C. B. & Bahnson, M. B., 1964b. Denial and repression of primitive impulses and of disturbing emotions in patients with malignant neoplasms. In: D. M. Kissen & I. I. Le Shan (eds), *Psychosomatic Aspects of Neoplastic Disease*. Philadelphia: Lippincott.

Bahnson, C. B. & Wardwell, W. I., 1962. Parent constellation and psychosexual identification in male patients with myocardial infarction. *Psychological Reports*, 10, 831-838.

Barnes, G. & Fishlinsky, M., 1976. Stimulus intensity modulation, smoking and craving for cigarettes. *Addictive Diseases: An International Journal*, 2, 484-499.

Bartmann, U. & Stäcker, K. H., 1974. *Psychologie des Raudhens*. Heidelberg: Omelle und Meyer.

Bartol, C., 1975. Extraversion and neuroticism and nicotine, caffeine and drug intake. *Psychological Reports*, 36, 1007-1010.

Bättig, K. (ed.), 1978. *Behavioural Effects of Nicotine*. Basel: S. Karger.

Bauer, F. W. & Robbins, S. L., 1972. An autopsy study of cancer patients. I. Accuracy of the clinical diagnosis (1955-1965). Boston City Hospital. *Journal of the American Medical Association*, 221, 1471-1474.

Beese, D. H. (ed.), 1968. *Tobacco Consumption in Various Countries*. Research Paper 6, 2nd edition. London: Tobacco Research Council. 1968.

Belcher, J. R., 1971. World-wide differences in the sex ratio of bronchial carcinoma. *British Journal of Diseases of the Chest*, 65, 205-221.

Belcher, J. R., 1975. The changing pattern of bronchial carcinoma. *British Journal of Diseases of the Chest*, 69, 247-258.

Bendien, J. & Groen, J., 1963. A psychological-statistical study of neuroticism and extraversion in patients with myocardial infarction. *Journal of Psychosomatic Research*, 7, 11-14.

Berge, T., 1974. Splenic metastases. Frequencies and patterns. *Acta Patholog. Microbiolog. Scand.*, 82A, 499-506.

Berkson, J., 1958. Smoking and lung cancer: some observations on two recent reports. *Journal of the American Statistical Association*, 53, 28-38.

Berkson, J., 1960. Smoking and cancer of the lung. *Proceedings of the Staff Meeting of the Mayo Clinic*, **35**, 367-385.

Berkson, J., 1962. Smoking and lung cancer: another view. *Lancet*, 807-808.

Berkson, J. & Elveback, L., 1960. Competing exponential risks, with particular reference to the study of smoking and lung cancer. *Journal of the American Statistical Association*, **55**, 415-428.

Berlyne, D. E., 1974. *Studies in the New Experimental Aesthetics*. New York: Wiley.

Best, J. A. & Hakstian, A. R., 1978. A situation-specific model for smoking behaviour. *Addictive Behaviors*, **3**, 79-92.

Betts, T. E. & Elson, L. A., 1974. The α_1-acute phase protein response in rats as a possible indicator of the relative smoking risks of different cigarettes. *Nature*, **248**, 709-710.

Bielianskas, L., Shekelle, R., Garron, D., Maliza, C., Ostfeld, A., Paul, O. & Rayner, W., 1979. Psychological Depression and cancer mortality. *Psychosomatic Medicine*, **41**, 77-78.

Blumenthal, J. A., Thompson, L. W., Williams, R. L. & Kong, Y., 1979. Anxiety-proneness and coronary heart disease. *Journal of Psychosomatic Research*, **23**, 17-21.

Brackenridge, C. J. & Bloch, S., 1972. Smoking in medical students. *Journal of Psychosomatic Research*, **16**, 35-40.

Brownlee, K. A., 1965. A review of 'Smoking and Health'. *Journal of the American Statistical Association*, **60**, 722-739.

Bulmer, M. G., 1970. *The biology of twinning in man*. London: Oxford University Press.

Burch, P., 1974. Does smoking cause lung cancer? *New Scientist*, 21 February, 458-463.

Burch, P. R. J., 1976. *The Biology of Cancer*. Lancaster: Medical and Technical Publishers.

Burch, P. R. J., 1978a. Are 90% of cancers preventable? *F. R. C. S. Journal of Medical Science*, **6**, 353-356.

Burch, P. R. J., 1978b. Coronary heart disease: risk factors and ageing. *Gerontology*, **24**, 123-155.

Burch, P. R. J., 1978c. Smoking and lung cancer: The problem of inferring cause. *Journal of the Royal Statistical Society*, **141**, 437-477.

Burch, P. R. J., 1979. Coronary disease: Risk factors, age, and time. *American Heart Journal*, **97**, 415-419.

Busbee, D., Shaw, C. R. & Cantrell, E., 1972. Enylhydrocarbon hydroxylase induction in human leukocytes. *Science*, **178**, 315-316.

Carney, R. E., 1967. Sex chromatin, body masculinity, achievement motivation and smoking behavior. *Psychological Reports*, **20**, 859-866.

Carter, G., 1974. Effects of cigarette smoking on learning. *Perception and Motor Skills*, **39**, 1344-1346.

Cattell, R. B., 1960. The multiple abstract variance analysis equation and solutions for nature-nurture research on continuous variables. *Psychological Review*, **67**, 353-372.

Cavalli-Sforza, L. L. & Feldman, M. W., 1973. Cultural versus biological inheritance: phenotypic transmission from parents to children (a theory of the effect of parental phenotypes on children's phenotypes). *American Journal of Human Genetics*, **25**, 618-637.

Cederlöf, R., 1966. *The twin method in epidemiological studies on chronic disease*. Stockholm: Karolinska Institute.

Cederlöf, R., Edfors, M., Friberg, L. & Jansson, E., 1967a. Hereditary factors, 'spontaneous cough', and 'smoker's cough'. *Archives of Environmental Health*, **14**, 401-406.

Cederlöf, R., Friberg, L. & Hrubec, Z., 1969. Cardiovascular and respiratory symptoms in relation to tobacco smoking. *Archives of Environmental Health*, **18**, 934-940.

Cederlöf, R., Friberg, L., Hrubec, Z. & Lorick, U., 1975. *The Relationship of Smoking and some Social Covariables to Mortality and Cancer Morbidity*. Stockholm: Karolinska Institute.

Cederlöf, R., Friberg, L. & Jonsson, E., 1967b. Hereditary factors and 'angina factors'. *Archives of Environmental Health*, **14**, 397-400.

Cederlöf, R., Friberg, L., Jonsson, E. & Kaij, L., 1961. Studies on similarity diagnosis in twins with the aid of mailed questionnaires. *Acta Genetica et Statistica Medica* (Basel), **11**, 338-362.

Cederlöf, R., Friberg, L., Jonsson, E. & Kaij, L., 1965. Morbidity among monozygotic twins. *Archives of Environmental Health*, **10**, 346-350.

Cederlöf, R., Friberg, L. & Lundman, T., 1977. The interactions of smoking, environment and heredity and their implications for disease etiology. *Acta Medica Scandinavia*, Supplement 612.

Cherry, N. & Kiernan, K., 1976. Personality scores and smoking behaviour—a longitudinal study. *British Journal of Preventive and Social Medicine*, **30**, 123-131.

Cherry, N. & Kiernan, K. E., 1978. A longitudinal study of smoking and personality. In: R. E. Thornton (ed), *Smoking Behaviour*. London: Churchill Livingstone.

Choi, N. W., Schuman, L. M. & Gullen, W. H., 1970. Epidemiology of primary central nervous system neoplasms. II. Case-control study. *American Journal of Epidemiology*, 91, 467-485.

Clark, T. J. H. & Cochrane, G. M., 1970. Effect of personality on alveolar ventilation in patients with chronic airways obstruction. *British Medical Journal*, 31 January 1970, 273-275.

Clausen, J., 1968. Adolescent antecedents of cigarette smoking: Data from the Oakland growth study. *Social Science and Medicine*, 1, 357-382.

Cohen, B. H. & Thomas, C. B., 1962. Comparison of smokers and nonsmokers. II. The distribution of ABO and Rh(d) blood groups. *Bulletin of the Johns Hopkins Hospital*, 110, 1-4.

Conteno, F. and Chiarelli, B., 1962. Study of the inheritance of some daily life habits. *Heredity*, 17, 347-359.

Coppen, A. & Metcalfe, M., 1963. Cancer and extraversion. *British Medical Journal*, 6 July, 1963, 18-19.

Corey, L. A., Kang, K. W., Christian J. C., Norton, J. A. Jr., Harris, R. E. & Nance, W. E., 1976. Effects of chorion type on variation in cord blood cholesterol of monozygotic twins. *American Journal of Human Genetics*, 28, 433-441.

De Faire, A., 1974. Ischaemic heart disease in death discordant twins. A study of 205 male and female pairs. *Acta Medica Scandinavia*, Suppl. 568, 1-109.

Dijl, H. van, 1979. Myocardial infarction patients and sociability. *Journal of Psychosomatic Research*, 23, 3-6.

Doll, R., 1974. Smoking, lung cancer, and Occam's razor. *New Scientist*, 61, 463-467.

Doll, R., & Hill, A. B., 1964. Mortality in relation to smoking: ten years' observations of British doctors. *British Medical Journal*, i, 1399-1410 and 1460-1467.

Dunbar, F., 1943. *Psychosomatic Diagnosis*. New York: Hoeber.

Eaves, L. J., 1969. The genetic analysis of continuous variation: a comparison of experimental design applicable to human data. *British Journal of Mathematical and Statistical Psychology*, 22, 131-147.

Eaves, L. J., 1970. Aspects of Human Psychogenetics. University of Birmingham, Ph.D. thesis.

Eaves. L. J., 1976a. A model for sibling effects in man. *Heredity*,

36, 205-215.

Eaves, L. J., 1976b. The effect of cultural transmission on continuous variation. *Heredity*, 37, 41-57.

Eaves, L. J. & Eysenck, H. J., 1974. Genetics and the development of social attitudes. *Nature*, 249, 288-289.

Eaves, L. J. & Eysenck, H. J., 1975. The nature of extraversion: a genetical analysis. *Journal of Personality and Social Psychology*, 32, 102-112.

Eaves, L. J. & Eysenck, H. J., 1976. Genetic and environmental components of inconsistency and unrepeatability in twins' responses to a neuroticism questionnaire. *Behavior Genetics*, 6, 145-160.

Eaves, L. J. & Eysenck, H. J., 1977. A genotype-environmental model for psychoticism. *Advances in Behaviour Research and Therapy*, 1, 5-26.

Eaves, L. J. & Gale, J. S., 1974. A method for analysing the genetic basis of covariation. *Behavior Genetics*, 4, 253-267.

Eaves, L. J., Last, Krystyna A., Martin, N. G. & Jinks, J. L., 1977. A progressive approach to non-additivity and genotype-environmental covariance in the analysis of human differences. *British Journal of Mathematical and Statistical Psychology*, 30, 1-42.

Eaves, L. J., Young, P. A., Last, Krystyna A. & Martin, N. G., 1978. Model fitting approaches to the analysis of human behaviour. *Heredity*, 41, 249-320.

Editorial—A surgical pathologist looks at cell type and lung cancer. *The Annals of Thoracic Surgery*. 1971, 12, 208-210.

Edwards, A. W. F., 1972. *Likelihood: An account of the statistical concept and its application to scientific inference*. Cambridge University Press.

Elgerot, A., 1977. *Note on sex differences in cigarette smoking as related to situational factors*. Reports from the Department of Psychology, University of Stockholm, No. 512.

Elson, L. A. & Betts, T. E., 1972. Sugar content of the tobacco and pH of the smoke in relation to lung cancer risks of cigarette smoking. *Journal of the National Cancer Institute*, 48, 1885-1890.

Elson, L. A., Betts, T. E. & Darcy, D. A., 1973 α_1—antitrypsin in cigarette smokers. In: W. Davis & C. Maltoni (eds), *Characterization of Human Tumours*. Amsterdam: Excerpta Medica.

Elson, L. A., Betts, T. E. & Passey, R. D., 1972. The sugar content and the pH of the smoke of cigarette, cigar and pipe tobaccos in relation to lung cancer. *International Journal of Cancer*, **9**, 666-675.

Emery, F. E., Hilgendorf, E. L. & Irving, B. L., 1968. *The psychological dynamics of smoking*. London: Tobacco Research Council, Research Paper 10.

Evans, R. B., Stein, E. & Marmorston, J., 1965. Psychological-hormonal relationships in men with cancer. *Psychological Reports*, **17**, 7-15.

Eysenck, H. J., 1954. *The Psychology of Politics*. London: Routledge & Kegan Paul.

Eysenck, H. J., 1957. *The Dynamics of Anxiety and Hysteria*. London: Routledge & Kegan Paul.

Eysenck, H. J., 1963a. Smoking, personality and psychosomatic disorders. *Journal of Psychosomatic Research*, **7**, 107-130.

Eysenck, H. J. (ed), 1963b. *Experiments with Drugs*. London: Pergamon Press.

Eysenck, H. J., 1965. *Smoking, Health and Personality*. London: Weidenfeld & Nicolson.

Eysenck, H. J., 1967. *The Biological Basis of Personality*. Springfield: C. C. Thomas.

Eysenck, H. J., 1970. *The Structure of Human Personality*. London: Methuen.

Eysenck, H. J. (ed), 1972. *Handbook of Abnormal Psychology*. London: Pitman.

Eysenck, H. J., 1973. Personality and the maintenance of the smoking habit. In: W. L. Dunn (ed), *Smoking Behavior: Motives and Incentives*. London: Wiley & Sons.

Eysenck, H. J., 1976a. *Sex and Personality*. London: Open Books.

Eysenck, H. J. (ed.), 1976b. *The Measurement of Personality*. Lancaster: Medical and Technical Publishers.

Eysenck, H. J., 1976c. Genetic factors in personality development. In: A. R. Kaplan (ed), *Human Behavior Genetics*. Springfield: C. C. Thomas.

Eysenck, H. J., 1977a. *Crime and Personality*. London: Routledge & Kegan Paul.

Eysenck, H. J., 1977b. *You and Neurosis*. London: Maurice Temple Smith.

Eysenck, H. J., 1978. The development of personality and its relation to learning. In: S. Murray-Smith (ed.), *Melbourne Studies in Education*. Melbourne: University Press.

Eysenck, H. J., 1979. Personality factors in a random sample of the population. *Psychological Reports,* 1979, 44, 1023-1027.

Eysenck, H. J. & Eysenck, S. B. G., 1969. *Personality Structure and Measurement.* London: Routledge & Kegan Paul.

Eysenck, H. J. & Eysenck, S. B. G., 1976. *Psychoticism as a Dimension of Personality.* London: Hodder & Stoughton.

Eysenck, H. J., & O'Connor, K., 1979. Smoking, arousal and personality. In: A. Remond & C. Izard (eds), *Electrophysiological effects of nicotine.* Amsterdam: Elsevier/North Holland.

Eysenck, H. J. & Rachman, S., 1964. *Causes and Cures of Neurosis.* London: Routledge & Kegan Paul.

Eysenck, H. J., Tarrant, M. & Woolf, M., 1960. Smoking and Personality. *British Medical Journal,* 1, 1456-1460.

Eysenck, H. J. & Wilson, G., 1978. *The Psychological Basis of Ideology.* Lancaster: Medical and Technical Publishers.

Falconer, D. S., 1964. *Introduction to quantitative genetics.* Edinburgh & London: Oliver & Boyd.

Feinstein, A. R., 1968. Clinical epidemiology. II. The identification rates of disease. *Ann. Internal Medicine,* 69, 1037-1061.

Feinstein, A. R., Gelfman, N. & Yesner, R., 1970. Observer variability in the histopathologic diagnosis of lung cancer. *American Review of Respiratory Disease,* 101, 672-684.

Feldman, M. W. & Cavalli-Sforza, L. L., 1975. Models for cultural inheritance: a general linear model. *Annals of Human Biology,* 2, 215-226.

Fisher, R. A., 1918. The correlation between relatives on the supposition of Mendelian inheritance. *Transactions of the Royal Society of Edinburgh,* 52, 399-433.

Fisher, R. A., 1957. Dangers of cigarette smoking. *British Medical Journal,* 2, 297-298.

Fisher, R. A., 1958a. Cigarettes, cancer and statistics. *Centennial Review,* 2, 151-166.

Fisher, R. A., 1958b. Lung cancer and cigarettes? *Nature,* 182, 108.

Fisher, R. A., 1958c. Cancer and smoking. *Nature,* 182, 596.

Fisher, R. A. 1959. *Smoking. The Cancer Controversy.* Edinburgh: Oliver & Boyd.

Fisher, R. A., 1960. *The Design of Experiments* (7th ed.). Edinburgh & London: Oliver & Boyd.

Floderus, B., 1974. Psycho-social factors in relation to coronary heart disease and associated risk factors. *Nordisk Hygienisk Tidskrift,* Supplement 6.

Frankenhaeuser, M., Myrsten, A. C., Post, B. & Johansson, G., 1971. Behavioural and physiological effects of cigarette smoking in a monotonous situation. *Psychopharmacologia*, **22**, 1-7.

Friberg, L., Kay, L., Dencker, S. J. & Jonsson, E., 1959. Smoking habits of monozygotic and dizygotic twins. *British Medical Journal*, **1**, 1090-1092.

Friedman, M., 1969. *Pathogenesis of Coronary Artery Disease*. New York: McGraw-Hill, 75-135.

Friedman, M. & Rosenman, R. H., 1959. Association of specific overt behaviour pattern with blood and cardiovascular findings. *Journal of the American Medical Association*, **269**, 1289-1296.

Friedman, G. D., Siegelaub, A. B., Dales, L. G. & Seltzer, C. C. Characteristics predictive of coronary heart disease in ex-smokers before they stopped smoking: comparison with persistent smokers and non-smokers. *Journal of Chronic Diseases*. In press.

Frith, C., 1967. The effects of nicotine on tapping. III. *Life Sciences*, **6**, 1541-1548.

Frith, C., 1968. The effects of nicotine on the consolidation of pursuit rotor learning. *Life Sciences*, **7**, 77-84.

Frith, C., 1971. Smoking behaviour and its relation to the smoker's immediate experience. *British Journal of Social and Clinical Psychology*, **10**, 73-78.

Fulker, D. W., 1975. Review of 'The Science and Politics of IQ'. *American Journal of Psychology*, **88**, 505-519.

Galton, F., 1876. The history of twins as a criterion of the relative powers of nature and nurture. *Journal of the Royal Anthropology Institution*, **5**.

German, J. L., 1974. *Chromosomes and Cancer*. New York: Wiley.

Glad, W., Adesso, V. J., 1976. The relative importance of socially induced tension and behavioral contagion for smoking behavior. *Journal of Abnormal Psychology*, **85**, 119-121.

Glass, D. C., 1977. *Behavior Patterns, Stress, and Coronary Disease*. Hillsdale, N. J.: Erlbaum.

Goldstein, L., Beck, R. A., Mundschenk, D. L., 1967. Effects of nicotine upon cortical activity of the rabbit brain: Quantitative analysis. *Annals of the New York Academy of Sciences*, **142**, 130-180.

Greer, S., 1979. Psychological enquiry: a contribution to cancer research. *Psychological Medicine*, **9**, 81-89.

Greer, S. & Morris, T., 1975. Psychological attributes of women who develop breast cancer: A controlled study. *Journal of Psychoso-*

matic Research, **19**, 147-153.

Gupta, A. K., Sethi, B. B. & Gupta, S. C., 1976. EPI and 16PF observations in smokers. *Indian Journal of Psychiatry*, **18**, 252-259.

Hagnell, O., 1962. *Svenska Lak-Tidn*, **58**, 492-498.

Hammond, E. C., 1966. *Smoking in relation to death rates of one million men and women*. Nat. Cancer Institute Monograph, **19**, 127-204.

Hamtoft, H. & Lindhardt, M., 1956. Tobacco consumption in Denmark. II. *Danish Medical Bulletin*, **3**, 150.

Hardy, D. R., 1968. Smoking and health: The importance of objectivity. In: E. F. Borgattu & R. R. Evans (eds), *Smoking, Health, and Behavior*. Chicago: Aldine.

Harvald, B. & Hauge, M., 1973. Hereditary factors elucidated by twin studies. In: J. V. Neel, M. W. Shaw & W. J. Schull (eds), *Genetics and the Epidemiology of Chronic Disease*. US Dept of Health, Education, and Welfare.

Hayley, D. C., 1952. *Estimation of the dosage mortality relationship when the dose is subject to error*. Technical Report No. 52, Stanford, Calif.: Contract No. ONR-25140: Univ. Stanford, Applied Mathematics and Statistics Laboratory.

Heasman, M. A. & Kipworth, L., 1966. *Accuracy of Certification of Cause of Death*. General Register Office, Studies on Medical and Population Subjects No. 20. London: HMSO.

Heimstra, N. W., 1973. The effects of smoking on mood change. In: W. L. Dunn (ed.), *Smoking Behavior*. Washington: Winston & Sons.

Heimstra, N. W., Cancroft, N. R. & De Kock, A. R., 1967. Effects of smoking upon sustained performance in simulated driving tasks. *Annals New York Academy of Sciences*, **142**, 295-307.

Higgins, M. W., Kjelsberg, M., Metzner, H., 1967. Characteristics of smokers and non-smokers in Tecumseh, Michigan. *American Journal of Epidemiology*, **86**, 45-59.

Higgins, I. T., Oldham, P. D., Drummond, R. J. & Bevan, B., 1963. Tobacco smoking and blood group. *British Medical Journal*, **2**, 1167-1169.

Hirayama, T., 1967. *Smoking in relation to the death rates of 265118 men and women in Japan*. National Cancer Center, Tokyo Research Institute, Epidemiology Division.

Hirayama, T., 1972. Huge Japanese study adds to smoking-death link. Reported in *Journal of the American Medical Association*,

222, 654-655.

Ikard, F. F., Green, P. E., Horn, D., 1969. A scale to differentiate between types of smoking as related to the management of affect. *International Journal of the Addictions*, 4, 649-659.

Jackson, L. G., 1978. Chromosomes and cancer: Current aspects. *Seminars in Oncology*, 5, 3-16.

Jacobs, M. A. & Spilken, A. Z., 1971. Personality patterns associated with heavy cigarette smoking in male college students. *Journal of Consulting and Clinical Psychology*, 37, 428-432.

Jamison, R. N., 1978. Personality, antisocial behaviour and risk perception in adolescents. London: University of London, unpublished Ph.D. thesis.

Jenkins, C. D., 1975. The coronary-prone personality. In: W. D. Gentry & R. B. Williams (eds), *Psychological Aspects of Myocardial Infarction and Coronary Care*. St Louis: C. V. Mosley Company, 5-23.

Jenkins, C. D., 1976. Recent evidence supporting psychological and social risk factors for coronary disease. *New England Journal of Medicine*, **294**, 987-994.

Jenkins, C. D., Rosenman, R. H., Friedman, M., 1967. Development of an objective psychological test for the determination of the coronary-prone behavior pattern in employed men. *Journal of Chronic Diseases*, **20**, 371-379.

Jenkins, C. D., Rosenman, R. H. & Zyzanski, S., 1974. Prediction of clinical coronary heart disease by test for coronary-prone behavior patterns. *New England Journal of Medicine*, **290**, 1271-1275.

Jenkins, C. D., Zyzanski, S. & Rosenman, R. H., 1978. Coronary-prone behavior: One pattern or several? *Psychosomatic Medicine*, **40**, 25-43.

Jinks, J. L. & Fulker, D. W., 1970. Comparison of the biometrical genetical, MAVA and classical approaches to the analysis of human behavior. *Psychological Bulletin*, **73**, 311-349.

Kagan, A., Gordon, T., Rhoads, G. & Schiffman, J. C., 1975. Some factors related to coronary heart disease incidence in Honolulu Japanese men: The Honolulu heart study. *International Journal of Epidemiology*, 4, 271-279.

Kahn, H. A., 1966. *The Dorn Study of smoking and mortality among U.S. veterans: report on eight and one-half years of observation*. National Cancer Institute Monograph, **19**, 1-125.

Kamin, L. *The Science and Politics of IQ.*, 1974. Potomac Md.: Lawrence Erlbaum Associates.

Kanekar, S. & Dolke, A. M., 1970. *Smoking, extraversion and neuroticism*, Psychological Reports, **26**, 384.

Kasriel, J. & Eaves, L. J., 1976. The zygosity of twins: further evidence on the agreement between diagnosis by blood groups and written questionnaires. *Journal of Biosocial Science*, **8**, 263-266.

Katz, L., 1969. Hearings on Cigarette Labeling and Advertising, part 2. US Committee on Interstate and Foreign Commerce, House of Representatives.

Katz, J., Kunofsky, S., Patton, R. E. & Altavan, N. C., 1975. Quoted by Levi & Waxman.

Kellermann, G., Luyten-Kellermann, M. & Shaw, C. R., 1973a. Genetic variation of amyl hydrocarbon hydroxylase in human lymphocytes. *American Journal of Human Genetics*, **25**, 327-331.

Kellermann, G., Cantrell, E. & Shaw, C. R., 1973b. Variations in extent of aryl hydrocarbon hydroxylase induction in cultured human lymphocytes. *Cancer Research*, **33**, 1654-1656.

Kellermann, G., Shaw, C. R. & Kellermann, M. L., 1973c. Aryl hydrocarbon hydroxylase inductibility and bronchogenic carcinoma. *The New England Journal of Medicine*, **289**, 934-937.

Kendall, M. G. & Stuart, A., 1961. *The advanced theory of statistics.* I. London: Charles Griffin & Co.

Kennedy, A., 1973. Relationship between cigarette smoking and histological type of lung cancer in women. *Thorax*, **28**, 204-208.

Kern, W. H., Jones, J. C. & Chapman, V. D., 1968. Pathology of bronchogenic carcinoma in long-term survivors. *Cancer*, **21**, 772-780.

Kessler, I. I., 1972. Epidemiologic studies of Parkinson's disease. III: A community based survey. *American Journal of Epidemiology*, **96**, 242-254.

Keys, A., 1962. Diet and coronary heart disease throughout the world. *Cardiological Practice*, **13**, 225-244.

Kissen, D. M., 1963a. Personality characteristics in males conducive to lung cancer. *British Journal of Medical Psychology*, **36**, 27-36.

Kissen, D. M., 1963b. Aspects of personality of men with lung cancer. *Acta Psychotherapeutica*, **11**, 200-210.

Kissen, D. M., 1964a. Relationship between lung cancer, cigarette smoking, inhalation and personality. *British Journal of Medical Psychology*, **37**, 203-216.

Kissen, D. M., 1964b. Lung cancer, inhalation and personality. In: *Aspects of Neoplastic Disease*. London: Pitman.

Kissen, D. M., 1967. Psychological factors, personality and lung cancer in men aged 55-64. *British Journal of Medical Psychology*, 40, 29-34.

Kissen, D. M., 1968. Some methodological problems in clinical psychosomatic research with special reference to chest disease. *Psychosomatic Medicine*, 30, 324-335.

Kissen, D. M. & Eysenck, H. J., 1962. Personality in male lung cancer patients. *Journal of Psychosomatic Research*, 6, 123-137.

Kissen, D. M. & Rowe, L G. 1969. Steroid excretion patterns and personality in lung cancer. *Annals of the New York Academy of Science*, 164, 476-482.

Knott, V. J., 1976. Effects of alcohol, smoking and smoking deprivation on the EEG. York: unpublished Ph.D. thesis, University of York.

Knott, V. J. Personality, arousal and individual differences in cigarette smoking. *Psychological Reports*. In press.

Knott, V. J. & Venables, P. H., 1977. EEG alpha correlates of non-smokers, smokers, smoking, and smoking deprivation. *Psychophysiology*, 14, 150-156.

Knudson, A. G., 1977. Genetics and etiology of human cancer. In: H. Harris & K. Hirschhorn (eds.), *Advances in Human Genetics*. London: Plenum Press.

Knudson, A. G., 1978. Retinoblastoma: A prototype hereditary neoplasm. *Seminars in Oncology*, 5, 57-60.

Knudson, A. G., Strong, I. C. & Anderson, D. E., 1973. Heredity and cancer in man. *Progress in Medical Genetics*, 9, 113-156.

Kozlowski, L. T., 1976. Effects of caffeine consumption on nicotine consumption. *Psychopharmacology*, 47, 165-168.

Krasnoff, A., 1959. Psychological variables in human cancer: a cross-validation study. *Psychosomatic Medicine*, 21, 291-296.

Kucek, P., 1975. Effect of smoking on performance underload. *Studia Psychologica*, 17, 204-212.

Kumar, R., Cooke, E. C., Lader, M. H. & Russell, M. A. H., 1977. Is nicotine important in tobacco smoking? *Clinical Pharmacology and Therapeutics*, 21, 520-529.

Lamb, D. & Reid, L., 1969. Goblet cell increase in rat bronchial epithelium after exposure to cigarette and cigar tobacco smoke. *British Medical Journal*, 1, 33-35.

Lange, K. & Elston, R. C., 1975. Extensions to pedigree analysis. I. Likelihood calculations for simple and complex pedigrees. *Human Heredity*, 25, 95-105.

Lange, K., Westlake, J. & Spence, M. A., 1976a. Extensions to pedigree analysis. II. Recurrence risk calculation under the polygenic threshold model. *Human Heredity*, 26, 337-348.

Lange, K., Westlake, J. & Spence, M. A., 1976b. Extensions to pedigree analysis. III. Variance components by the scoring method. *Annals of Human Genetics*, London, 39, 485-491.

Langford, A., 1976. Smoking, drinking and personality: a study of twins and foster families. University of Birmingham: M.Sc. Thesis.

Lasogga, F., 1978. Persönlichkeitsmerkmale und Rauchverhalten Jugendlicher. *Zeitschrift für Klinische Psychologie*, 7, 162-171.

Lebovitz, B. & Ostfeld, A., 1971. Smoking and personality: A methodological analysis. *Journal of Chronic Diseases*, 23, 813-821.

Levi, R. N. & Waxman, S., 1975. Schizophrenia epilepsy, cancer, methionine, and folate metabolism. Pathogenesis of schizophrenia. *The Lancet*, 5 July 1975, 11-13.

Liljefors, I., 1970. Coronary heart disease in male twins: hereditary and environmental factors in unicordant and discordant pairs. *Acta Medica Scandinavia*, Suppl. 511.

Liljefors, I., 1977. Coronary heart disease in male twins: Seven-year follow-up of discordant pairs. *Acta Genetica Medica Gemelli.*

Loehlin, J. C. & Nichols, R. C., 1976. *Heredity, Environment, and Personality.* Austin: University of Texas Press.

Lombard, H. L. & Snegireff, L. S., 1959. An epidemiological study of lung cancer. *Cancer*, 12, 406-413.

Lord, F. M. & Novick, M. R., 1968. *Statistical Theories of Mental Test Scores.* Reading, Mass.: Addison-Wesley.

Lundman, T., 1966. *Smoking in relation to coronary heart disease and lung function in twins.* Stockholm: Karolinska Institute.

Lynch, H. T. (ed.), 1976. *Cancer Genetics.* Springfield: C. C. Thomas.

Lyon, R., Tong, J., Leigh, G. & Clare, J., 1975. The influence of alcohol and tobacco on the components of choice reaction time. *Journal for the Study of Alcohol*, 36, 581-596.

McArthur, C. et al., 1958. The psychology of smoking. *Journal of Abnormal and Social Psychology*, 56, 267-275.

McCarthy, E. G. & Widmer, G. W., 1974. Effects of screening by consultants on recommended elective surgical procedures. *The*

New England Journal of Medicine, **291**, 1331-1335.

McKennell, A. C., 1970. Smoking motivation factors. *British Journal of Social and Clinical Psychology,* **9**, 8-22.

McMichael, J., 1979. Fats and atheroma: an inquest. *British Medical Journal*, 173-175.

Mausner, B. & Platt, E. S., 1971. *Smoking: A behavioral analysis*. Toronto: Pergamon Press.

Mainland, D. & Herrera, L., 1956. The risks of biased selection in forward going surveys with non-professional interviewers. *Journal of Chronic Disease*, **4**, 240-244.

Marmot, M. G., Syme, S. L., Kagan, A., Kato, H., Cohen, J. B. & Belsky, J., 1975. Prevalence of coronary and hypertensive heart disease and associate risk factors. *American Journal of Epidemiology*, **102**, 514-525.

Martin, N. G., Eaves, L. J., Kearsey, M. J. & Davies, P., 1978. The power of the classical twin study. *Heredity*, **40**, 97-116.

Martin, N. G. & Martin, P. G., 1975. The inheritance of scholastic abilities in a sample of twins: I. Ascertainment of the sample and diagnosis of zygosity. *Annals of Human Genetics*, **39**, 213-218.

Maruyama, T. & Yasuda, N., 1970. Use of graph theory in computation of inbreeding and kinship correlations. *Biometrics*, **26**, 209-220.

Matarazzo, J. D. & Saslow, G., 1960. Psychological and related characteristics of smokers and nonsmokers. *Psychological Bulletin,* **57**, 493-513.

Mather, K., 1943. Variation and selection of polygenic characters. *Journal of Genetics*, **41**, 159-193.

Mather, K., 1949. *Biometrical Genetics*. 1st edition. London: Methuen.

Mather, K., 1966. Variability and selection. *Proceedings of the Royal Society of London (Series B)*, **164**, 328-340.

Mather, K., 1967. *The Elements of Biometry*. London: Chapman & Hall.

Mather, K., 1974. Non-alletic interaction in continuous variation of randomly breeding populations. *Heredity*, **32**, 414-419.

Mather, K. & Jinks, J. L., 1971. *Biometrical Genetics: The Study of Continuous Variation*. London: Chapman & Hall.

Mathews, A. G., 1975. Ischaemic heart disease: possible genetic markers. *The Lancet*, **2**, 681-682.

Miles, H. H., Waldvogel, S., Barrahee, E. C. & Cobb, S., 1954.

Psychosomatic study of 46 young men with coronary artery disease. *Psychosomatic Medicine*, 16, 455-462.

Mittman, C. (ed.), 1972. *Pulmonary Emphysema and Proteolysis*. New York: Academic Press.

Moran, P. A. P. and Smith, C. A. B., 1966. *Commentary on R. Fisher's paper on the Correlation between Relatives on the Supposition of Mendelian Inheritance*. Cambridge: Cambridge University Press.

Morrison, D. F., 1967. *Multivariate Statistical Methods*. New York: McGraw-Hill.

Morton, N. E., 1974. Analysis of family resemblance: I. Introduction. *American Journal of Human Genetics*, 26, 318-330.

Mulvihill, J. (ed.), 1977. *The Genetics of Human Cancer*. New York: Raven.

Myrsten, A. & Anderson, K., 1973. *Interaction between effects of alcohol intake and cigarette smoking*. Stockholm: Reports from the Psychological Laboratory, No. 402.

Myrsten, A., Anderson, K., Frankenhaeuser, M. & Elgerot, A., 1975. Immediate effects of cigarette smoking as related to different smoking habits. *Perceptual and Motor Skills*, 40, 515-523.

Nefzger, M. D., Quadfasel, F. A. & Karl, V. C., 1968. A retrospective study of smoking in Parkinson's disease. *American Journal of Epidemiology*, 88, 149-158.

Nelder, J. A., 1975. *General Linear Interactive Modelling*. Oxford: Numerical Algorithms Group.

Nelder, J. A. & Wedderburn, R. W. M., 1972. Generalised linear models. *Journal of the Royal Statistical Society (Series A)*, 135, 370-384.

Nesbitt, P. D., 1972. Chronic smoking and emotionality. *Journal of Applied Social Psychology*, 2, 187-196.

Nesbitt, P. D., 1975. Smoking, physiological arousal, and emotional response. *Journal of Personality and Social Psychology*, 25, 137-144.

Newman, H. H., Freeman, F. N. & Holzinger, K. J., 1937. *Twins: a study of heredity and environment*. Chicago: Chicago University Press.

Nichaman, M. Z., Hamilton, H. B., Kagan, A., Grier, T., Sacks, S. T. & Syme, S. L., 1975. Distribution of biochemical risk factors. *American Journal of Epidemiology*, 102, 491-501.

Nichols, R. C. & Bilbro, W. C., Jr., 1966. The diagnosis of twin zygosity. *Acta Genetica Basel,* **16**, 265-275.

Nilsson, A. & Tibbling, L., 1972. Personality correlates of smokers with differing consumption of cigarettes. Lund University: *Psychological Research Bulletin,* **XII**: 1.

Numerical Algorithms Group, 1977. *NAG Fortran Library Manual.* Oxford: NAG.

O'Connor, K. The contingent negative variation and individual differences in smoking behaviour. *Personality and Individual Differences.* In press.

Ostfeld, A. M., Lebovitz, B. Z., Shekelle, R. B. & Paul, O., 1964. A prospective study of the relationship between personality and coronary heart disease. *Journal of Chronic Disease,* **17**, 265-272.

Partanen, J., Bruun, K. & Markkanen, T., 1966. *Inheritance of drinking behavior.* Helsinki: The Finnish Foundation for Alcohol Studies, 14.

Passey, R. D., 1962. Some problems of lung cancer. *The Lancet,* **ii**, 107-112.

Passey, R. D., Blackmore, M., Warbrick-Smith, D. & Jones, R., 1971. Smoking risks of different tobaccos. *British Medical Journal,* **4**, 198-201.

Pearl, R., 1928. *The Rate of Living.* New York: A. A. Knopf.

Pearson, K., 1900. On the correlation of characters not quantitatively measurable. *Philosophical Transactions of the Royal Society (Series A),* **195**, 1-47.

Petrie, A., 1967. *Individuality in Pain and Suffering.* Chicago: Chicago University Press.

Pettingale, K. W., Greer, S. & Tee, D. H. H., 1977. Serum IGA and emotional expression in breast cancer patients: *Journal of Psychosomatic Research,* **21**, 395-399.

Phelps, J. W. & Gerdes, E. B., 1978. Cigarette smoking and performance failure: Psychophysiological and subjective effects. *Psychophysiology,* **16**, 178-179.

Pike, M. C. & Doll, R., 1965. Age at onset of lung cancer: significance in relation to effect of smoking. *The Lancet,* 27 March 1965, 665-668.

Pikkarainen, J., Tukkunen, J. & Kulonen, E., 1966. Serum cholesterol in Finnish twins. *American Journal of Human Genetics,* **18**, 115-126.

Powell, G. E., 1977. Psychoticism and social deviancy in children. *Advances in Behaviour Research & Therapy,* **1**, 27-56.

Powell, G. E., Stewart, R. A. & Grylls, D. G., 1979. The personality of young smokers. *British Journal of Addiction,* **74**, 311-315.

Prieto, F., 1976. Lung disease and the environment. *New Scientist.* 4 March 1976, 504-506.

Raaschou-Nielsen, E., 1960. Smoking habits in twins. *Danish Medical Bulletin,* 7, 82-88.

Rae, G., 1975. Extraversion, neuroticism and cigarette smoking. *British Journal of Social and Clinical Psychology,* **14**, 429-430.

Rae, G. & McCall, J., 1973. Some international comparisons of cancer mortality rates and personality: a brief note. *The Journal of Psychology,* **85**, 87-88.

Rake, R. H., Herwig, L. & Rosenman, R. H., 1978. Heritability of Type A behavior. *Psychosomatic Medicine,* **40**, 478-486.

Rao, D. C., Morton, N. E. and Yee, S., 1976. Resolution of cultural and biological inheritance by path analysis. *American Journal of Human Genetics,* **28**, 228-242.

Rao, L. G. S., 1970. Discriminant function based on steroid abnormalities in patients with lung cancer. *The Lancet,* 29 August 1970, 441-445.

Rao, L. G. S., 1971. Effect of resection of lung tumours on the steroid abnormalities in patients with lung cancer. *British Medical Journal,* 4, 588-590.

Rao, L. G. S., 1972. Lung cancer as an endocrine disease. *Nature,* **135**, 220-221.

Rassidakis, N. C., Kelepouris. M., & Fox, S., 1971. Malignant neoplasms as a cause of deaths among psychiatric patients. I. *International Mental Health Research Newsletter,* **13**, 3-6.

Rassidakis, N. C., Kelepouris, M., Goulis, K. & Karaiossefidis, K., 1972. Malignant neoplasms as a cause of death among psychiatric patients. II. *International Mental Health Research Newsletter,* **14**, 3-6.

Rassidakis, N. C., Erotokristow, A., Validou, M. & Collaron, T., 1973a. Anxiety, schizophrenia and carcinogenesis. *International Mental Health Research Newsletter,* **15**, 3-6.

Rassidakis, N. C. et al., 1973b. Schizophrenia, psychosomatic illnesses and malignancy. *International Mental Health Research Newsletter,* **15**, 3-6.

Rassidakis, N. C. et al., 1973c. Malignant neoplasms as a cause of death among psychiatric patients. III. *International Mental Health Research Newsletter,* **15**, 3-6.

Rassidakis, N. C. Grotoerton, A. & Validou, M., 1973a. An essay on the study of the etiology and pathogenesis of schizophrenia, the psychosomatic illnesses, diabetes melitus and cancer. *International Mental Health Research Newsletter*, 15, 3-8.

Record, R. G., McKeown, T. & Edwards, J. H., 1970. An investigation of the difference in measured intelligence between twin and single births. *Annals of Human Genetics*, 34, 11-20.

Reid, D. D., 1975. International studies in epidemiology. *American Journal of Epidemiology*, 102, 469-476.

Reid, D. D. & Rose, G. A., 1964. Assessing the comparability of mortality statistics. *British Medical Journal*, 2, 1437-1439.

Report, International Symposium., 1971. Twin Registries in the Study of Chronic Disease. *Acta Medica Scandinavia*, Supplementum 523.

Rhoads, G., Balckwelder, W. C., Stemmermann, G., Hayashi, T. & Kagan, A., 1978. Coronary risk factors and autopsy findings in Japanese-American men. *Laboratory Investigation*, 38, 304-311.

Rigdon, R. H., Kirchoff, H., 1953. Smoking and cancer of the lung — let's review the facts. *Texas Reports on Biology & Medicine*, 11, 715-727.

Rimé, B. & Bonami, M., 1979. Overt and covert personality traits associated with coronary heart disease. *British Journal of Medical Psychology*, 52, 77-84.

Roos, S. S., 1977. A psychophysiological re-evaluation of Eysenck's theory concerning cigarette smoking. Part 1. The Central Nervous System. Part 2. The Autonomic Nervous System. *South African Medical Journal*, 52, 237-240, 281-283.

Rose, G., 1977. Ischaemic heart disease. *Journal of Medical Genetics*, 114, 330-331.

Rosenblatt, M. B., 1969. The increase in lung cancer: epidemic or artifact? *Med. Counterpoint*, 1, 29-39.

Rosenblatt, M., 1974. Lung cancer and smoking — the evidence re-assessed. *New Scientist*, 9 May 1974, 332.

Rosenblatt, M. B., Teng, P. K., Kerpe, S. & Beck, I., 1971a. Causes of death in 1000 consecutive autopsies. *N. Y. State Journal of Medicine*, 71, 2189-2193.

Rosenblatt, M. B., Teng, P. K., Kerpe, S. & Beck I., 1971b. Prevalence of lung cancer: disparity between clinical and autopsy certification. *Medical Counterpoint*, 3, 53-59.

Rosenman, R. H., 1967. Emotional patterns in the development of cardiovascular disease. *Journal of the American College Health Association*, 15, 211-219.

Rosenman, R. H., Brand, R. J. & Jenkins, C. D., 1975. Coronary heart disease in the Western Collaborative Group Study: Final follow-up experience of 8½ years. *Journal of the American Medical Association*, 233, 872-877.

Rosenman, R. H., & Chesney, M. A., 1980. The relationship of type of behaviour to coronary heart disease. *Activitas Nervosa Superior,* 22, 1-45.

Rosenman, R. H., Friedman, M. & Strauss, R., 1964. A predictive study of coronary heart disease: The Western Collaborative Group Study. *Journal of the American Medical Association*, 189, 15-22.

Rothman, K. J. & Monson, R. R., 1973. Epidemiology of trigeminal neuralgia. *Journal of Chronic Disease*, 26, 3-12.

Royal College of Physicians, 1962. *Smoking and Health*. London: Pitman.

Royal College of Physicians, 1971. *Smoking and Health Now*. London: Pitman.

Royal College of Physicians, 1977. *Smoking or Health*. London: Pitman.

Royce, J. R., 1973. The conceptual framework for a multi-factor theory of individuality. In: J. R. Royce (ed.), *Multivariate Analysis and Psychological Theory*. London: Academic Press, pp. 305-407.

Russell, M. A., Peto, J. & Patel, V. A., 1974. The classification of smoking by factorial structure of motives. *Journal of the Royal Statistical Society (Series A)*, 137, 313-346.

Rustin, R. M., Kittel, F., Dramaix, M., Kornitzer, M. & Backer, G., 1978. Smoking habits and psycho-social-biological factors. *Journal of Psychosomatic Research*, 22, 89-99.

Saunders, N. A., Heilpern, S. & Rebuck, A. S., 1972. Relation between personality and ventilatory response to carbon dioxide in normal subjects: a role in asthma? *British Medical Journal,* 18 March 1972, 719-721.

Schachter, S., 1973. Nesbitt's Paradox. In: W. L. Dunn (ed.), *Smoking Behavior: Motives and Incentives*. London: Wiley & Sons.

Schaeppi, V., 1967. Effects of nicotine administration to the cat's lower brain stem upon electro-encephalographic and autonomic system. *Annals of the New York Academy of Science*, 142, 40-49.

Schubert, D. S. P., 1965. Arousal seeking as a central factor in tobacco smoking among college students. *The International Journal of Social Psychiatry*, 11, 221-225.

Schwartz, D., Flamanti, R., Lellouch, J. & Denoix, P. F., 1961. Results of a French survey on the role of tobacco, particularly inhalation, in different cancer sites. *Journal of the National Cancer Institute*, 26, 1085-1108.

Sehrt, E., 1904. *Beiträge zur Kenntnis des primären Lungencarcinoma*. Leipzig: George.

Seltzer, C. C., 1963. Morphologic constitution and smoking. *The Journal of the American Medical Association*, 183, 639-645.

Seltzer, C. C., 1967. Constitution and heredity in relation to tobacco smoking. *Annals of the New York Academy of Sciences*, 142, 322-330.

Seltzer, C. C., 1968. An evaluation of the effect of smoking on coronary heart disease. *The Journal of the American Medical Association*, 203, 193-200.

Seltzer, C. C., 1970. The effect of cigarette smoking on coronary heart disease. *Archives of Environmental Health*, 20, 418-423.

Seltzer, C. C., 1972a. Differences between cigar and pipe smokers in healthy white veterans. *Archives of Environment and Health*, 25, 187-191.

Seltzer, C. C., 1972b. Critical appraisal of the Royal College of Physicians report on smoking and health. *The Lancet*, 243-248.

Seltzer, C. C., 1975. Smoking and coronary heart disease in the elderly. *The American Journal of the Medical Sciences*, 269 309-315.

Seltzer, C. C., Siegelaub, A. B., Friedman, G. D. & Collen, M. F., 1974. Differences in pulmonary function related to smoking habits and race. *American Review of Respiratory Disease*, 110, 598-608.

Seth, M. & Saksena, N. K., 1977. Personality of patients suffering from cancer, cardiovascular disorders, tuberculosis and minor ailments. *Indian Journal of Clinical Psychology*, 4, 135-140.

Shields, J., 1962. *Monozygotic Twins*. London: Oxford University Press.

Siltanen, P., Lauroma, M., Nikko, O., Punsar, S., Pyörälä, K., Tuominen, H. & Vanhala, K., 1975. Psychological characteristics related to coronary heart disease. *Journal of Psychosomatic Research*, 19, 183-195.

Slack, J. & Evans, K. A., 1966. The increased risk of death from ischaemic heart disease in first degree relatives of 121 men and 96 women with ischaemic heart disease. *Journal of Medical Genetics*, 3, 239-241.

Smith, G. M., 1967. Personality correlates of cigarette smoking in students of college age. *Annals of the New York Academy of Sciences*, 142, 308-321.

Smithers, D. W., 1953. Facts and fancies about cancer of the lung. *British Medical Journal*, i, 1235-1239.

Snedecor, G. W. & Cochran, W. C., 1967. *Statistical methods*. 6th ed. Ames, Iowa: Iowa State Press.

Stavraky, K. M., 1968. Psychological factors in the outcome of human cancer. *Journal of Psychosomatic Research*, 12, 251-260.

Stebbings, J. H., 1971. Chronic respiratory disease among non-smokers in Hagerstown, Maryland. II. Problems in the estimation of pulmonary function values in epidemiological surveys. *Environmental Research*, 4, 163-192.

Stell, P. M., 1972. Smoking and laryngeal cancer. *The Lancet*, ii, 617-619.

Stemmermann, G. A., Steer, A., Rhoads, G., Lee, K., Hayashi, T., Nakashima, T. & Keehn, R., 1976. A comparative pathology study of myocardial lesions and atherosclerosis in Japanese men living in Hiroshima, Japan and Honolulu, Hawaii. *Laboratory Investigations*, 34, 592-600.

Sterling, T. D., 1973. The statistician *vis-à-vis* issues of public health. *The American Statistician*, 27, 212-217.

Steward, L. & Livson, N., 1966. Smoking and rebelliousness. *Journal of Consulting Psychology*, 30, 225-229.

Stocks, P. 1970. Cancer mortality in relation to national consumption of cigarettes, solid fuel, tea and coffee. *British Journal of Cancer*, 24, 215-225.

Surgeon General, 1971, 1972, 1973. *Health Consequences of Smoking*. US Department of Health, Education and Welfare.

Surgeon General's Advisory Committee, 1964. *Smoking and Health*. US Department of Health, Education and Welfare.

Syme, S. L., Marmot, M. G., Kagan, A., Kato, H. & Rhoads, G., 1975. Epidemiologic studies of coronary heart disease and stroke in Japanese men living in Japan, Hawaii and California: Introduction. *American Journal of Epidemiology*, 102, 477-480.

Tallis, G. M., 1962. The maximum likelihood estimation of correlation from contingency tables. *Biometrics*, 18, 342-353.

Tarrière, C. & Hartemann, F., 1964. Investigation into the effects of tobacco smoke on a visual vigilance task. *Ergonomics, Proceedings of 2nd I.E.A. Congress, Dortmund*, 525-530.

Theorell, T., Faire, U. de, Schalling, D., Adamson, U. & Askevold, F., 1979. Personality traits and psychophysiological reactions to a stressful interview in twins with varying degrees of coronary heart disease. *Journal of Psychosomatic Research*, **23**, 89-99.

Thomas, C. B., 1968. On cigarette smoking, coronary heart disease, and the genetic hypothesis. *The Johns Hopkins Medical Journal*, **122**, 69-76.

Thomas, C. B., 1976. Precursors of premature disease and death. *Annals of Internal Medicine*, **85**, 653-658.

Thomas, C. B., 1978. Personality differences between smokers and nonsmokers. *Maryland State Medical Journal*, **114**, 84-87.

Thomas, C. B. & Cohen, B. H., 1955. The familial occurrence of hypertension and coronary disease, with observations concerning obesity and diabetes. *Annals of Internal Medicine*, **42**, 90-95.

Thomas, C. B. & Cohen, B. H., 1960. Comparison of smokers and nonsmokers. I. A preliminary report on the ability to taste phenylthiourea (P.T.C.). *Bulletin of the Johns Hopkins Hospital*, **106**, 205-208.

Thomas, C. B. & Duszynski, K. R., 1974. Closeness to parents and the family constellation in a prospective study of five disease states. *The Johns Hopkins Medical Journal*, **134**, 251-270.

Thomas, C. B. & Greenstreet, R. L., 1973. Psychobiological characteristics in youth as predictors of five disease states. *The Johns Hopkins Medical Journal*, **132**, 16-43.

Thomas, C. B., Ross, D. C. & Higginbottom, C., 1962. Precursors of hypertension and coronary disease among healthy medical students: Discrimination function analysis. II. Using parental history as the criterion. *Bulletin of the Johns Hopkins Hospital*, **115**, 245-251.

Thornton, R. E. (ed.), 1978. *Smoking Behaviour*. London: Livingstone.

Thouless, R. H. 1935. The tendency to certainty in religious belief. *British Journal of Psychology,* **26**, 16-31.

Thurlbeck, W. M., Anderson, A. E., Jarvis, M., Mitchell, R. S., Pratt, P., Restrepo, G., Ryan, S. F. & Vincent, T., 1968. A cooperative study of certain measurements of emphysema. *Thorax*, **23**, 217-228.

Todd, G. F., 1966. *Reliability of statements about smoking habits*. London: Tobacco Research Council, Research Paper 2A.

Todd, G. F. & Mason, J. I., 1959. Concordance of smoking habits in monozygotic and dizygotic twins. *Heredity*, 13, 417-444.

Tokuhata, G. K., 1964. Familial factors in human lung cancer and smoking. *American Journal of Public Health*, 54, 24-32.

Tokuhata, G. K., 1973. Cancer of the lung; host and environmental interaction. In: H. T. Lynch (ed.), *Cancer Genetics*.

Tokuhata, G. K. & Lilienfeld, A. M., 1963a. *Familial aggregation of lung cancer among hospital patients*. Public Health Reports, Washington, 78, 277-283.

Tokuhata, G. K. & Lilienfeld, A. M., 1963b. Familial aggregation of lung cancer in humans. *Journal of the National Cancer Institute*, 30, 289-312.

Tomkins, S. S., 1966. Psychological model for smoking behavior. *American Journal of Public Health*, 56, 17-20.

Tomkins, S., 1968. A modified model of smoking behavior. In: E. F. Borgatta & R. Evans (eds), *Smoking, Health and Behavior*. Chicago: Aldine.

Tong, J., Knott, V., McGraw, D. & Leigh, G., 1974a. Alcohol, visual discrimination and heart rate: Effects of dose activation and tobacco. *Quarterly Journal for the Study of Alcohol*, 35, 1003-1022.

Tong, J., Knott, V., McGraw, D. & Leigh, G., 1974b. Smoking and human experimental psychology. *Bulletin of the British Psychological Society*, 27, 533-538.

Ure, D. M., 1969. Negative association between allergy and cancer. *Scottish Medical Journal*, 14, 51-54.

Vetta, A. & Smith, C. A. B., 1974. Comments on Fisher's theory of assortative mating. *Annals of Human Genetics*, 38.

Wakefield, J., Yule, R., Smith, G. & Adelstein, A. M., 1973. Relation of abnormal cytological smears and carcinoma of cervix uteri to husband's occupation. *British Medical Journal*, 21 April 1973, 142-143.

Warburton, D. M. & Wesnes, K., 1978. Individual differences in smoking and attentional performance. In: R. E. Thornton (ed.), *Smoking Behaviour*. London: Churchill Livingstone.

Warwick, K. & Eysenck, H. J., 1963. The effects of smoking on the CFF threshold. *Life Sciences*, 4, 219-225.

Waters, W. E., 1971. Smoking and neuroticism. *British Journal of*

Social Medicine, **25**, 162-164.

Westlund, K. 1970. Distribution and mortality time trend of multiple sclerosis and some other diseases in Norway. *Acta Neurologica Scandinavia*, **46**, 455-483.

Weyer, M. (ed.), 1967. The effects of nicotine and smoking on the central nervous system. *Annals of the New York Academy of Sciences*, **142**, 1-333.

Whitby, W. T., 1979. *Smoking is good for you*. Sydney: Common Sense Publications.

Whitlocks, J. P., Cooper, H. L. & Gelbrin, H. V., 1972. Axyl hydrocarbon (benzopyrene) hydroxylase is stimulated in human lymphocytes by mitogens and benz (*a*) anthracene. *Science*, **177**, 618-619.

Willis, R. A., 1967. *Pathology of Tumours*. 4th edition. London: Butterworths.

Wilson, E. B. & Burke, M. H., 1957. Some statistical observations as a co-operative study of human pulmonary pathology. *Proceedings of the National Academy of Sciences*, **43**, 1073-1078.

Winkelstein, W., Kagan, A., Kato, H. & Sacks, S. T., 1975. Blood pressure distributions. *American Journal of Epidemiology*, **102**, 502-513.

World Health Organization, 1960. *Epidemiology of Cancer of the Lung*. World Health Organization Technical Report, Series 192.

Worth, R. M., Kato, H., Rhoads, G. G., Kagan, A. & Syme, S. L., 1975. Mortality. *American Journal of Epidemiology*, **102**, 481-490.

Wright, S., 1934. The method of path coefficients. *Annals of Mathematical Statistics*, **5**, 161-215.

Yesner, R., 1973. Observer variability and reliability in lung cancer diagnosis. *Cancer Chemotherapy Reports*, **4**, 55-57.

Yesner, R., Geostl, B. & Anerbach, O., 1965. Application of the World Health Organization classification of lung carcinoma to biopsy material. *The Annals of Thoracic Surgery*, **1**, 33-49.

Yesner, R., Selfman, N. A. & Feinstein, A. R., 1973. A reappraisal of histopathology in lung cancer and correlation of all types with antecedent cigarette smoking. *American Review of Respiratory Disease*, **107**, 790-797.

Young, P. A., Eaves, L. J. & Eysenck, H. J., 1980. Intergenerational stability and change in the causes of variation in personality. *Journal of Personality and Individual Differences*, 1

Index